Views of Mt. Fuji

Views of Mt. Fuji

Katsushika Hokusai

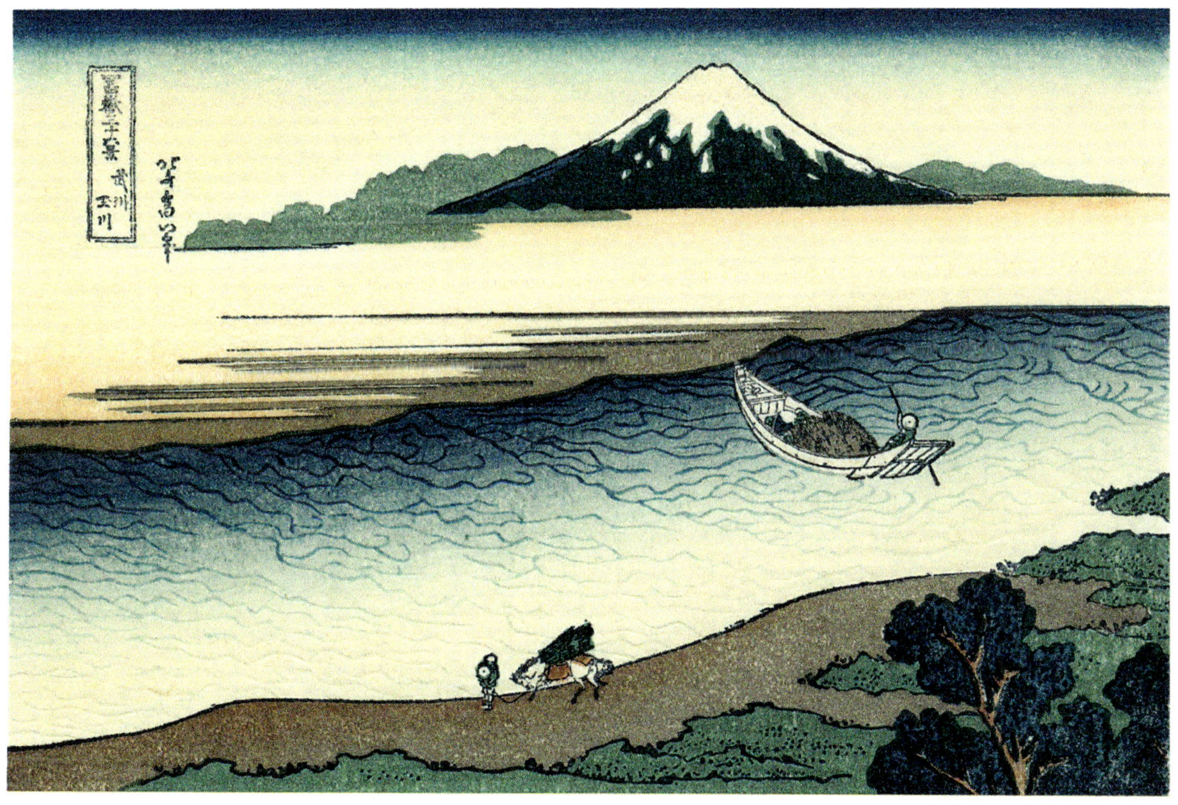

DOVER PUBLICATIONS, INC.
MINEOLA, NEW YORK

Bibliographical Note

This Dover edition, first published in 2013, is an a unabridged republication of *One Hundred Views of Mt. Fuji,* originally published by Frederick Publications, New York, 1960, and all the plates from *The Thirty-Six Views of Mt. Fuji,* originally published by Takamizawa Ukiyoe Co., Ltd., Tokyo, n.d. The Introduction to *Thirty-Six Views of Mt. Fuji,* found on pages 241–250, was reprinted from *Hokusai's 36 Views of Mt. Fuji,* originally published by Toto Shuppan Company, Ltd., Tokyo, 1959.

Library of Congress Cataloging-in-Publication Data

Katsushika, Hokusai, 1760-1849.
  [Prints. Selections]
  Views of Mt. Fuji / Katsushika Hokusai.
     p. cm.
  Summary: "Kasushika Hokusai was one of the foremost ukiyo-e artists of his generation and his Thirty-six Views of Mt. Fuji one the best know series in all of Japanese woodblock printing. Mt. Fuji had and continues to have a mythical hold on the Japanese imagination, and Hokusai depicts the endless depth and variety the mountain conveys through its situation in landscape, season, and time of day. This Dover book reprints the Thirty-six Views of Mount Fuji series in color along with Hokusai's later black & white series, One Hundred Views of Mount Fuji. A must for all lovers of Japanese art and the woodblock prints of the floating world"—Provided by publisher.
  "This Dover edition, first published in 2013, is an a unabridged republication of One Hundred Views of Mt. Fuji, originally published by Frederick Publications, New York, 1960, and all the plates from The Thirty-Six Views of Mt. Fuji, originally published by Takamizawa Ukiyoe Co., Ltd., Tokyo, n.d. The Introduction to Thirty-Six Views of Mt. Fuji found on pages 241-250, was reprinted from Hokusai's 36 Views of Mt. Fuji, originally published by Toto Shuppan Company, Ltd., Tokyo, 1959."
  ISBN-13: 978-0-486-49758-7 (pbk.)
  ISBN-10: 0-486-49758-5
  1. Katsushika, Hokusai, 1760-1849. Thirty-six views of Mt. Fuji. 2. Katsushika, Hokusai, 1760-1849. Hundred views of Mount Fuji. 3. Fuji, Mount (Japan)—In art. I. Title.

NE1325.K3A4 2013
769.92—dc23

          2013015606

Manufactured in the United States by Courier Corporation
49758502   2014
www.doverpublications.com

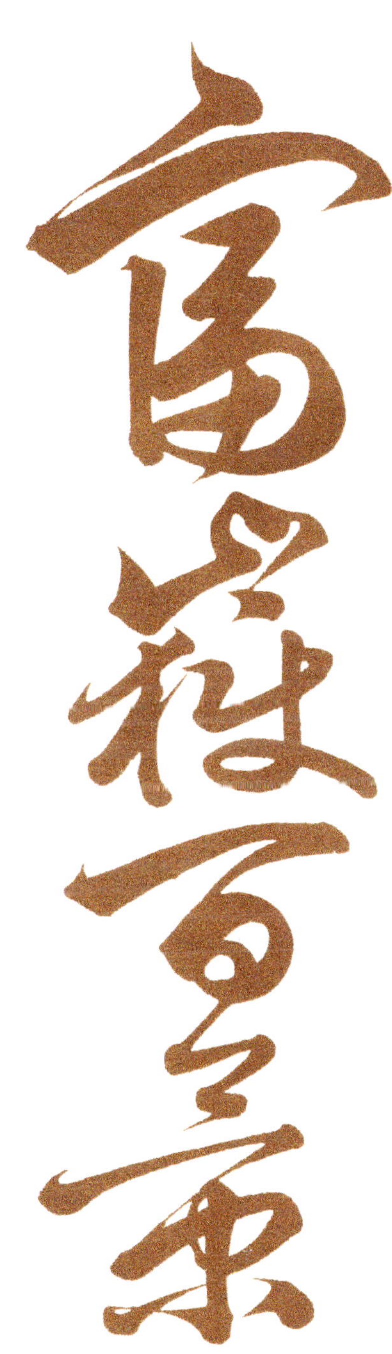
富嶽百景

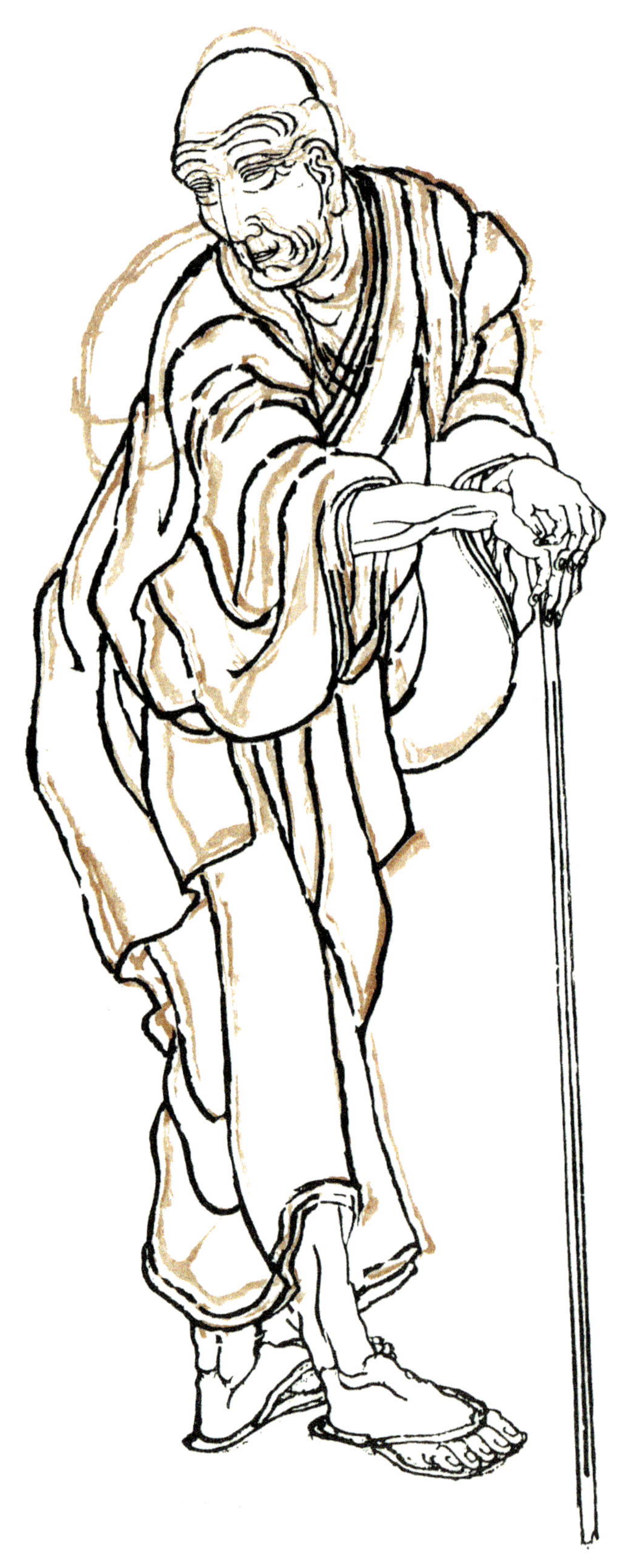

富嶽百景

One Hundred Views of Mt. Fuji

Katsushika Hokusai

INTRODUCTION

In the years 1830 to 1833, Hokusai was at the height of his powers. An old but incredibly productive man of over seventy, he had behind him a series of achievements in a variety of mediums and styles, culminating in the superb series of colour-prints, the "Thirty-six Views of Fuji", the "Waterfalls", the "Bridges" and the "Flowers", now recently completed. At this peak, he turned as to a monumental labour of love and homage, to the preparation of a book of designs devoted to the Peerless Mountain. From the first, it was conceived consciously as his masterwork: it was to be a final expression of faith such as another might have dedicated to a religious cause. It was to sum up his artistic philosophy and practice: it was to express the whole gamut of his experience, from the meanness of his fellow creatures toiling for a handful of rice, to the sublimity of the great mountain stark against the empty sky.

To appreciate the greatness of Hokusai's book, we must know something of the veneration, amounting to idolatry, of this mountain peak among the Japanese; and something, too, of the art of the picture book in Japan.

The bald geographical and geological facts about Fuji are briefly stated. A quiescent volcano, last active in 1707/8, it is 12395 feet at Ken-ga-mine, the highest point of the crater wall at the summit, and is thus the highest mountain in Japan. In circumference, at the base, it is one hundred miles. In shape, seen from afar, it approximates to a cone, but the sides are not equal, and each makes a sweeping catenary curve forming, with the broken apex, an assymetrical pattern so utterly Japanese in spirit that one feels that if Fuji did not exist in actual fact, Japanese artists would have created it. Arising as it does, isolated, in the midst of a broad plain, it is a dominant feature of the landscape of many surrounding districts, and a popular map is the Fuji-mi Jusanshu, the "Thirteen Provinces whence Fuji can be viewed". The ascent of Fuji, not particularly arduous or dangerous in the summer months, is a pilgrimage that every good Japanese makes at least once during his life-time.

Fuji, in fact, has from earliest times been nothing less than an obsession with the Japanese. Other countries have natural features universally known within and outside their borders—the Niagara Falls and the Table Mountain are instances that come to mind—but none of these features has a significance to the inhabitants of those countries comparable to that of Fuji to the Japanese. It is more than simply a symbol of the homeland, such as the Dome of St. Pauls is to Londoners, or the Eiffel Tower to Parisians; it is more than the abode of the Gods, as Olympus was to the ancient Greeks. It signifies the long history and the aspirations of the race; it is a token of all the scenic beauty of the land,

*and by inference, represents the impressibility of the people to
nature. Among national symbols, perhaps the Statue of Liberty
comes nearest to this summing up of a people's ideals, but that
was man-made to represent those ideals.*

*Some of the first poems in the native language show that
already, in the 8th century, Fuji was revered with superstitious
awe. In the Nara anthology called Manyoshu, the "Collection of
One Thousand Leaves", is an anonymous poem that contains
these lines:*

> *"No words may tell of it, no name know I that is fit
> for it,*
> *But a wondrous deity it surely is!*
> *... It is the peace giver, it is the god, it is the treasure.*
> *On the peak of Fuji, in the land of Suruga,*
> *I never weary of gazing."*

*The earliest scrolls of the true Japanese style of painting,
the Yamato-e of the 12th and 13th centuries, contain memorable
depictions of Fuji, isolated in grandeur, or a back-drop to tem-
pestuous events in the foreground. It is drawn with studied reverence, girt with clouds that crown it as, in western painting, a
nimbus marks the saintly head. In verse and scroll, it almost
seems that as the new nation became aware of itself, Fuji was
chosen as an emblem of artistic, as well as national, independence.*

*In the field of the decorative arts, especially in metalwork
and lacquer, Fuji recurs again and again, on the large ink-box
and on the exquisitely-made inro, on sword-guard and stiletto-
haft—whether for writer or warrior, Fuji was equally appropriate.
It is a favourite subject in landscape netsuke, accompanied sometimes by Saigyo, the mediaeval poet, looking towards it for inspiration, or by Yoritomo, leader of the Minamoto clan in the*

12th century, shown boar-hunting with Nitta, his retainer, at the foot of the mountain. As one of the Three Lucky Things, (Fuji, Falcon and Egg-plant, to dream of which was a mark of good-fortune), Fuji often figured on surimono, the New Year's Greeting Cards. It is a frequent motif in brocade pattern; in bonzai (dwarf gardens): in porcelain decoration; in the decoration of practically everything the Japanese ever used or wore. It is like a signature tune denoting "Japan". It may be difficult to account for this predominant place in the people's hearts, but then we are, after all, far from accounting for a number of their customs and for many of the traits of their character—the idolatry of the Emperor, for example, or that strange duality of personality which permits a callousness to human suffering and a hyper-sensitiveness to the fine arts to co-habit in the same individual. It is a fact we must accept.

Hokusai was a sort of self-styled encyclopoedist of Japanese life and custom. Birth, inclination and artistic gifts predestined him to such a function. He was steeped in the lore of his country, in its traditions, its poetry, the associations of each place-name. Like Shakespeare, he makes us wonder how one so low-born and so apparently ill-educated, could have attained to so universal a knowledge. Hardly any aspect of life in the diverse provinces that make up Japan escaped his notice, and it is not surprising that the form of Fuji appears as a leit-motif in his work from the very first book-illustrations of the 1780's to the last drawings of his old age, nearly seventy years later.

In this period he was concerned in the production of upwards of two hundred books. To some, like the poetry albums of his early years, he contributed only a single design in company with leading contemporaries like Eishi, Utamaro and Shigemasa. Most publications, however, called for a large number of drawings. The kibyoshi or "yellow-backs", also of his early years, were cheap-jack novelettes of three to five small booklets, with pictures helping out the text as in a strip-cartoon. More serious literature, such as Bakin's interminably long novels, ran usually to multiples of five volumes, each with five or six illustrations, and when they extended, as in one case, to ninety volumes, they represented a vast output of designs. But these works of illustratoin, powerful as they are and of great value in elucidating the texts, are of secondary importance to the albums and books in which Hokusai had a free hand. This type of book, consisting of a bound series of prints, in monochrome or colour, with a minimum of text, is uniquely Japanese. It could be a set of landscapes, or a fashion magazine; a pictorial anthology of verse, or an advertisement, with portraits, of the ladies to be hired at the Yoshiwara, or licensed quarter, a serious manual of instruction for art students, or a collection of slapstick caricatures. Hokusai's ehon, "picture books", are among the most remarkable. There are disconnected sketches brought together in book form by admiring pupils, of which the immortal Manga is the best known; there are books of warriors and derring-do; books of drawing-instruction; and above all, albums of landscape prints, such as the "Range upon Range of Mountains" of 1803, the "Panoramic Views along Both Banks of the Sumida River" of 1804/5; and the "One Hundred Views of Fuji", the last and finest work of this kind.

When we handle a Japanese picture-book, the very feel of it, the strangeness of its format, even the opening from left to right instead of right to left as in our own books, has a certain appeal. It is light, it has soft covers, it opens easily, using the whole "spread" of the book for some prints with a frank acceptance of the gap for the binding in the centre. When to these qualities we add the texture of the mulberry-bark paper, silky yet strong; the vivacity of the brush-drawn calligraphy, (moveable type was only very rarely used); and the beauty of the wood-block illustrations, we begin to realize that part of our pleasure is due to the book being a hand-made article throughout, in the production of which paper-maker, book-binder, publisher, artist, block-cutter and printer all joined forces. For once we may perhaps allow ourselves a superlative generalisation: Japanese illustrated books, at their finest, are the most beautiful in the world.

The "One Hundred Views of Fuji" is printed in monochrome, but so exquisitely that the gradations of the black and grey of the ink give the effect of a wide range of colour. The principal engraver, Egawa Tomekichi, was one whom Hokusai especially admired for his skill. Although any detailed bibliographical consideration of the book would be out of place here, it must be emphasized that only the first edition of each of the first and second volumes is printed in this superfine way and does complete justice to the splendid designs. The first edition of volume 1, which appeared in 1834, bears a title-label with decoratives lines at the top resembling a feather, and this has led it to be called the "Falcon's Feather" edition. The covers of this edition are salmon pink and embossed by gauffrage, or blind printing, with a landscape design. The colophon bears the proud inscription "75 years old, formerly Hokusai I-itsu, now changing his name to the Old Man About Drawing, Manji" with a red seal depicting a stylised Fuji in white reserve. The second volume is dated 1835, and has similarly distinguishing label and covers, signature and seal. The third volume, for a reason never explained, was not published until after a long interval in fact, on the evidence of the introduction, (for the volume is undated), not until Hokusai "had outlived his 90th year". This can only mean in 1849, when, by Japanese computation, which makes a man a year old at birth, Hokusai was ninety: the year of his death. By that time, the standard of printing had fallen below the extreme refinement of the first and second volumes. At the issue of the third volume, the first and second volumes were reprinted, and there is a marked difference in the impressions of the 1834/5 editions and the 1849.

As to the title of the work, an obvious question arises. Why One Hundred Views of Fuji? Why, in the earlier colour-printed set of broadsheets, Thirty-six Views? It is one of the more curious foibles of the Japanese to adopt a sort of numerical classification for things as diverse as ancient poets, natural landscape features, and events in the lives of the saints. There are the Six Jewel Rivers; the Eight Views of Lake Omi; the Seven Scenes from the Life of Ono no Komachi, the Poettess; the Twenty-four Examples of Filial Piety; the Seven Gods of Good Luck; the Eight Taoist Immortals; and so on. We are not immune from a similar sort of reliance on the magic of numbers—there are the Seven Wonders of the World and the Nine Worthies, for instance—but with the Japanese (and the Chinese for that matter) these groupings are much more common. The establishment of the canon, the fixing of the runic number, is invariably traced back to a remote antiquity. The orthodox number of Views of Fuji became fixed at either thirty-six or one hundred, but nobody seems to know·when or how. It is rather a coincidence that two of the numerical categories most frequently referred to are the 36 Poets of Antiquity, and the 100 Poems by 100 Poets, and it *may be that the Views of Fuji were linked to these; it would be quite in keeping with the national flair for associating incompatibles—they personified the 53 Stations of the Tokaido with portraits of the reigning beauties, and thought nothing of turning the Eight Views of Lake Biwa into Eight Views of Elegant Boudoirs.*

The Preface to the first volume of Hokusai's book refers to the "100 Chapters on Fuji" by Keichu, and the "100 Sections on Fuji", by Toko, and might have gone on, more appositely, to draw attention to another artist's "One Hundred Views". These are by Minsetsu, a minor artist of the classical school, and appeared in a block-printed book published in 1785, when Hokusai was a young man of 25. It is more likely that the book was known to him, and may even have been remembered by him when he came to compile his own "One Hundred Views". But a comparison, if one can be made at all between the two versions, would only be to point out the orthodoxy of Minsetsu's unimaginative prints and the extreme originality of Hokusai's.

For Hokusai's "Views" are nothing more or less than the pictorial setting of an obsession. There is a quiet opening to the first volume, a picture of the Sublime Goddess, Bringer of Fruit and Flowers, serving as a prologue that hints at the genesis of the mountain from the chaos and mists of antiquity. The next picture shows the mythical creation of the mountain, an event supposed to have taken place in the year corresponding to B.C. 285. From then on, the theme having been announced, Hokusai uses it like the great composer he was, bringing it into the foreground with sonorous brass, or veiling it with contrapuntal themes that all but disguise it, digressing only very infrequently with a reference to legend or history. Fuji straddles right across the page, or recedes to the far distance; it is white against a dark sky, or black under sunset clouds; it is seen through the stems of bamboos, or through the strips of dyed cloth hanging on poles to dry; it is even seen as a reflection or shadow in lake or sea ,or, with typical Hokusai whimsicality, upside down in the wine-cup of an old tippler.

The technique is almost that of the motion picture. We are switched from viewpoint to viewpoint, with a deliberate choice of "angle", that, for all the wealth of incident, focusses our attention on the mountain, so insists on its inevitability that when it is not prominent, our eyes search for it. Everything revolves around that immortalised cone of volcanic rock. The mood and the tempo change as swiftly as the viewpoint, from the sublime to the trivial, from the slow pace of peasants trudging under heavy loads, to the dash of a great wave breaking in a crest of foam. The element of surprise, the trick of astounding us, is another of Hokusai's stratagems. There is often something quite unexpected, imprevu, about the way Fuji is introduced into the picture. It is glimpsed through the mesh of a fisherman's net, or beneath the arch of a bridge, faintly through a downpour of rain, or framed in a hole in a rock. The excitement of the Japanese in catching sight of the mountain is conveyed a number of times—best of all, perhaps, in the picture entitled "The first kakemono (hanging-picture) of Fuji", where an old man flings out his hands in ecstasy at the vision of Fuji through an opened window. Occasionally, one almost hears the impressario's roll of drums, the clap of thunder that precedes a stupendous feat of showmanship: most powerful of these, I think, is the troupe-l'oeil of Fuji and a village at its foot caught in a blinding flash of lightning during a gale.

One could continue to dwell on the devices employed by Hokusai to gain his effects, to hold our attention, to vary the composition, and other technical considerations, but it is doubtful if it would bring us any nearer to accounting for the affection and the admiration we have for this collection of prints. In many respects, Hokusai was a Japanese of the Japanese, and some of the pictures in his book have overtones for his countrymen that must fail to register with us. His artistic style is a curious amalgam of native, of Chinese, and even of European elements, a quite personal blend that the connoisseurs of his own country have often pronounced distasteful, or praised only when they found that it was admired by the west. The appeal to us of his artistry is more immediate in the colour-prints, where the daring of the designs and the patterning of arbitrary colour dictated by the wood-block medium are seen to anticipate certain trends of modern art, especially the artist's right to subjugate natural forms and not to be dominated by them. In the "One Hundred Views" there are occasional successes of this kind but on the whole we are more conscious of the virility of the line and the subtlety of the washes expressing vast vistas so economically—stylistic features of the purely oriental kind that in another artist might have awakened only a faint response in us, enured as we are to western styles and techniques. No: it is not style alone, nor a capacity for skilful draughtsmanship, nor a genius for the misen-page—all of which Hokusai shared with a number of his fellow-countrymen —that gives the "One Hundred Views" its universal acceptance: ultimately, it is the human element, the feeling that these are peopled landscapes, that beneath this sublime peak and upon its slopes, men and women, mostly of a humble, near-to-earth order, are living out their lives. It is what we call the "common touch", which Hokusai, like Rembrandt, unknowingly possessed. The men and women are not quite in our likeness—they have an anatomy and a physiognomy devised as much by Hokusai as by Mother Nature—but the fishermen, coopers, tea-pickers, builders, boatmen, signwriters, umbrella-makers, the revellers, the pilgrims, the travellers, all are recognisably fellow human-beings, enlisting our sympathy or raising our laughter.

The human element is not even lacking in those half-a-dozen or so prints from which man and his works are absent, when we are shown Fuji in the majesty of isolation against a sky barred with cloud, or across a great waste of grasses under a full moon: for the mind carries over a thought of the poorly-clad peasants and artisans who people other pages of the book, and we realize that the sublimity of the mountain, the awe that these great transcripts of nature inspires in us, were felt also by these humble toilers and travellers at the sight of the actual Fuji. Hokusai has left them out of these pictures and depicted instead the uplift that the sight of the mountain brought to them, the sigh of wonder at the beauty of the land they lived in.

Hokusai, we can be sure, had no preconceived philosophic intent in depicting the life of these poor people against the immutable shape of Fuji, and yet the Peerless Mountain becomes in this series of prints a symbol of permanency underlining the transience of the men and women of the "Floating World" who look up to it with such reverence. Looked at in this way, it is far more than simply "One Hundred Views of Fuji": it becomes a commentary on man's relationship to nature, and assumes the stature of an epic.

JACK HILLER

PREFACE TO THE FIRST VOLUME.

(Translation.)

In the " Fuji-hiyakushu " (Hundred Chapters on Fuji) of
Keichiu was described the rugged loftiness of the Mountain:
in the " Fuji-hiyakuku " (Hundred Sections on Fuji) of Tôko
we are taught to admire the high Peak hidden amid gorgeously-
hued clouds; and now the brush of our late venerable Master
Hokusai (Sen Hokusaiô), in the Hundred Illustrations that
follow, fills us afresh with the sense of the beauty and majesty of
the Peerless Mountain.   As Fuji is lifted high in solitary
grandeur over all the high hills around, so shall we not say that
the productions of the genius of Hokusai stand alone in
unapproachable excellence.   Not only in the fifteen provinces
that lie within sight of him who gazes from the summit of Fuji,
but throughout the length and breadth of the land, dare we
foretell—'tis no rash prophecy — that these volumes will bring
home to thousands the marvellous and beautiful aspects of the
Mountain.   Ten titles* did the Master bestow upon Fuji, after

* The following are among these :—*Fuji*, peerless; *Fuji*, the hill of the
Felicity-Sage ; *Fugaku*, Felicity or Prosperity Peak ; *Tama-yama*, or *giyo-
kuzan*, Precious Mountain; *Giyokuhô*, Precious Summit ; *Hôrai-zan*, the hill
where the Artemisia (species of Moxa plant) may be gathered ; *Fu-yô-zan*,
Hibiscus (mutabilis) Hill.   Fuji is often written, too, with characters meaning
" Deathless," in allusion probably to the tale of Jofuku given above.

17

heedful comparison of the various names that the admiration of the people had given to the Peerless Hill. Men shall never tire of turning over these pages, and as we are shown in them the high, bare peak, viewed from the near shore of Tago, or seem to gaze upon the Great Mountain from the distant Cape of Miho, our hearts expanding in the broad moonlight, our souls penetrated with a delight subtle as the perfume that opening flowers lend the passing breeze ; or are persuaded that we are admiring the majesty of Fuji as we rest on our staff on the remote plain of Fujimi, or alight from our "kago" at the top of the pass of Shiwomi : whether a glimpse of the vast snow-clad slope is granted us through the drooping willow-branches, or the mighty cone is shown towering high o'er a billowy sea breaking in angry surf upon a rocky coast; whether we have pictured for us hollow valleys hidden in rolling mists, or the arduous climb up the craggy mountain-side, or the perilous descent from the rugged top,—we see the genius of the Master revealed in every effort of his brush !

In these volumes are depicted bare peaks and thickly-wooded hills and jagged mountain tops, such as are to be seen in the picture books of the day—and the sketches of the Master are no whit inferior, I trow, to the best productions of the priestly author of the " Hiyakushu."

Composed by Riutei Tanehiko, calligraphed by Tôsai, in the month of abundant verdure (fourth month, May-June) of the fourth year of the "nengo," (year-period) *Tempo* (Celestial Protection) A.D. 1834.

DESCRIPTION OF PLATES.

PLATE I.

MOKUGE-HIRAKU-YA-HIME-NO-MIKOTO.

Sublime Goddess, generatrix or developer of Flowers and Trees.

THIS is probably Toyo-uke-bime-no mikoto (Sublime
Goddess of Plenteous Food), who shares with Amaterasu
no ohongami (the Great Lord Heaven-shiner) the head-
ship over the deities of Ise, and who, by a sort
of fissiparous self-division, became Kukunochi-no-kami
(originatrix of trees), and Kayana-hime-no-kami (originatrix of
grasses). In her right hand she holds a white metal mirror,
which is to a woman what a sword is to a man. In her left
hand she bears a "tamagushi," a branch of the "sakaki" tree
(*Cleyera japonica*, a sweet-smelling, white-flowered low tree, allied
to the tea, camellia, and other ternstræmiaceous genera), with
strips of paper attached to it, symbolic of the "magatama," or
sacred jade ornaments, which in ancient times formed part of
the "tamagushi." Those versed in Japanese mythology will
remember that upon the occasion of the Sun Goddess, angered
by the insult offered her by her brother, Sosa-no-o no mikoto, who
threw a reeking horse's hide upon her as she sat at her loom,
retiring in her wrath into a cave, and so depriving the world of
light, the god Amanokoyane pulled up a "sakaki" tree by its roots,
and by attaching to it divers strips of cloth, a metal mirror, and
a number of "magatama" strung together, formed the original
"gohei," by which among other attractions the goddess was
induced to peer forth from her retreat, when the god Tajikara

(Strongi'th'arms) dextrously prevented the closing of the door, and drew forth the unwary deity into the open air. At the present day "gohei" are merely strips of white paper cut in an alternately notched fashion, and hung across the entrance to a "miya" (shrine) or fastened to a rod or bamboo switch. They are intended to attract the local deity to his sacred abode (miya), about which, with the same object, "sakaki" trees are commonly planted, together with "hisakaki" (*Eurya japonica*), a member of the same natural order as the "sakaki," an evergreen with small, ill-smelling green flowers, the odour of which is supposed to keep off wild boars.

In her hair the goddess carries an ornament resembling in form a "chôchô," or butterfly, a symbol of womanhood, as a horse is a mark or symbol of manhood. Underneath, on her forehead, are two black signs or patches—"hohotsu," or more commonly "bôbô" (the word "hohotsu" seems to be connected with "honoka," dark, dusky), worn of old by ladies of rank, and even by nobles of the Mikado's Court, and said to have been intended to replace the eyebrows, which it was then the custom among persons of rank to shave off at a certain age. The custom is still not uncommon among married women of all classes, but is beginning to fall into desuetude. In the background, dim mists and vapoury clouds show the beginning of the development of the kosmos out of the primeval chaos of Japanese and Chinese mythology.

FUJI-MINE SHUTSUGEN.

The Manifestation of the Peak of Fuji in the Fifth year of the period Kôrei (B.C. 285).

The legend of the sudden creation of Fuji has been already related. The amazement of the figures in the foreground is graphically though conventionally portrayed. On the right are the "mura-yakunin," or village authorities, one of whom is drawing up a sort of procès-verbal of the wonderful event. To the left are seen the high officials of the district, seated on "koshô" or military campstools, from which the general in the days of old Japan watched and directed the course of the battle. Behind are their henchmen, holding their "katana" or long swords, always removed from the "obi" or girdle upon occasions of ceremony. The time is the grey of the morning, probably of that following the night upon which the marvellous upheaval took place. The slope of the Mountain is lit up by the earliest rays of the rising sun. Japanese authors tell us that for a long time the Mountain remained without a name, and assert that the term "Fuji" is nothing else than the "kun," or Japanese rendering of the character "Tô" of the name Marutô, of a former celebrated "Kannushi" or priest of the mountain-god. That character denotes the *Wistaria chinensis*, called in Japanese "Fuji no ki," and as this beautiful tree (for in Japan it is as often a low tree as a mere shrub) is very plentiful on and about the slopes of Fuji, it is possible that some connection exists between the name of the Mountain and that of the tree. But commonly the word Fuji is represented by two Chinese characters, meaning no-two, sanspareil, or peerless, though occasionally these are replaced, as in the title of the present work, by characters signifying Prosperity Peak.

PLATE III.

Yen no Ubasoku Fugaku Sôsô.

The Manifestation of the Peak of Fuji and the Ubasoku Yen.

The term " Ubasoku " (in Sanscrit, Upâsaka) was given by the Indian Buddhists to lay members of their Church, who, without entering upon monastic life, paid close observance to the principal requirements of the faith (Eitel. Handbook Chin. Buddhism).

The full name of the saint is Yen no Shôkaku, and the following account of him, taken from the seventy-third volume of the great Japanese and Chinese Encyclopædia, " Wa-kan-sanzai-dzuye " (Illustrations of the Three Powers, Heaven, Earth, and Man), may be of interest :—

" Yen no Shôkaku belonged to the noble family of Kamoyen (now known as Takakamo), and was born at the village of Ihobara, in the district of Katsura-no-kami, in the province of Yamato, on New Year's day, of the fifth year of the reign of the Emperor Jomei (A.D. 633). As a boy he was both intelligent and studious. At the age of thirty he devoted himself to the study of the doctrines of Buddhism, and abandoned the world to dwell upon Mount Katsuraki in Yamato. There for over thirty years he made his home in a cave, clothed himself in the leaves of the Fuji (*Wistaria sinensis*) and the Katsura (*Cercidiphyllum japonicum*), and nourished himself upon the young shoots of the common pine (*Pinus massoniana*). He occupied his time in chanting the liturgies of the god Kujaku-Miyôwô, and in passing from place to place at his pleasure, riding upon a cloud. He compelled the spirits of the mountain to yield him their obedience, and serve him as his servants. Once he laid upon

them the following behest : 'From the summit of Katsuraki
to Mount Kimpô the way is rough and perilous, fling ye a stone
bridge across, that the path may become easy.' The mountain
spirits obeyed, and worked hard night after night in collecting huge
rocks and constructing the bridge with them. Shôkaku, however,
was displeased with their slowness, and spoke angrily to them,
asking how it was that they were so long about the task. They
replied, ' Really, we are hindered by that monster demon
Hitokotonushi ; we dare not work by day, we can only work by
night, and thus it happens that we are but tardy in fulfilling the
task laid upon us.' Upon this Shôkaku sought out Hitokotonushi
and reviled him, but to no purpose. At this want of success he
became enraged, and, casting a spell upon the demon, paralysed
him, and threw him into a deep valley. In revenge, Hitokotonushi, through the servants of his shrine, spoke thus to the
Emperor Bummu, or Mommu (A.D. 697-707): 'I am the god
worshipped by all who harbour rebellious thoughts; Yen no
Shôkaku is a secret fomenter of disorders, public and private ;
seize thou him, lest perils come upon thee.' Shôkaku was
accordingly summoned, and came riding through the air to obey
the call. It was determined to seize his mother (as a kind of
hostage), and he, seeing there was no help for it, delivered himself
up a prisoner. This took place in the fifth month of the third
year of the Emperor Bummu. He was banished to Ôshima, an
island off the coast of Idsu. Shôkaku remained three years at
Ôshima, keeping within the limits of the island during the day,
but every night visiting Fujisan. He walked across on the
surface of the sea, just as if he were on dry land ; so quick was
his pace that no bird could have kept up with him. This marvel
occurred in the first year of Daihô (A.D. 701). At last he was
recalled from banishment, and returned to Kiyôto. He after-

wards dwelt by Mount Minôômo (commonly known as Minô), where he built a temple not far from a cascade known as Minôdera. Finally he made a raft of sods, and, embarking upon it, accompanied by his mother, whom he placed in a large bowl, on the seventh day of the sixth month of the first year of Daihô (A.D. 701), voyaged Chinawards. He died at the age of seventy."

The hermit or saint is represented squatting on a piece of coarse "goza," or thin matting, apparently on the edge of the fuming crater. It may here be remarked, parenthetically, that no true Japanese willingly sits or squats upon bare boards, or upon the bare ground. Over the curiously-patterned underdress is worn the black garment of a priest. In the left hand is carried a sort of staff, resembling the "shakujô" of mendicant Buddhist priests, but without the metal rings by clashing which the latter try to attract the benevolent attention of the faithful. Round the neck hangs a rosary, "judsu," and the accessories show the saint to have been a follower of the "Riyôbu" (or "both-sorts") doctrine, which is simply Buddhism into which more or less of Shintôism has been incorporated. In the foreground are a pair of wooden "geta" or pattens.

With a peculiar gesture of both hands, the fingers of which are held in a particular position, the holy man is exorcising a whirlwind of demons ("mafû," or demon-blast) issuing from the crater, whose terrible features are quaintly shadowed forth in the storm-driven fumes in the background. On the ghostly vapour-whirl his staff throws a faint shadow.

The following, among other prodigies, is related of Shôkaku. On one occasion a wayfarer passed by the spot where the hermit was sojourning, just as a flock of wild geese were flying by overhead. Shôkaku asked him if he were hungry, and upon the

traveller signifying that he was, offered to provide him with a
meal. The offer was accepted, and, with a wave of the hand,
the holy man brought down several of the birds to his feet, and
roasted them, and gave of them to the wayfarer to eat, himself
partaking of the meal. After a time he said to his guest that his
hunger was now stayed, and then, opening his mouth, blew out
all the birds he had eaten, who rose up in the air and flew
away. He next breathed upon the place where the geese had
been cooked, and, wonderful to relate, the remainder of the birds
that he had brought down appeared, and, flapping their wings,
mounted rapidly into the air.

PLATE IV.

KUWAI-SEI NO FUJI.

Fuji on a bright Day.

The Great Mountain is seen from the south, perhaps from
Tago no ura, or the mouth of the swift Fujigawa. High into the
clear blue, tempered by long bars of fleecy clouds, towers
the lofty peak, within the jagged outline of which yawns the wide,
deep crater, quiet at last, after having built up so vast a monument
of the fiery energy that the ruddy tints of the rough and cindery
cone still seem to bear witness to. The higher slopes are hidden
under a smooth mantle of gleaming snow; about the foot cluster
rugged hills, and precipitous wooded ranges run down to the
broken coast-line. A few birds are soaring high in the air, and
the fishermen's boats on the tranquil sea of the foreground tell us
of human life.

PLATE V.

The Opening of the Mountain.

The "Opening" of Fuji took place on the first day of the sixth month of the Old Calendar: it is now celebrated in the early days of August, by which time the snow has commonly altogether disappeared, save in unsunned nooks and crannies, and under wind-blown heaps of dust and cinders. From this period up to the end of September those who are under vows of pilgrimage ("giyôja") to adore the mountain-gods ("sankei") may make the ascent. The crowd of votaries represented by the Master is a purposed exaggeration. On each pilgrim's hat ("kasa") are inscribed the Chinese characters "no-two" (peerless), pronounced by the Japanese "fu-ji." The multitude have emerged from the forest that clothes the lower slopes, and are toiling up the steep gullies, overgrown with *Eurya japonica* and other low bushes, that separate the lava streams, ere they enter upon the severer climb up the bare portion of the dead, or rather sleeping volcano, by winding paths over slippery lava beds and treacherous heaps of loose ash and cinder.

PLATE VI.

KUDARI.

The Descent.

Here the Master has drawn for us, with his wonted force and directness, a sketch, in amusing contrast with the preceding one, of the headlong descent of the returning pilgrims down the cinder-strewn, steep slopes of the bare upper portion of the volcanic cone. Staff in hand they leave the winding beaten track, and with long stride or leap drop down the loosely-heaped talus, eager

to find themselves back at their "yadoya," in one of the seven
villages that occupy the seven Mountain-approaches (" yama-no-
kuchi") whence they started the day before, and where a boiling
hot bath and a good meal shall make them forget the toilsome
climb and the comfortless night spent in the draughty stone huts
that cluster round the bleak edge of the crater itself.

PLATE VII.

Hôyei-zan Shiutsugen.

The Upthrow of Mount Hôyei.

I.

Such is the name bestowed upon the hump on the southwestern slope of Fuji, well seen from Yedo and Yokohama. The
flank eruption which gave birth to it took place on the twenty-
sixth day of the last month but one of the fourth year of the
"nengo" or epoch Hôyei (Precious Longevity), that is, of the year
1707 of our era, whence the name. Some account of this event
will be found in the description of Fuji, given above, and taken
from the " Wa-kan-sanzai-dzuye."

The Plate depicts the terror and disaster the earthquake that
accompanied the outburst spread through the villages that cluster
about the foot of the Mountain, nestling among the low wooded
hills or half hidden amid clumps of bamboos or camellias on the
skirts of the great undulating plain that stretches from the base of
Fujisan to the shores of the Gulf of Yedo and the Pacific Ocean.
The horror of the catastrophe is admirably rendered, and its
various incidents are told with a vigour which, to those who know
Japanese life, will appear not unworthy of comparison with that of
Hogarth. A furious gale rages through the thick gloom. Rocks
and stones, hurled forth from the new crater, are showered down

in destructive abundance.   Men, women, and children are tossed
aloft by the sudden upheaval, and, with the debris of their ruined
homes, fall miserably on the wreck-strewn ground.   Huge beams
and rafters jostle in the air with fragments of tea-jars, with tubs
and masses of thatch, with tiles and uptorn patches of flooring,
and even heavy wooden mortars are spun round in the wild
confusion.   The paper panes of the broken "shoji," or window-
frames, flutter aimlessly in all directions.   Vainly do the terror-
struck peasants try to escape ; some dragging after them their
fainting wives, others carrying on their backs aged folk or little
infants. One man has his account-book under one arm, while with
the other he seeks, but ineffectually, to help a woman, perhaps his
wife, who has fallen forwards with her child on her back ; another
grasps a box containing his scanty possessions, which he is yet
unwilling to lose.   The whole forms a terrible picture of the panic,
ruin, and despair the most sudden, the most unforeseeable, and
the most tragic of the convulsions of nature brings upon helpless
man.

PLATE VIII.

Hôyei-zan Shiutsugen.

The Upthrow of Mount Hôyei.

II.

Wayfarers and country people are discussing the marvellous
event, now that all is once more quiet. The time is early morning,
and against a background of unflecked blue stand out in a flood
of light the sun-illumined slopes of Fuji; the rugged hills that
cluster about the base are still in the shade, save their ridges just
touched by the sun, and a few vigorous strokes of the brush
indicate rather than represent the deeply-ravined and undulating
plain that lies between the ancient coast line and the shores of the

Pacific. The figures in the foreground reproduce with wonderful sincerity and truth Japanese gesture, attitude, and carriage—travellers, wearing sword or dagger; rustics, hoe in hand or bamboo pole on shoulder; pedlars and servants, all with their loins girt up ready for work or road. The last personage but one to the rustics' left is not afflicted with a tumour on the neck; what appears such is the bottom of an upturned "hiyôtan" or gourd.

PLATE IX.

Muchiu no Fuji.

Fuji seen through the Morning Mists,—probably from Utsu no Tôge, the Pass of Utsu, on the Tokaidô (Eastern seaway) or high road between the two capital cities of Yedo and Kiyôto, re-named of late Tôkiyô (Eastern Capital) and Saikiyô (Western Capital) respectively. Peasants are climbing a rugged hill, on their way to cut fodder. In the valley bottom flows the Ôi river, on the waters of which, obscured by the mist, float spectral-looking boats. On the further bank is dimly to be seen a hamlet, buried among machilus, camellia, and pine trees; beyond, solemn cryptomeriæ rear their tall forms, and in part hide from view the shining cone of Fuji.

PLATE X.

Yamanaka no Fuji.

Fuji from the Hills.

The time is the close of autumn. Two hunters are reloading their matchlocks, while women are gathering the "kikurage" (a kind of edible fungus, *Tremella auriculata, L.* ?) that are growing

abundantly upon the decaying bark of a gnarled and ancient
pine. Tall reeds, probably Eulaliæ, stripped of their feathery
inflorescence, cluster thickly at the foot of a lofty precipice, and
Fuji towers high in the distance against a cloudless sky. The
wild, chilly aspect of an autumn landscape in Japan is admirably
rendered.

PLATE XI.

RIUTO NO FUJI.

Fuji from the Willow Bank.

A rising ground, planted with willows ("yanagi"), some few miles
east of the Riyôgoku Bridge in Yedo, much resorted to by holiday
folk. The wayfarer to the extreme left, painfully trudging along
with the help of a staff, is a victim to ophthalmia, the sequel
probably of an attack of small-pox, and is hastening to the
" Yashiro " or shrine of Miyôken, within the precincts of which
stands an ancient pine tree, in the decayed and hollow trunk
whereof the white snake Hakuda has made his lair, whom the
faithful afflicted with eye-disease propitiate by due prayers and
offerings on the eighth of the first month. The other figures well
represent every-day life in the suburbs of Yedo. A petty
gentleman, wearing his two swords, is followed by a single
servant bearing his baggage. A pair of holiday makers enjoy a
morning pipe as they contemplate the distant Mountain, which no
true Japanese ever tires of regarding ; pedlars carry their packs
wrapped in cloths knotted round their necks ; peasants, hoe on
shoulder, are trudging to their fields ; a lazy " mago " (packhorse
man) rides his beast, not yet fatigued with the day's labour ; a
mother, child on back and pipe in mouth, is probably carrying to
her husband in the ricefields his morning meal.

TANABATA NO FUJI.

Fuji seen over the House-tops on the Loom-Worker's Night.

On the evening of the seventh day of the seventh month is held the Feast of Tanabata, or the Loom-Worker (lit. handloom), when the lover-stars, Shokujo (Chinese Chih-nü, the Star a Lyra) and Kengiu (Chinese Ki'en-niu, a close group rather than a single star, situate partly in Capricornus, partly in Sagittarius; or according to some β,γ of Aquila), are adored. Bamboo poles are set up on the roofs, to which are tied bundles of variously coloured strips of paper, on which are writ stanzas, such as :—

"Ama no gawa	"What time on Heaven's stream,
kayou uki-ki ni	floats by the drifting log,
koto towan :	one thing I fain would ask :
momiji no hashi wa	the Bridge, like autumn's sere leaves,
chiru ya chiradzu ya ?"	is it scattered, or (endureth it still) unscattered?"

The allusions in the above verse will be made clear by what follows.

In the "Nen-chiu-koji-yôgen," a Japanese treatise in seven volumes, on the origin and signification of some of the principal festivals and customs of the year, it is said that the two stars, Shokujo or the Loom-Woman, and Kengiu or the Herdsman, are separated from each other by the River of Heaven (under which name the Milky Way is known to the Japanese and Chinese), and that on the seventh night of the seventh month Shokujo goes forth as a bride and seeks Kengiu as her bridegroom, crossing the River of Heaven by a bridge formed of the close-set wings of a line of " ujaku " (magpies?)   A legend is then given identical with the one cited by Mr. Mayers in his most useful Chinese Reader's Manual, Art. 311, from the "Peh-wuh-sze" or Record of the Doings of Peh. Peh was the title bestowed upon Chang K'ien, a minister of Wan-wu-ti, who flourished in the second century before our era, and was the first Chinese to explore the countries lying west of the Middle Kingdom. He is said to have made treaties with the Kings of Turkestan, and to have introduced the grape-vine from Persia, with the art of making wine. The legend runs that Chang K'ien was ordered to explore the sources of the Yellow River (Hoang Ho). He sailed up the stream accordingly on a log or raft, provided with a year's provisions, and, on arriving at a certain place, saw there a good-wife weaving, and an oxherd leading his beast to the water. On asking the name of the place, the woman gave him her shuttle, and told him to return to his own country, and there to seek out an astrologer, named Kün-p'ing, who, on seeing the shuttle, would answer his enquiry. He followed her directions, and Kün-p'ing, after informing himself of the exact day and hour of the occurrence, made the proper calculations, and declared that at that very moment he had observed a wandering star come between Shokujo and Kengiu. Hence it was clear that Chang K'ien had reached the Milky Way, of which the Hoang Ho was in truth nothing less than a continuation upon earth.

On Tanabata night, the "Nenchiu-Koji" goes on to advise us, the inner court should be swept, and set with clean matting, on which we may place ourselves and watch the heavens. Should we be fortunate enough to catch the two lover-stars in conjunction, we may rely on attaining whatever wishes we may be holding in our heart. It is equally lucky to see the five hues sparkling in the Milky Way by daylight on the seventh of the seventh month. Whoever, too, shall light upon a spider spinning its web about a melon, will do great deeds. And a variety of other fortunate omens are mentioned, which, however, it would be tedious to set forth here.

The Feast of Tanabata or Shisseki (Seventh Evening) is sometimes called "Kikkô," which means, "Praying for Valour and Virtue." Various offerings are made, and the verses above alluded to ought to be written with ink rubbed up with dew gathered in the morning from the leaves of the "imo" or yam (*Colocasia antiquorum*). The feast is said to have been instituted in the "nengo" Tempei Shôhô (Celestial Peace, Power, and Wealth), A.D. 749-757.

PLATE XIII.

SODE GA URA.

View of Fuji over the Point of Sode.

A picturesque promontory about halfway between Yenoshima and the Cape of Inamura, near which Yuranoske, the hero of the Chiushingura, or the Loyal League, landed, with his companions, on their journey to Kamakura (the then capital of Eastern Japan, now a mere village) to wreak vengeance for the self-dispatch of their lord Yenya upon his enemy Moronawo, by whose arrogance and malice the ruin of their lord and clan had been brought about.

Near Cape Inamura the path strikes inland from Yenoshima to Kamakura and the great bronze statue of Daibutsu, in the vicinity of which two English officers of the 20th Regiment, Major Baldwin and Lieutenant Bird, were murdered in 1864, under circumstances of peculiar atrocity, by a couple of Japanese fanatics, who were afterwards executed. Up to this point the path skirts the foot of a low range of wind-blown sand-hills that overlook a beach of loose volcanic sand, known as "Shichi ri no hama," or the seven-league Beach. Here in due season the shore is brilliant with the yellow flowers of *Ixeris repens,* and various kinds of creepers mingled with the pink corollas of a pretty convolvulus (*Calystegia soldanella*). The damp hollows among the sand-hills are filled with a tangled growth of species of Astragalus and purple-flowered Lathyrus, with here and there the straight, leafless, scaly stem of an Orobanche, topped by a spike of large, ringent flowers of a pale lilac hue. The lower slopes of the dunes show a glory of red azalea blossoms, amid which the fragrant, white, waxlike inflorescence of *Pittosporum tobira,* and a species of Photinia, afford an agreeable relief.

At the foot of the promontory extends a water-worn irregular floor of rock, over which, when the wind blows from south or east, the vast Pacific tide surges in mighty, foam-flecked humps and whirls of vitreous brine, to break in showery spray high up against the cliff-face, retreating the next moment in swift backward rush, with a long hiss, as it were, of baffled rage, to meet and struggle with the advancing flood. At the base of the precipice has been hollowed out a shelter for a pair of images of local deities, and under the protection of the well-wooded point nestles a pretty hamlet.

PLATE XIV.
Bishiu Fujimi-hara.
Fuji from the Plain of Fujimi in Bishiu (Owari), famous for the numerous cranes which haunt the marshy moor.

PLATE XV.
Yama mata Yama.
Hills upon Hills.
A fanciful sketch, somewhat clumsy both in conception and execution, designed to show the immensity of Fuji under contrast of the Mountain with a procession of ordinary hills.

PLATE XVI.
ÔMORI.
Fuji from Ômori.

A low-lying tract, between Yedo and the village of Kawasaki, so familiar to old Yokohama residents as the limit of their rides in the early days of the settlement. Yokohama itself might be descried from the stand-point of the spectator, to the left of the Mountain in the further shore of the bay, the hither boundary of which is the long, low strip of land running out in the middle distance far into the waters of the Gulf of Yedo. The character of the coast scenery is well rendered, despite the almost bare simplicity of the means employed.

PLATE XVII.
DÔCHIU NO FUJI.
View of Fuji from the Mouth of a Cavern.

The time is autumn. The middle-plan of the sketch is occupied by conventional mist rising from the valley-bottom. A couple of woodcutters are resting from their toil, and enjoying a friendly chat over a pipe of tobacco.

PLATE XVIII.
MATSUYAMA NO FUJI.
View of Fuji over the Pine Hills.

A familiar prospect to all who have walked from Yenoshima to Kamakura by the pretty path striking inland from near Cape Inamura, towards the poor village that now occupies the site of the mediæval capital of the Ashikaga Shôguns. The figures of holiday folk in the foreground are drawn with the Master's usual vigour, sincerity, and wealth of incident, but the foliage of the pine trees is lamentably conventional.

PLATE XIX.

INCHIU NO FUJI.

View of Fuji through the Smoke of a Bonfire, lit in the chill, latter autumn time, when the maples are shedding their yellow, brown, and scarlet leaves, by a couple of wayfarers and a pack-horse man, who avails himself of the chance of a puff (ippuku) at his pipe. On the stone tablet are inscribed Chinese characters, pronounced "Seimen Gongo," the Green-Visaged Diamond (Club) Wielder, a name, perhaps, of Indra, the Brahmanic deity, who became a protector of Buddhism.

PLATE XX.

DEMMEN (TA-OMO) NO FUJI.

Fuji mirrored in the Rice Marshes.

The wild geese (" gan ") are not drawn with Hokusai's usual skill.

PLATE XXI.

ROCHIU IKADA NO FUJI.

Fuji from the Reedy River.

Probably the Ôi River. The rapid movement of the broad, shallow, rippling stream is well rendered by a few dexterous strokes. The reeds bow their feathery heads to a slight breeze. In the background towers Fuji, against a cloudless sky of deep blue. Rafts are being toilsomely guided with the stream, while idlers are lazily fishing from an unfinished raft on the bank.

PLATE XXII.

KOGARE NO FUJI.

Fuji from an old Tree-stump.

This is one of the most vigorous of the hundred sketches. A high wind is blowing over the upland fields, rattling loudly the clappers hung on strings to scare away the birds from the ripening crops. The thatch is almost torn from the roof of the hut of the watcher, whose duty it is to guard the fields from thieves, and to work the clappers when the wind does not perform the task for him. The wayfarers have much ado to keep their legs against the furious blast. The distant hills are just touched by the first rays of the rising sun, and long bars of cloudy mist are beginning to veil Fuji from view.

PLATE XXIII.

GUWAN-TAN NO FUJI.

Fuji on New Year's Morn, seen over the heads of a group of holiday-makers : gentlemen accompanied by their servants on their way to pay the usual congratulatory visits of the season ; monkey-leaders with pole and hoop, "manzai" dancers, &c. &c. In one corner is a kite, on which is inscribed the character "fuku" (good luck.)

PLATE XXIV.

YEDO NO FUJI.

A view, probably, over the roof of a " shiro " or mansion, or over the gable-end of a portal adorned with a " shachihoko," commonly distinctive of the residence of a member or vassal of the Tokugawa family. The " shachihoko " is often in bronze, and represents a fish, possibly a " koi " or pike, conventionalised

and with the tail uppermost.   The signification of this ornament
or badge I have been unable to discover.   The pike is said to be
common in the Yedo rivers, especially, the "Yedo-mi-yage" tells
us, in the Yedogawa, whence however the vulgar were forbidden
to take it, so that to ordinary, that is non-noble, folk, its flavour
was unknown.

PLATE XXV.

KIYO-DAI NO FUJI.

Sunset behind Fuji (mirror and stand).

Towards the close of summer, the sun, seen from Yedo, sets
directly behind the Great Mountain, the triangular outline of
which is then fancifully compared to the stand of a Japanese
mirror, itself represented by the shining orb.   The spectator is
supposed to be placed somewhere on the banks of the Sumida
river, perhaps near Mukojjima, celebrated for its wild-plum and
cherry orchards.   To the right, in the middle plain, a glimpse is
caught of the Asakusa pagoda.   The rough wave-lines are rather
clumsily suggestive of the irregular rush of the stream.   On the
right are two manure-tubs.

PLATE XXVI.

URA FUJI.

The other Side of Fuji.

The view is from the hilly province of Kai.   In the foreground, at the back of a farmer's hut, an impossible horse is being
groomed, his packsaddle is lying on the ground beside him.
Tobacco leaves are hung up to dry, and a woman with a child
on her back (ombo) is preparing homespun cotton yarn for the
loom.   The whole forms an admirably faithful picture, rich in
incident, of village life.

PLATE XXVII.

Kasa Fuji.

Fuji with its Cap on.

The view is from a ford on the Baniu river, so well known to residents of Yokohoma, who cross the stream on their annual trips to the Lake of Hakoné to escape the summer heats of the plain.

The chill peak of Fuji not seldom so condenses the moisture in the currents of air that play about it, as to surround itself with a sort of wreath or curl of cloud, constantly changing in form, and drifting vanishingly to leeward, affording an appearance often of smoke issuing from the long inactive crater.

PLATE XXVIII.

Kumo-obi no Fuji.

Cloud-begirdled Fuji.

The Buddhist Saint, Saigiyô Hôshi (Teacher of the Law), is fancifully presented in an old Priest crossing a bridge on the Tôkaidô, riding on a bullock, and contemplating with a sort of ecstasy the Great Mountain rising high above belts of fleecy cloud. In the left corner of the sketch is a party of coolies, bearing a huge government chest, in charge of an officer.

PLATE XXIX.

Kuwa-kan no Fuji.

Fuji seen amid the opening blooms of Spring. This is, perhaps, the most charming sketch in the "Hundred Views." A picnic party at Mukôjima, on the banks of the Sumida river, are enjoying a holiday in the early days of Spring among the cherry-groves, now in full flower. A "geisha" is regaling them with the plaintive music of the "samisen." The sky is free from all clouds ; the air is warm and full of sunlight ; around them the picturesquely-branched and as yet leafless cherry-trees are laden with snowy masses of tender blooms. In the distance rises the shapely cone of Fuji, still white with the winter's snow.

PLATE XXX.

Hôsaku no Fuji.
View of Fuji across the fruitful Rice-fields.

A country path over the paddy-land in the later autumn time. On the hill to the right is a shrine to Inari, the patron of rice farmers, sometimes identified with one of the Seven Gods of Happiness, Benzaiten, who, however, is commonly regarded as a goddess. The hill is very likely a mound or tumulus (dzuka) marking the last resting-place of some ancient hero. The gaunt-looking trees, with their trunks swathed in rice straw, probably serve to show the boundaries of properties. In the middle place stands a notice board, protected by a sort of roof or coping, on which perhaps the tax-assessment is made public. In the distance are seen the roofs of a small hamlet, and the horizon is broken by the bold outline of Fuji.

PLATE XXXI.

Senkin Fuji.
Mountains of Wealth (lit. Thousand-pieces-of-gold Fuji).

A fancifully allegorical sketch. In the distance is the real Fuji—written in the title of the sketch with characters signifying Sage of Wealth. In the foreground are two Fuji-like pyramidal heaps of rice-bags, symbolical of riches, covered each with a protecting mat. Small birds (chidori?) are fluttering about looking out for stray grains of rice.

End of Vol. I.

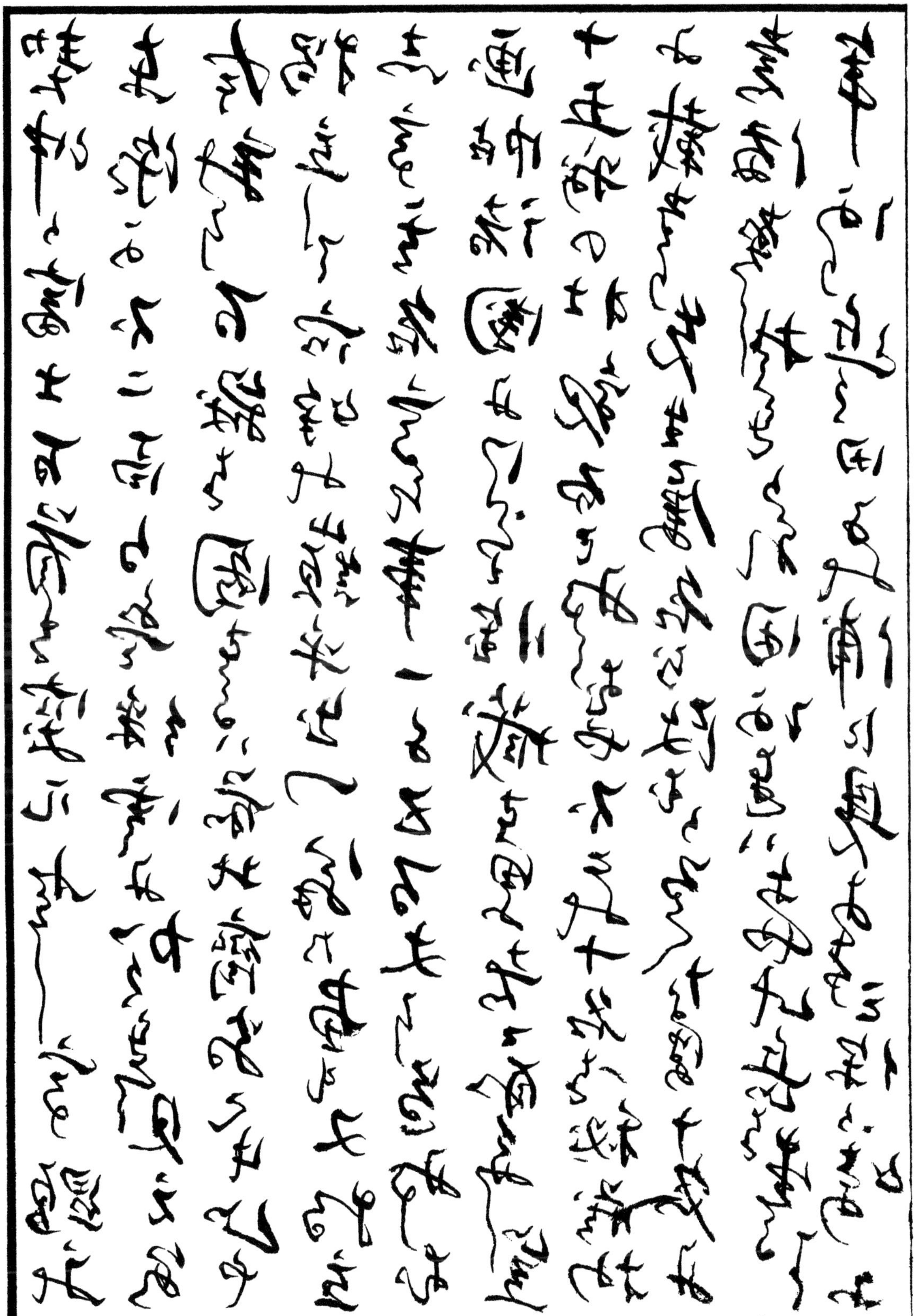

[illegible]
[illegible]
[illegible]
[illegible]
[illegible]
[illegible]
[illegible]
[illegible]

[illegible]

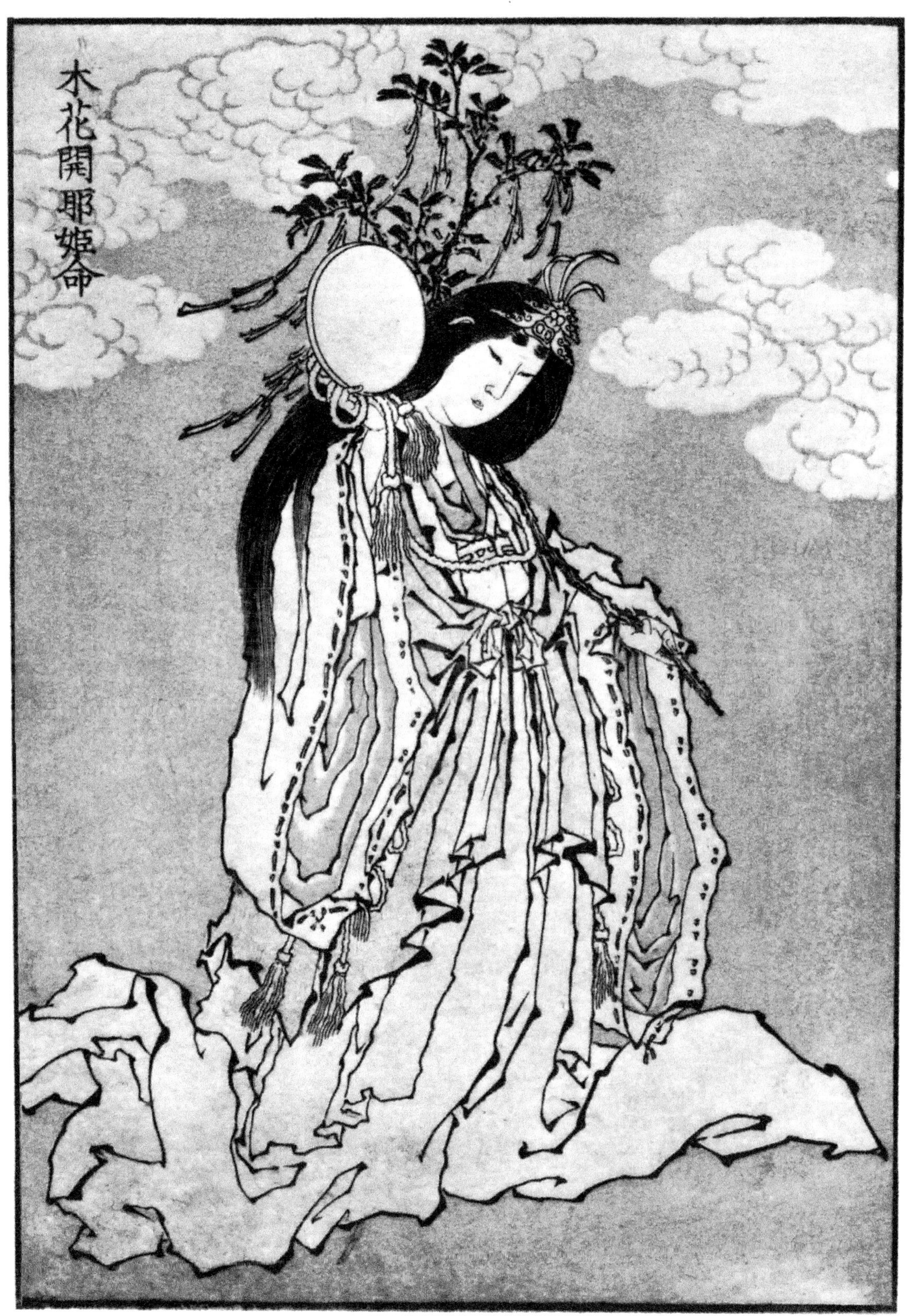

Plate I

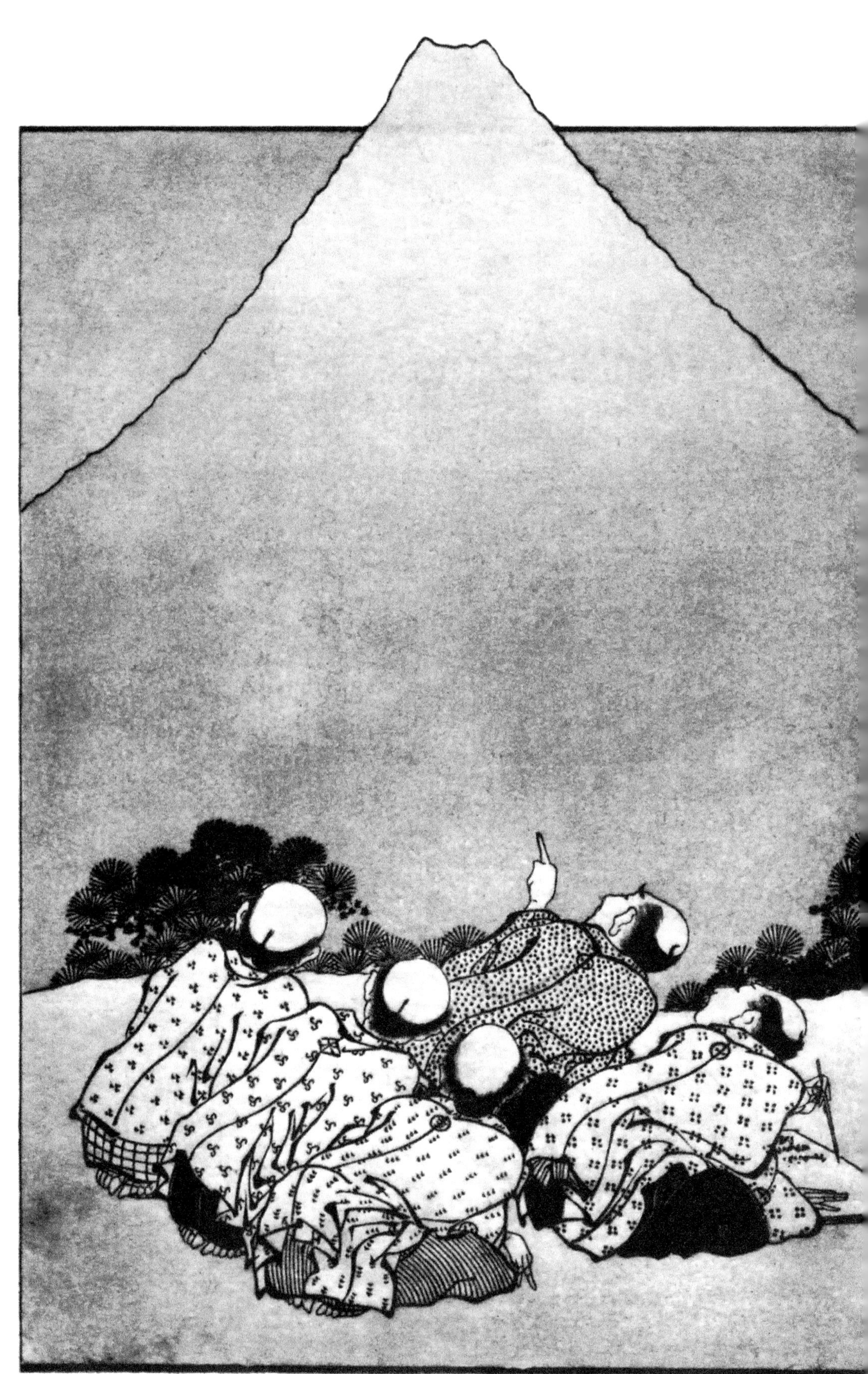

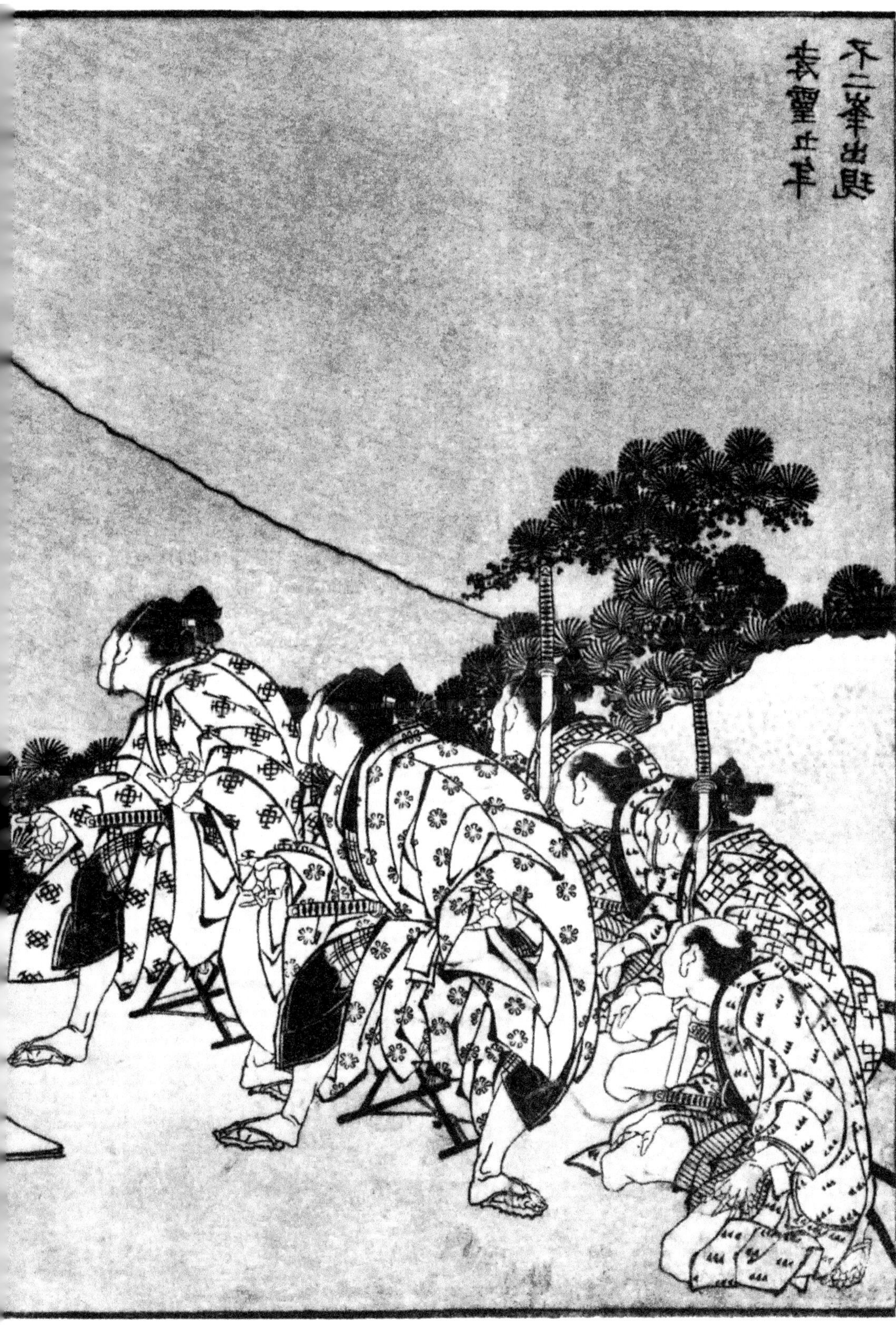

Plate II

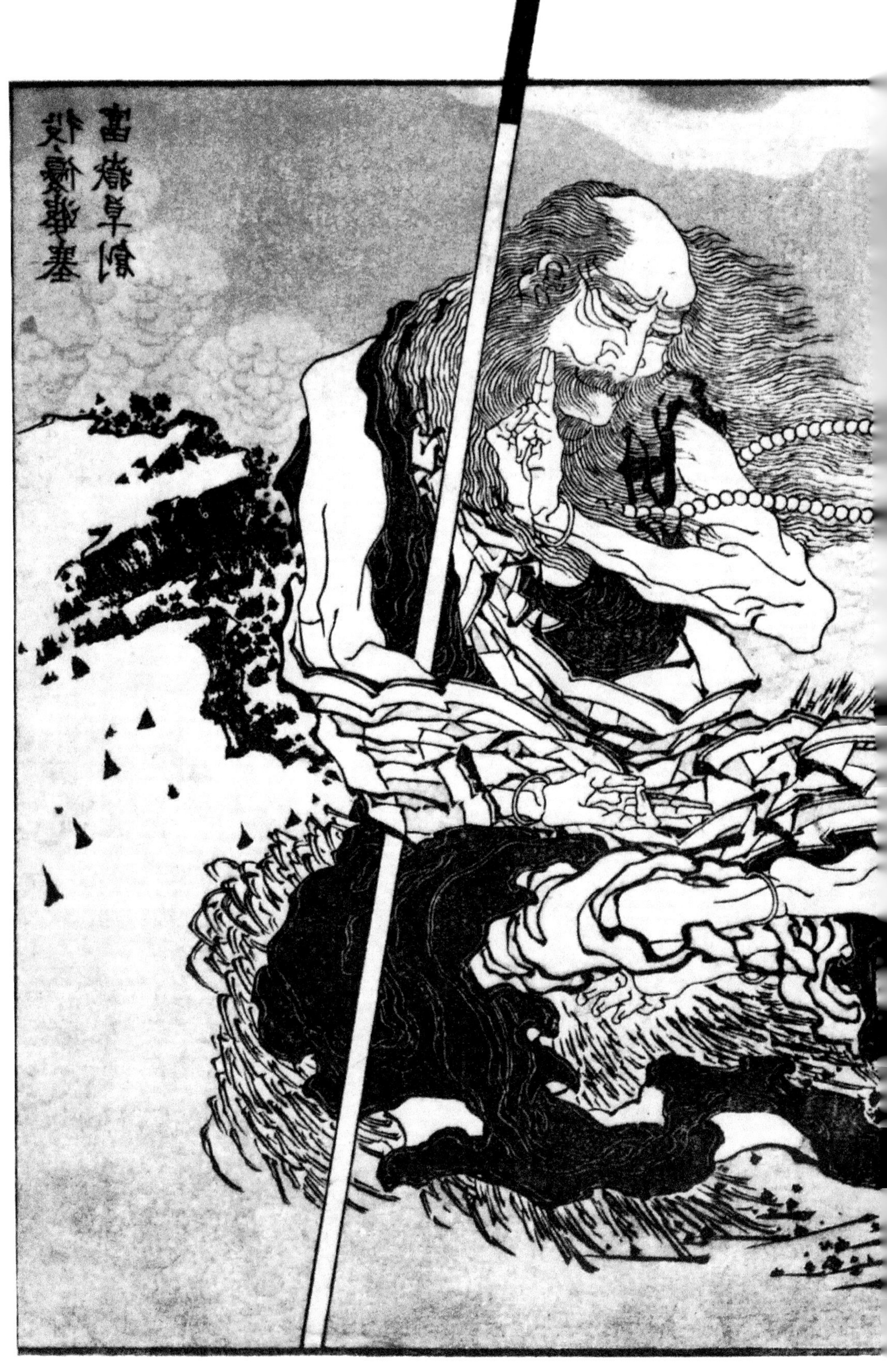

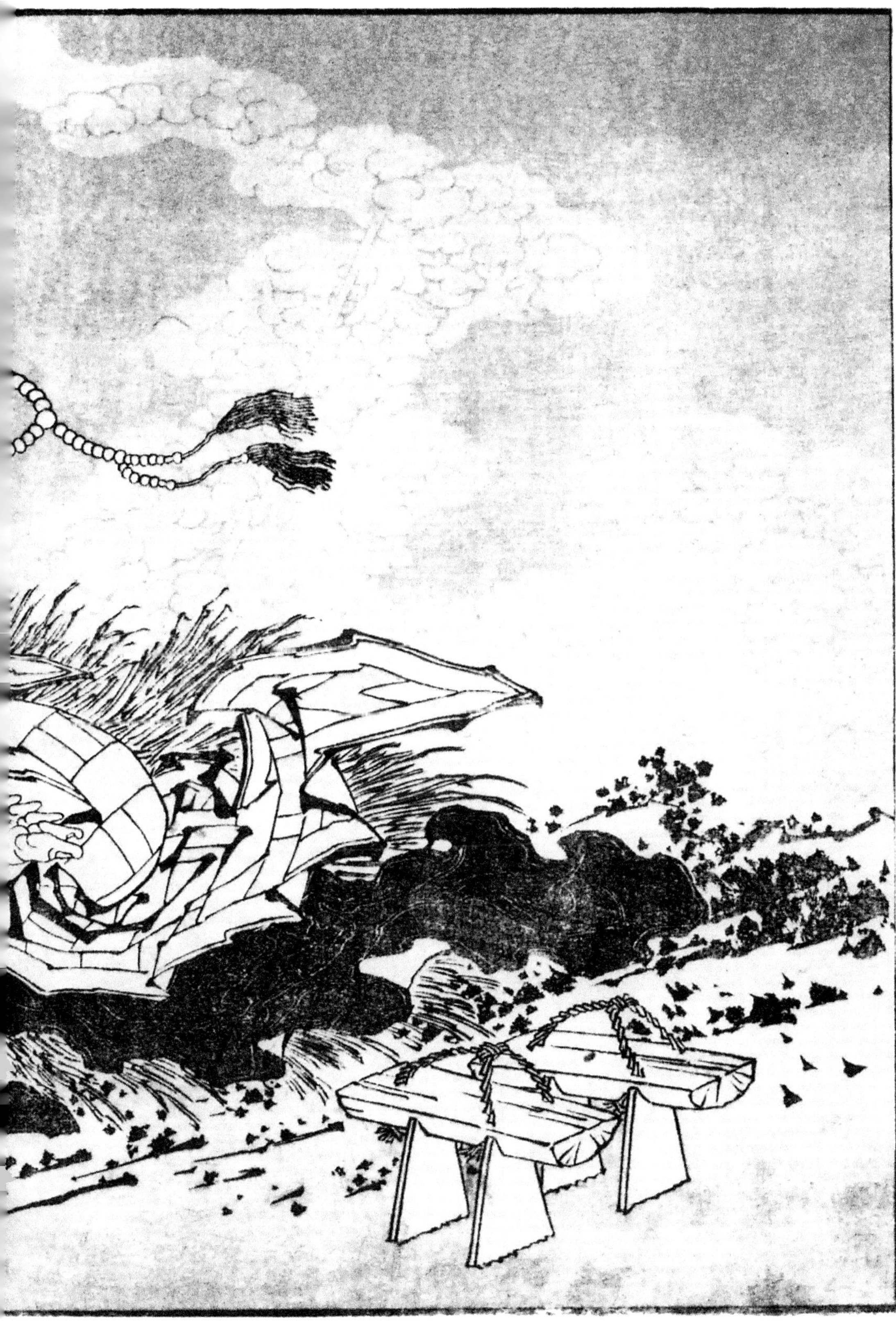

Plate III

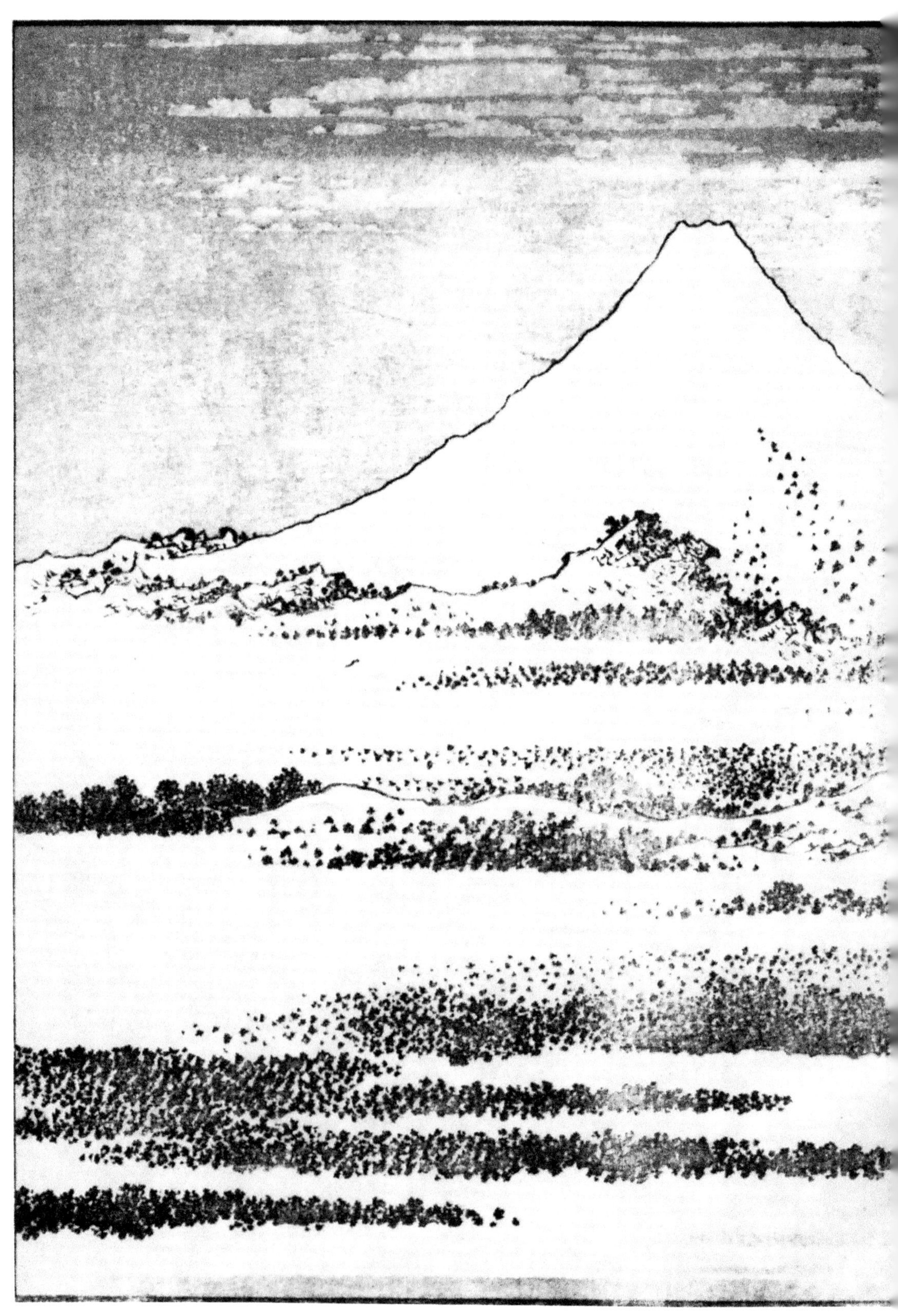

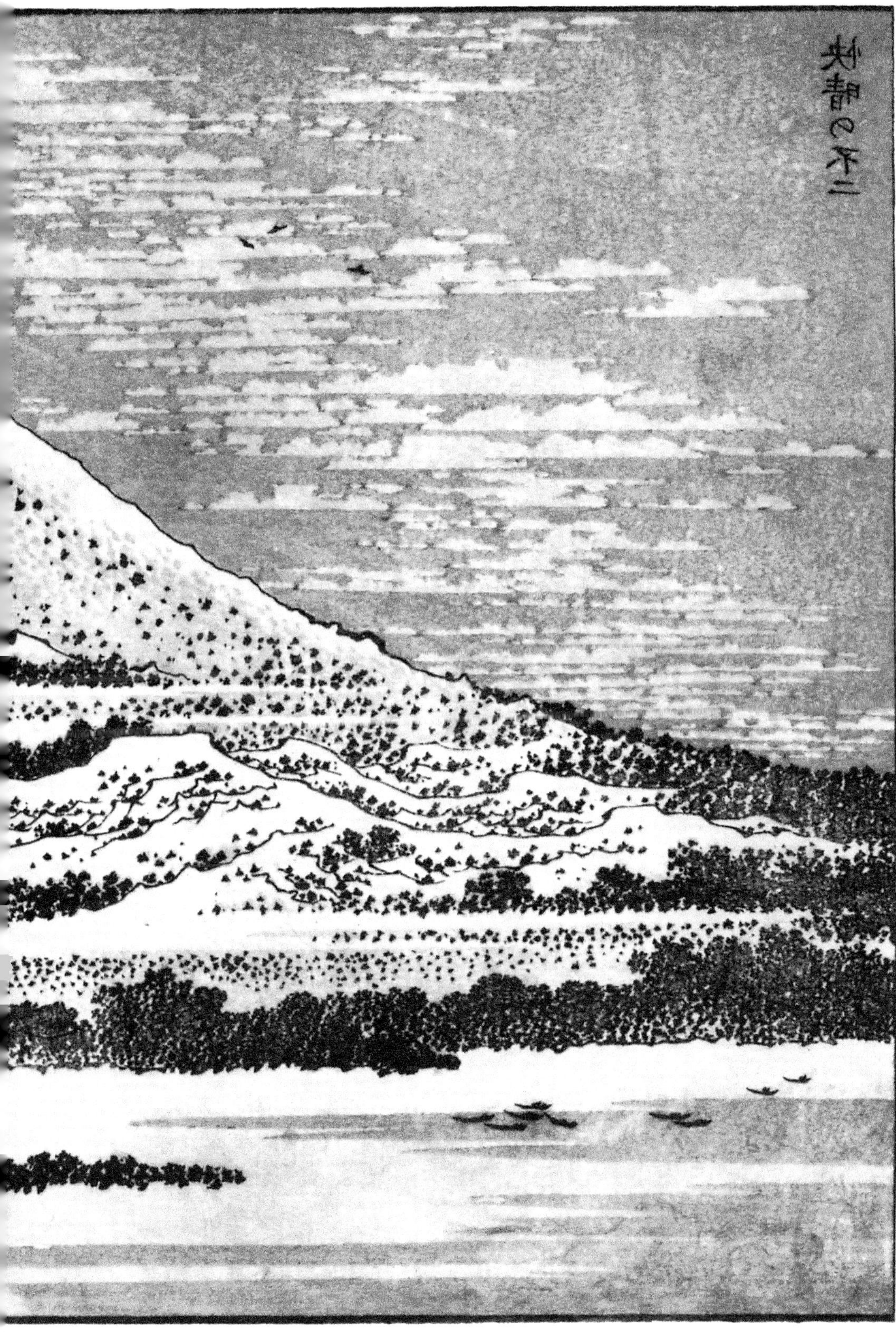

Plate IV

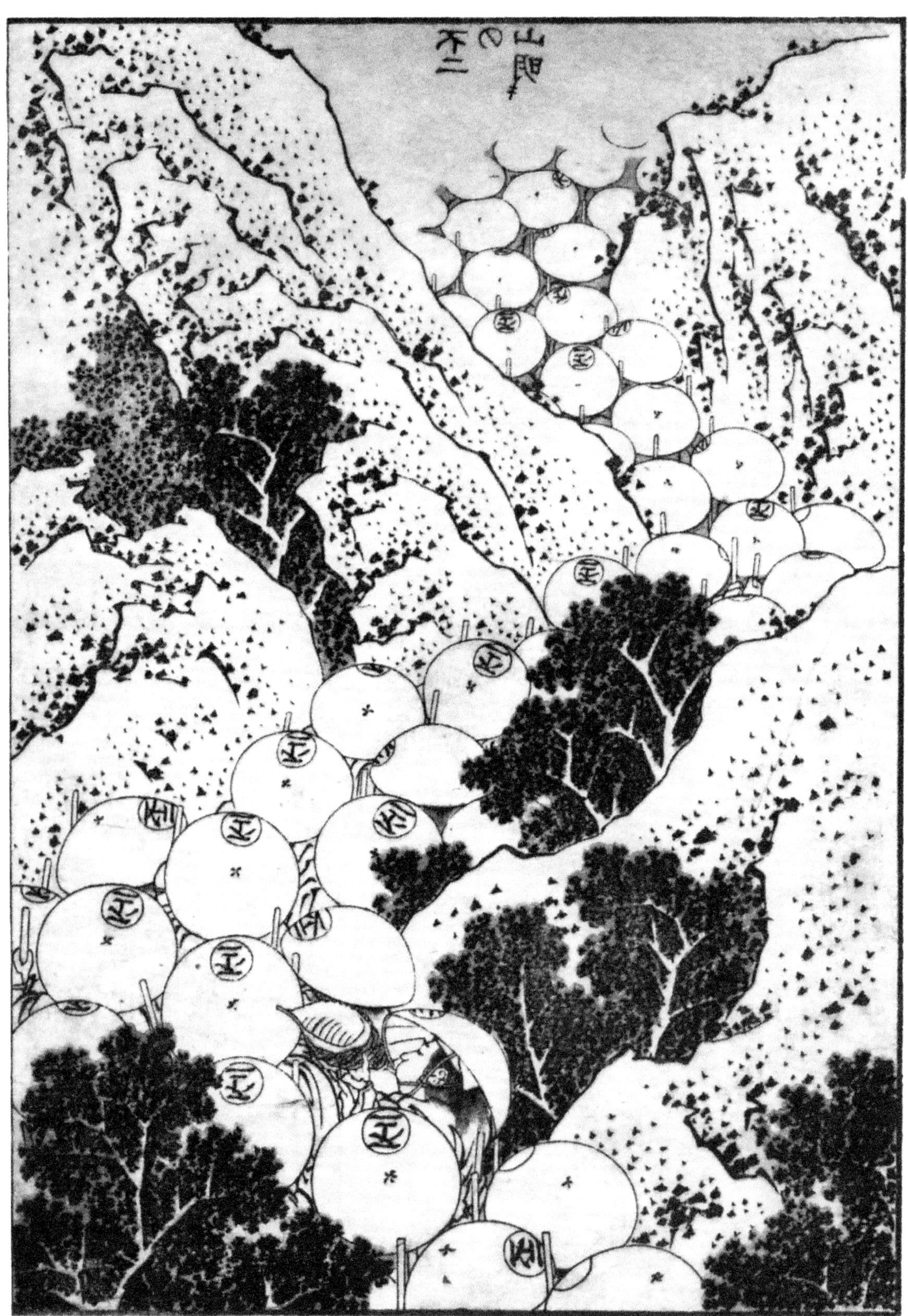

Plate V

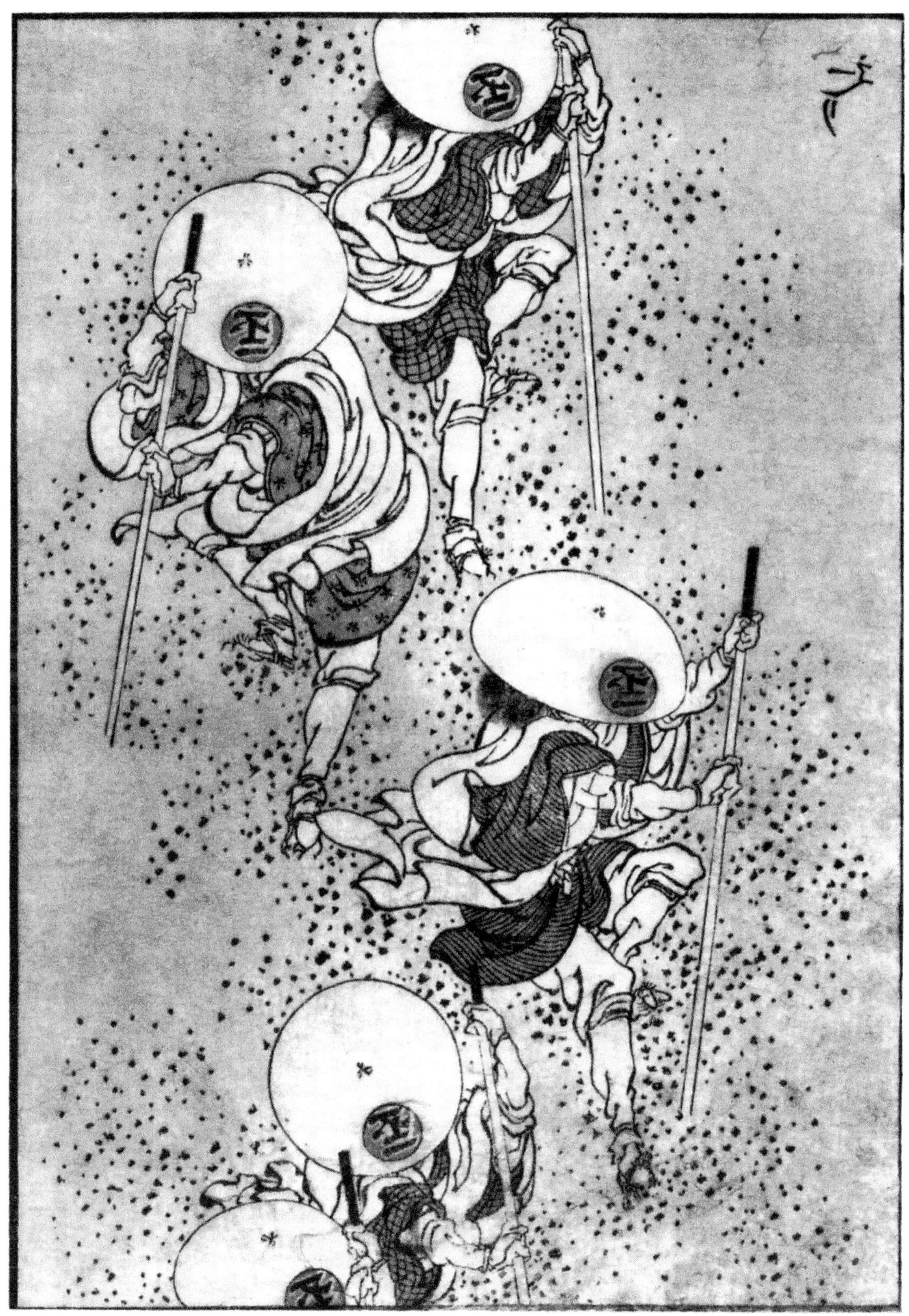

Plate VI

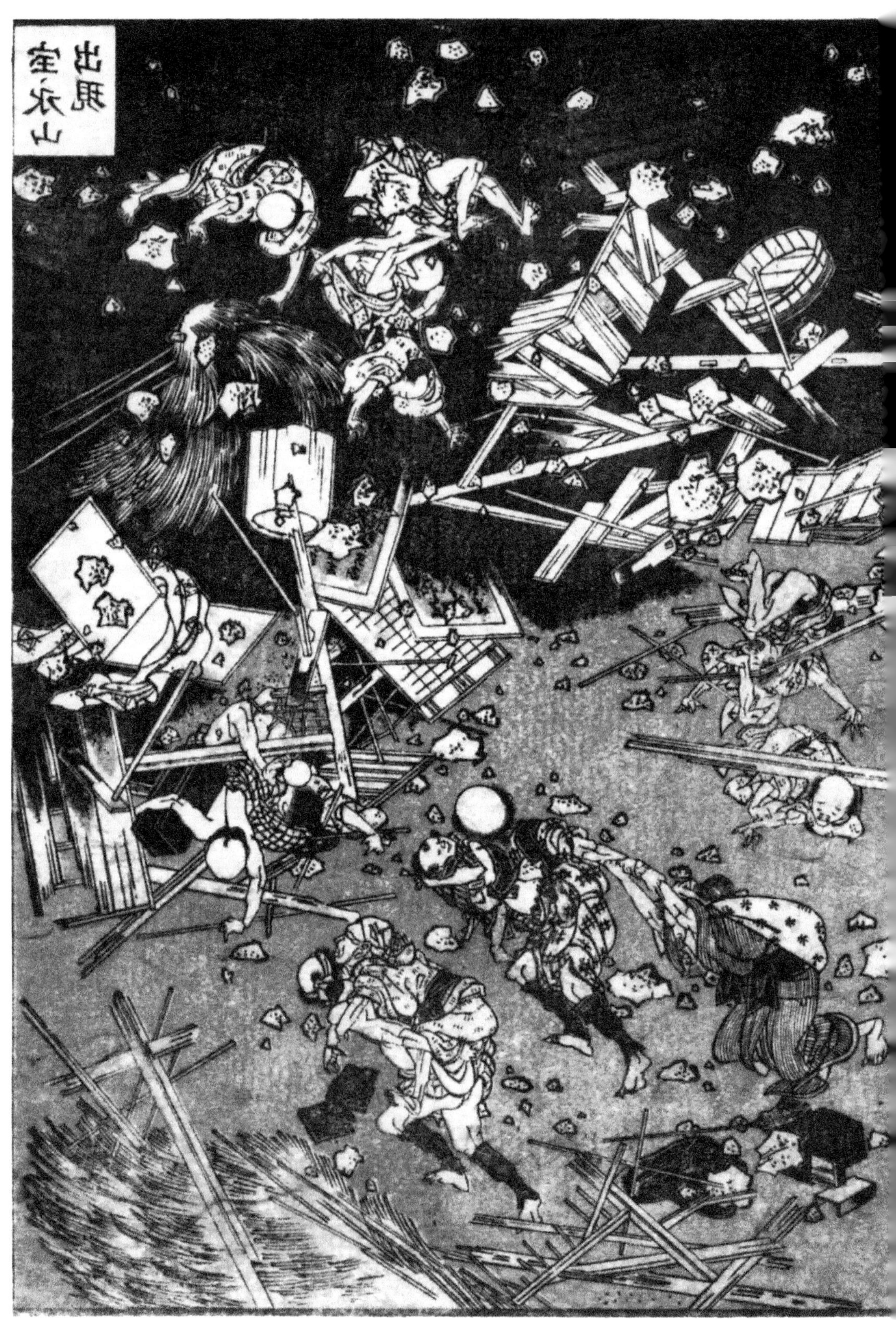

出羽
室衣山

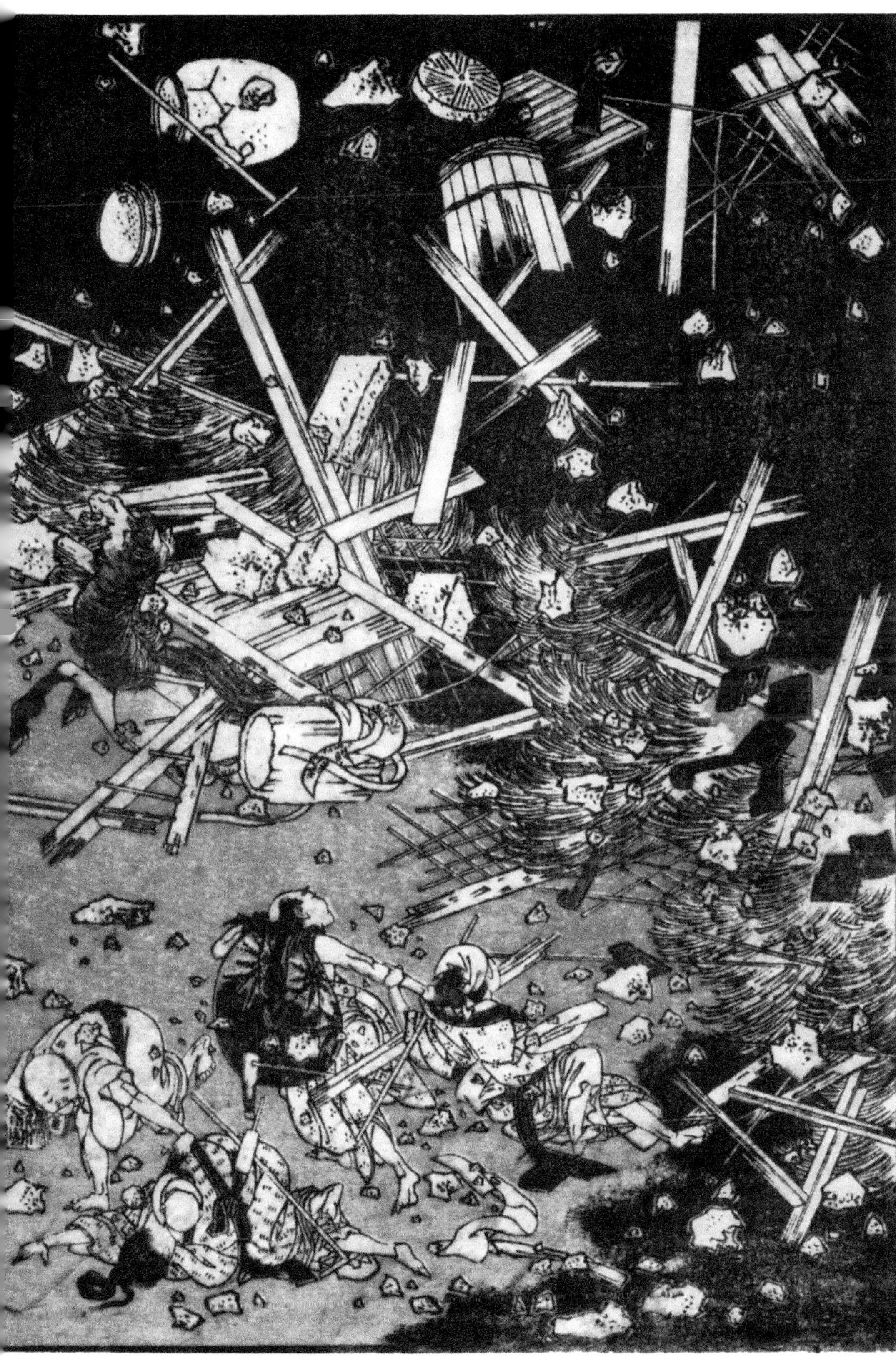

Plate VII

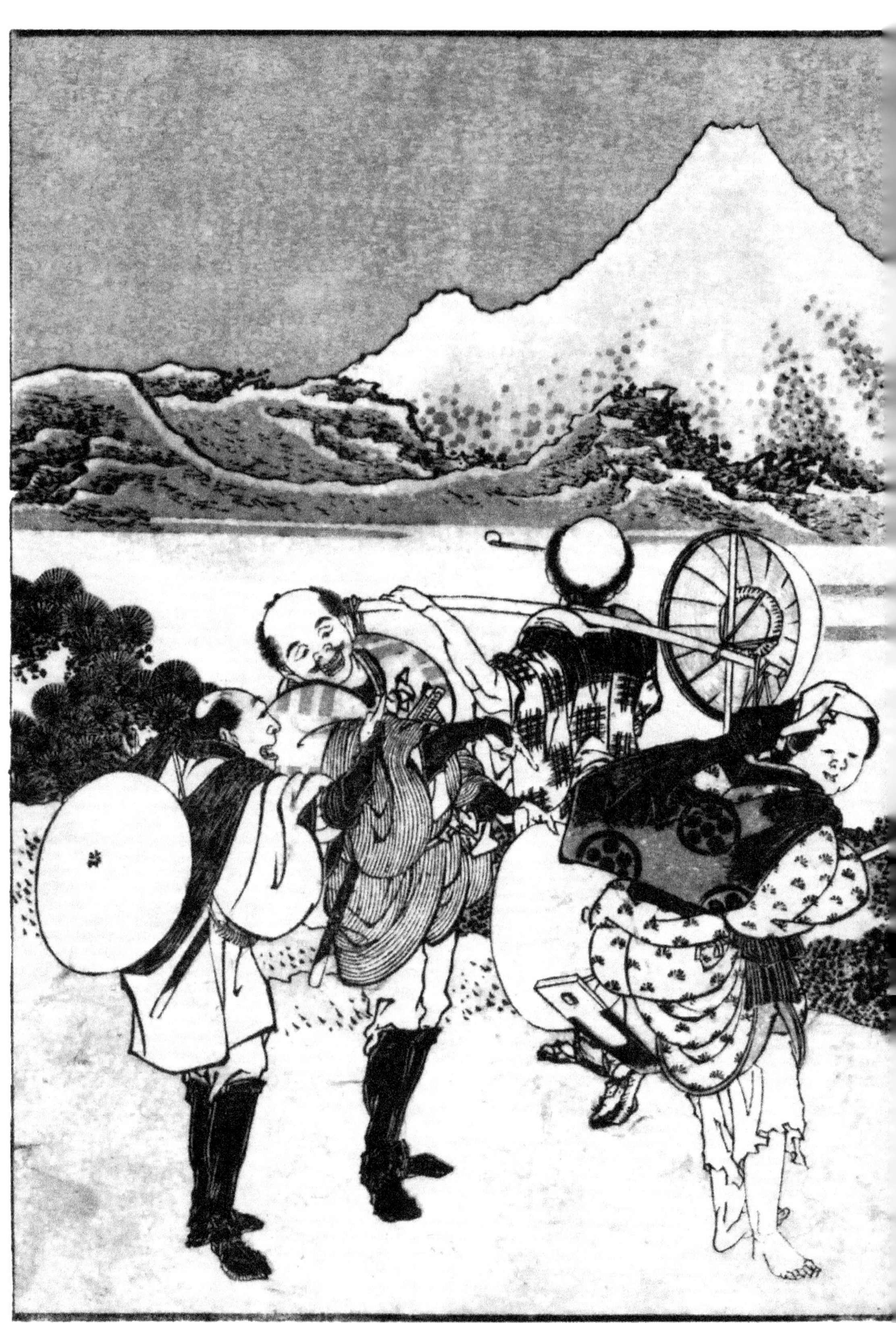

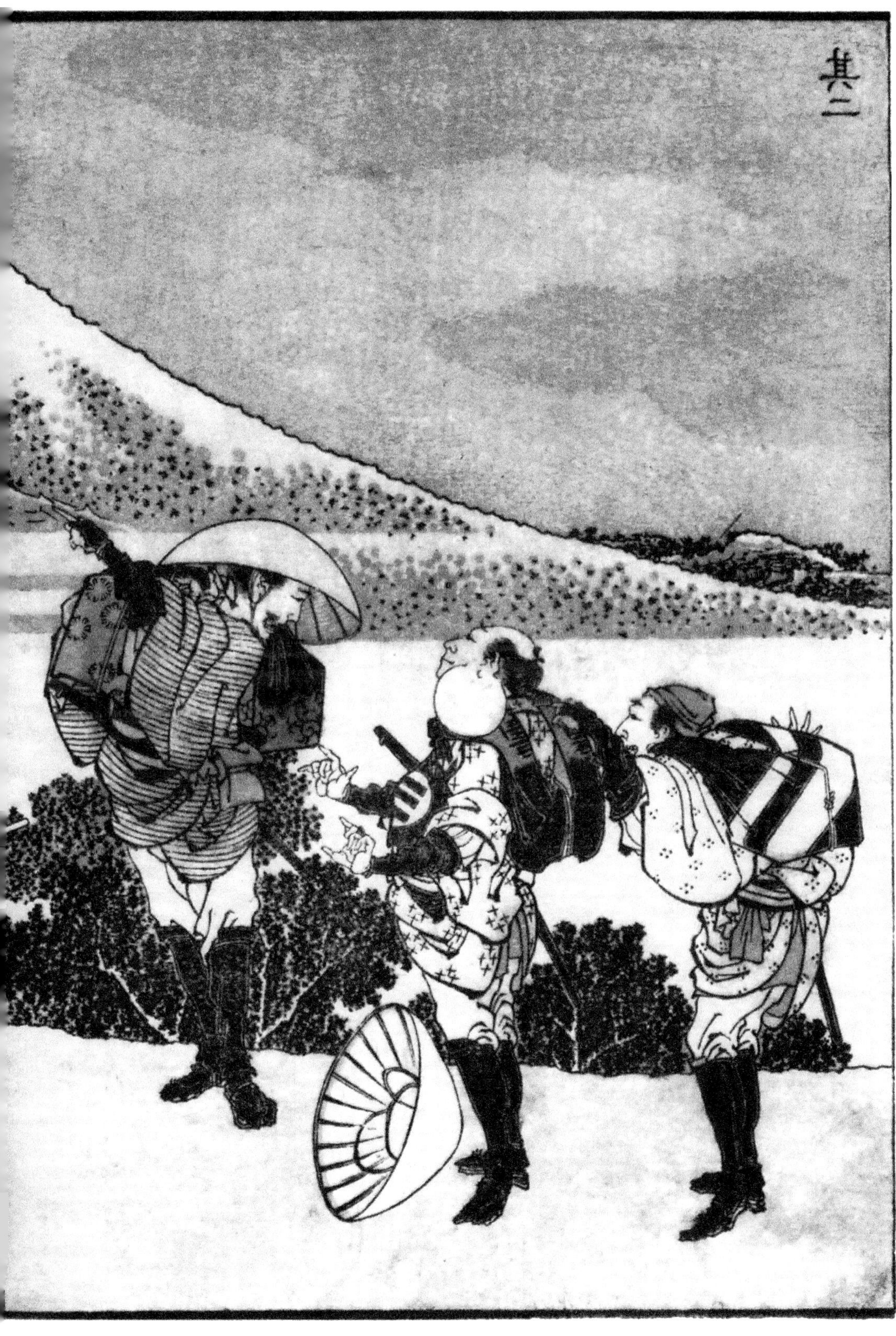

Plate VIII

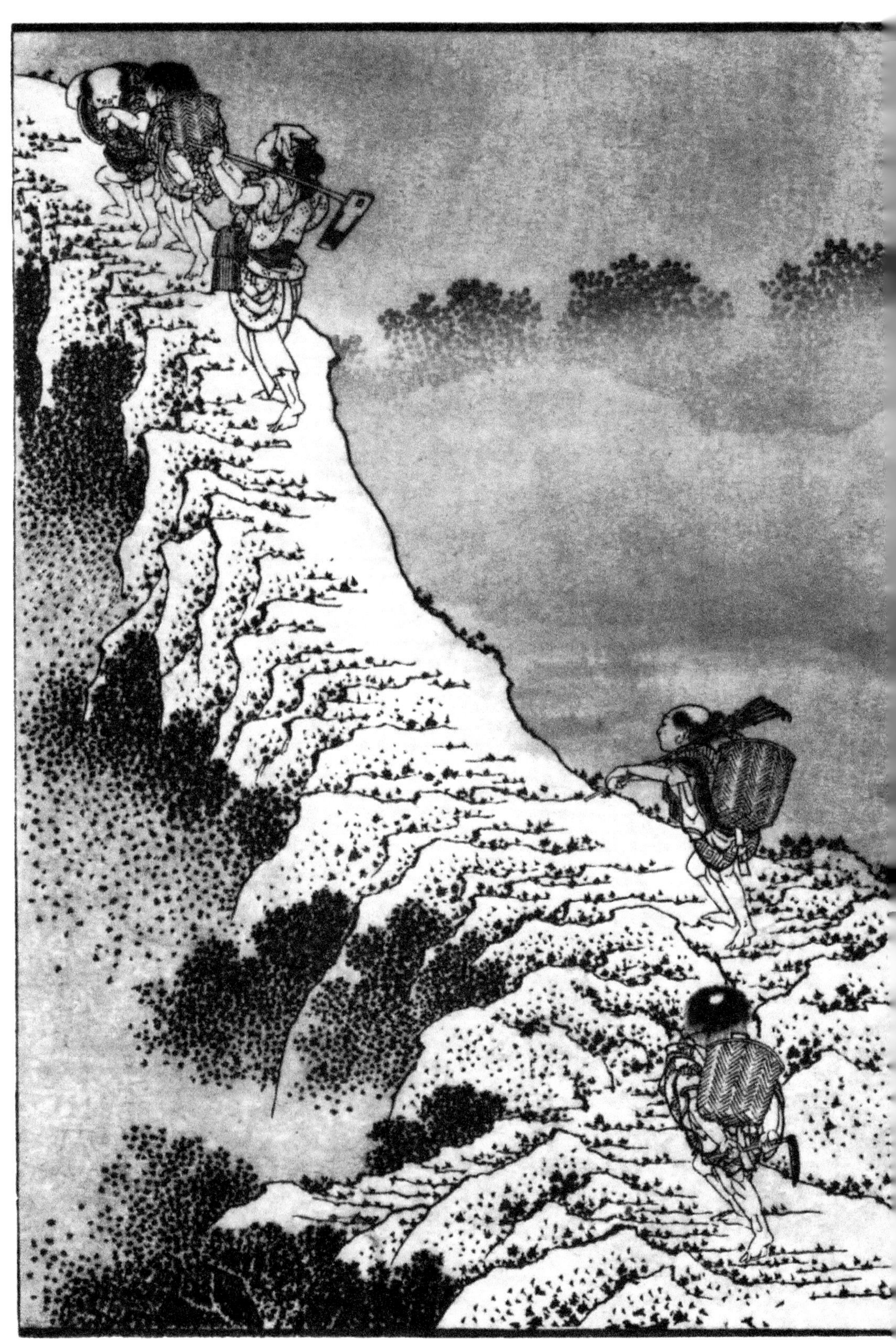

Plate IX

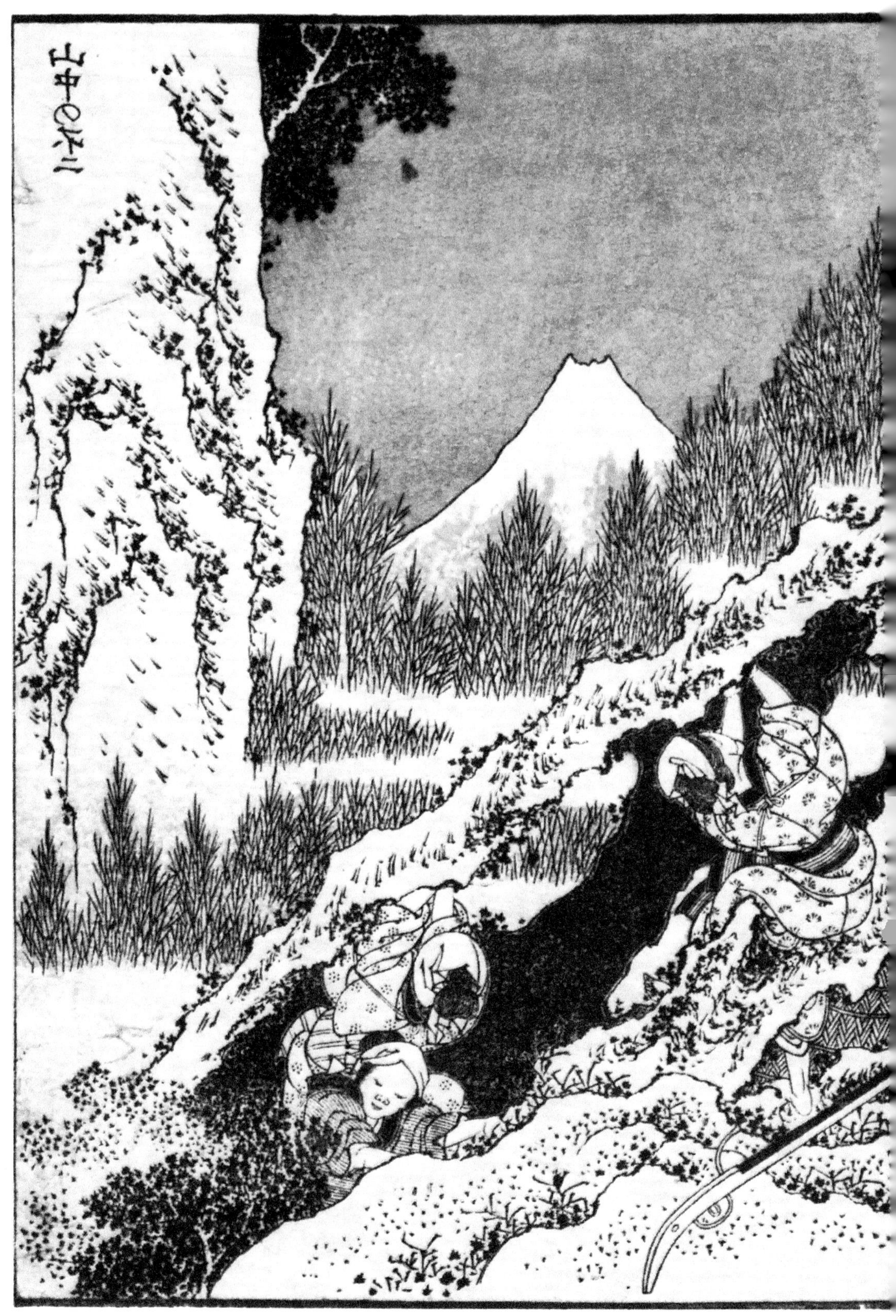
二代目のおいて

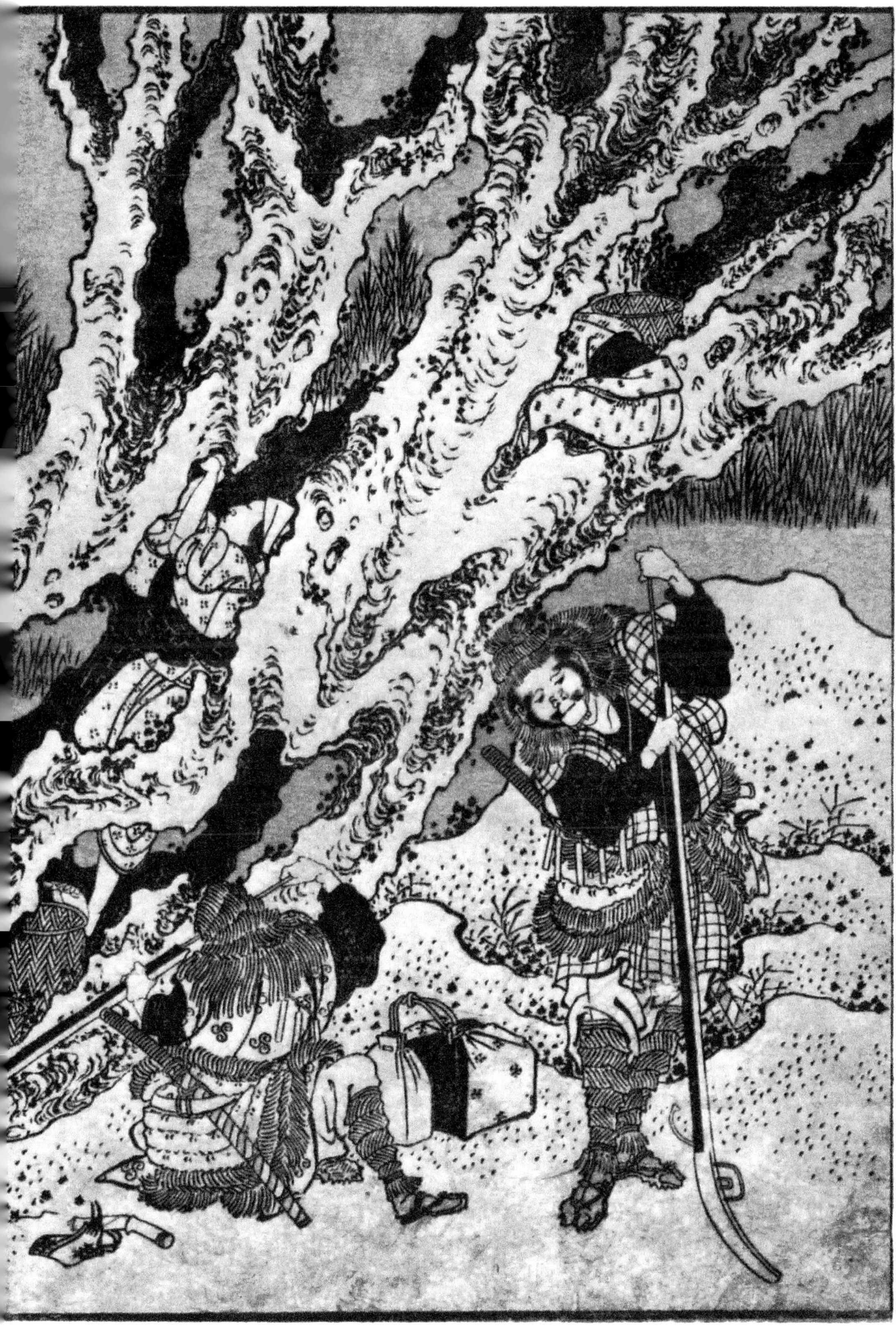

Plate X

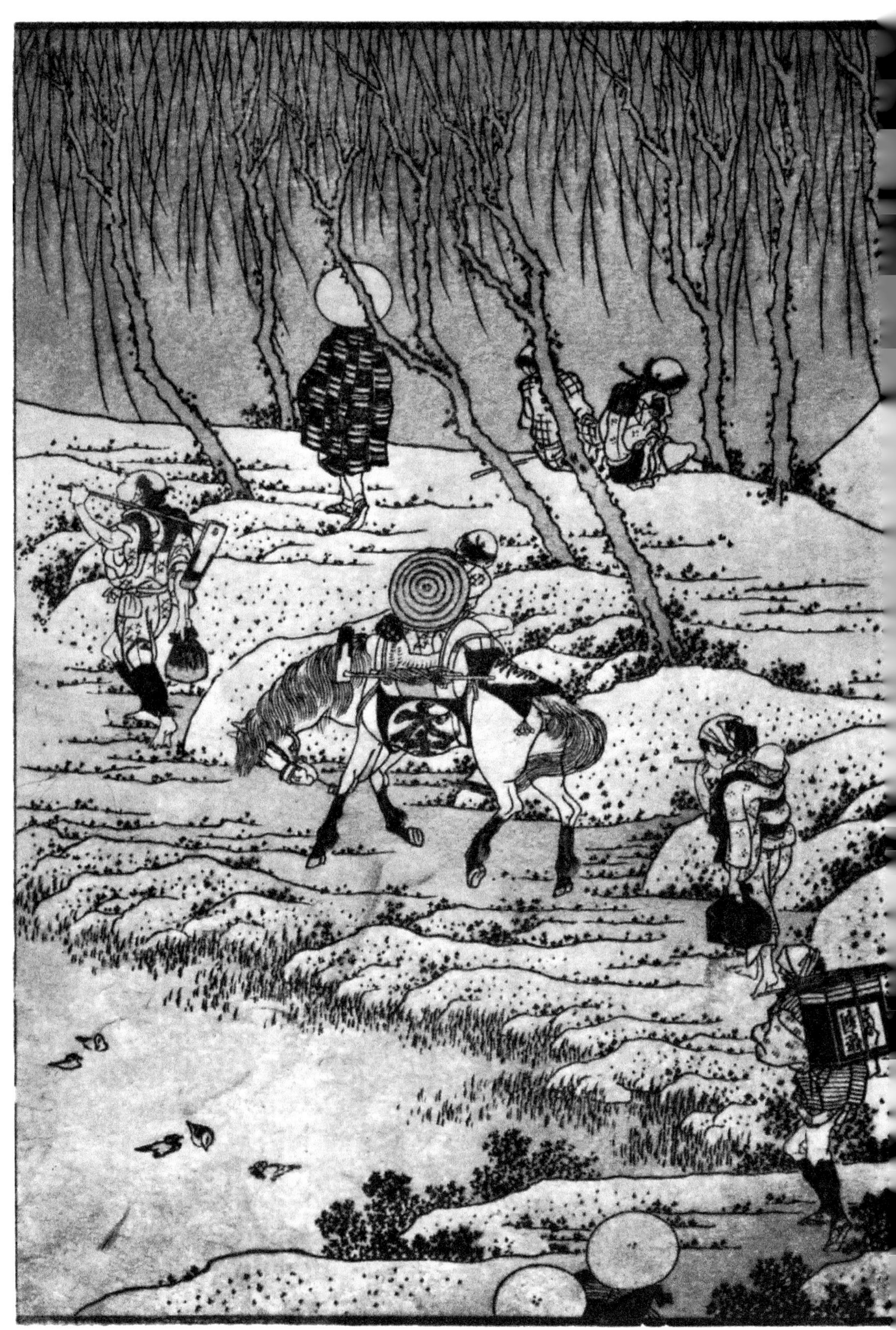

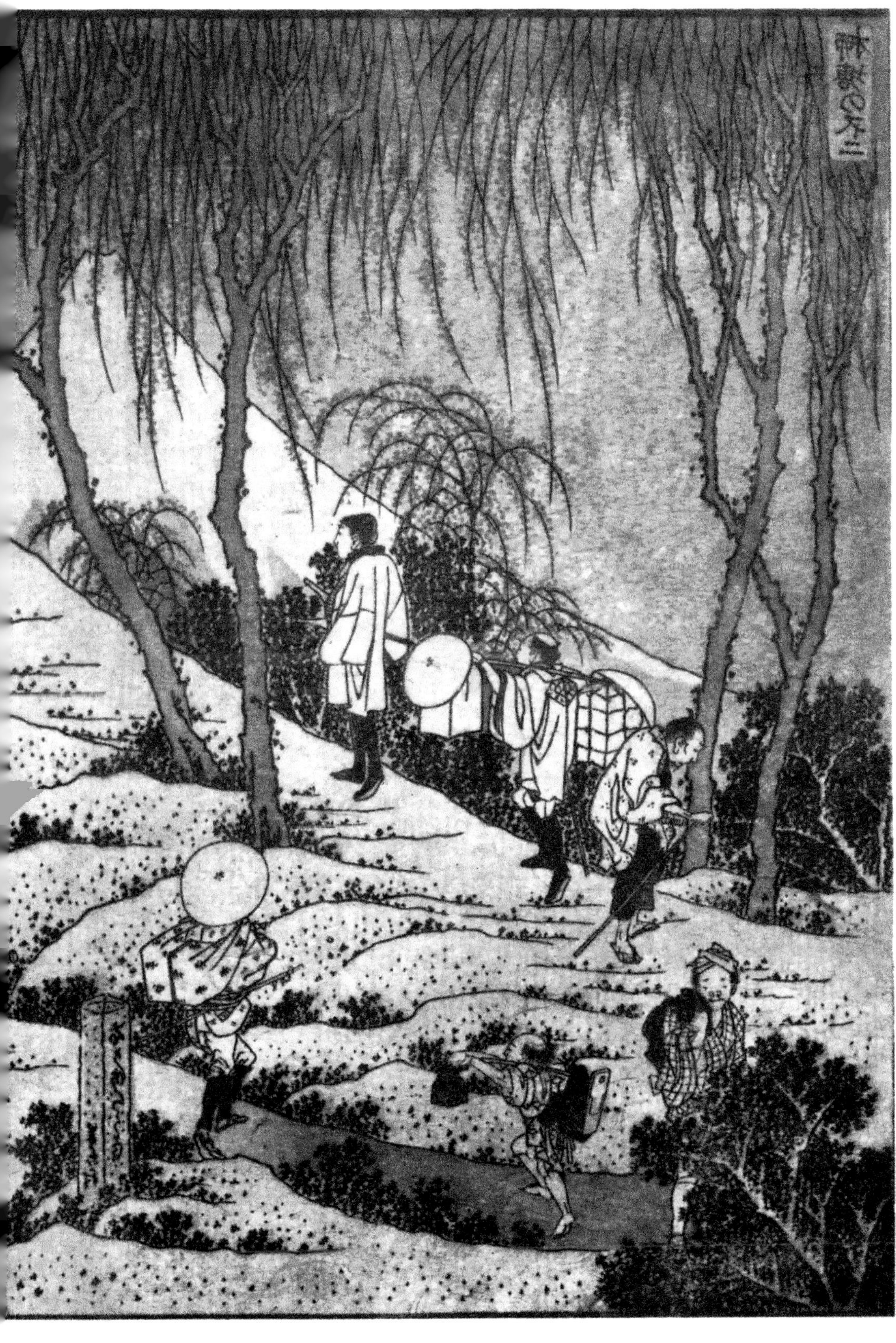

Plate XI

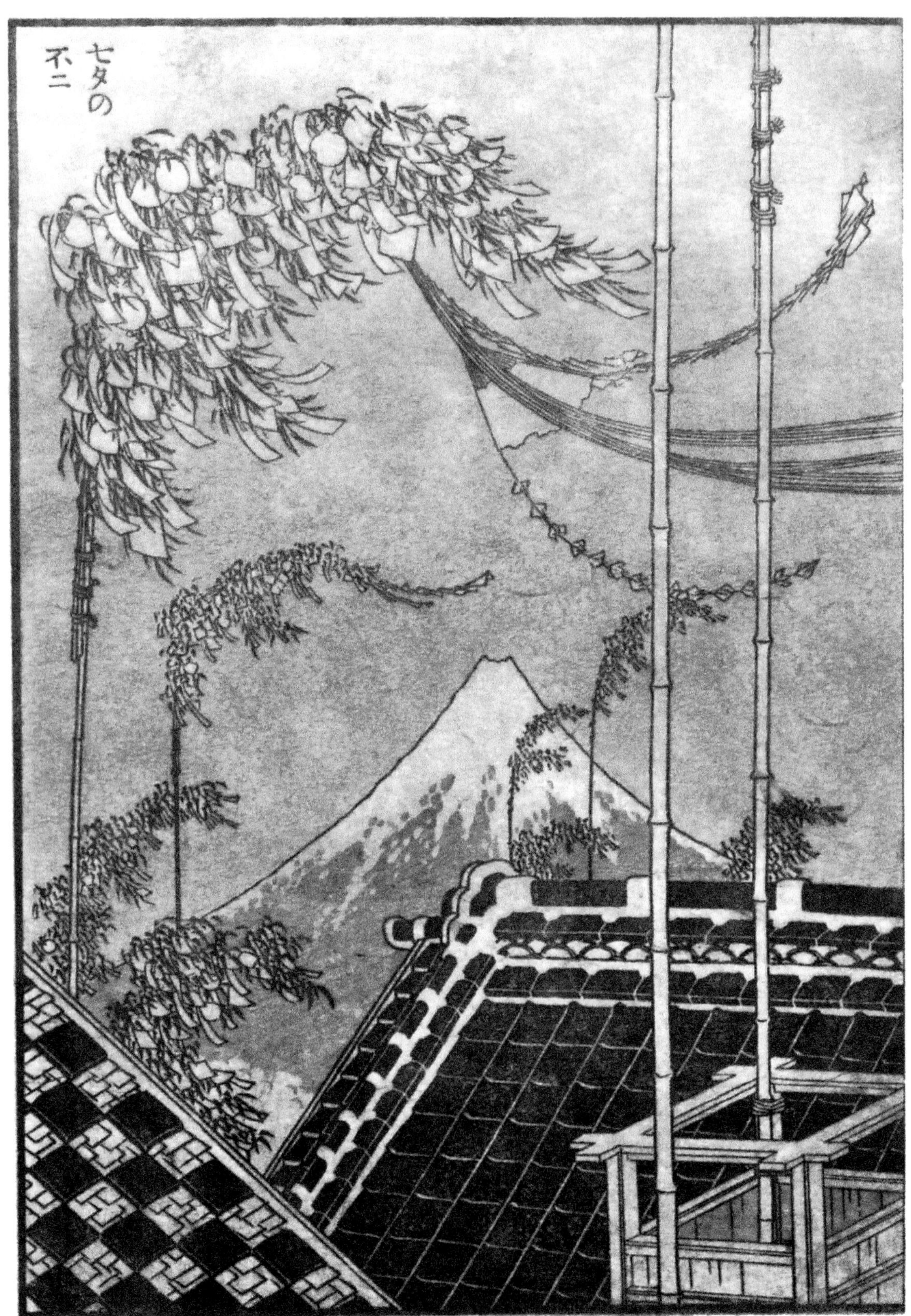

Plate XII

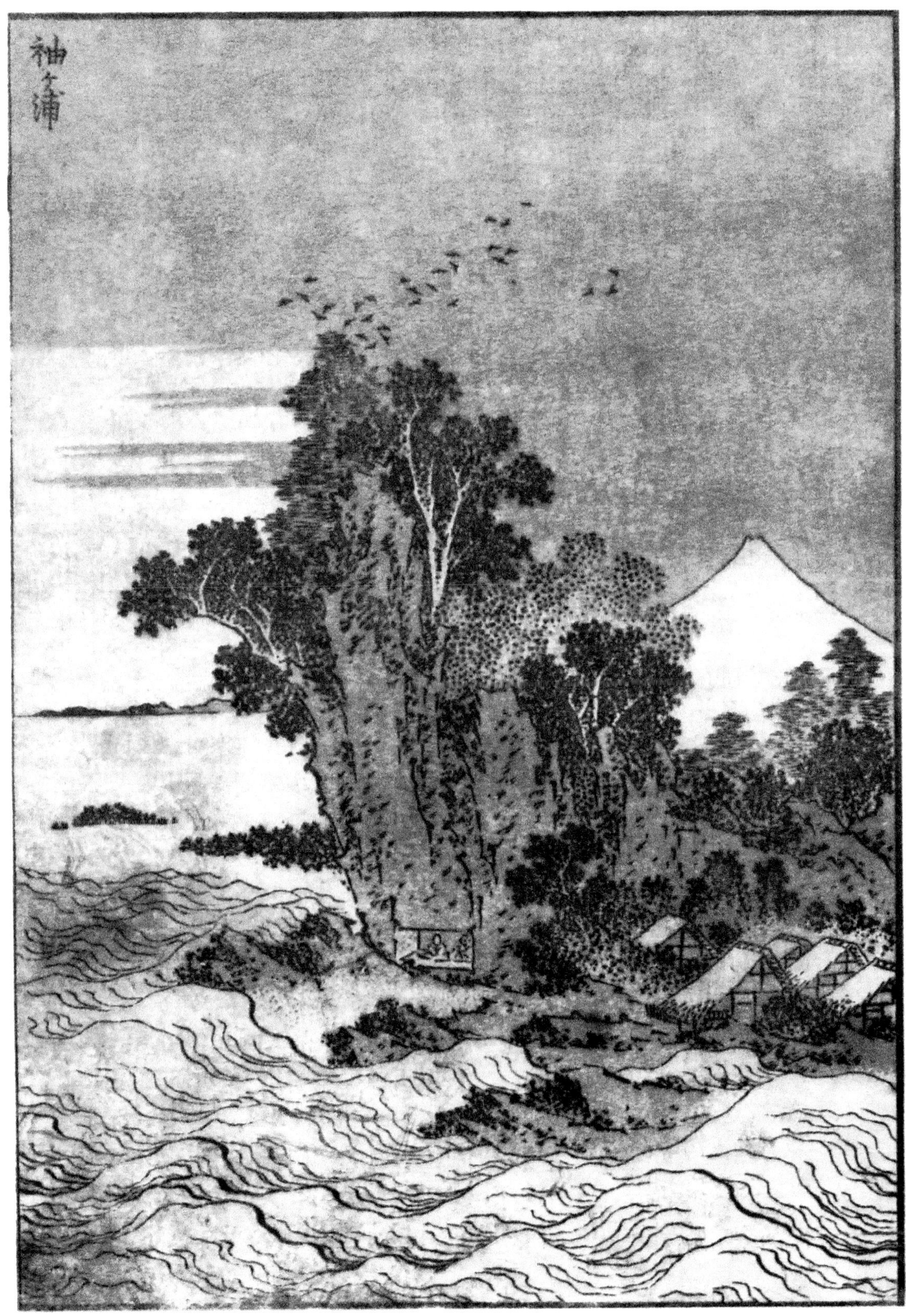

Plate XIII

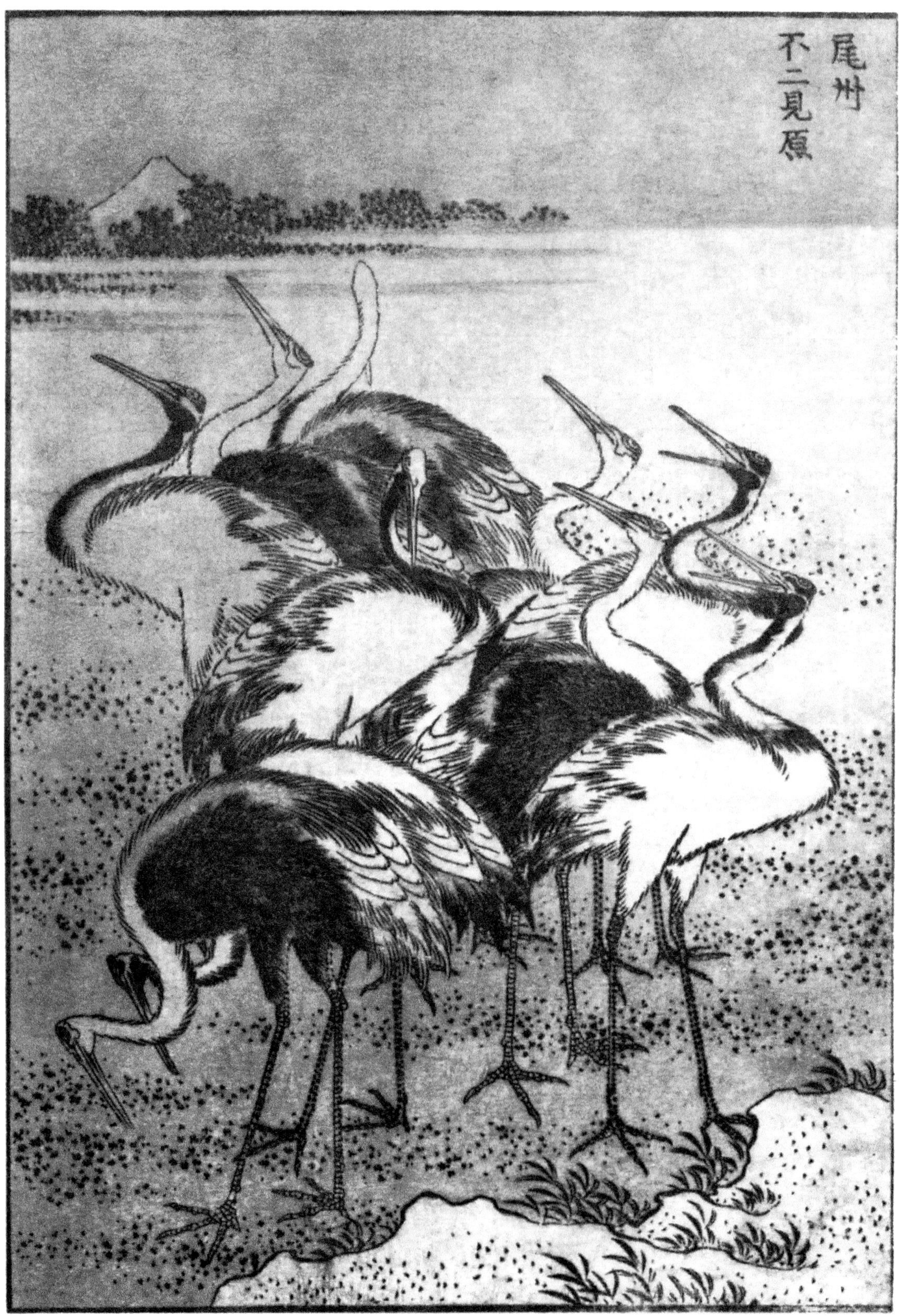

Plate XIV

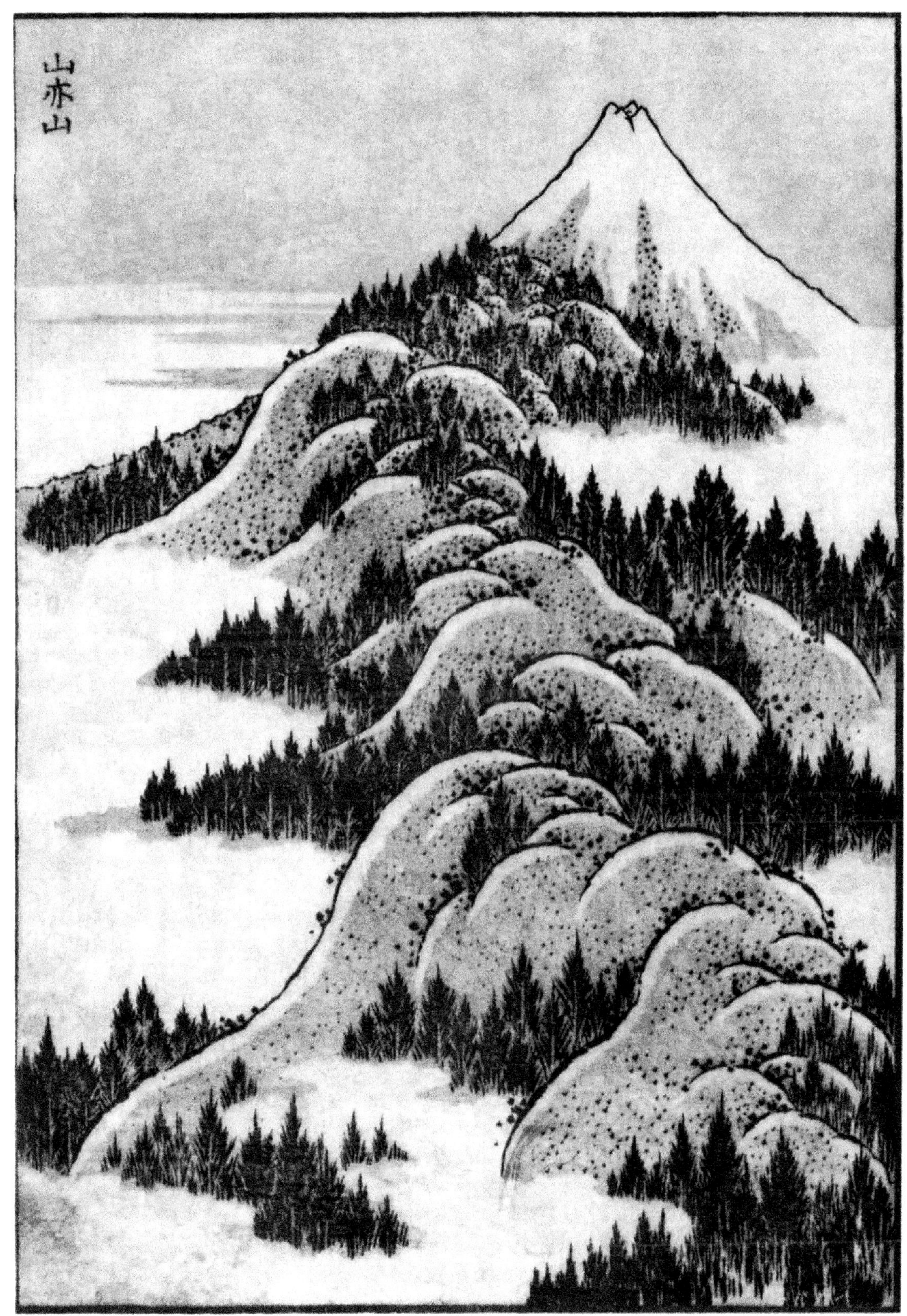

Plate XV

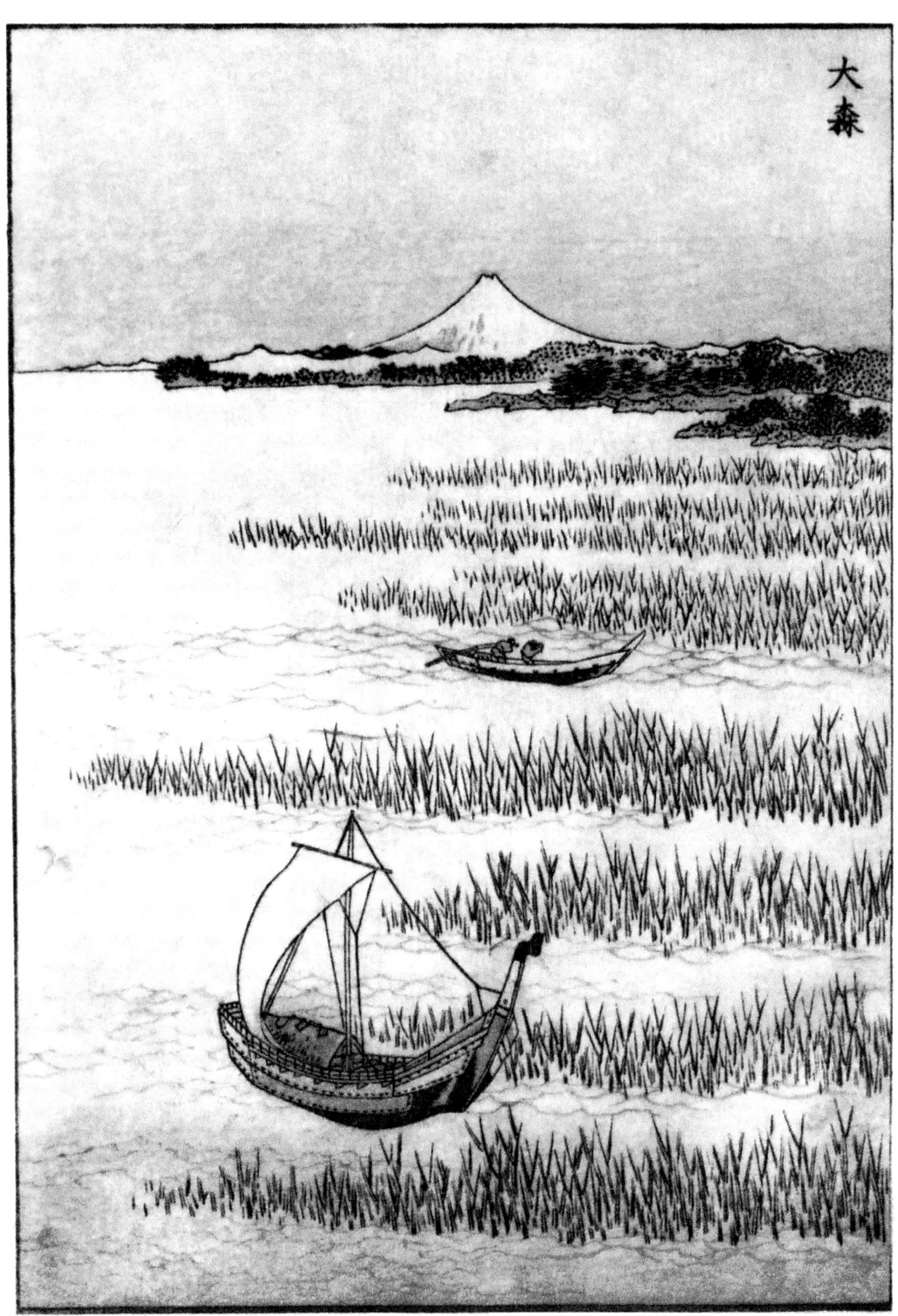

Plate XVI

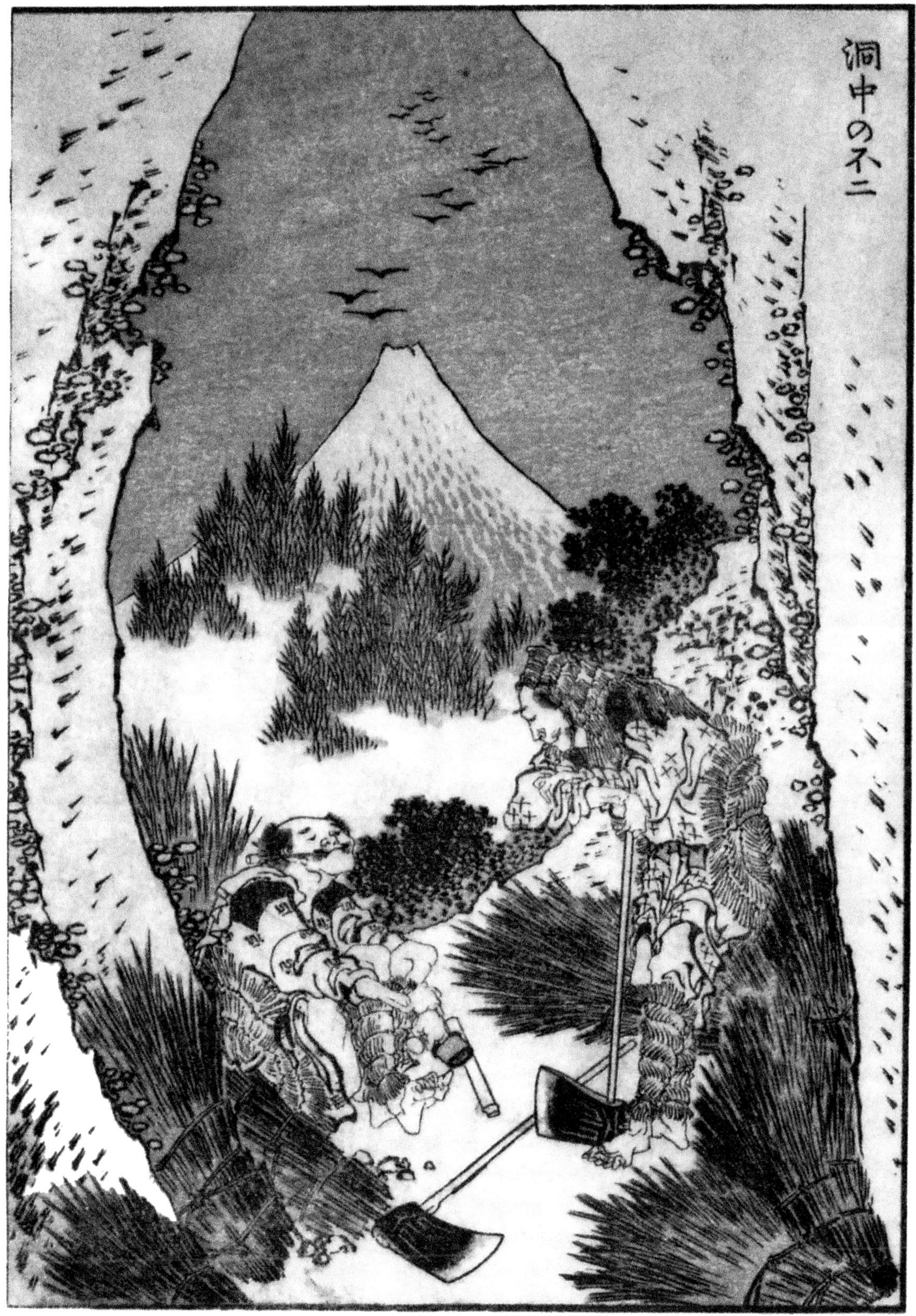

Plate XVII

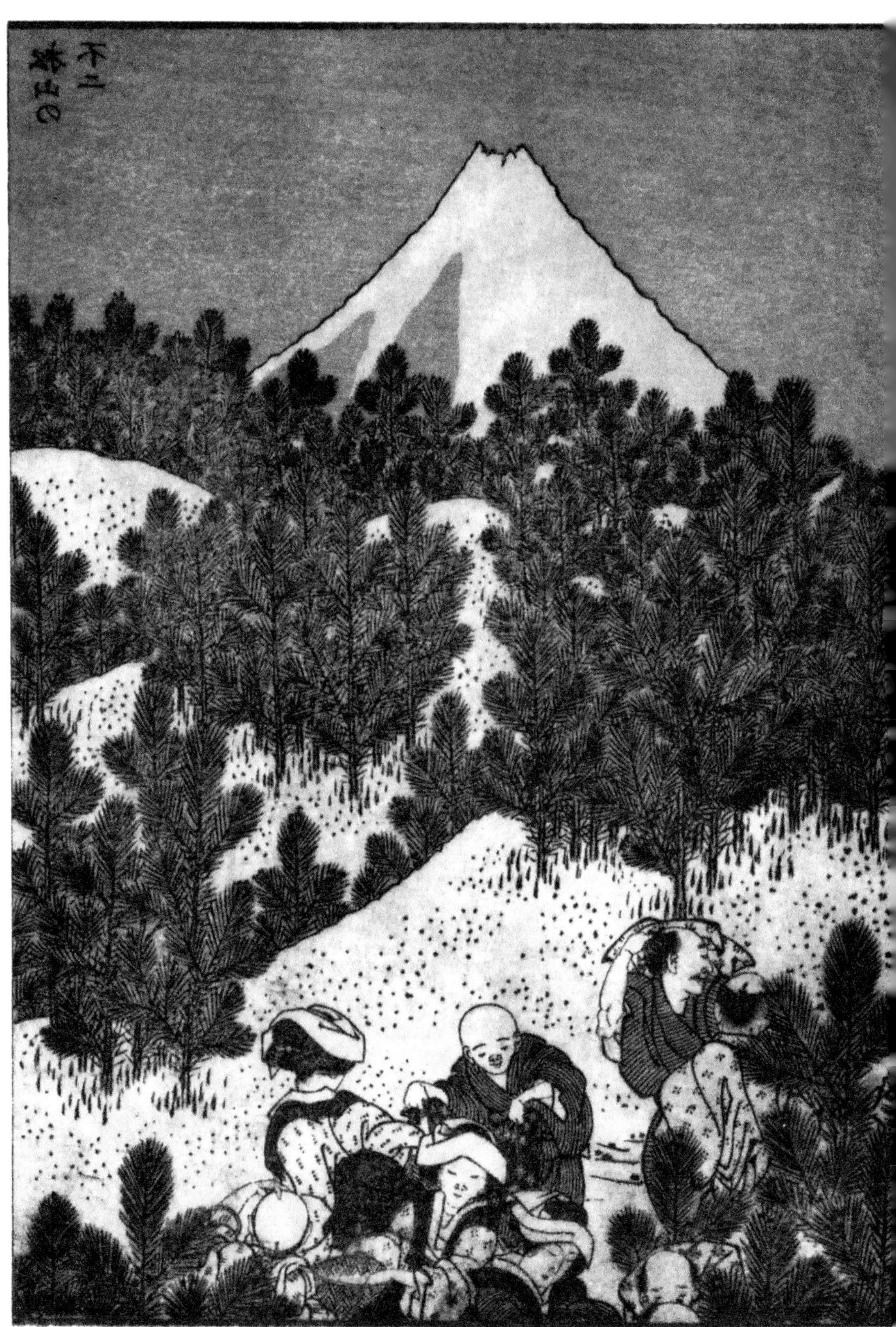

不二
養山の

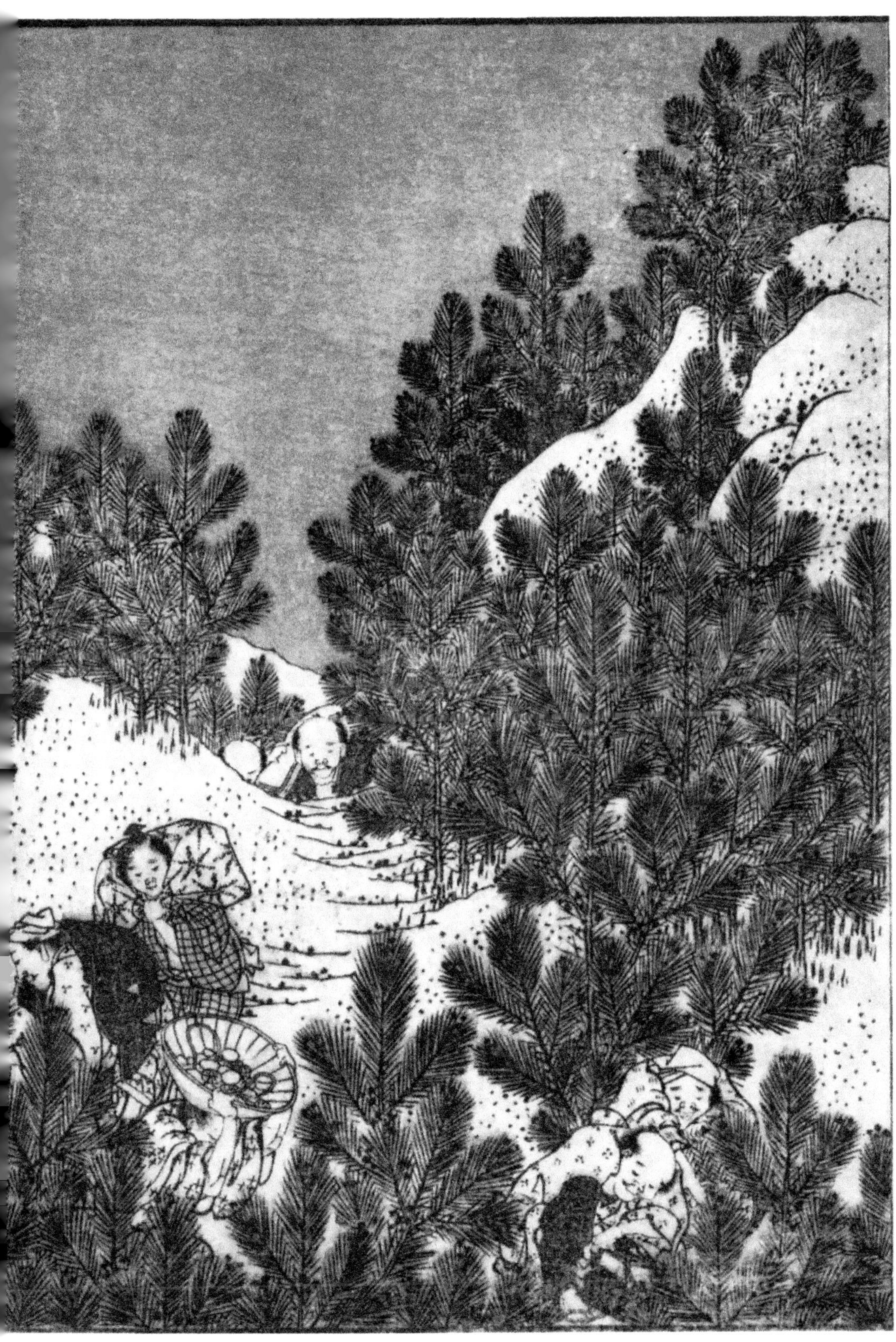

Plate XVIII

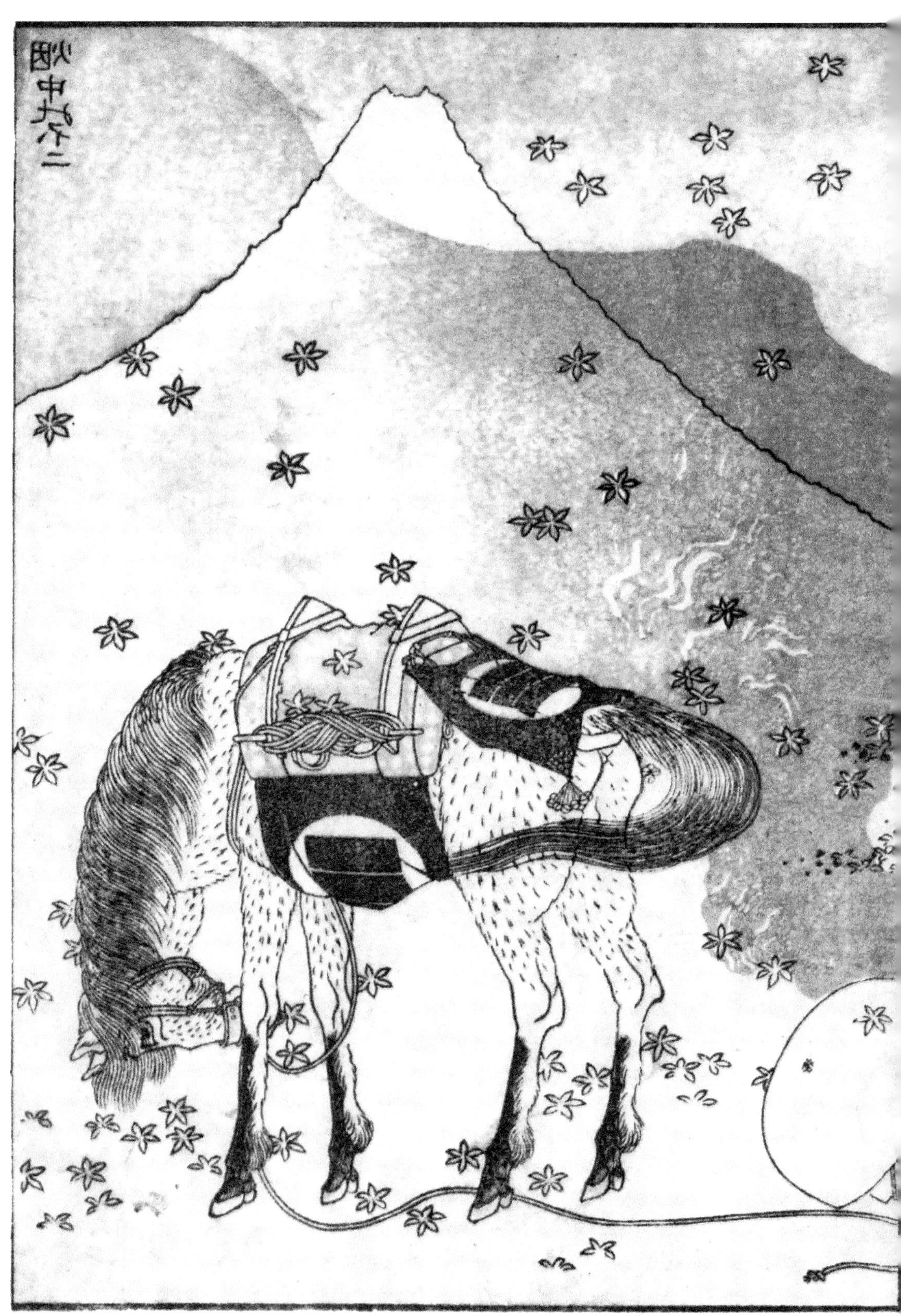

火中かん二図

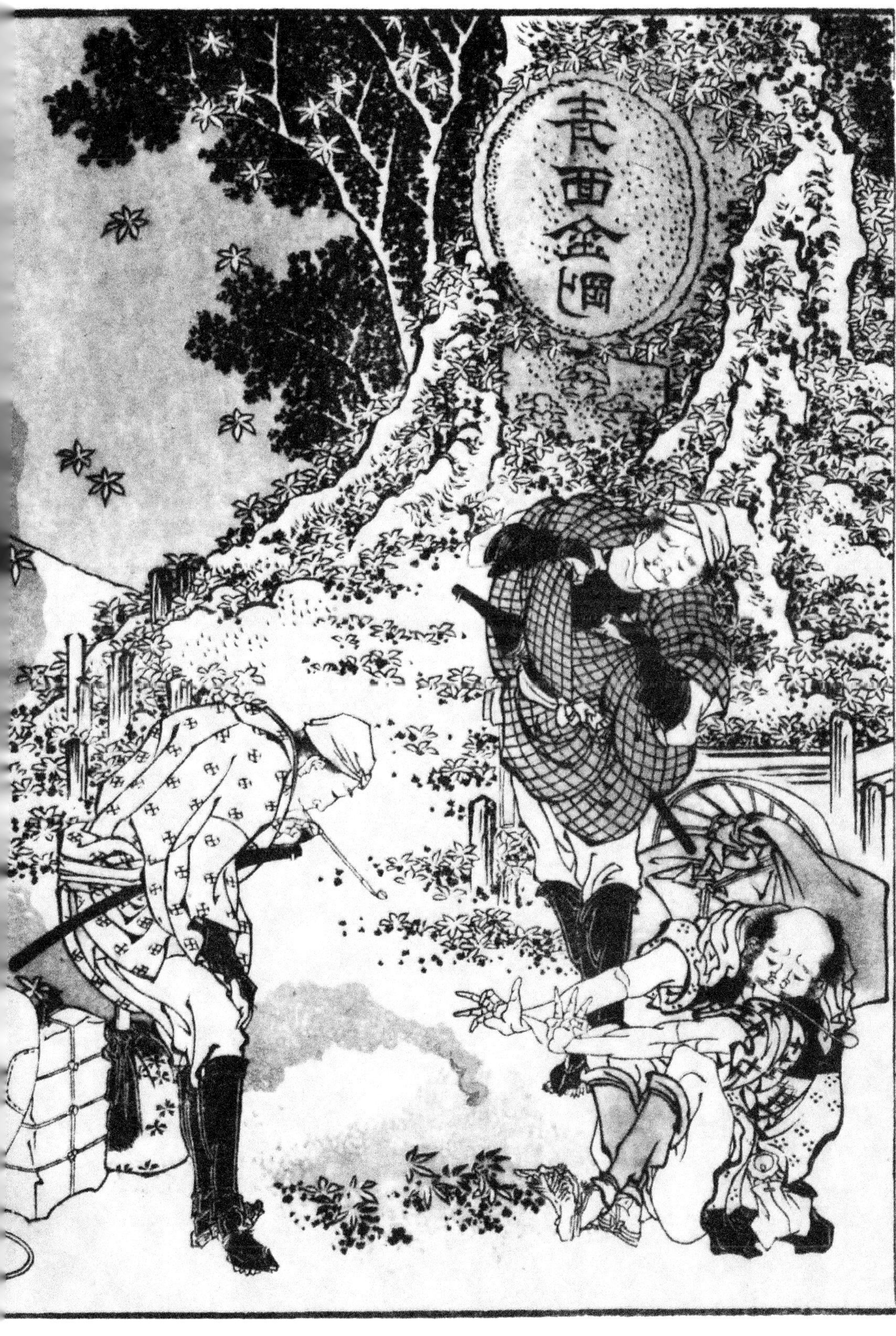

Plate XIX

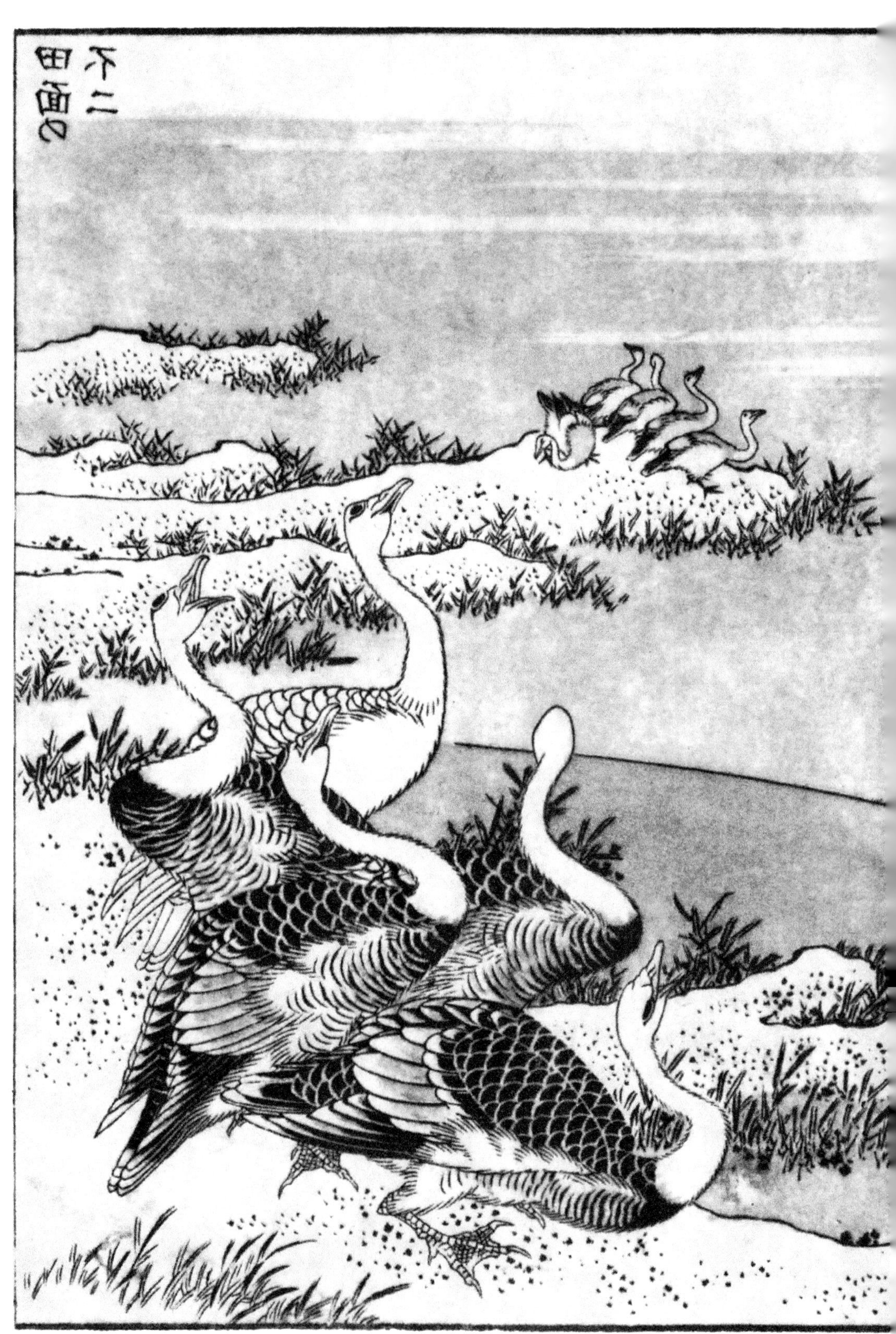

下二
畫の

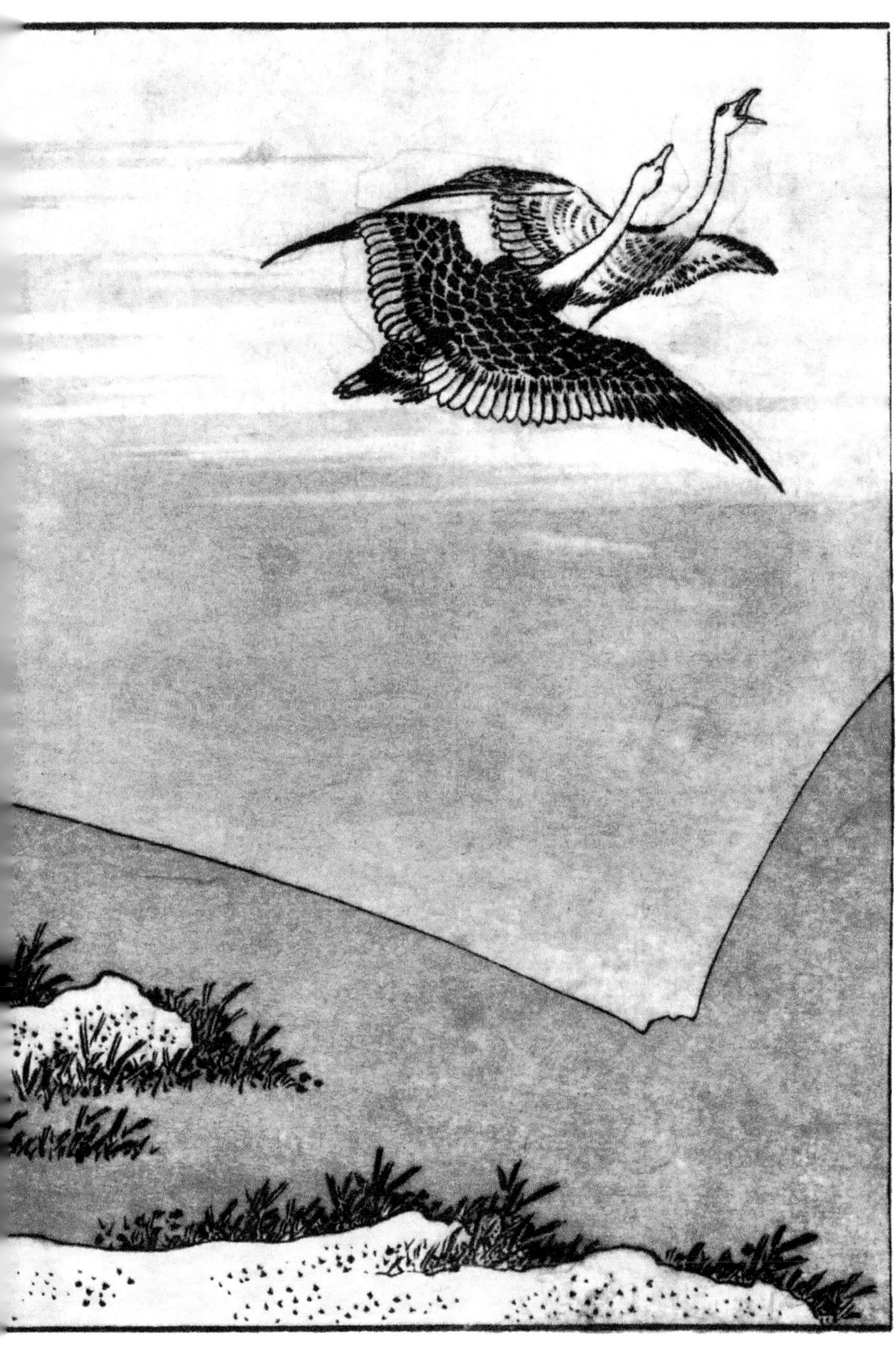

Plate XX

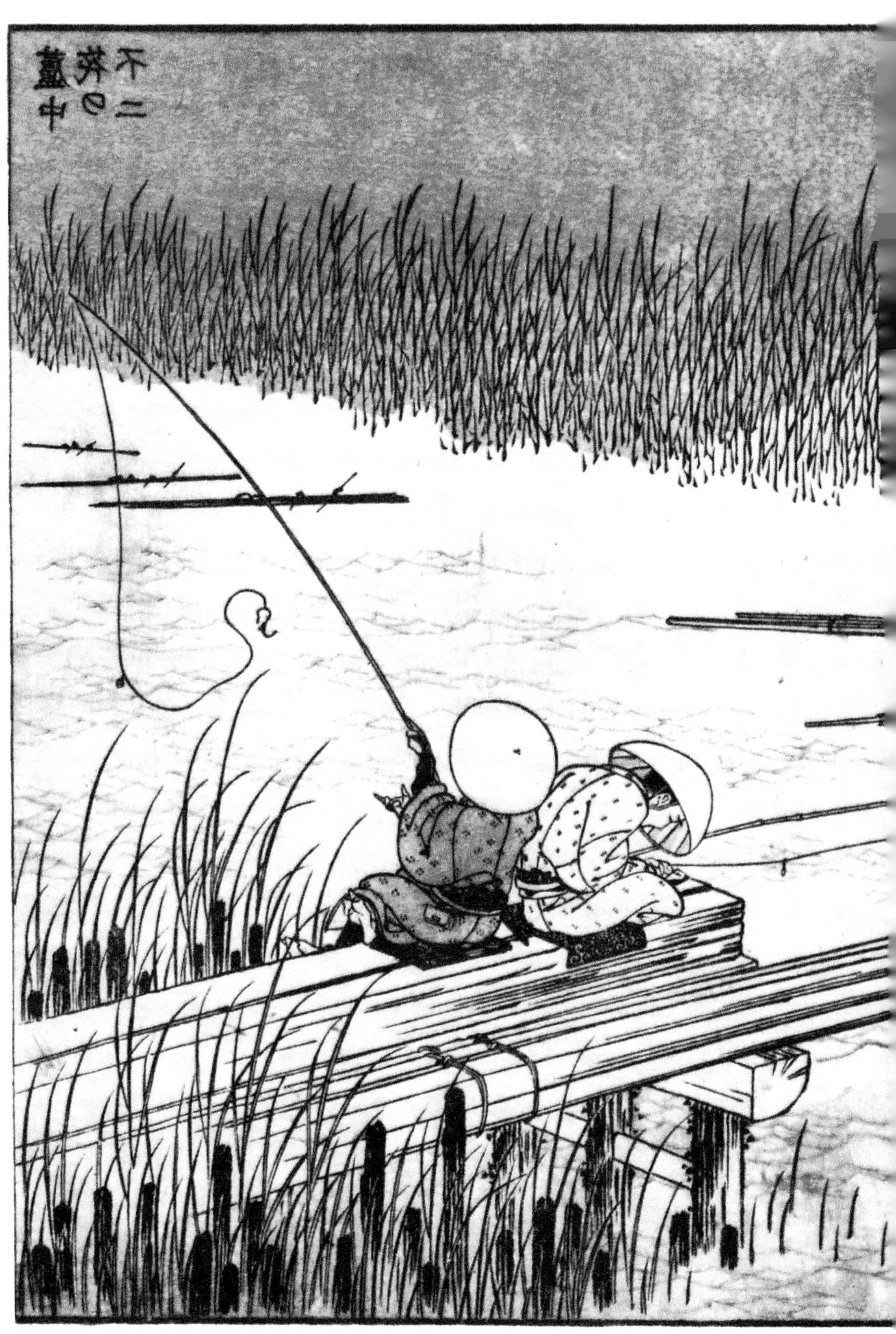

不二芽の蘆中

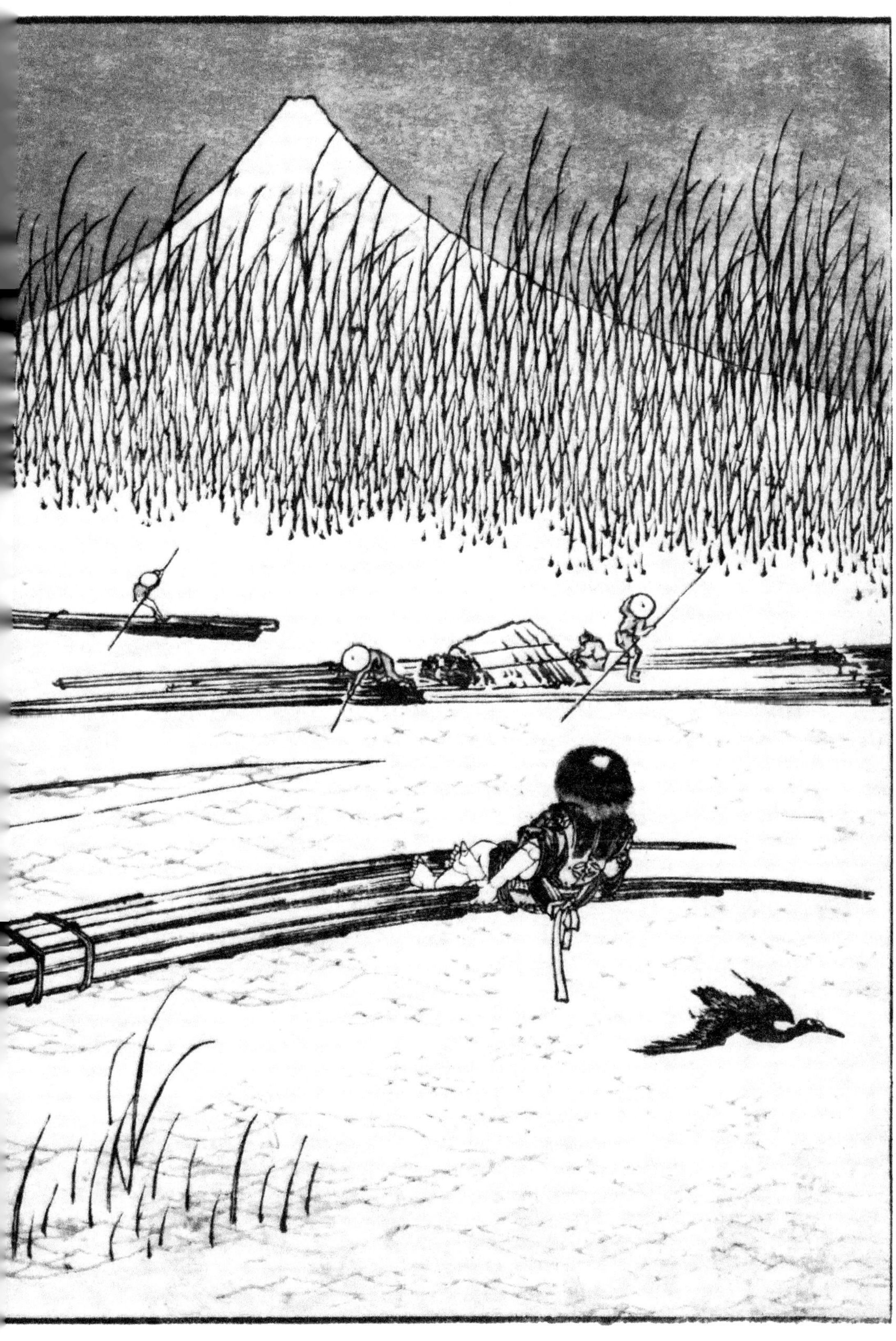

Plate XXI

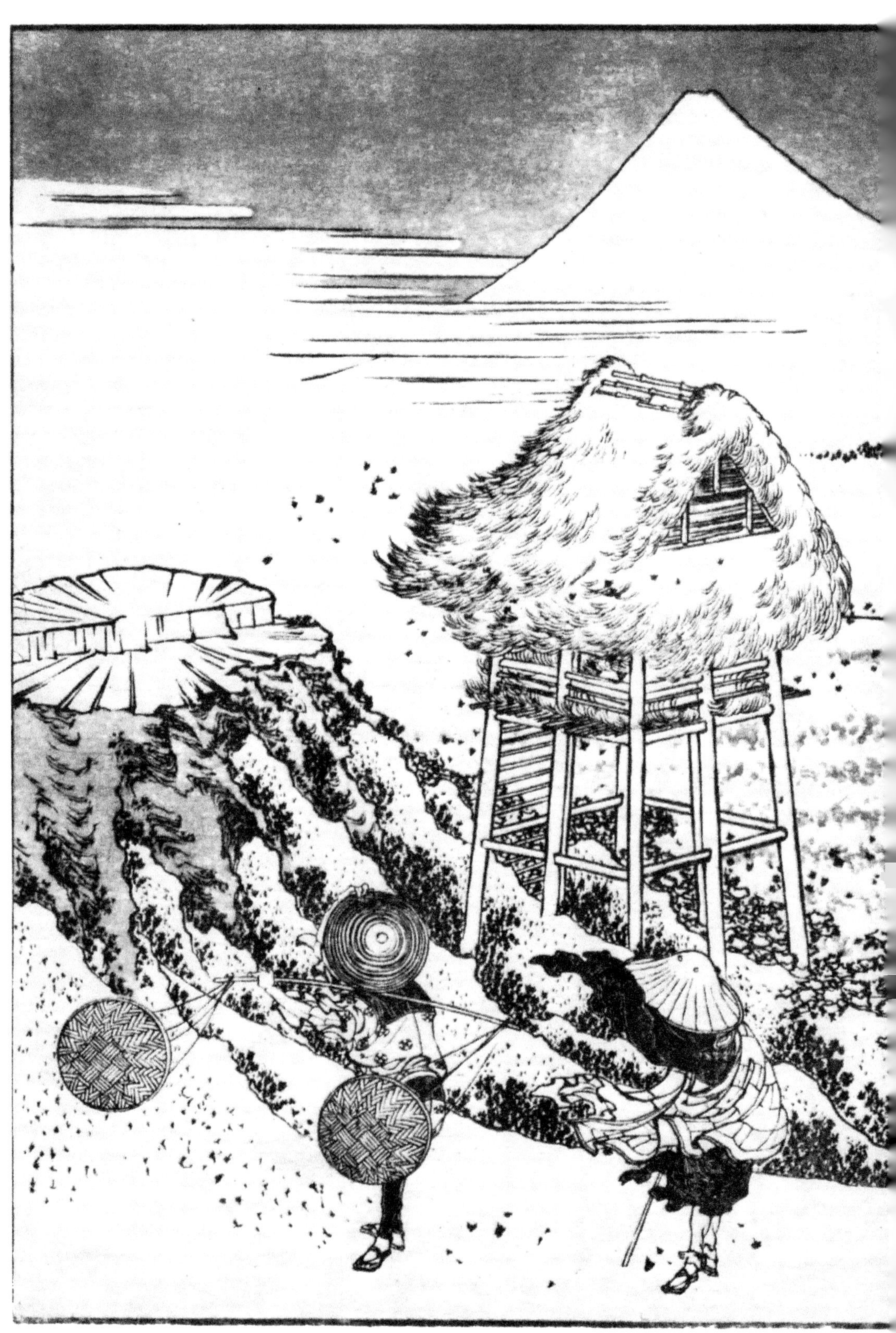

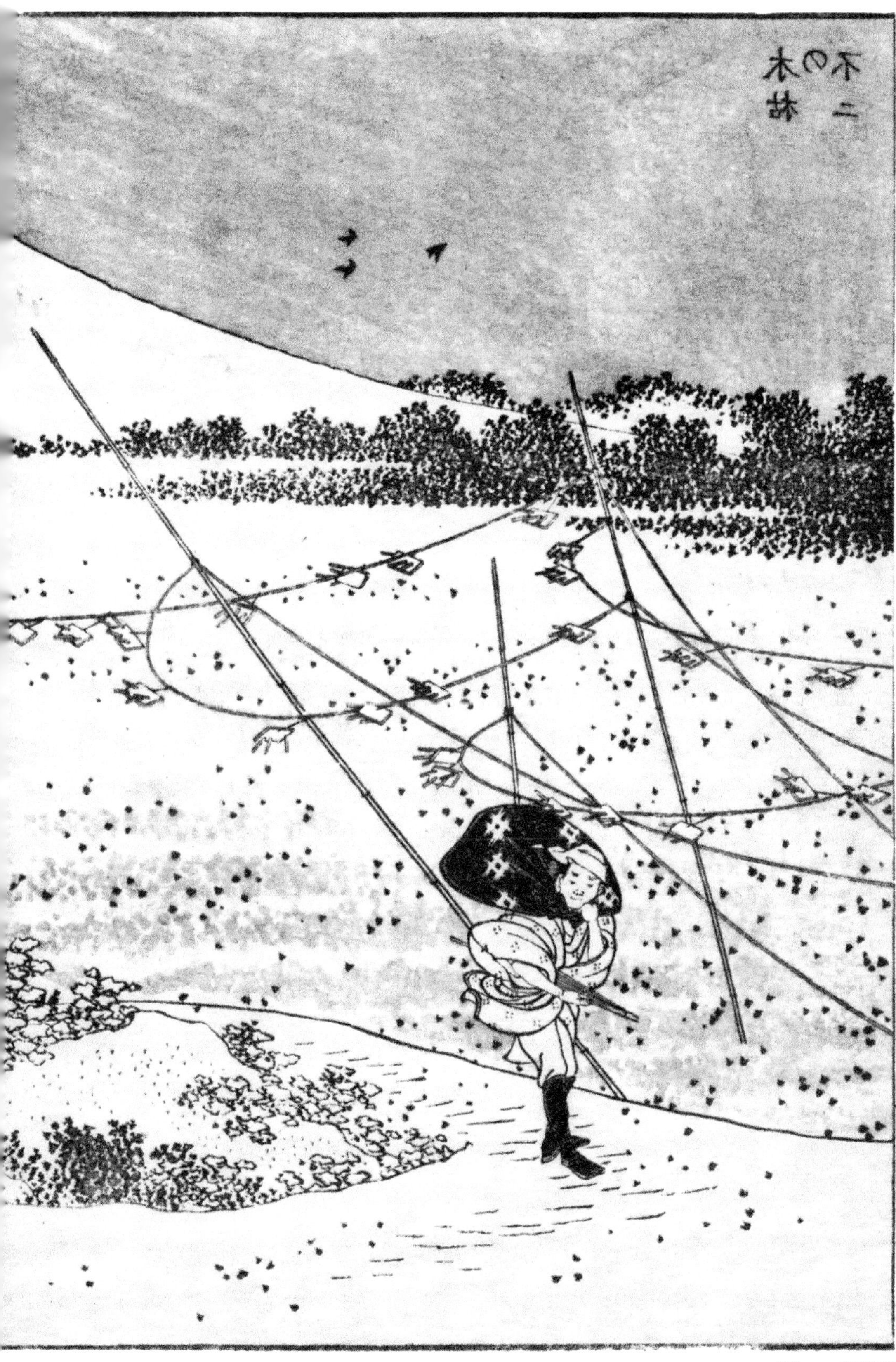

不
の
木
二
株

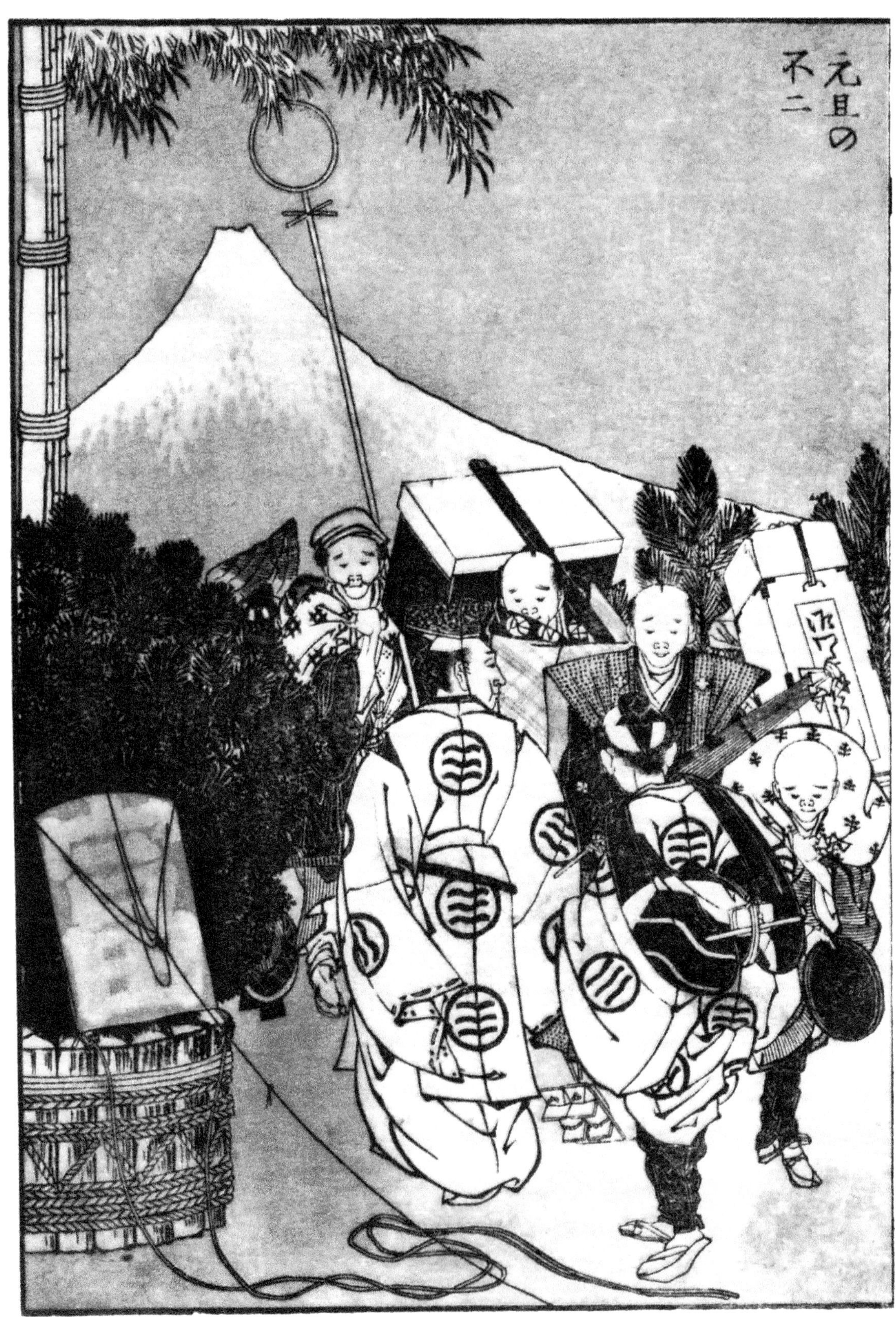

Plate XXIII

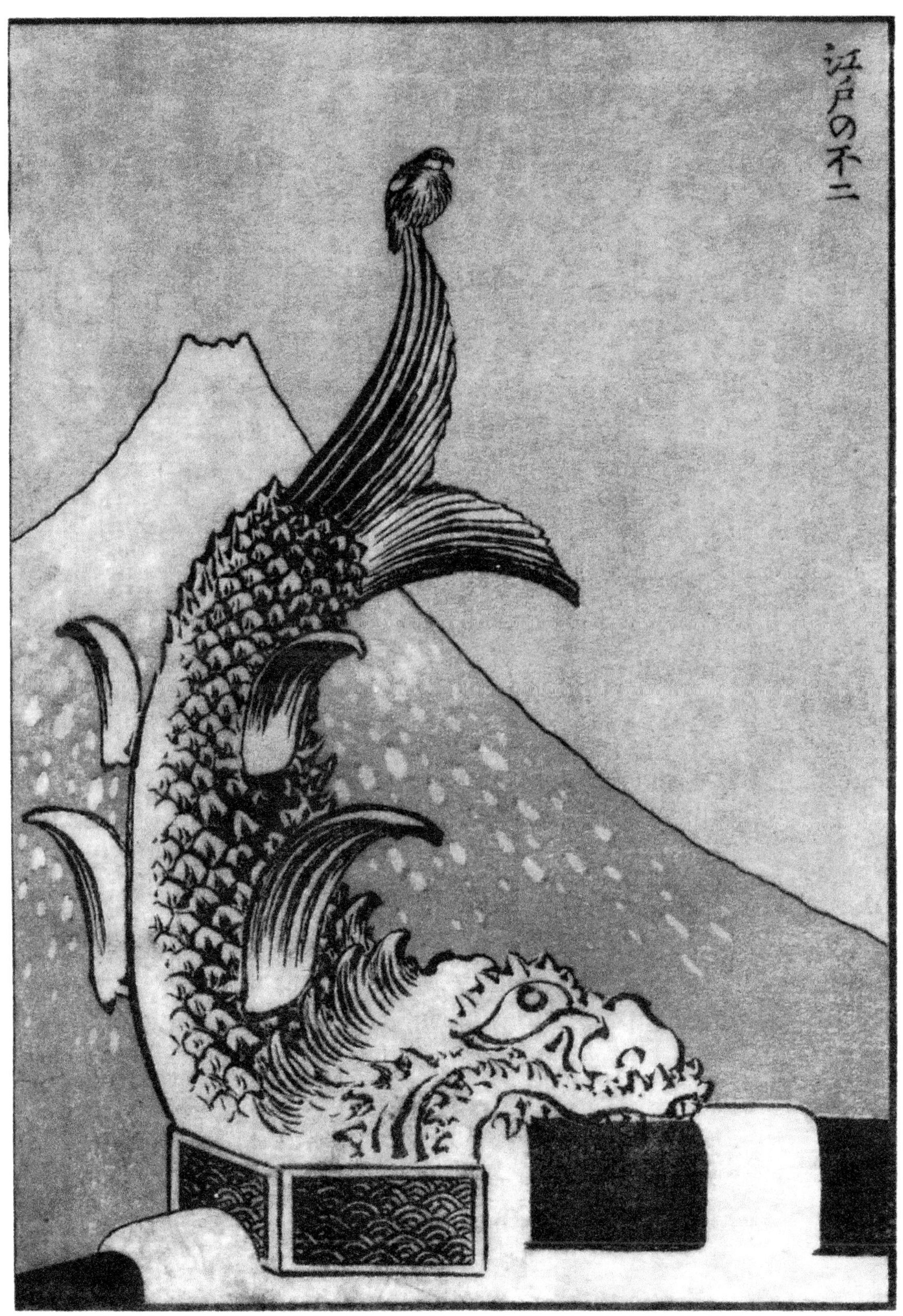

Plate XXIV

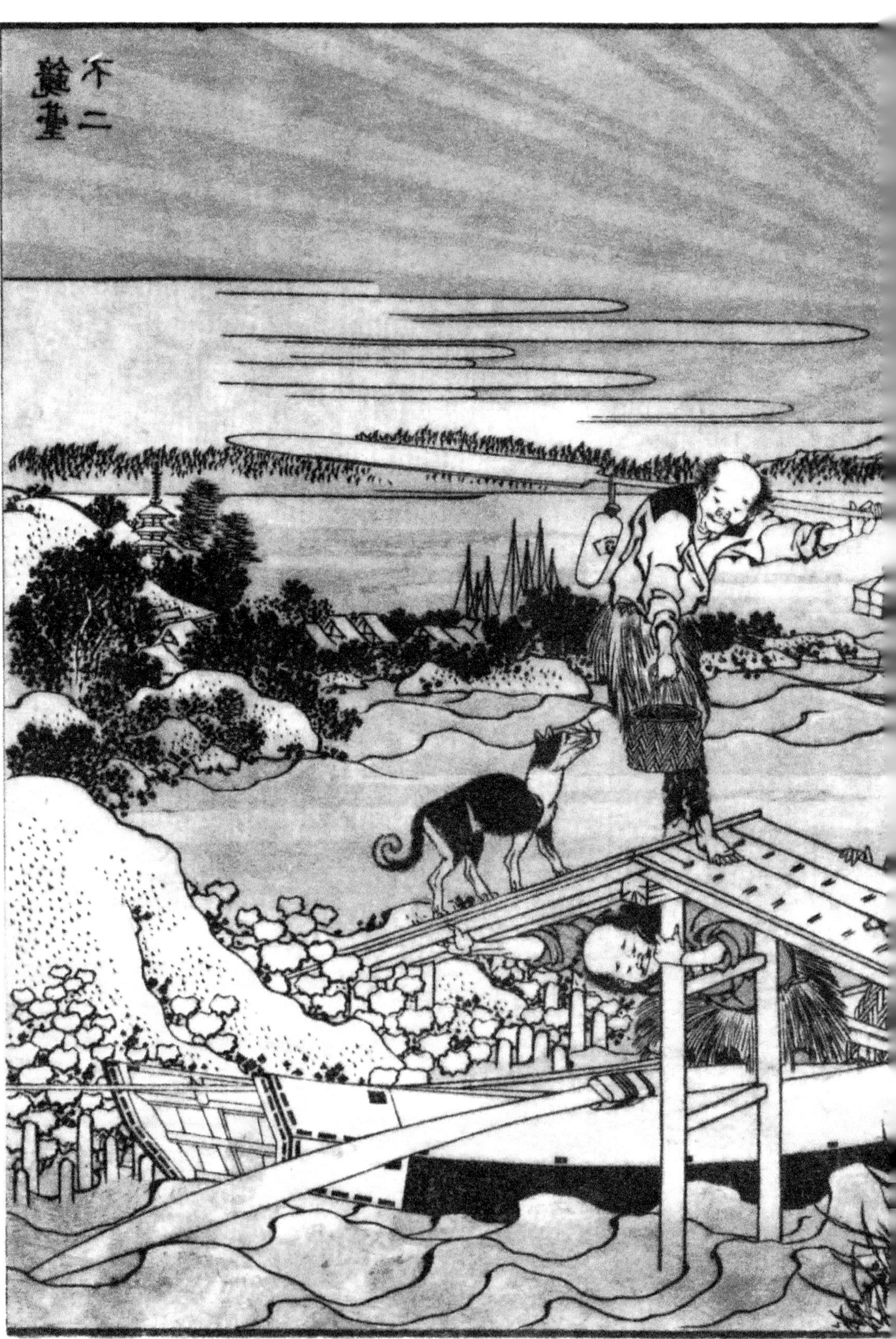

不二
鵲橋

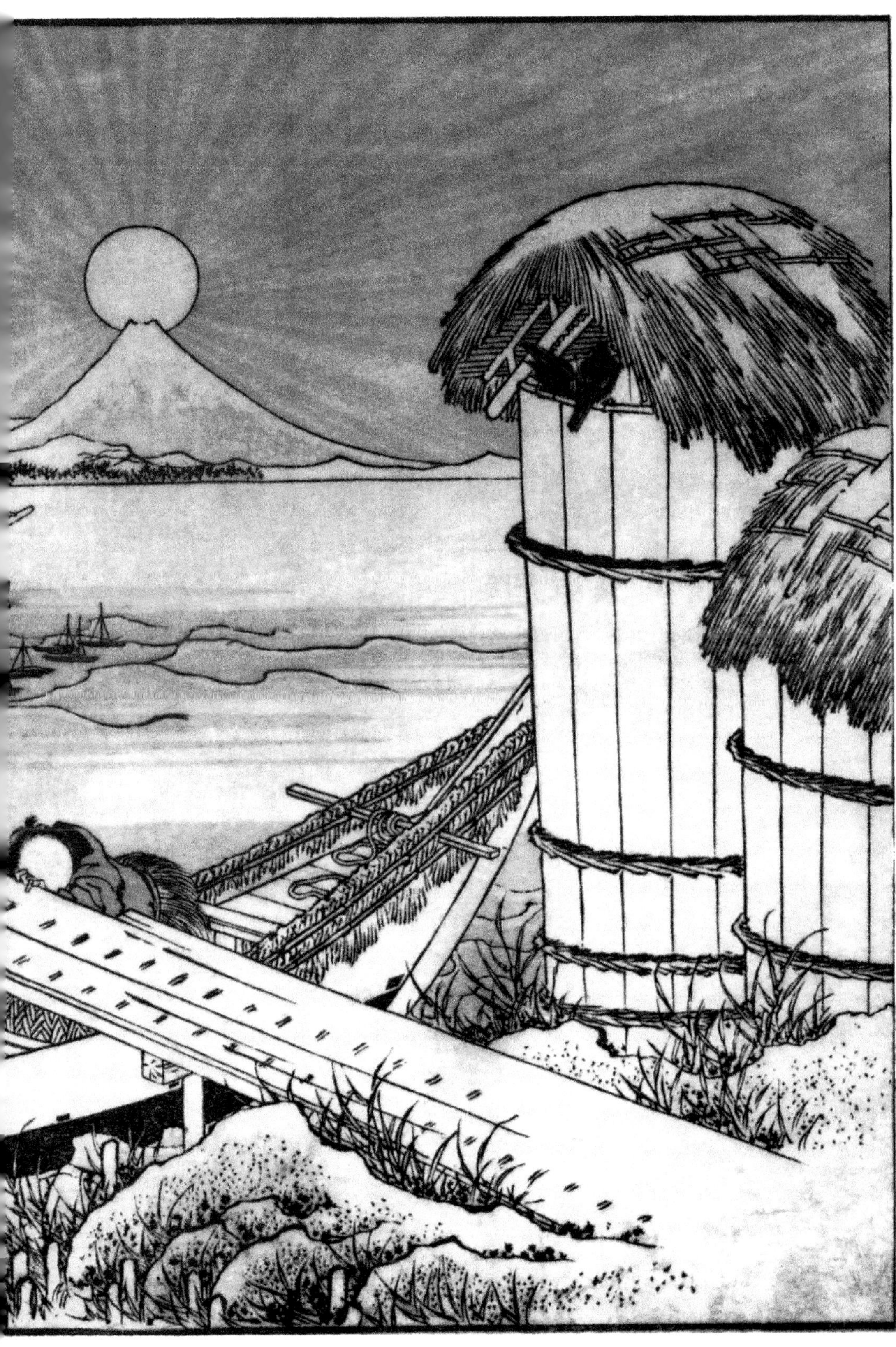

Plate XXV

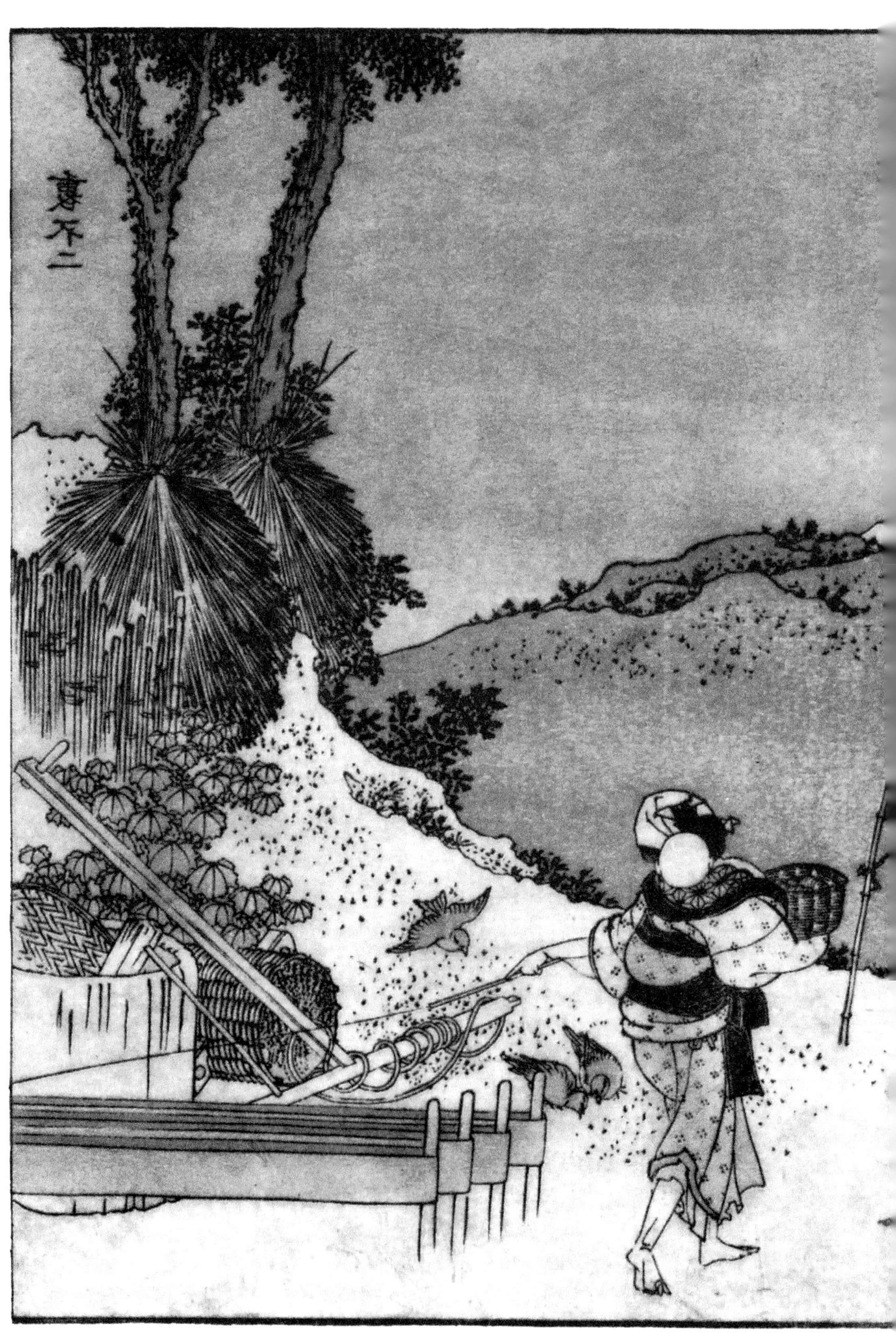

喜不二

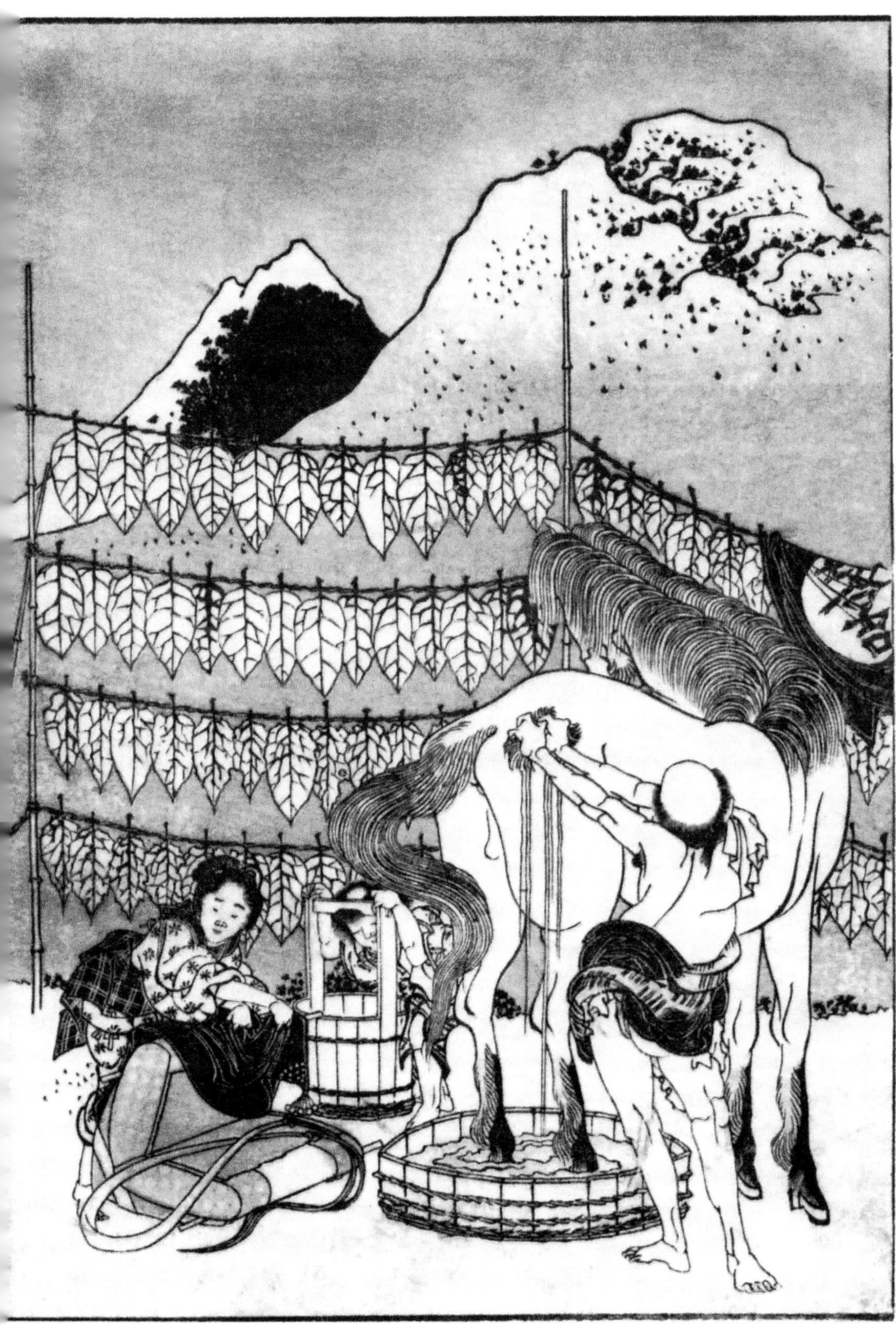

Plate XXVI

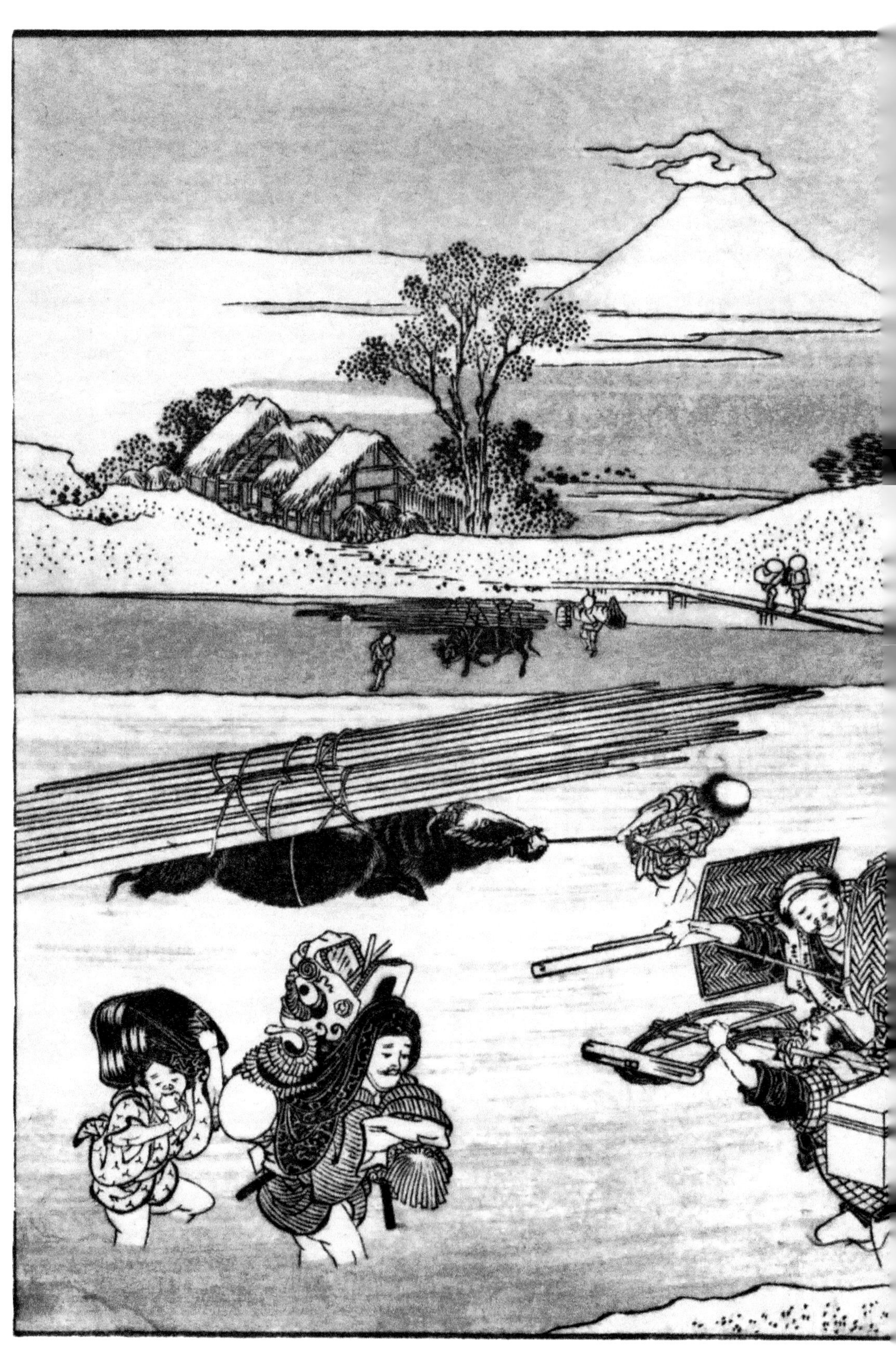

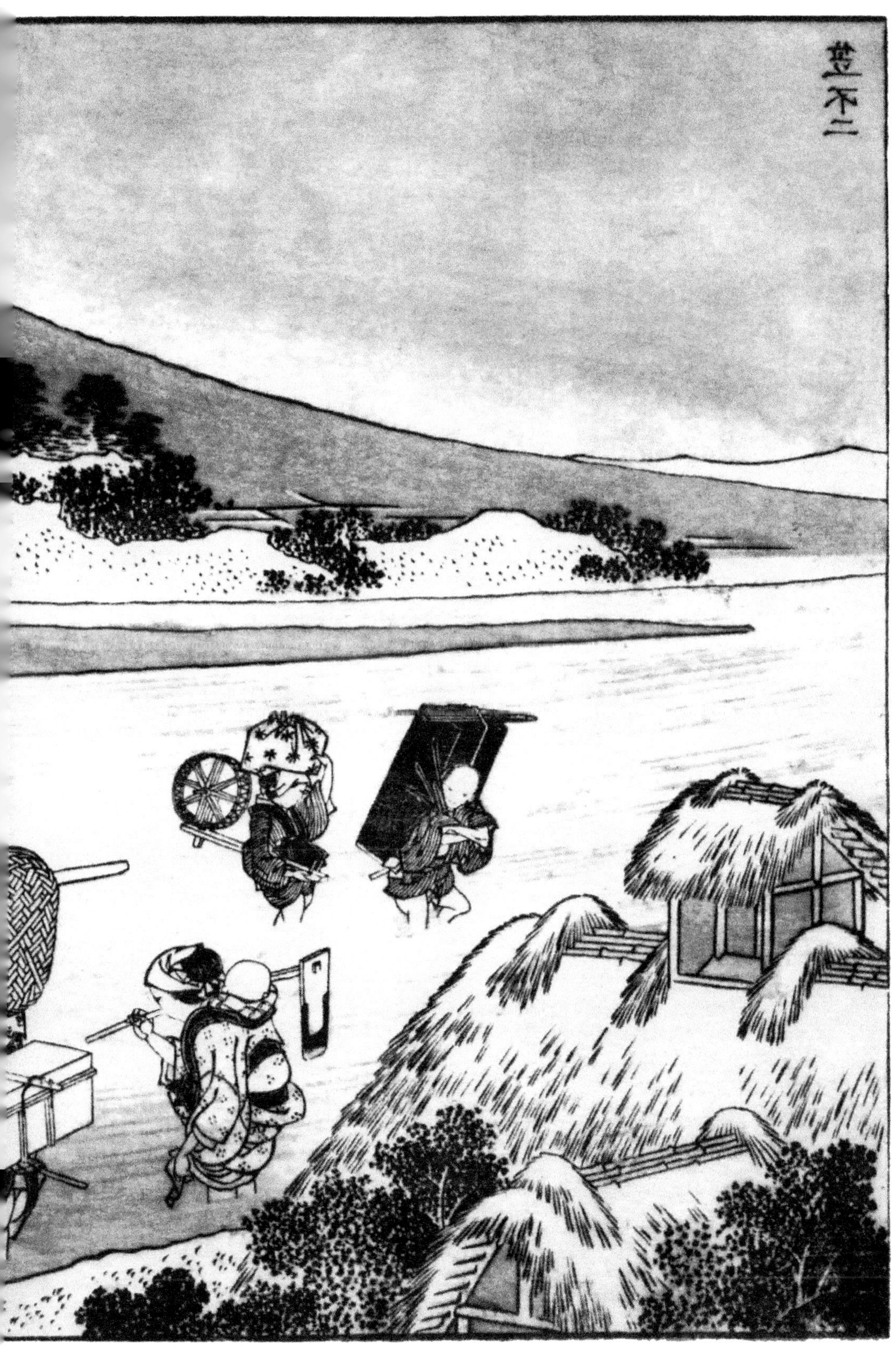

Plate XXVII

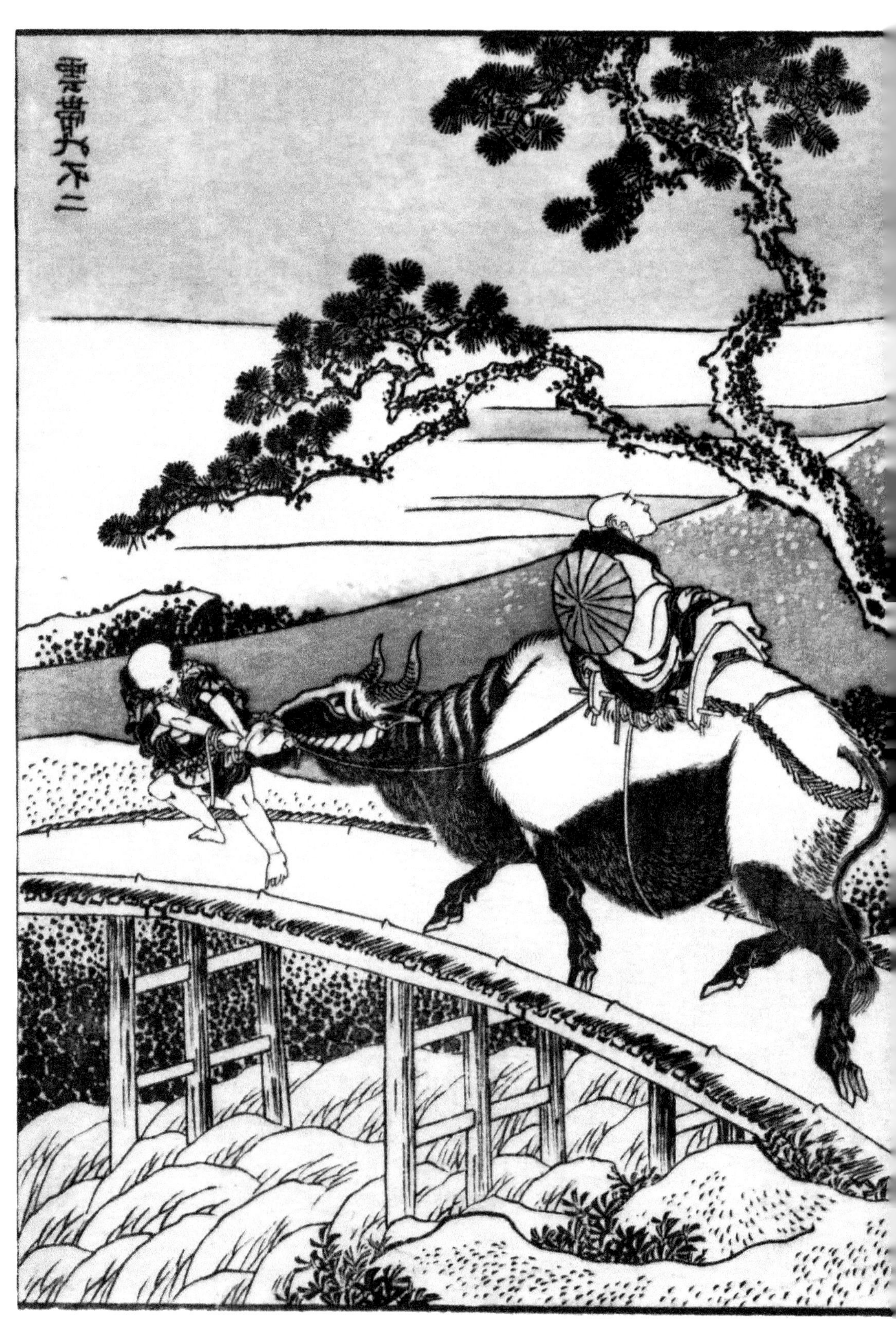

聖帝天下二

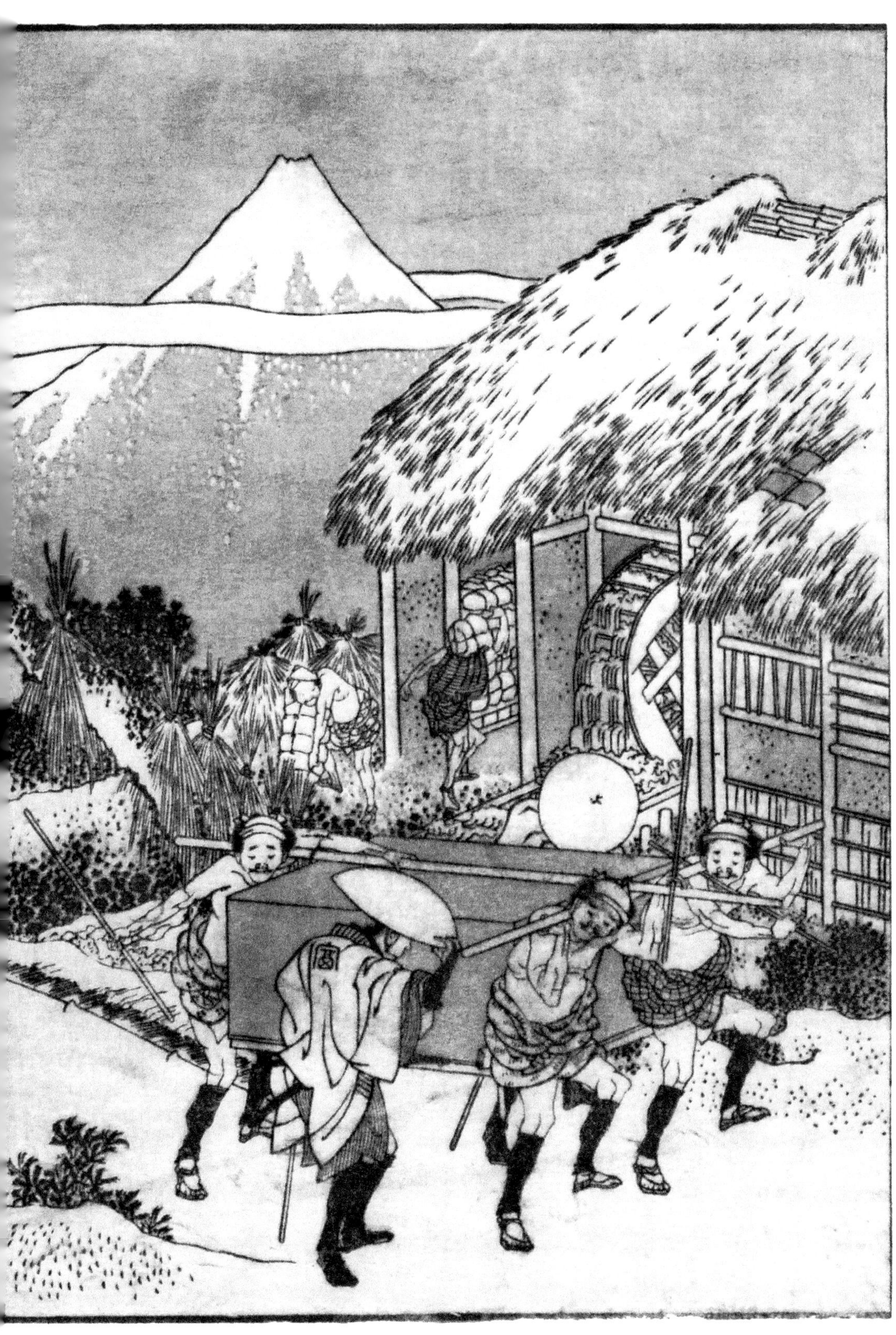

Plate XXVIII

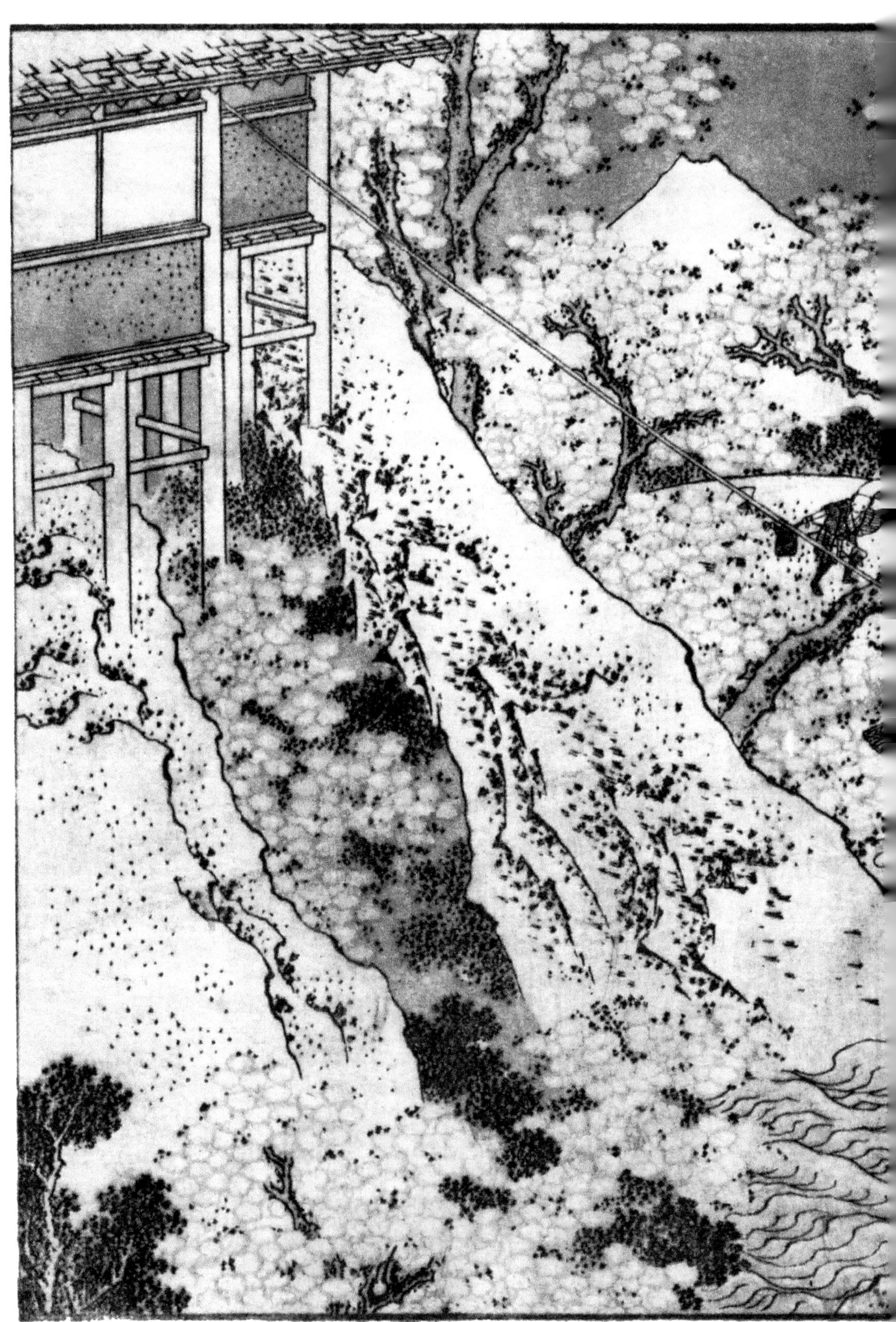

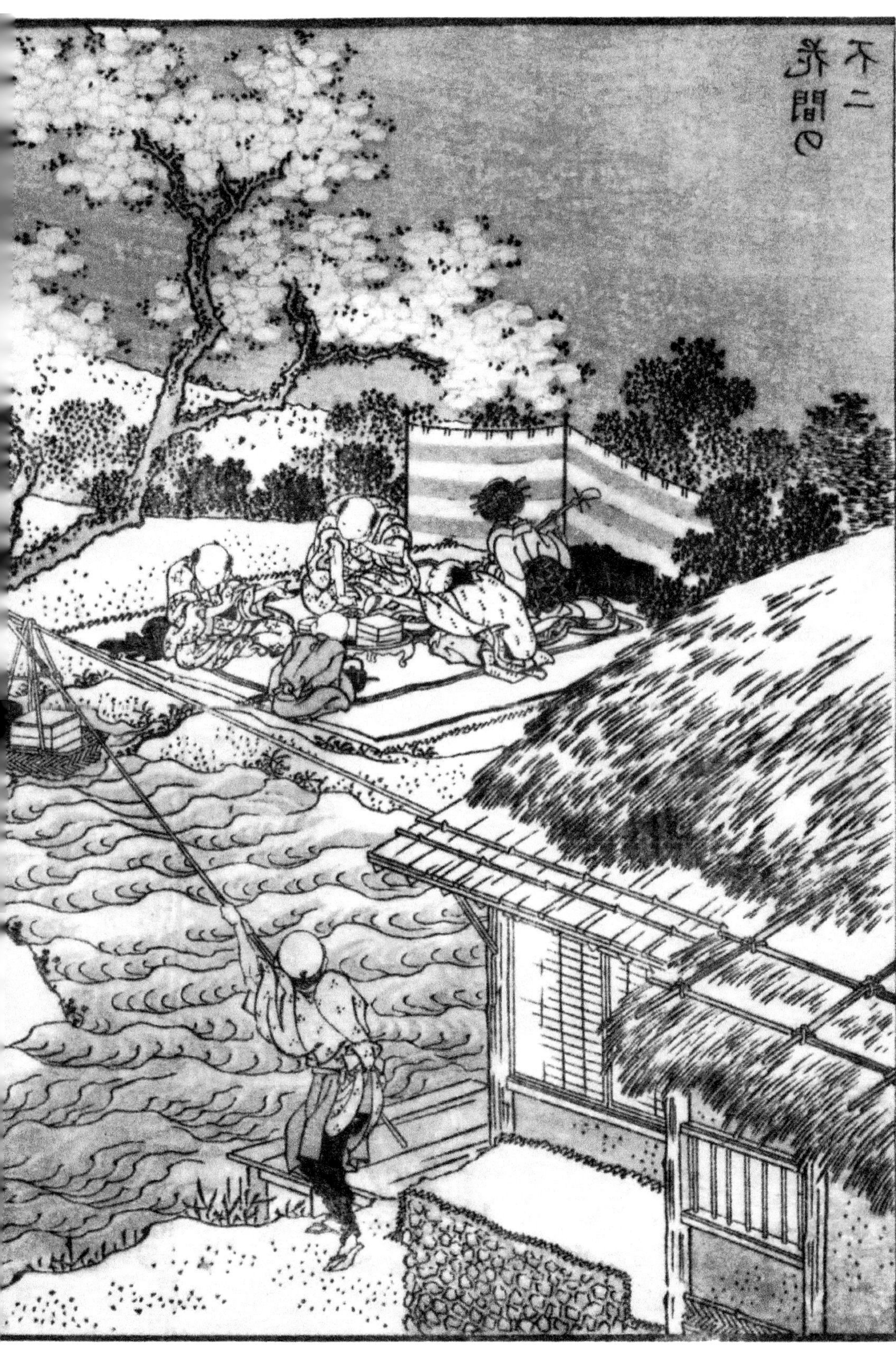

Plate XXIX

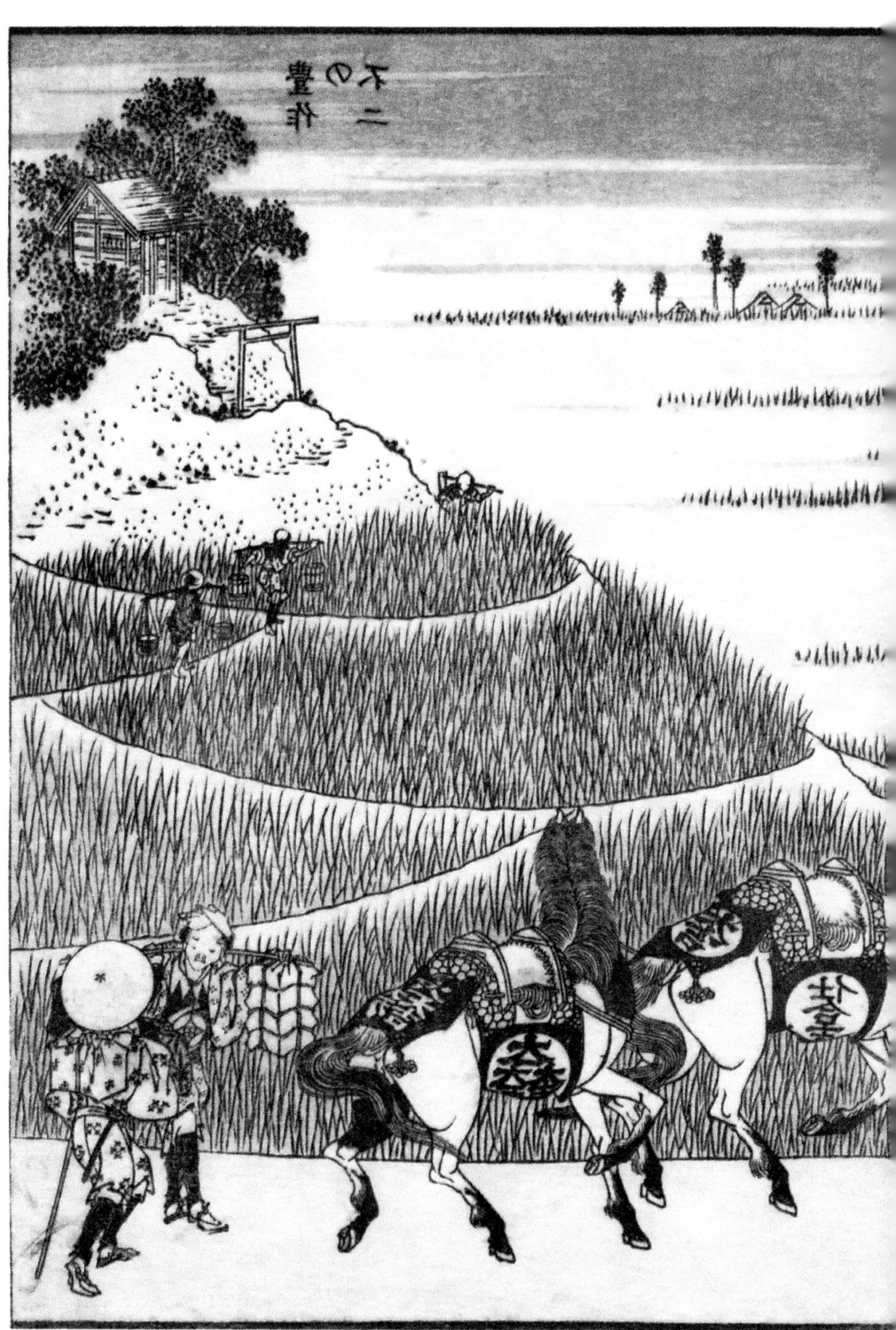

不二の
豊里

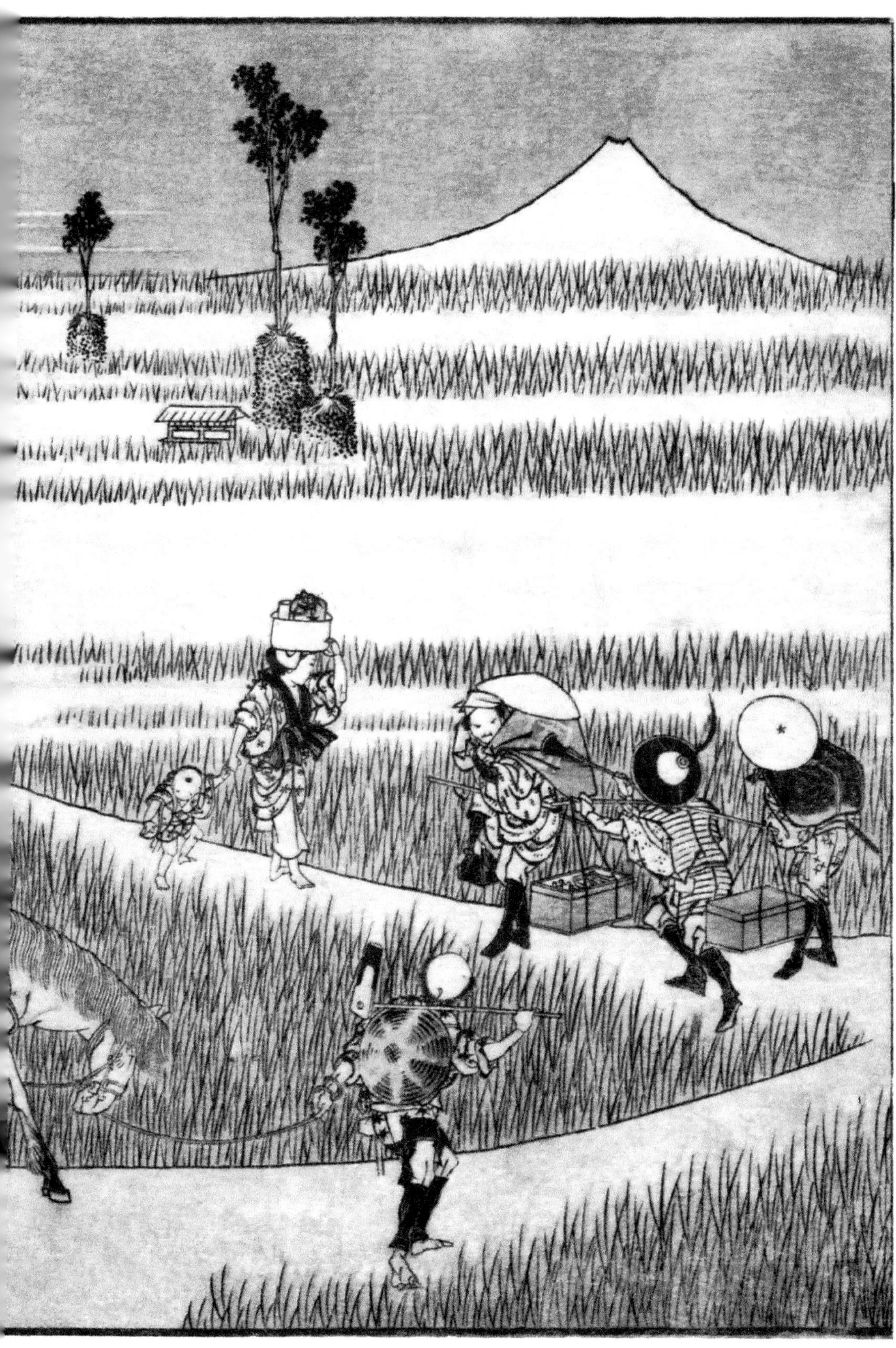

Plate XXX

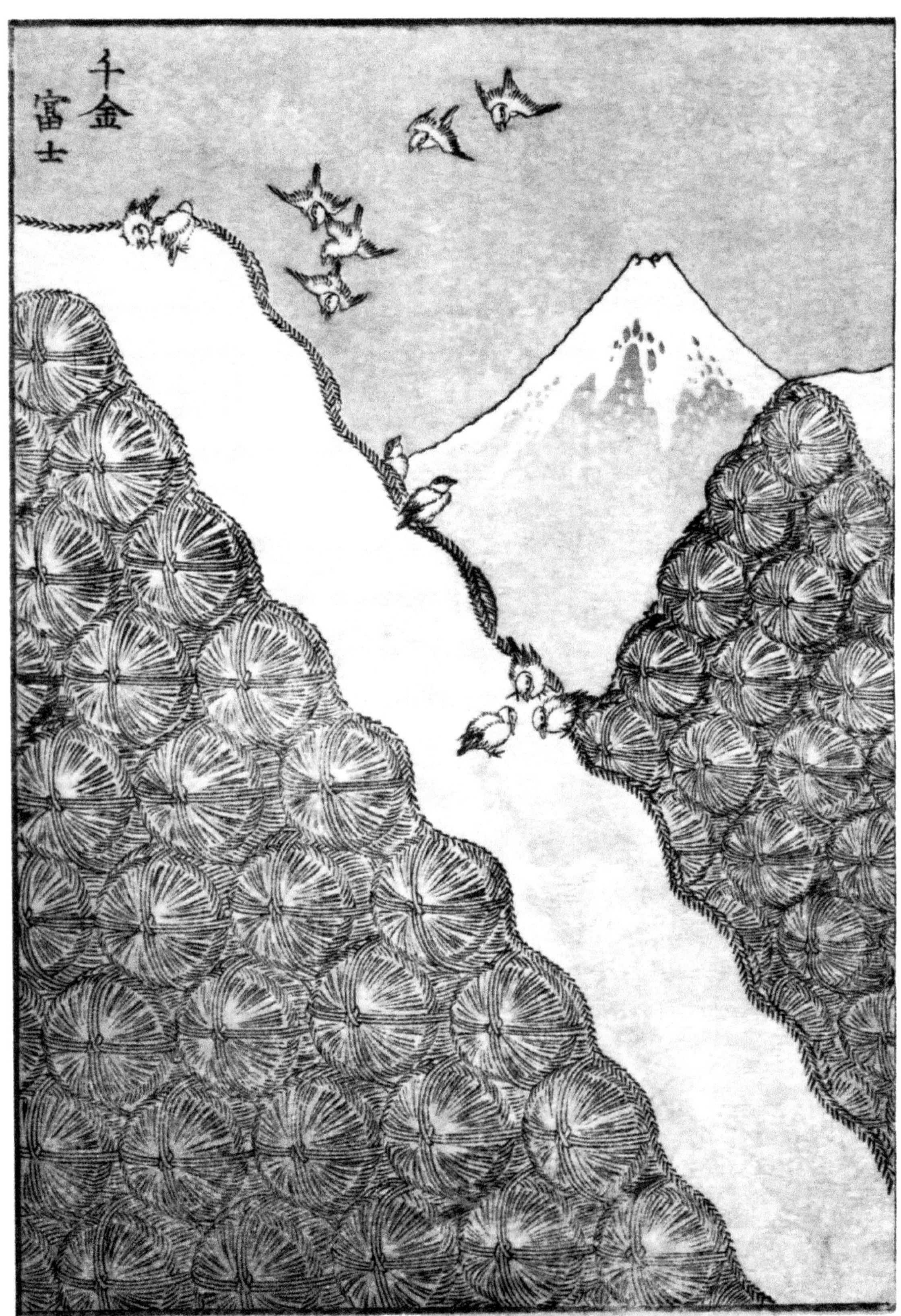

Plate XXXI

PREFACE TO THE SECOND VOLUME.

(Translation.)

LIKE that of a carefully worked gem is the form of Fuji; its hue is that of polished silver. From whatever quarter beheld, it is seen to rise, not sheer into the sky, but as a perfect cone, not more inclined on one side than on another. Eight are the sloping faces of Fuji; the pure, gem-like Mountain, standing out against the blue sky like a lotus-flower emergent from the surface of a pool. Exalted over all high hills is the lofty summit of Fuji, majestic monarch of our land. How splendid is the Peerless Mountain illumined by the red rays of the rising sun! how beautiful its purple mass set in the midst of the glory of sunset! —at birth and death of day, alike calling forth the wonder and admiration of men.

It changes in hue and form as we approach it or recede from it. A hundred aspects has the Great Mountain; in spring its peak is tipped by spiral cloud-wreaths; in autumn the vast mass is blown by the winds clear of all mist. Now vapours encircle its top, now haze clings round its base.

Here we have a Hundred Views of the Mountain, sketched by the venerable Hokusai. He who turns over these pages cannot but admire the genius with which the hundred beauties of Fuji are portrayed.

Composed by Rozankô, in the first month of the sixth year of the " nengo " *Tempo* (A.D. 1836.)

DESCRIPTION OF PLATES.

PLATE I.

IDO-KUMI NO FUJI.

Fuji and the Well-drawer.

A somewhat clumsy, and certainly far-fetched conceit. The outline of Fuji is suggested as traced by the ascending and descending portions of the well-rope. The sun has but lately risen, and the lower slopes of the Mountain are still shrouded in the morning mists. The exaggerated attitude of the well-drawer, so peculiarly Japanese, and typically Hokusaiesque, is yet distinguished by truthful, though grotesquely rendered, energy.

PLATE II.

SHINSHIU YATSUGATAKE NO FUJI.

View of Fuji over the Eight Peaks of Shinano.

The lake in the foreground is, probably, that of Suwa, but from no portion of this inland sheet of water could Fujisan be seen in the position given in the sketch, which we must therefore take to be an imaginary composition, intended to present the great lake and the famous mountain range of Shinano in combination with the grand volcano of Suruga.

PLATE III.

CHIKURIN (TAKEBAYASHI) NO FUJI.

View of Fuji through a Bamboo-grove.

Only the Peak is illumined by the newly-risen sun. None of the features of the intervening landscape are given, lest the

attention should be distracted from the shapely form of the
Mountain, and the graceful curves and foliage of the bamboos.

PLATE IV.

TSUTSUMI-GOYE NO FUJI.

View of Fuji as one crosses a Dike.

The great plain of Yedo, extending from the shores of the
gulf to the foot of the mountain-ranges, of which Nantai-zan,
Asamayama, Fujisan, and Ôyama are the most prominent peaks,
is intersected by many broad and rapid rivers, such as the
Tonegawa and the Tamagawa, and numerous smaller streams, all
peculiarly liable to inundations ; as a protection against which,
solidly-constructed dikes, often faced with stone, and generally
topped by a narrow path for foot-travellers and packhorses, were
built up during the reigns of the great Shôgun Iyeyasu and
his successors, and are still maintained for the most part in
excellent repair.

PLATE V.

TÔRIU NO FUJI.

The Manifestation of the Dragon on Fuji.

The monster, enveloped in rolling masses of cloud, seeks to
climb towards the light out of the horrid darkness where his
genesis takes place. The mountain is obscured by misty vapours,
exhaled from the dragon's lair, save on one extreme edge, where
a glimpse of unsullied sunshine is perhaps intended to symbolise
fair Hope, who so rarely abandons even the most wretched of
mankind. The sketch illustrates with energetic simplicity a
superstition common to the Japanese and their Celestial
neighbours.

There were four principal mythical animals celebrated among
the Chinese. These were the Lin, · or K'i-lin (Japanese Kirin), a
sort of unicorn, supposed to symbolise perfection, to live for a
thousand years, and to resume in itself the five elements (fire,
water, earth, metal, and wood); the Féng (Japanese Hô) in form
partaking of the characters of a peacock and a pheasant, and a
harbinger of the advent of a good sovereign; the Kwei (Japanese
Ki), or tortoise, symbolic of longevity; and lastly the Lung
(Japanese Riyô), the chief of the four, possessing the attribute of
Imperial Majesty as conferred by Heaven upon the Rulers of the
Middle Kingdom. A variety, the yellow dragon, rising from
the waters of the Hoang Ho (yellow river) bore to Fuh-hi the
founder of the Chinese Empire (B.C. 2852—2738) a roll on which
were inscribed diagrams, whence was elaborated the system of
Chinese characters. There are other dragons, such as the
Heaven-dragon, who supports the mansions of the gods; the
Spirit-dragon, governing the distribution of wind and rain;
the Earth-dragon, determining the course and flow of rivers and
streams; and the Treasure-dragon, that keeps guard over the
precious things which mortal eyes may not see (*vide* Mayers).

PLATE VI.

UNERI NO FUJI.

The Distortion of Fuji.

A strange conceit this, truly! The form of the great Mountain
is mirrored in a rippling sea or lake, and the wavy image is
admiringly contemplated by one half of the party in the boat,
while the remainder regard with ecstasy the lofty cone itself.

Koya machi no Fuji.

View of Fuji from the Dyer's Street in Yedo.

The outline of the Mountain is seen interrupted by pendent pieces of cotton cloth, drying in some dyer's yard after having been—not in the vat, but under the brush—of the dyer.

PLATE VIII.

Haichiu no Fuji.

All Fuji in a Saucer.

A hunter or wayfarer, apparently—possibly some historical or legendary personage—is resting under a pine-tree, and with exaggerated gesture shows his delight at the image of the Mountain, of which he has caught an unexpected glimpse, reflected on the surface of the water with which he has just filled the saucer from the gourd carried at his girdle.   In the basket in the background is a Hô bird (phœnix).

PLATE IX.

Kaijô no Fuji.

View of Fuji over the Ocean.

The particles of spray dashed from the crest of the breakers rolling in upon the cedar-fringed beach are fancifully supposed to be transformed into the small birds (chidori), that haunt the sea-shore in flocks, flying low just over the line of surf.

PLATE X.

SUSAKI NO FUJI.

View from the Cape of Su, on the Eastern bank of the Sumida River, where it enters the Gulf at Yedo.

The Mountain stands out, a cone of dark purple, against the low-massed crimson cloud-bars that catch the last rays of the sun to throw them across a steely sky. All is calm ; the ferry-boat has wellnigh reached her anchorage, the day's work done, with the aid of the dying breeze under which the shallow water still heaves, while the shore-birds are winging a final flight seawards, ere betaking themselves to their wonted shelter for the night.

A few rapid strokes of the brush, and firm, bold sweeps in two tints of grey, have sufficed for the Master to render, with exquisite truthfulness and feeling, the solemn and tender peace of a summer twilight.

PLATE XI.

YUME NO FUJI.—*A Dream of Fuji.*

Allusion to the popular belief that the sleeper who sees in a dream the Mountain, with a pair of falcons and three brinjals ("ichi fuji, ni taka, san nasubi"), may hope for a long, happy, and prosperous life.

PLATE XII.

SAMPAKU NO FUJI.

The Mountain as one of the Three Perfections of Whiteness.

The other two are snow and the crane. The simplicity of the means by which the characteristic aspects of winter are rendered in the sketch, with singular directness and force, is worthy of remark.

PLATE XIII.

KAKEMONO NO HOTTAN.

Which may be freely rendered "*The First Hanging Picture
(kakemono) of Fuji.*"

The paper-paned sash or panel has just been removed from
a window, revealing a view of the Great Mountain dominating
the landscape, apparently in the neighbourhood of Matsuho.
The servant calls the attention of the guest — for the scene
seems laid at an inn—who throws up his hands in ecstasy at
the charm of the picture thus suddenly displayed, *encadré* in the
framework of the window-opening, as a " kakemono " is by its
embroidered silk borders, broad above and below, and narrow
at either side.

PLATE XIV.

MATSU-GOYE NO FUJI.

Fuji seen through the Pine-trees.

The picture is somewhat spoiled by the conventional rigidity
and symmetry of the foliage.   The pine much resembles the
stone-pine of Italian coasts (*P. maritima*), but is the species
known to botanists as *P. massoniana*.

PLATE XV.

FUJI NO MURO.--*A shelter on Fuji.*

Partly natural, partly built up in a rude manner, with rough
blocks of lava. There are many huts on the several tracks by
which pilgrims make the ascent, at some of which hot tea, at
others merely cold water, can be procured.

PLATE XVI.

Shashin no Fuji.

The Portraiture of Fuji.

A delightful sketch, to which the details of Japanese life in the foreground lend additional interest. The artist is absorbed in the contemplation of his subject, while his servants are busied about unpacking his baggage, and preparing his luncheon, a small bottle of "saké" being at the same time warmed over a hastily-lit fire of sticks. The bird perched on the boundary-post gives the grotesque element which the quaint humour of the Master hardly permits to be wholly absent from any of his productions.

PLATE XVII.

Nana hashi ichiran no Fuji.

Fuji and the Seven Bridges.

An ideal combination, probably, of elements taken from the familar scenery of the great plain lying north and east of Yedo. The fact of seven bridges being visible at once seems to have struck the Master as one likely to interest his admirers : possibly some allusion is intended by the picture. The bridge in the foreground shows with great accuracy of detail how the Japanese put these structures together. The human figures represent with singular truth and spirit the types of Japanese life commonly met with in the neighbourhood of the capital—the petty gentle-man, the small trader, and the peasant.

PLATE XVIII.

Taiseki ji no Sanchiu no Fuji.

View of Fuji from the mountain-path leading to the Temple of Taiseki (Big-Rock) in the Province of Mino.

The wayfarers are probably pilgrims, the leader of whom is gazing at the rocky mass whence the temple towards which they are hastening has its name.

PLATE XIX.

Shimada ga hana sekiyô Fuji.

Evening View of Fujisan from the Ness of Shimada, a Town on the Tôkaidô.

The close of a summer day. All toil has ceased ; the fishing boats are at anchor, the nets hung up to dry, and idlers are amusing themselves with rod and line, or with saunter and chat on the pile-protected embankment. Fuji is already of a dark purple hue, partly concealed by low-lying long bars of tinted clouds, while the shadowed roofs show that the short twilight is about to merge in night. An air of indescribable peace and tranquillity reigns over the whole scene.

PLATE XX.

Fumoto no Fuji.—*At the foot of the Mountain.*

An ideal sketch, designed to strike the beholder with a proper sense of the precipitous and rugged character of the ancient volcano. It would seem to be early morning : the peasants are starting for a day's grass-cutting.

PLATE XXI.

Yuudachi no Fuji.

A Thunder-storm at the foot of Fuji.

Lightning is flashing through the dark shadow of the over-hanging rain-cloud, the ominous outline of which is shown on the still sunlit slope of the Mountain. A furious gale—one almost hears the roar of it—howls through the humble hamlet: the first puffs scare the scanty population into a rush for shelter. , The onslaught of the tempest is depicted with great spirit; the first folds of coming gloom enwrap the village, around which the elements are waking up to strife, while beyond all is yet light and peace.

PLATE XXII.

Tôtomi Yama Naka no Fuji.

View from among the Hills of the Province of Tôtomi.

In the foreground woodmen are felling or lopping a huge timber-tree, either a pine or a retinospora ; possibly an oak. The exaggerated attitudes of the two axemen are characteristic.

PLATE XXIII.

Hi no Fuji.

Fujisan under the Watery Arch of a Sluice-fall.

The mellow light dancing on the surface of the rapid river, bathing in yellow glory the grassy slopes beyond, and filtering in flashing dots and bars through the foliage of the laurels and cedars ; the dark purple hue of the distant Mountain, up the bare cone of which the mists are creeping, while long, low lines of cloud are slowly settling down upon it, show that the time is

evening. Some of the wayfarers are drinking in the beauty of
the scene, to others nature displays one of her loveliest aspects
in vain. The path leads up an embankment by a cutting, the
sides of which are faced with large polygonal blocks of black
basalt.

PLATE XXIV.

Gekka no Fuji.—*Fuji by Moonlight.*

The gaunt wolf on the hill, baying at the moon, somewhat
mars the picture, otherwise true and impressive enough. Below,
in the full radiance of the silvery satellite, women are beating
the newly-woven cotton homespun, that the cloth may be soft
and supple. The landscape is mostly hidden by rising mists,
white in the pale moonlight, streaming upon the thatch roof
of the farm-house, and the granite of the small shrine. Over
the orb itself droop a few leaves of the willow, while the Mountain
lies in the blackest shadow.

PLATE XXV.

Yuki no tan no Fuji.—*A Snow Fuji,*

Heaped up in some farm-yard, to the amusement not only
of the urchin hid under an immense hat, and carrying a pail
in one hand, in the other a number of empty saké-bottles, but
of his seniors as well, who stand by idly watching the building
up of the snow Fuji, on the soft mass of which a couple of
puppies are disporting themselves.

PLATE XXVI.

Bumpen no Fuji.—*Fuji of the Poet.*

A screen picture. Kakinomoto no Hitomaro, seated on a mat, contemplates with rapture the lofty Peak towering high over a landscape of which the village of Matsuho, famed for its brine-pans, forms the foreground. Kakinomoto was the son of Kosho, the Fifth of the Ninwo, or Human Kings, the third of the national dynasties, and was so named from a " kaki "-tree (*Diospyros kaki* — species of *persimmon*), said to have overshadowed his birth-place. Hitomaro is simply the designation of a rank. The following is a free version of an example of the poet's power, taken from the " Hiyaku-nin isshiú :"—

> " On Matsuho's shore, our meeting-place,
> As darkens e'en I pining wait
> To clasp thee, sweet, in my embrace ;
> Ah ! why dost linger still so late ?
> Than Matsuho's furnaces the fire
> That burns within me rages higher."*

PLATE XXVII.

Buhen no Fuji.—*Fuji of the Warrior.*

The prowess of Nitta Yoshitsune (?) a retainer of Yoritomo, at a boar-hunt in the neighbourhood of Fuji. The animal had turned upon its pursuers, trampling them under foot, when Nitta, jumping on its back, slew the brute with his short sword. A common version of the story, often seen in "netsuke" groups representing it, is that Nitta seized the boar by the tail, and forced it to turn round before killing it.

---

* There is a word-play connected with Matsuho, which may mean the place of waiting (matsu, to wait), or the place of pines (matsu, a pine).

PLATE XXVIII.

Kizami no Fuji.—*The Mountain seen through a Trellis.*

In the foreground of this sketch, more curious than artistic, is represented an iron "kama" or cauldron, out of which a bag of rice is being lifted to be placed upon a bamboo drainer. In the left-hand corner unboiled rice is being shaken from a piece of thin matting into a shallow tub, to be there washed with water and so prepared for boiling. Under the cauldron is a rude sort of furnace, lined with irregular blocks of black basalt.

PLATE XXIX.

Sôchiu no Fuji.—*Window-framed Fuji.*

The old priest, who seems to be amusing his leisure with poetical composition, throws up his arms in ecstasy at the beauty of the Mountain, of which he has caught a sudden glimpse with the sun shining full upon it, as he looks up from his task. A flight of crows crosses the cone, reminding him of the Raven's Bridge of the legend of the Lover-stars of Tanabata night (*vide* page 23).

PLATE XXX.

Tani-ma no Fuji.—*View of Fuji from the head of a Valley.*

A couple of faggot-cutters are just reaching the top of the toilsome ascent, a third is resting himself against the cliff, and changing his worn-out "waraji" or straw sandals for fresh ones. Hard by a peasant is filling his tub with manure from a receptacle hollowed out of the foot of the cliff, composed of a soft volcanic conglomerate.

END OF VOLUME II.

富嶽百景

[illegible]

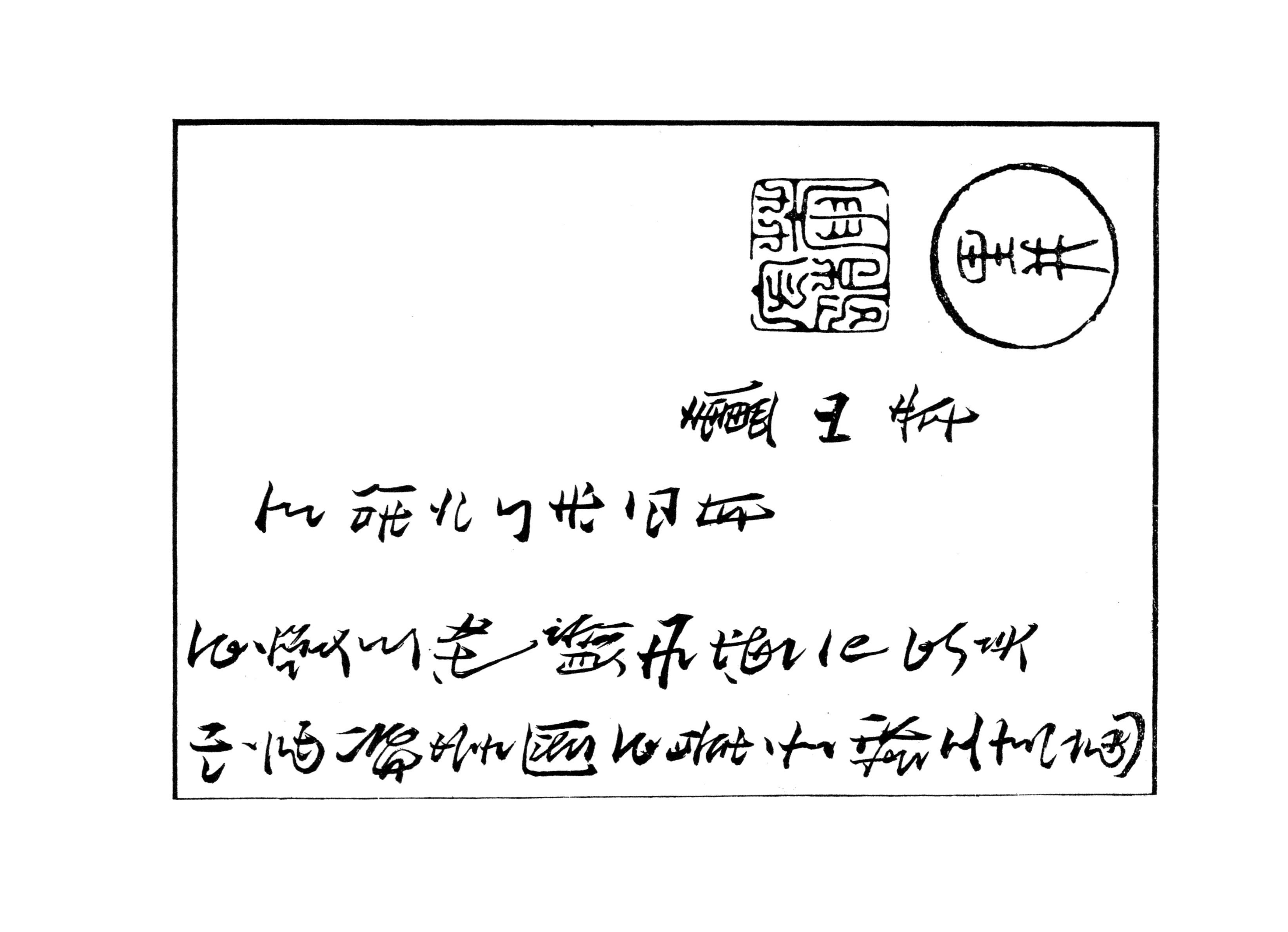

[illegible]

[illegible]

[illegible]

[illegible]

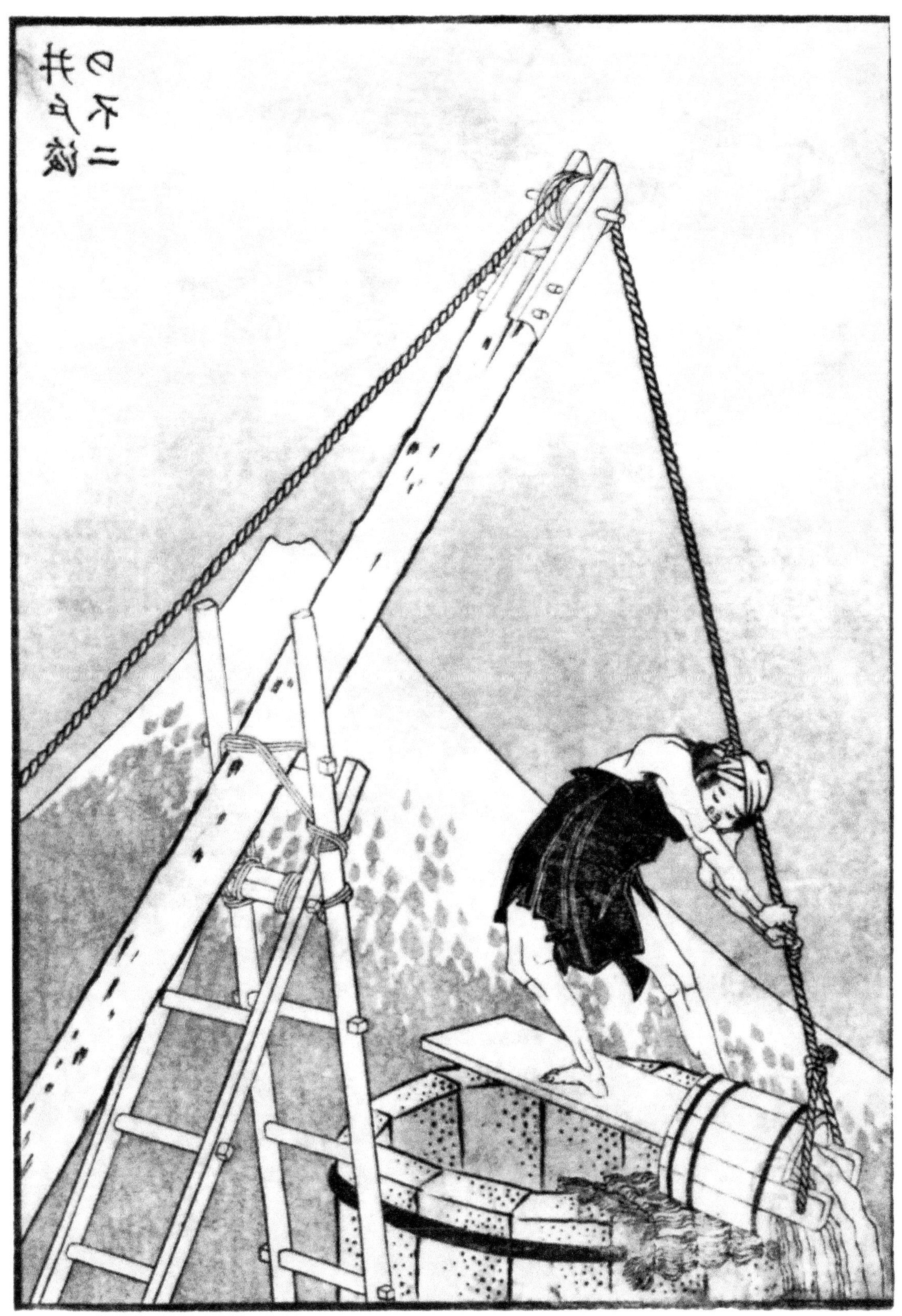

Plate I

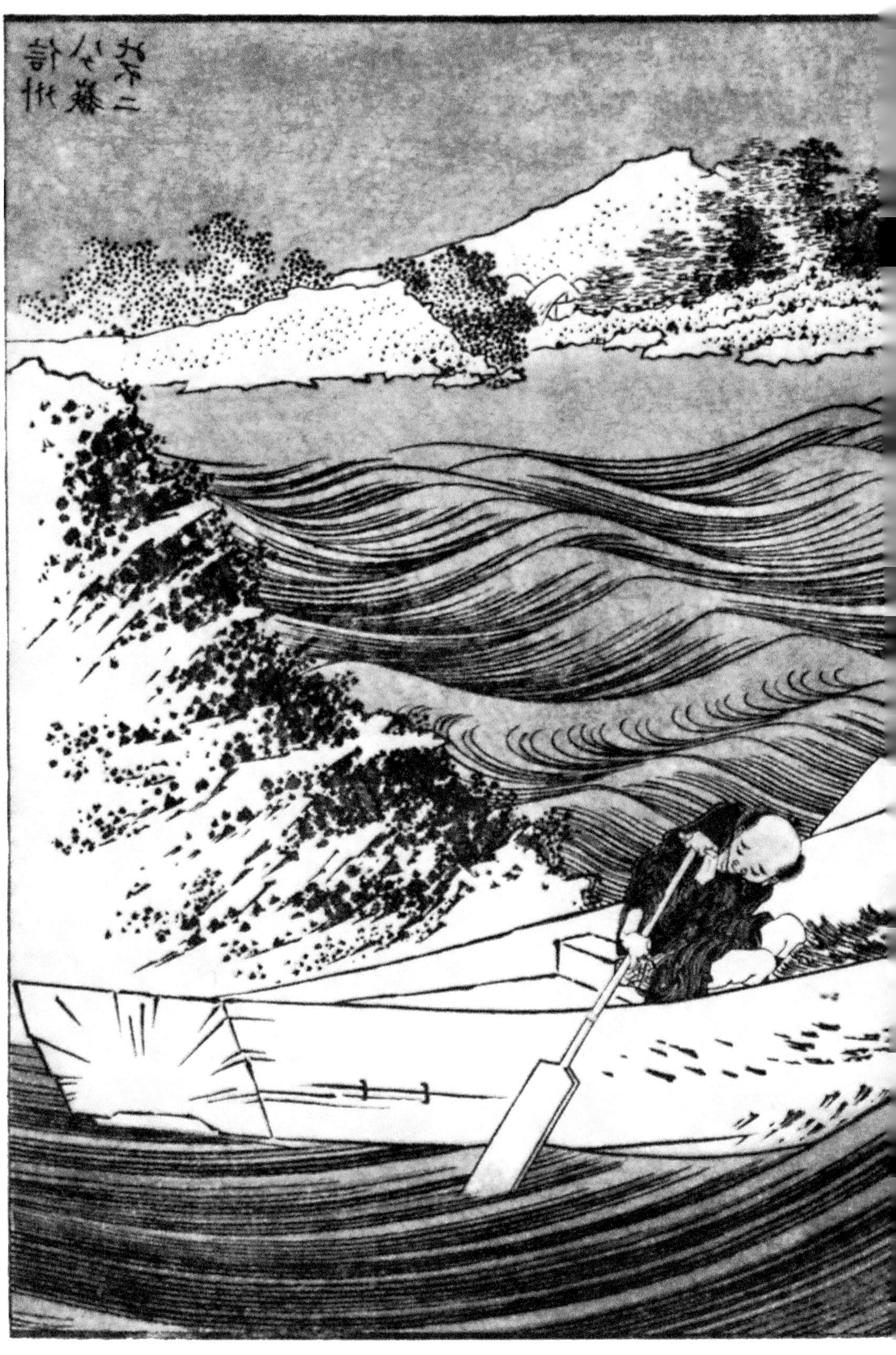
茶木二
ん藤
計代

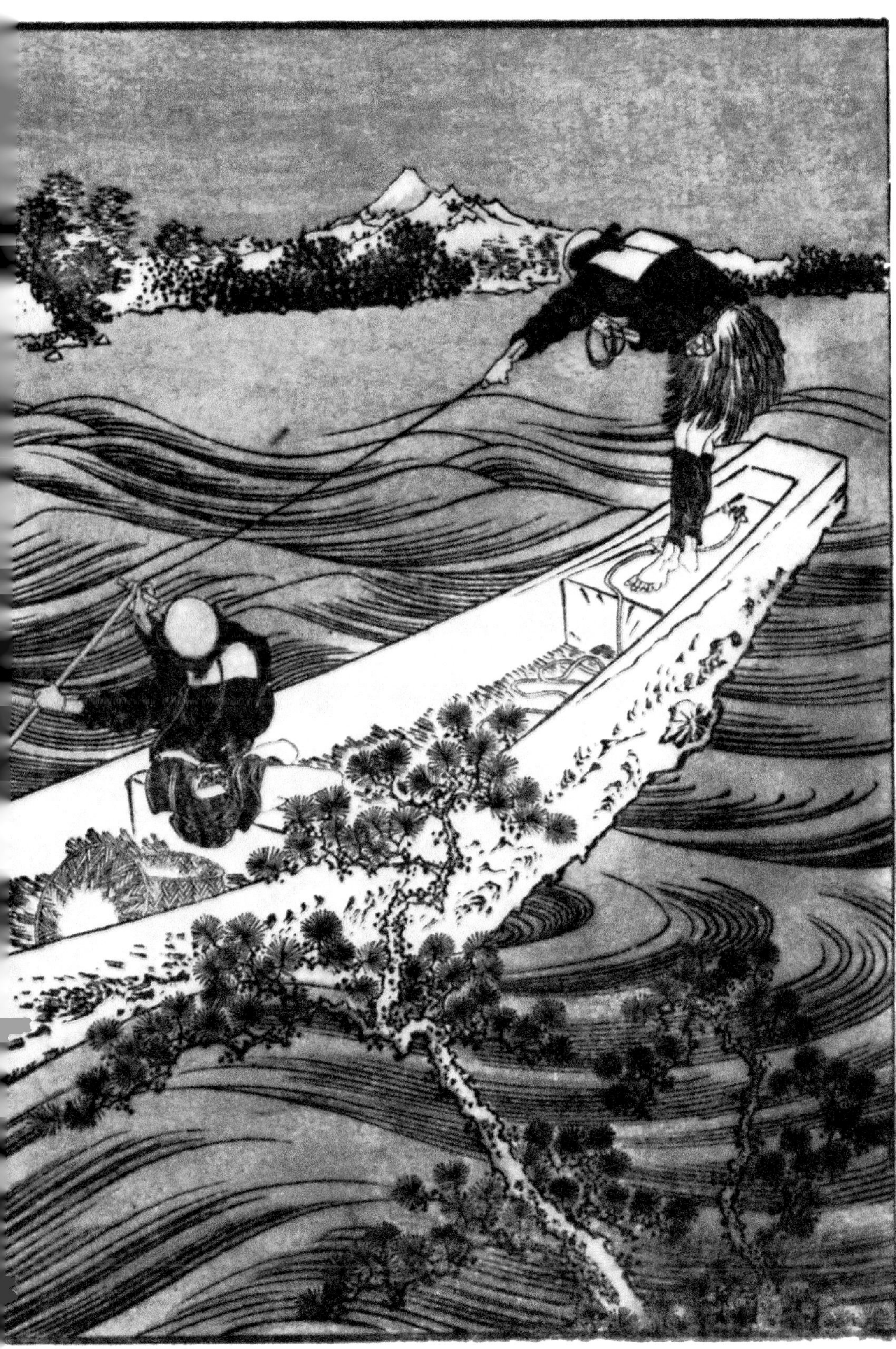

Plate II

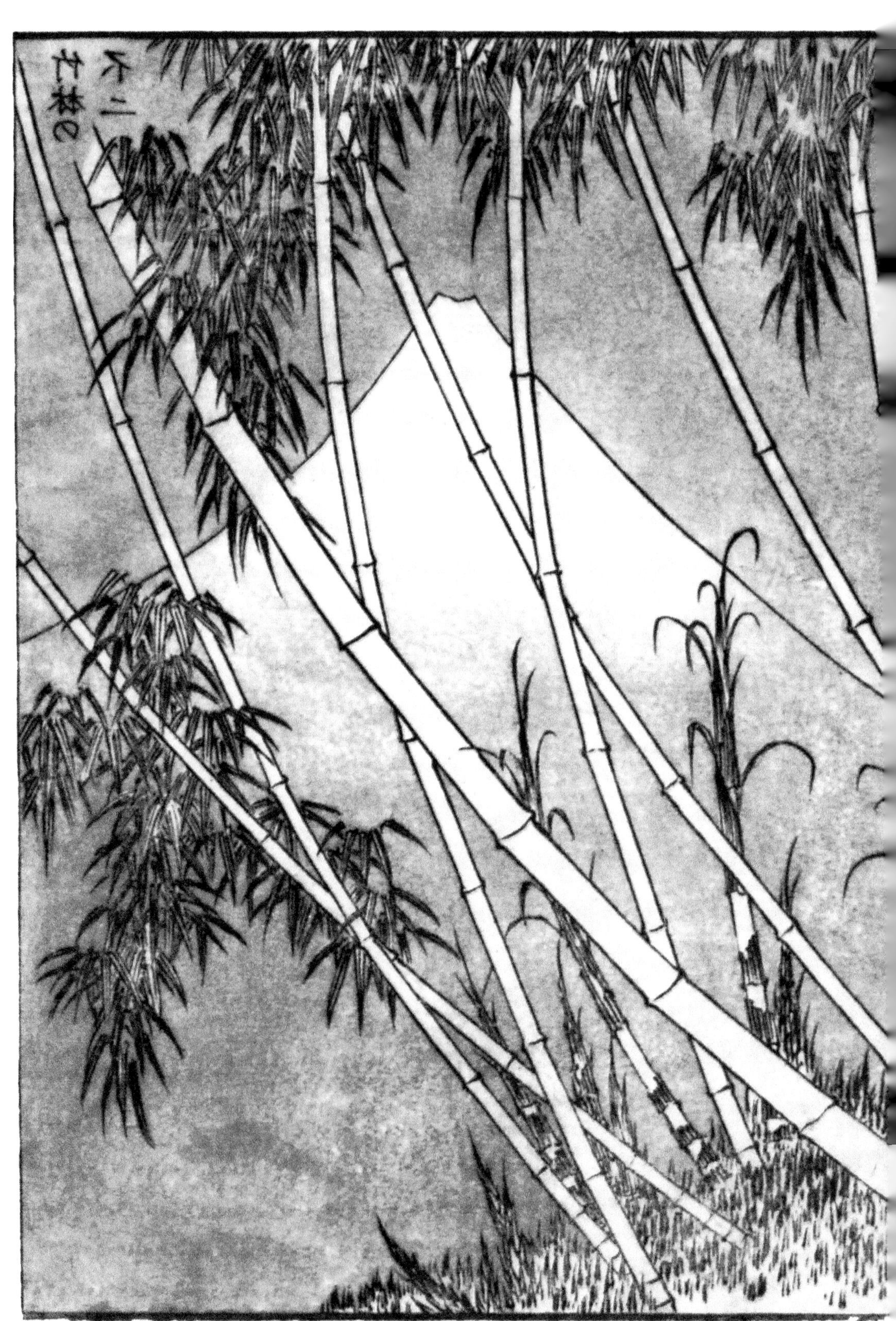

不二
竹林の

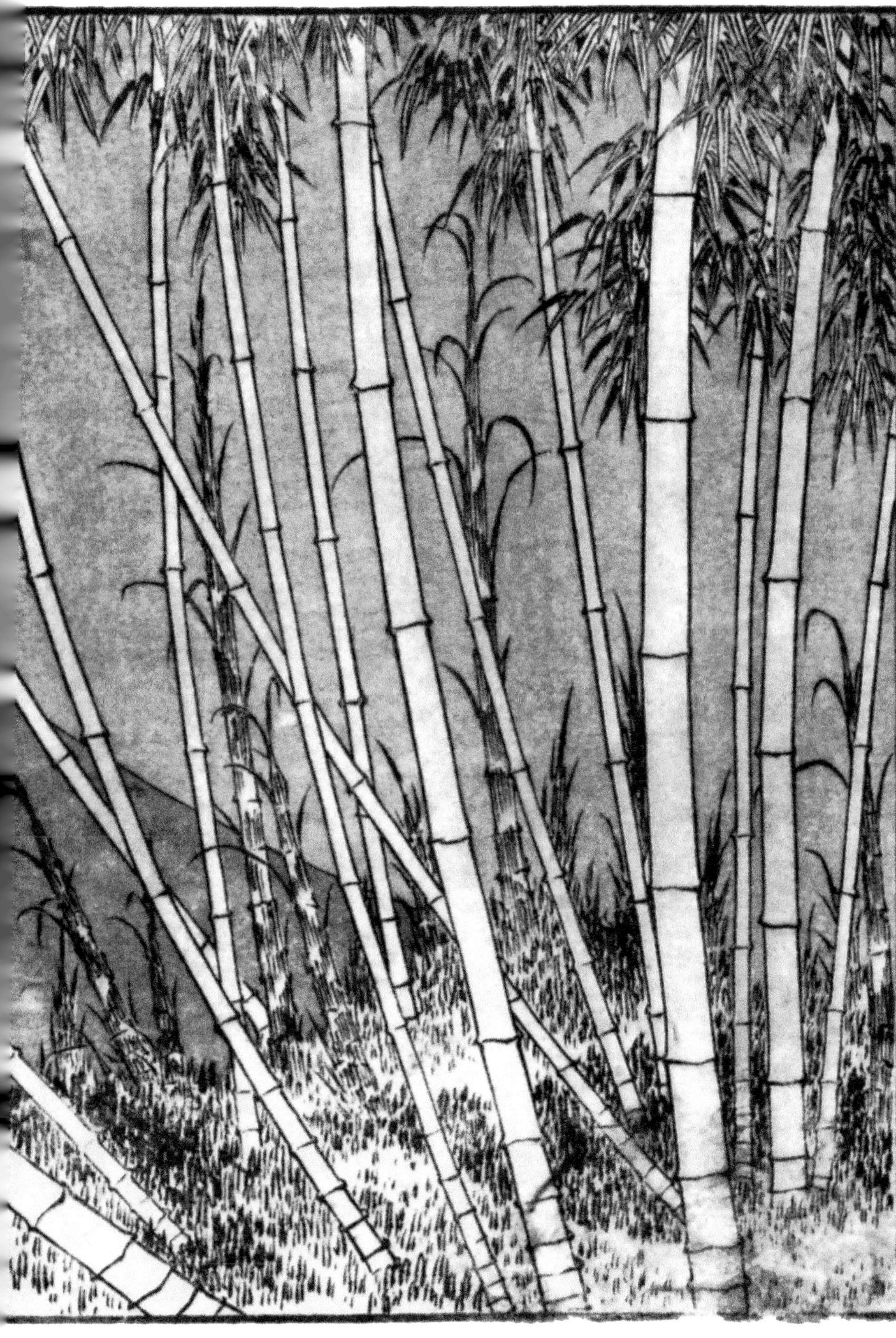

Plate III

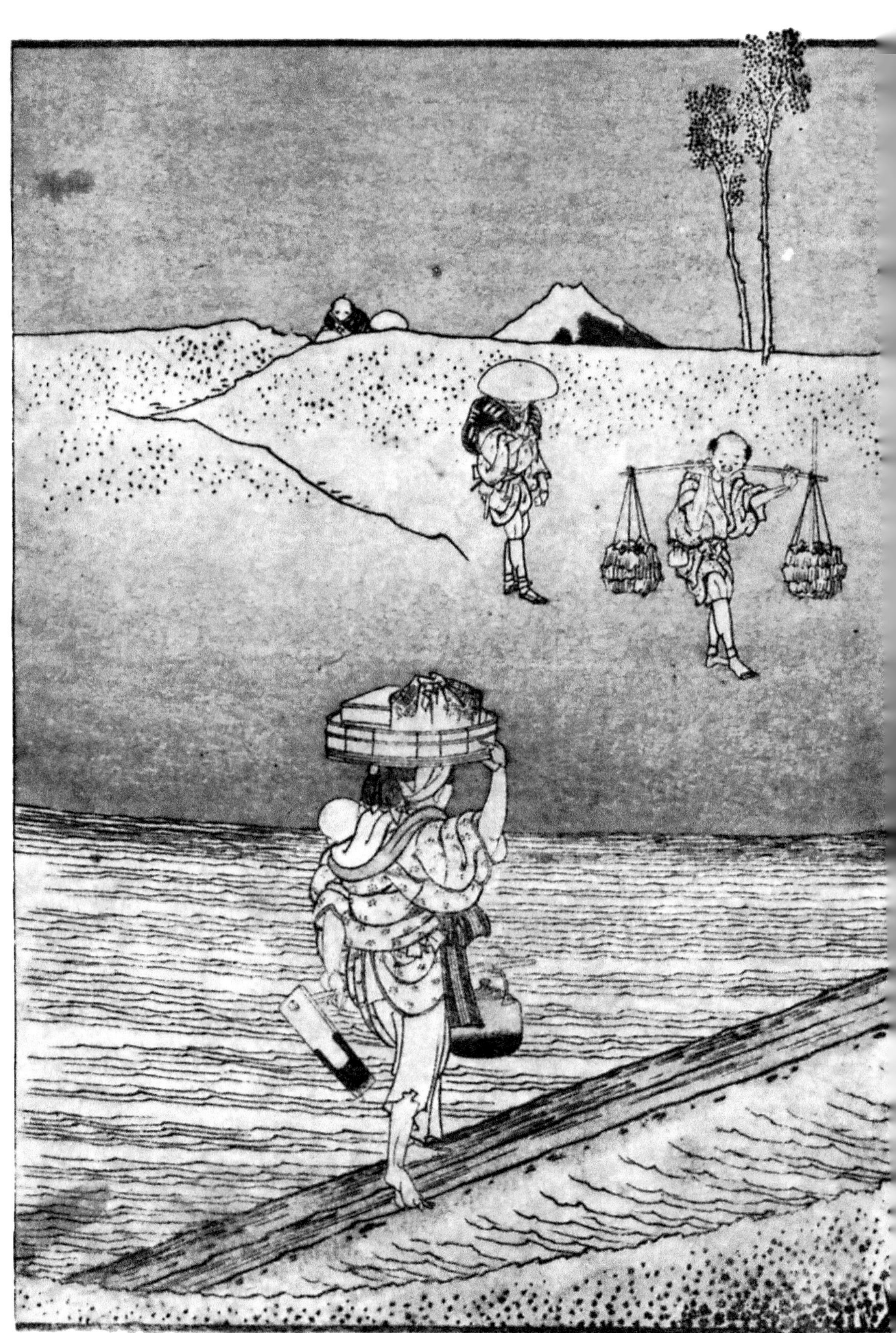

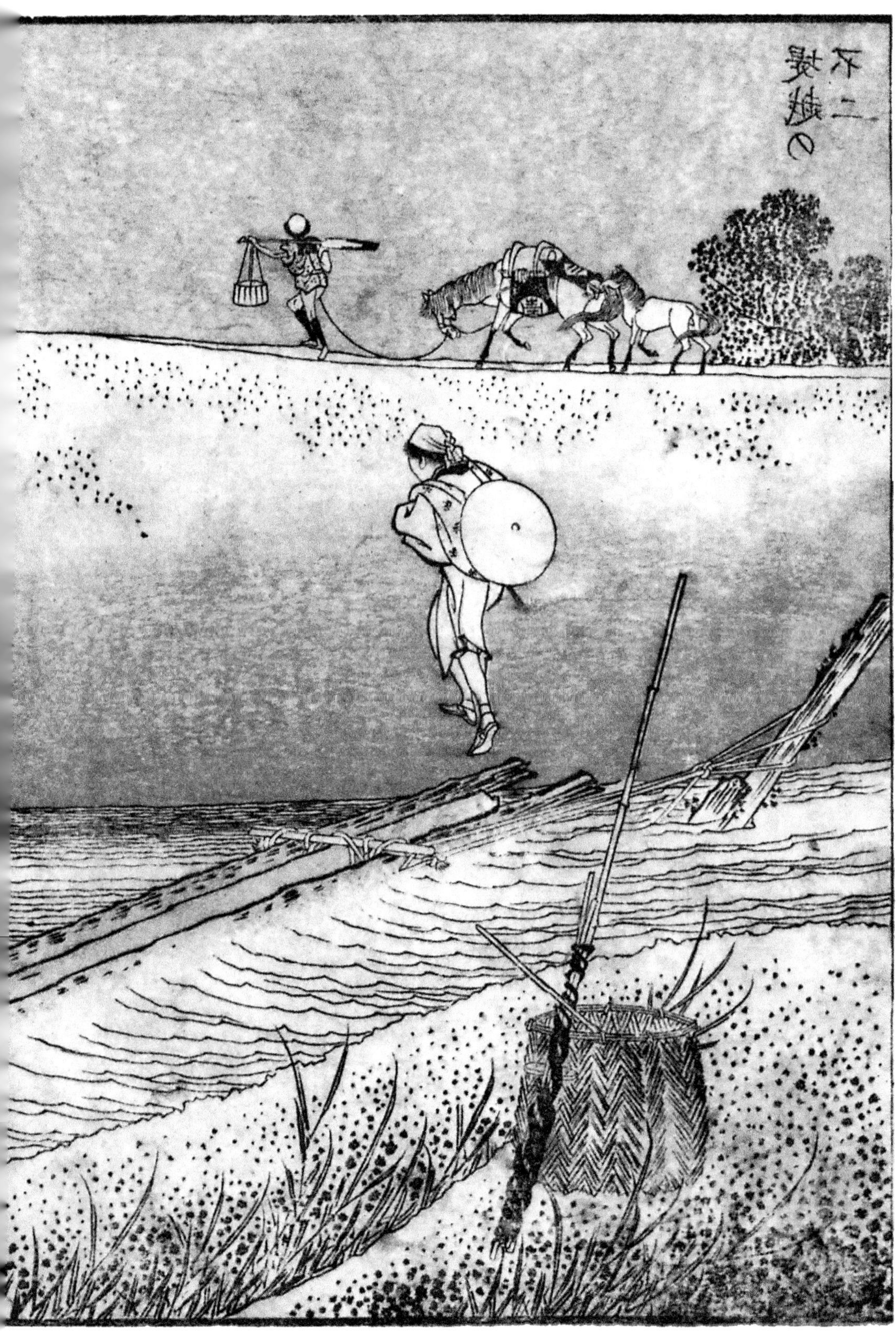

Plate IV

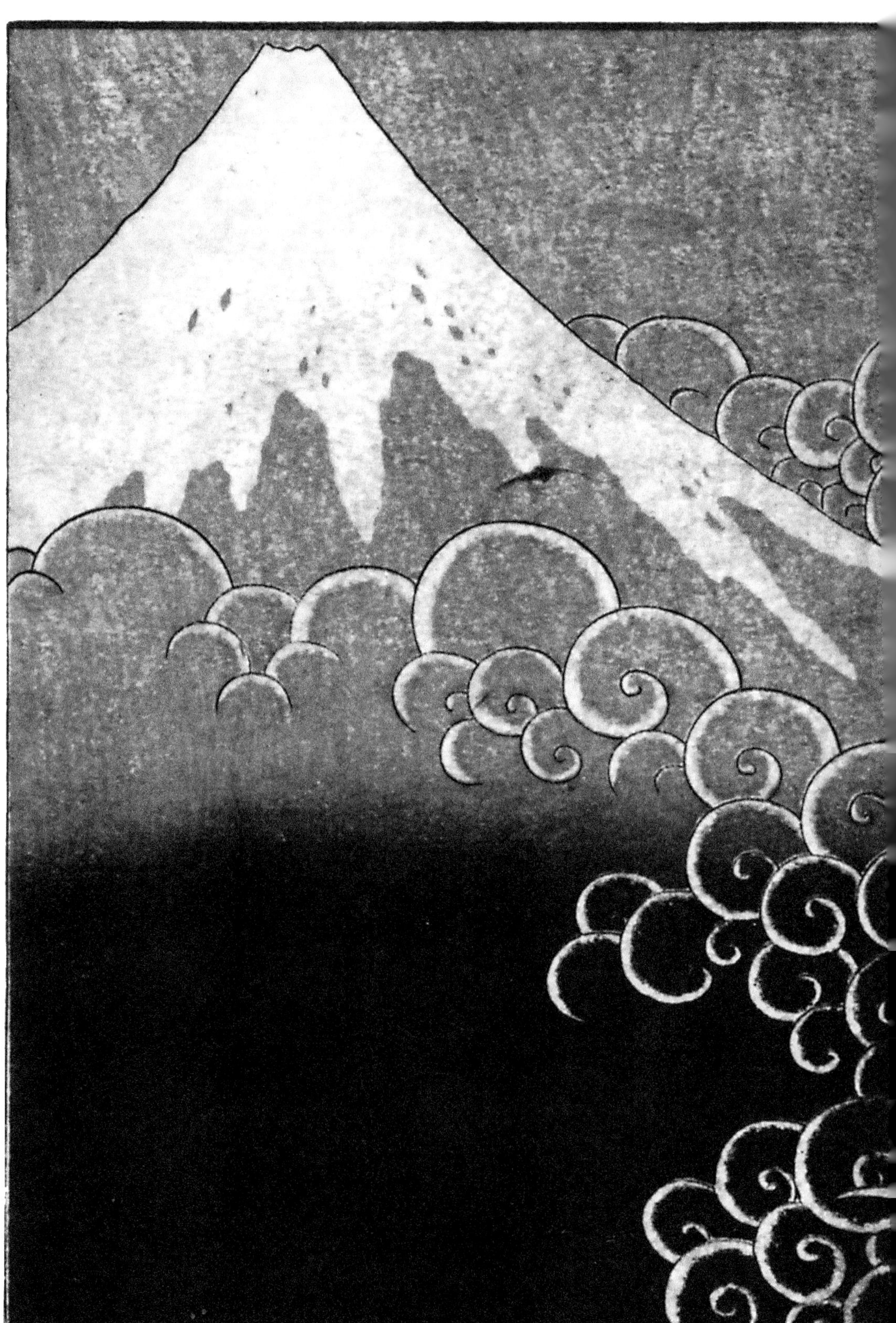

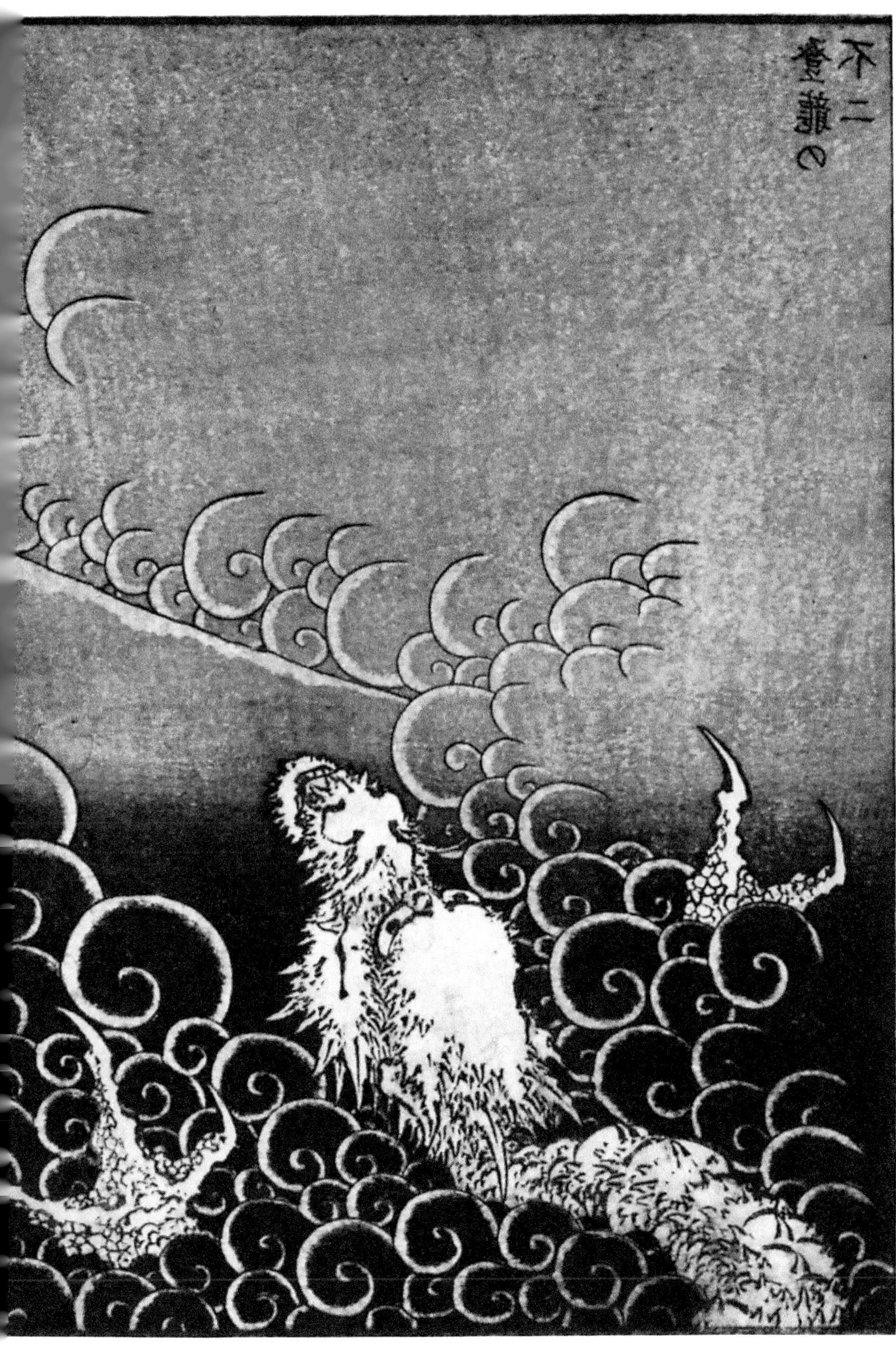

Plate V

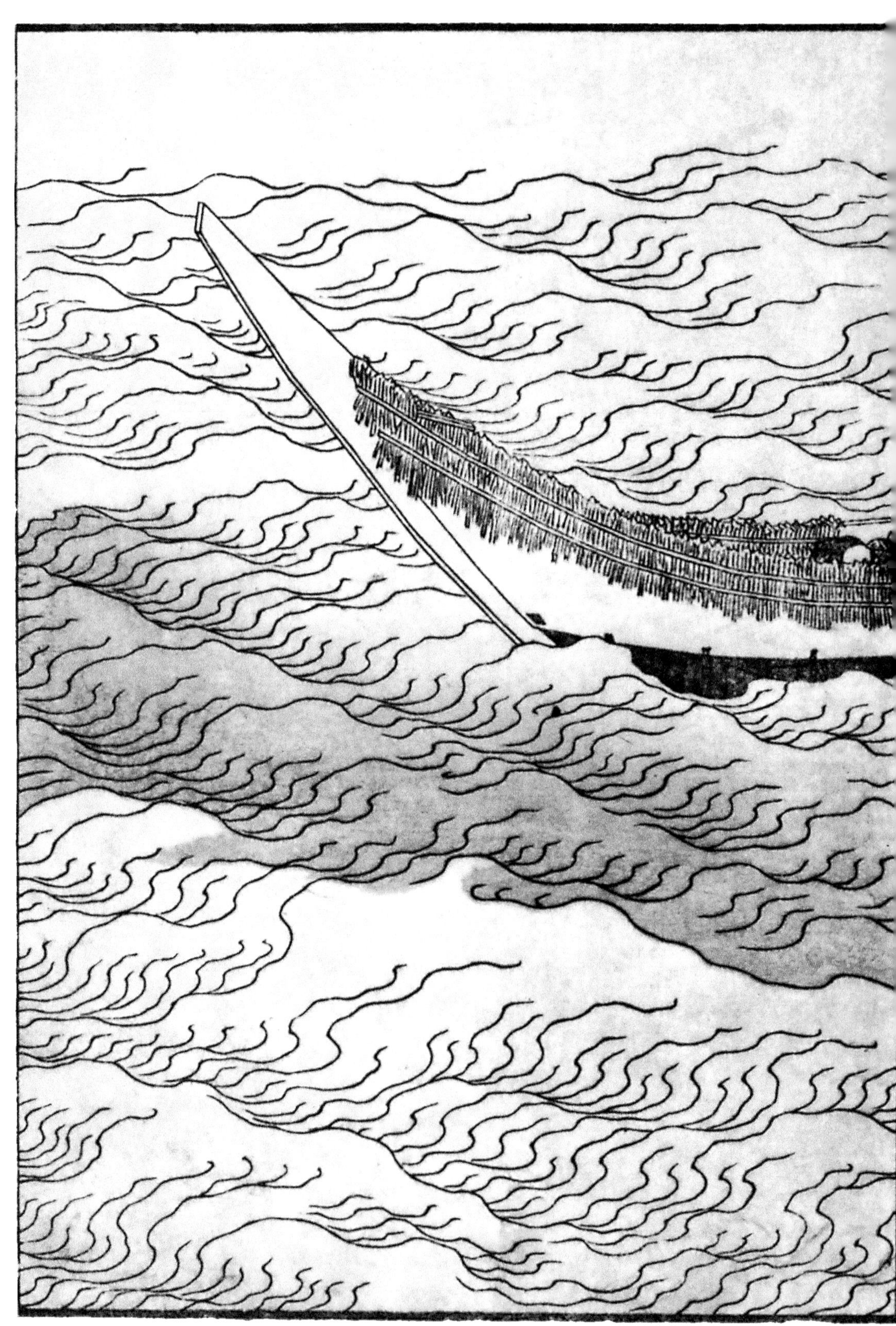

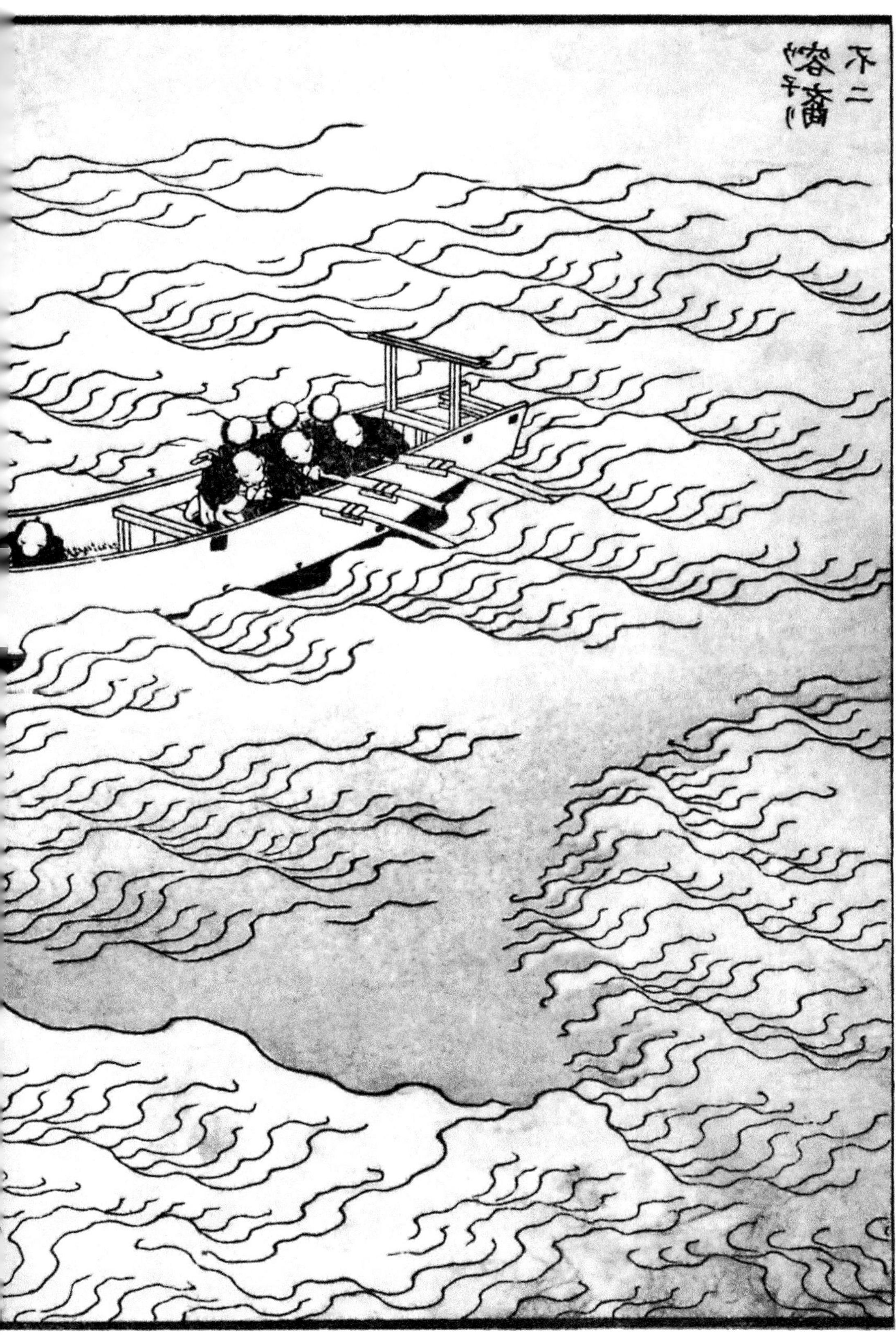

Plate VI

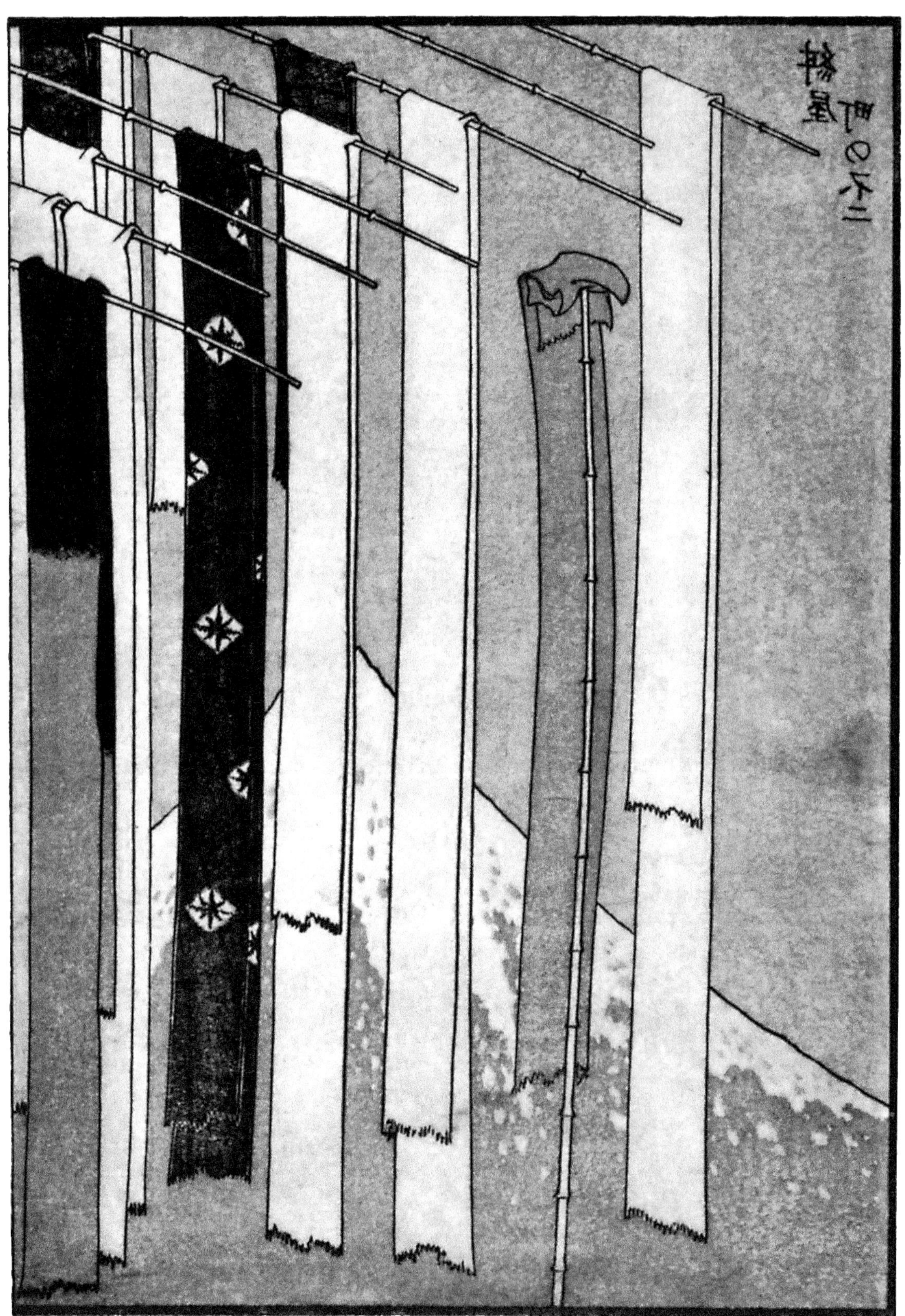

Plate VII

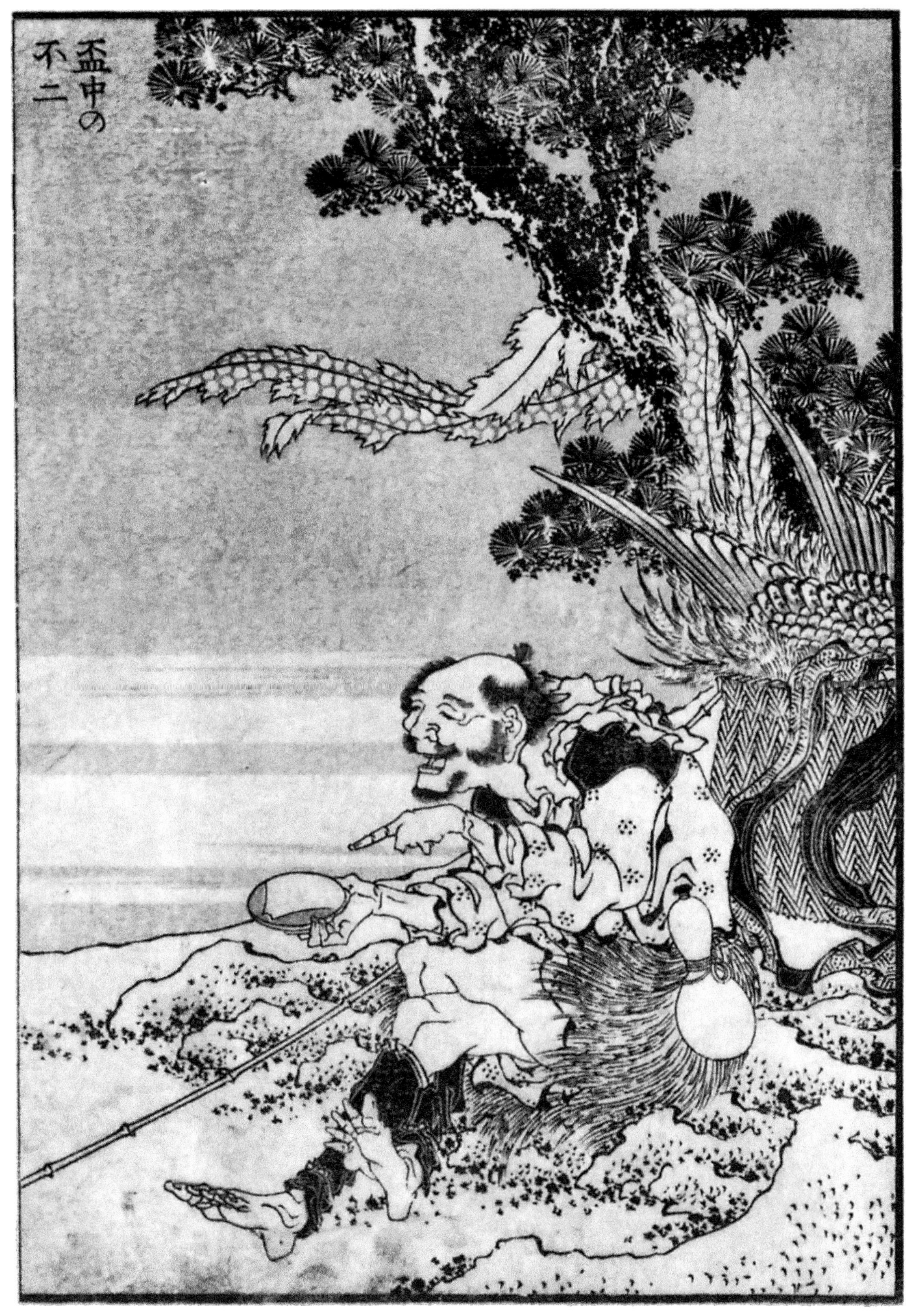

Plate VIII

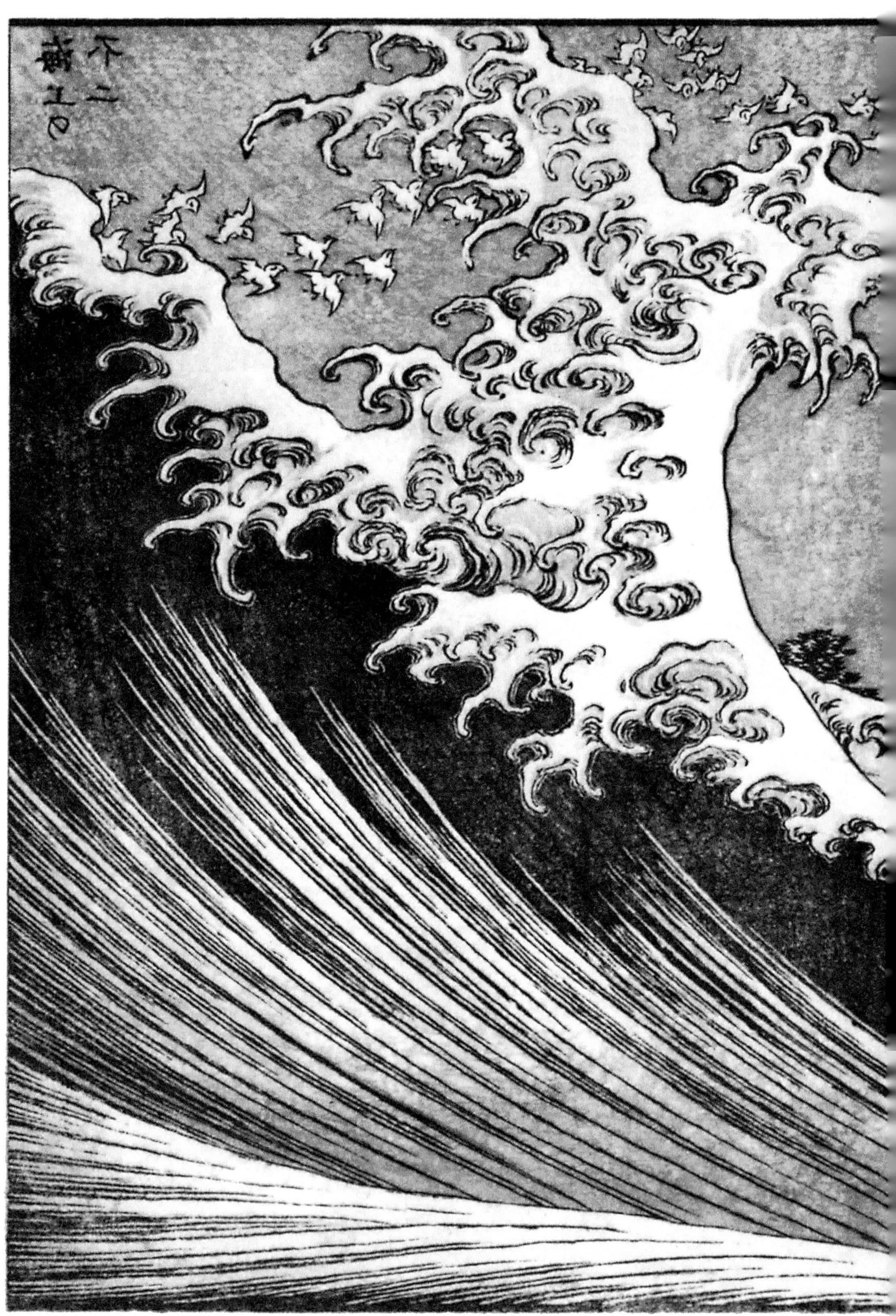

不二
蔵王の

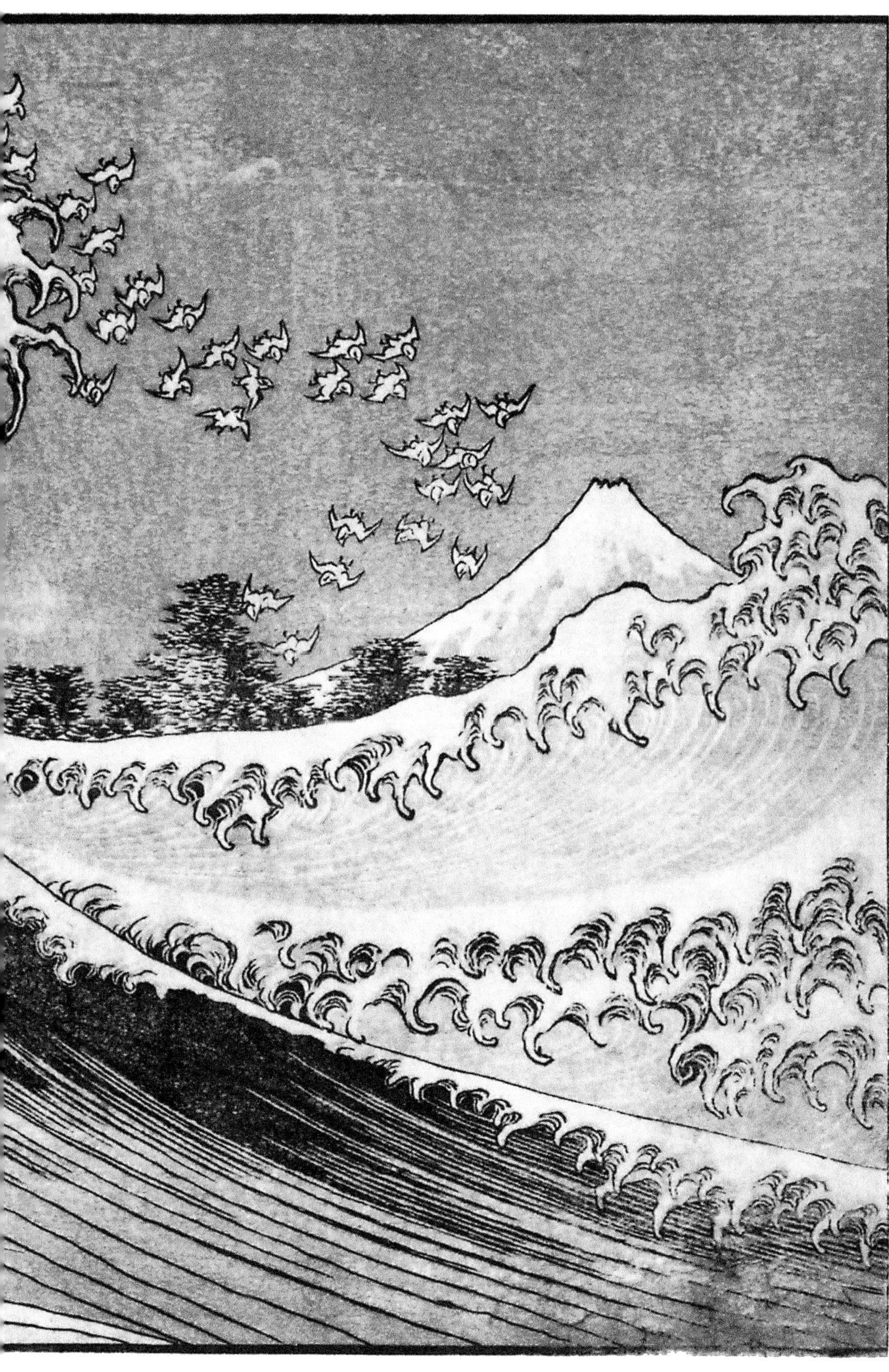

Plate IX

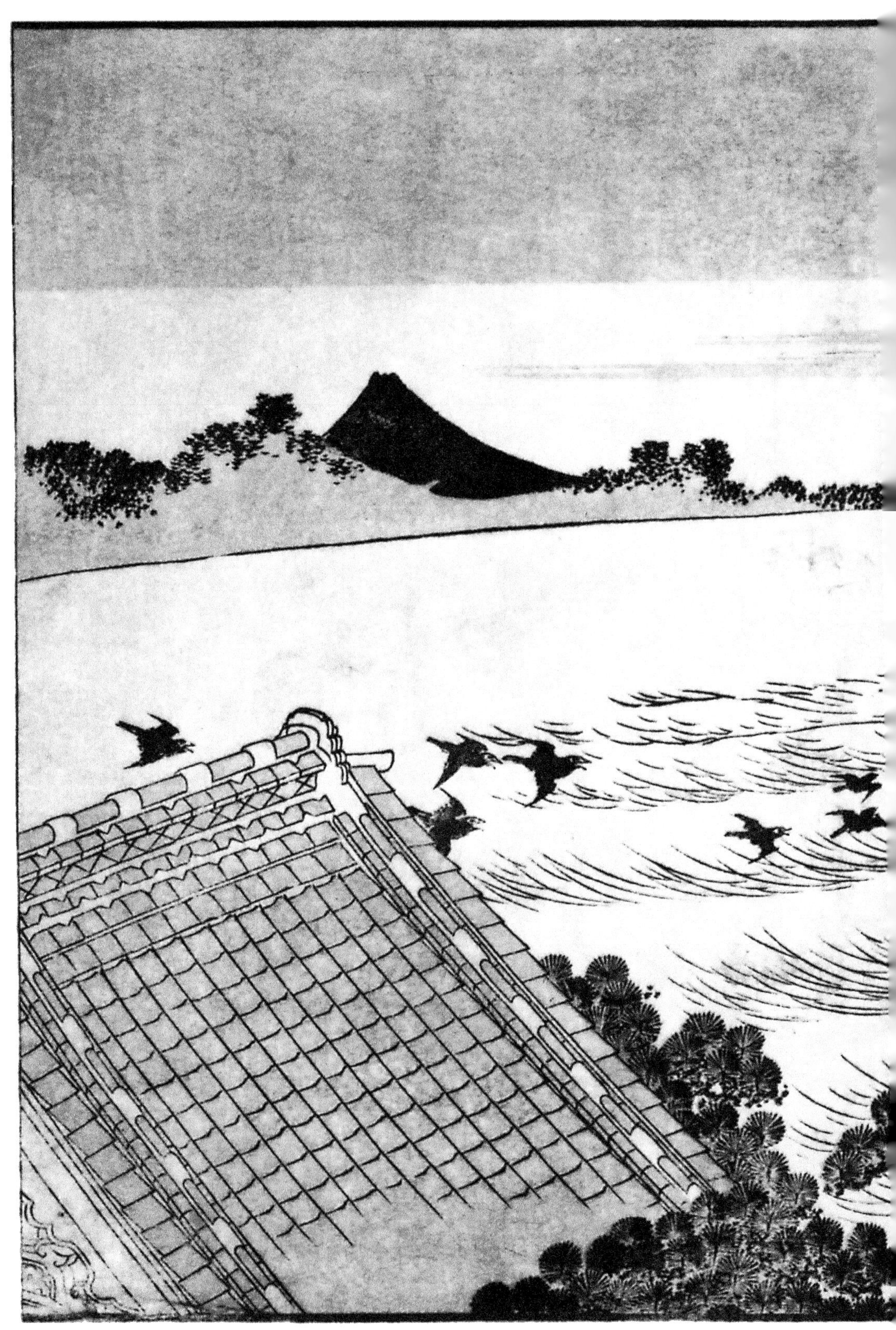

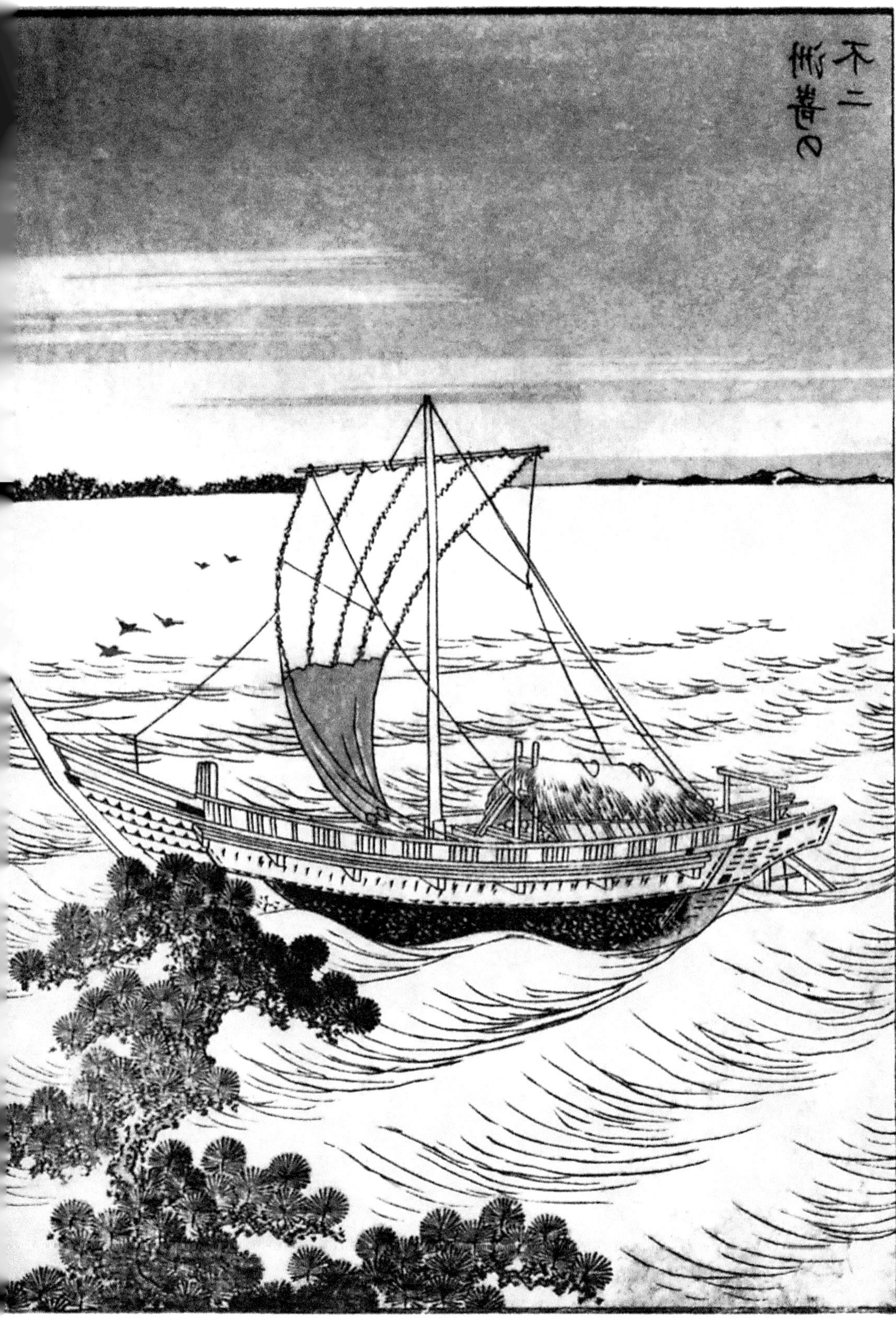

Plate X

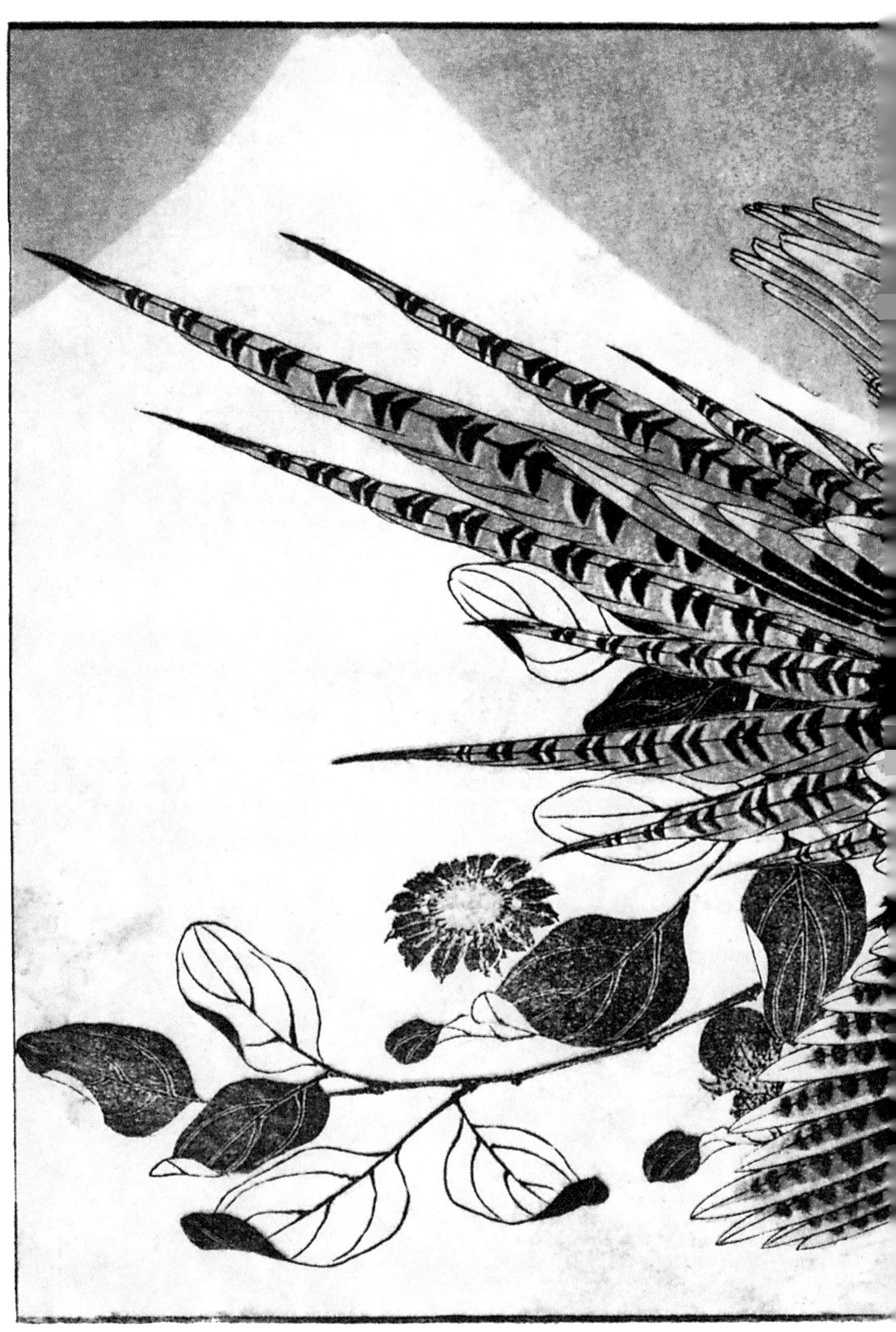

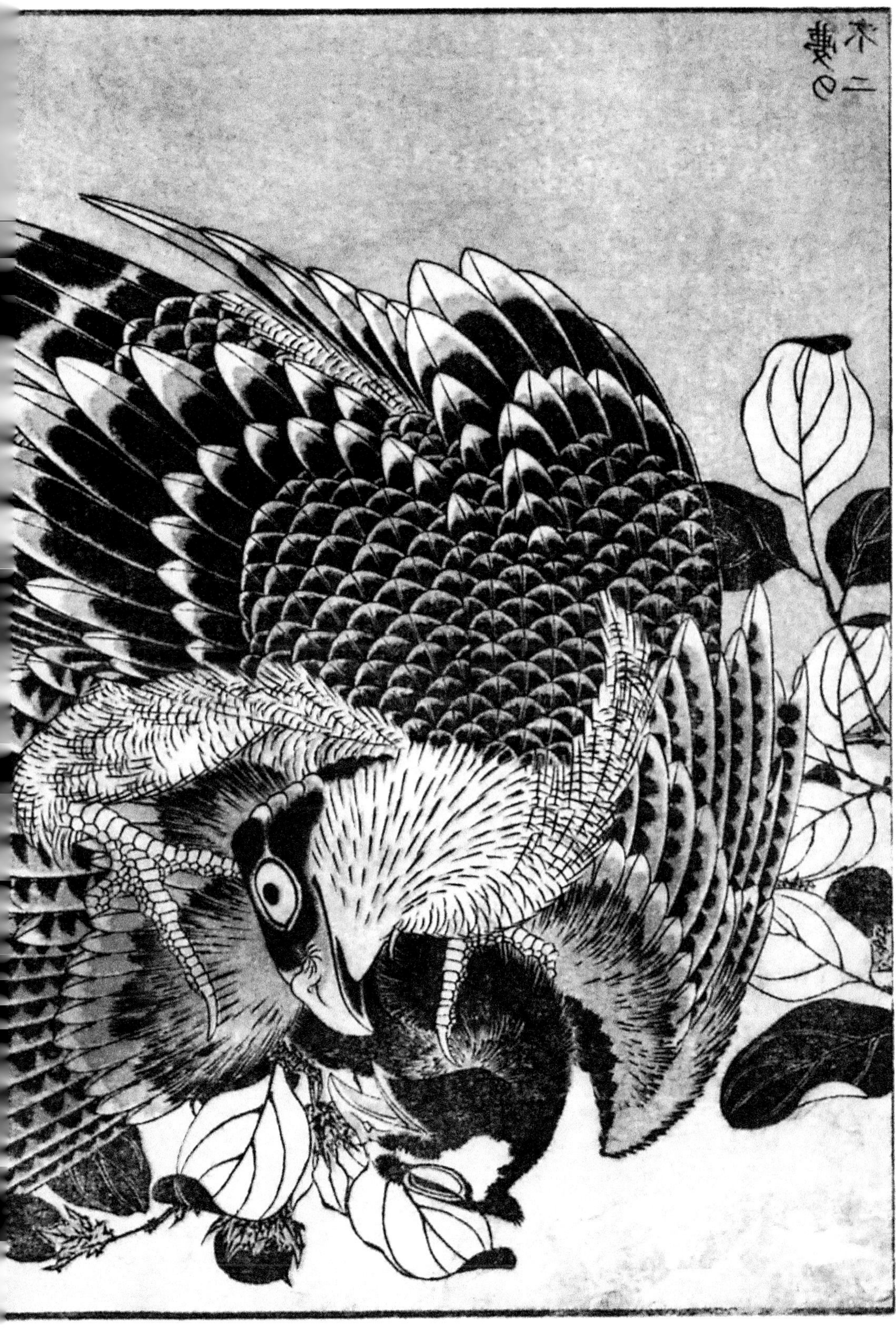

Plate XI

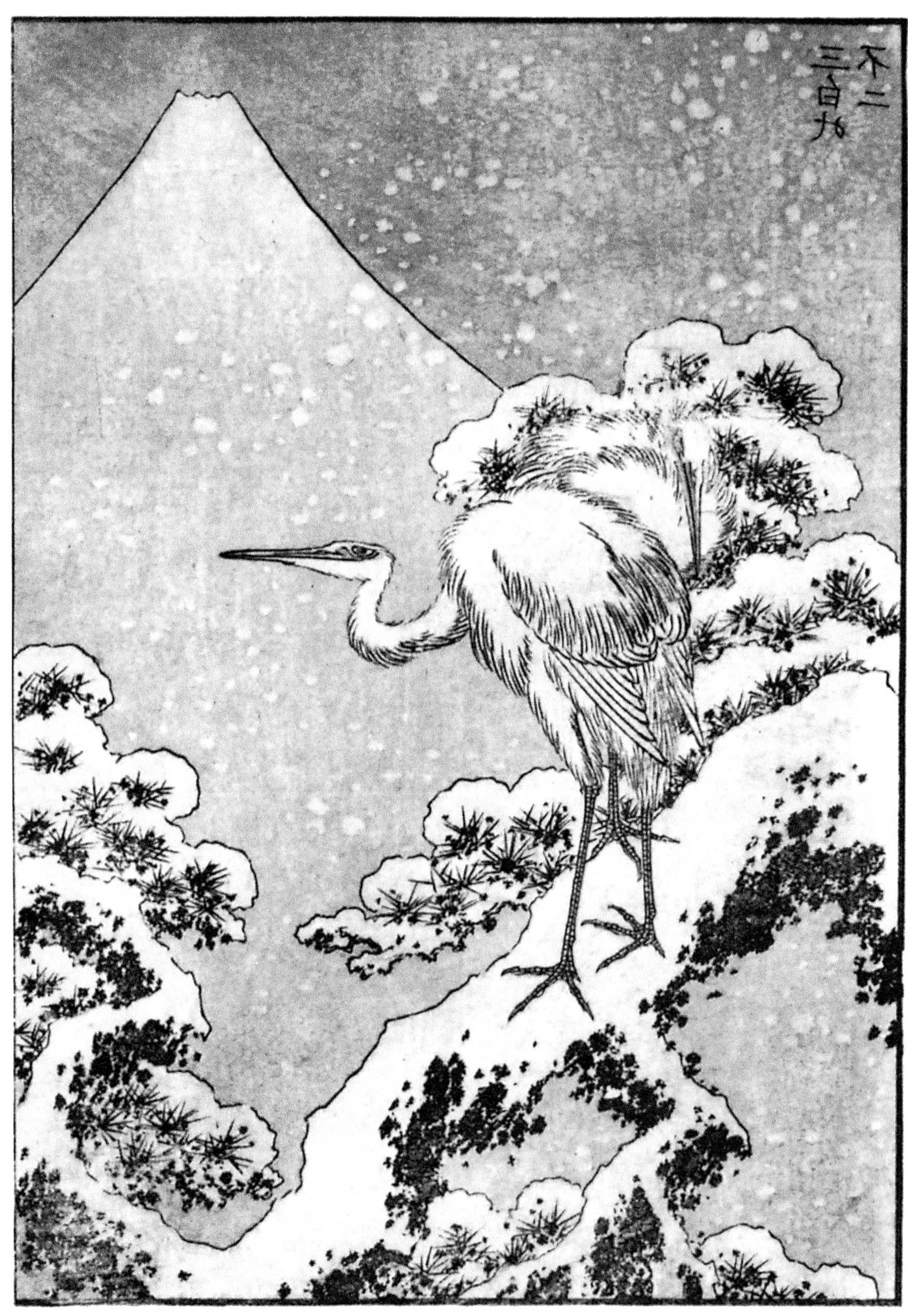

Plate XII

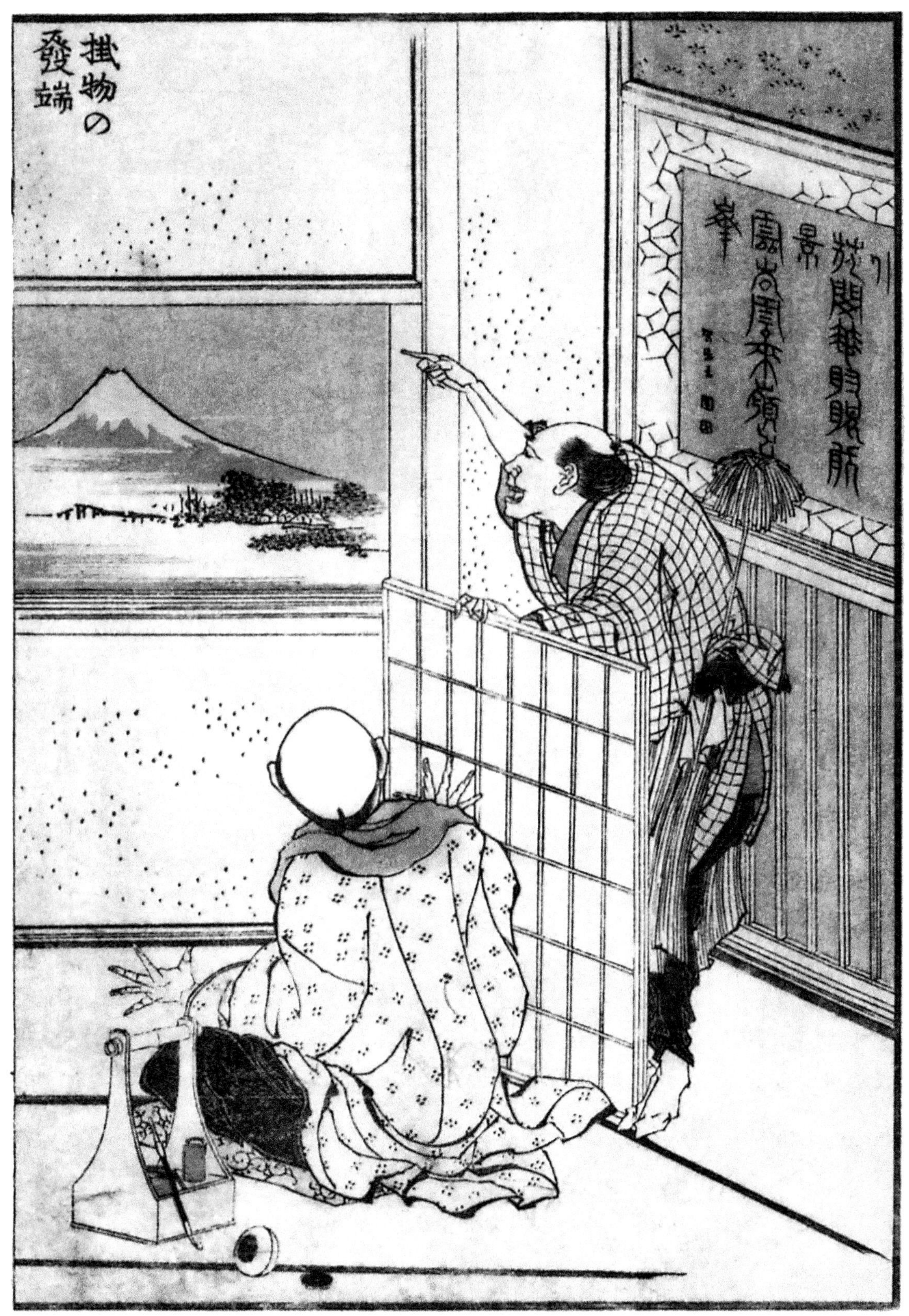

Plate XIII

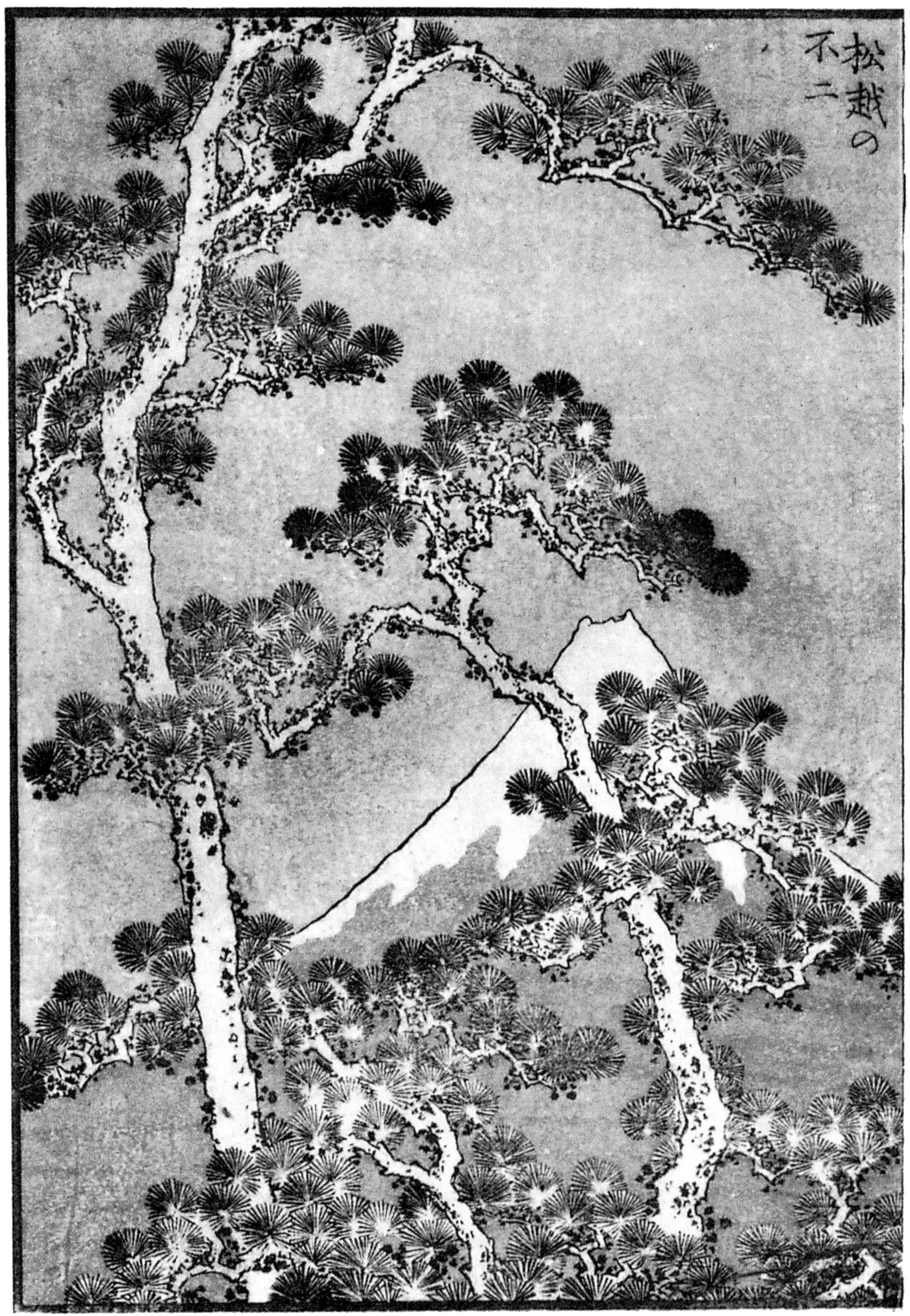

Plate XIV

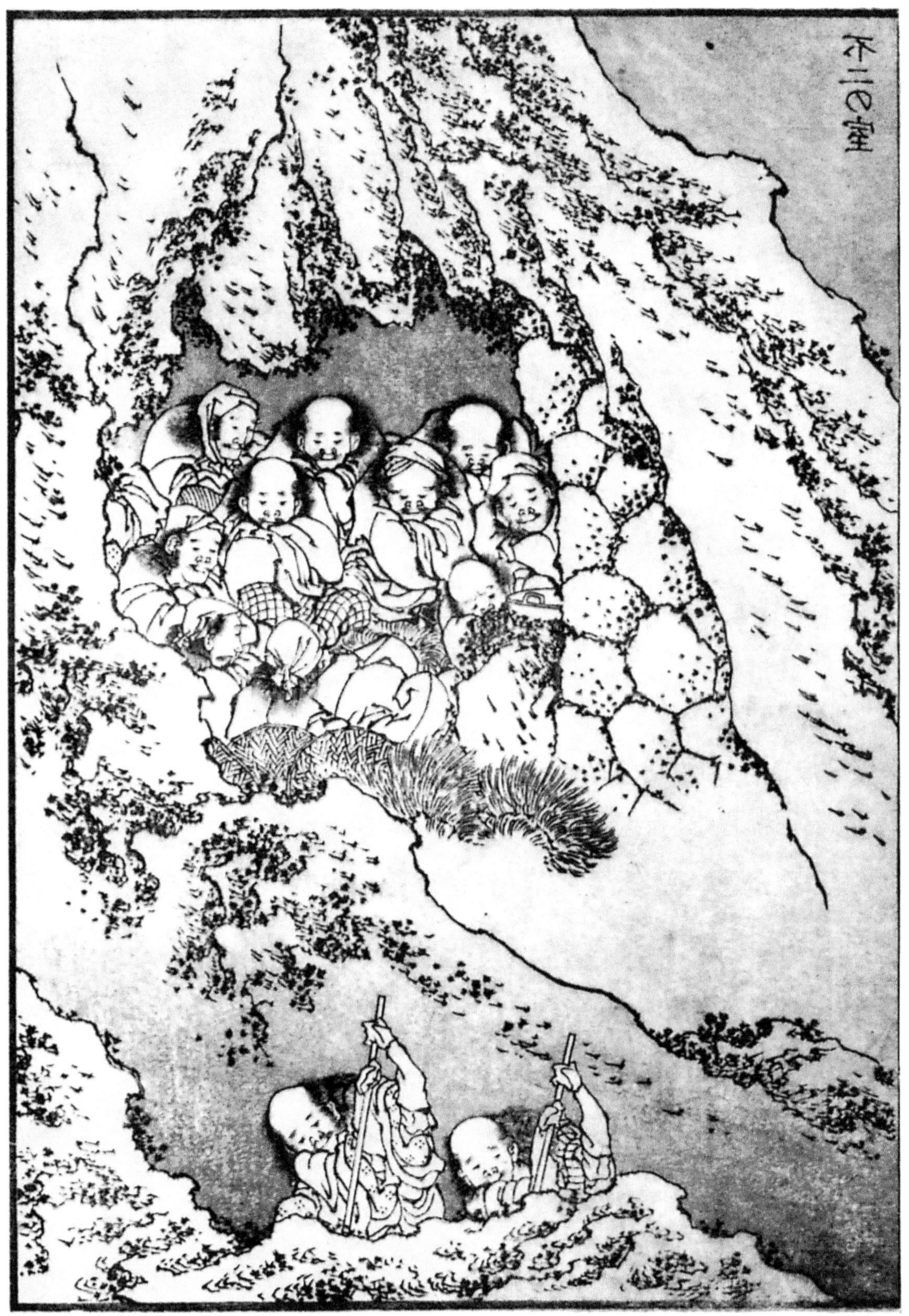

Plate XV

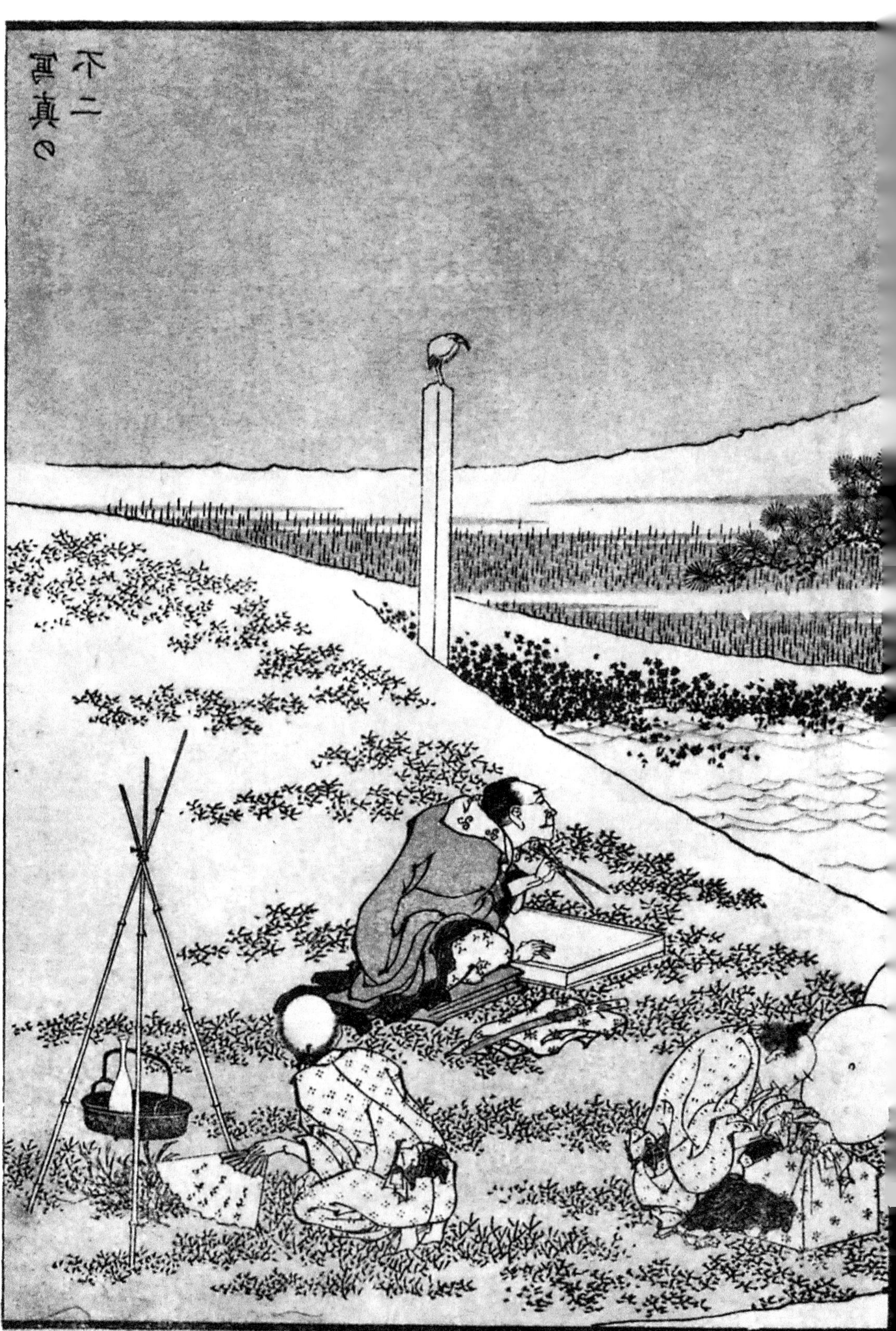

不二
寫真の

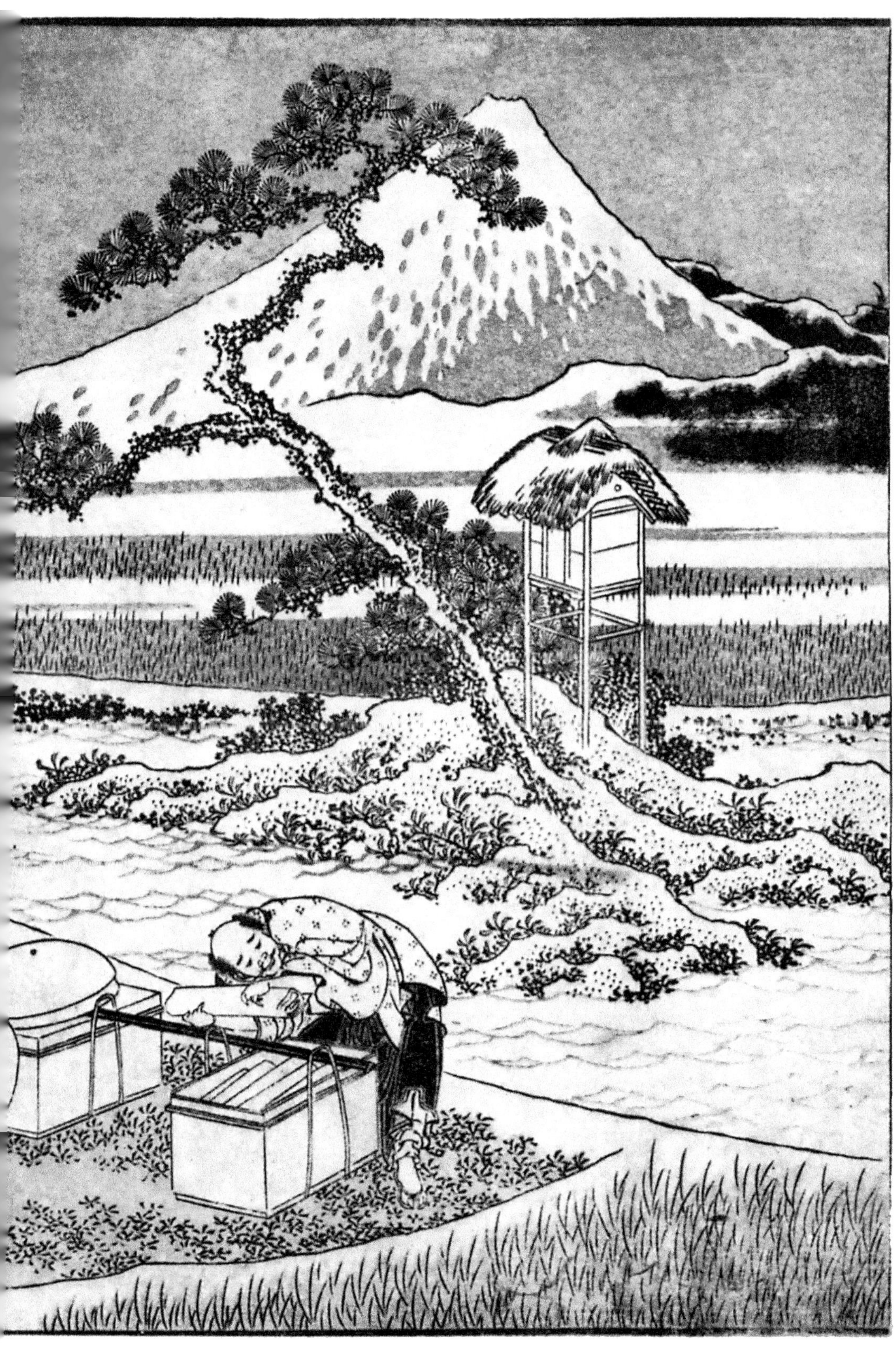

Plate XVI

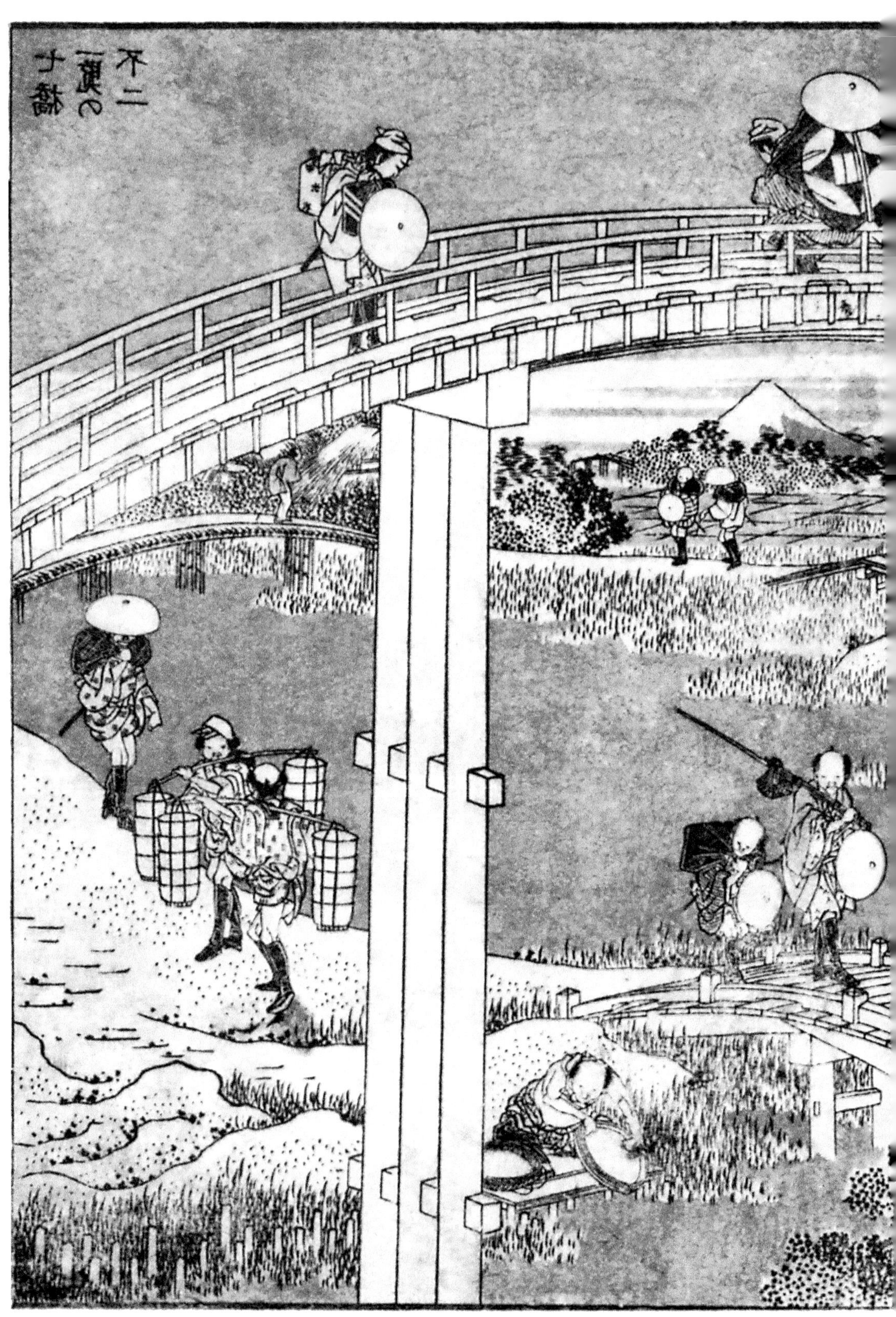

不二
裏の
十謌

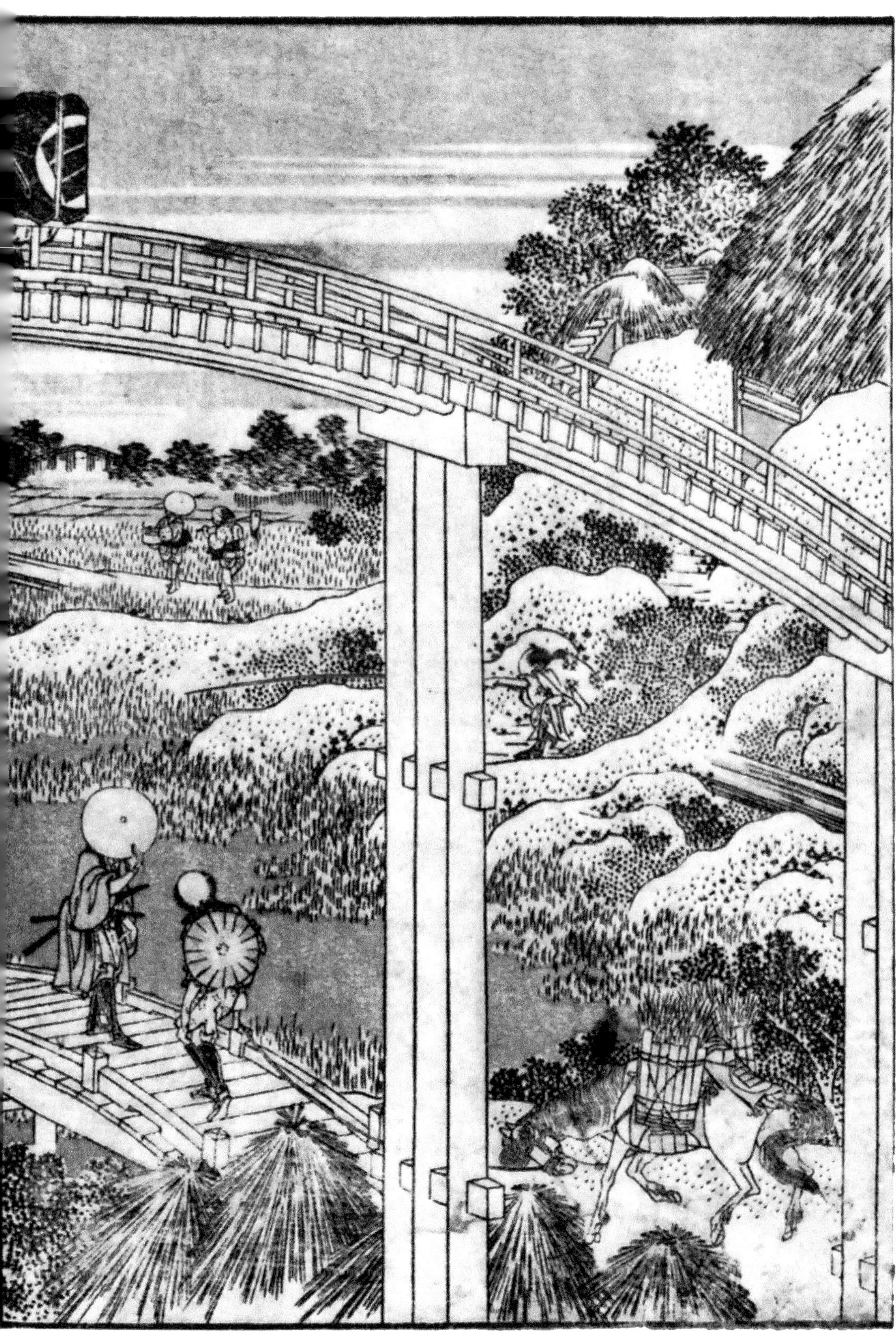

Plate XVII

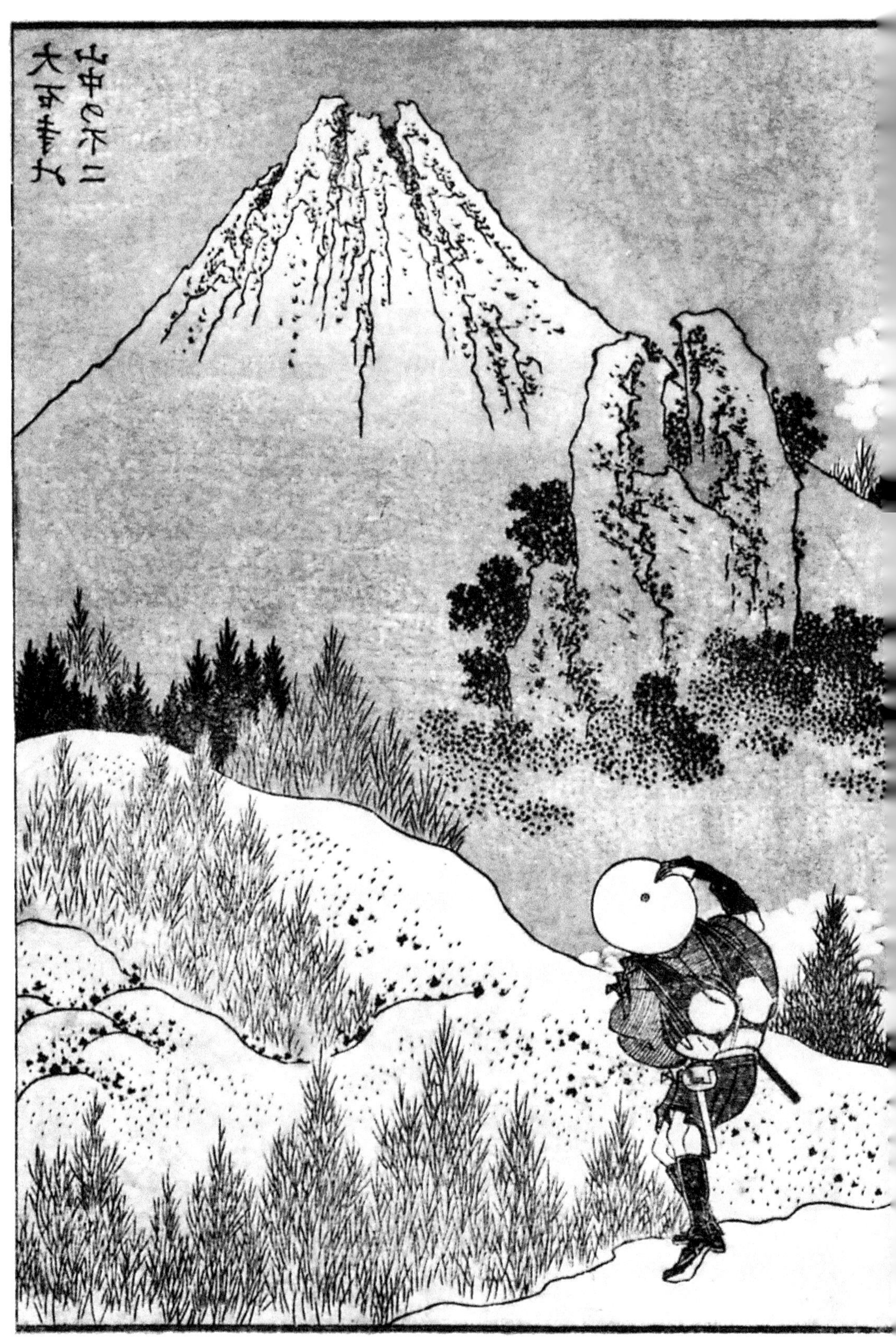
山中の不二
大石美大

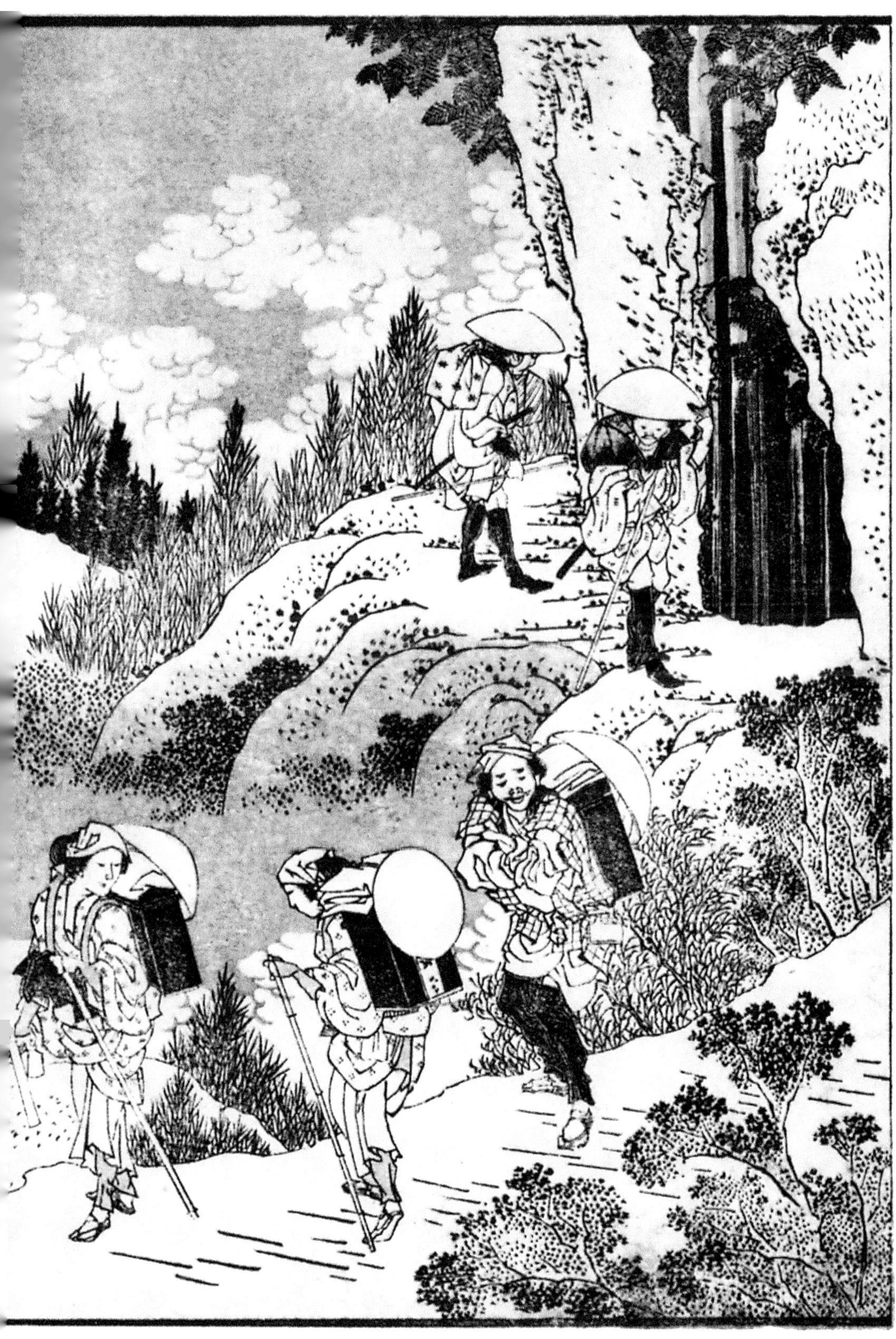

Plate XVIII

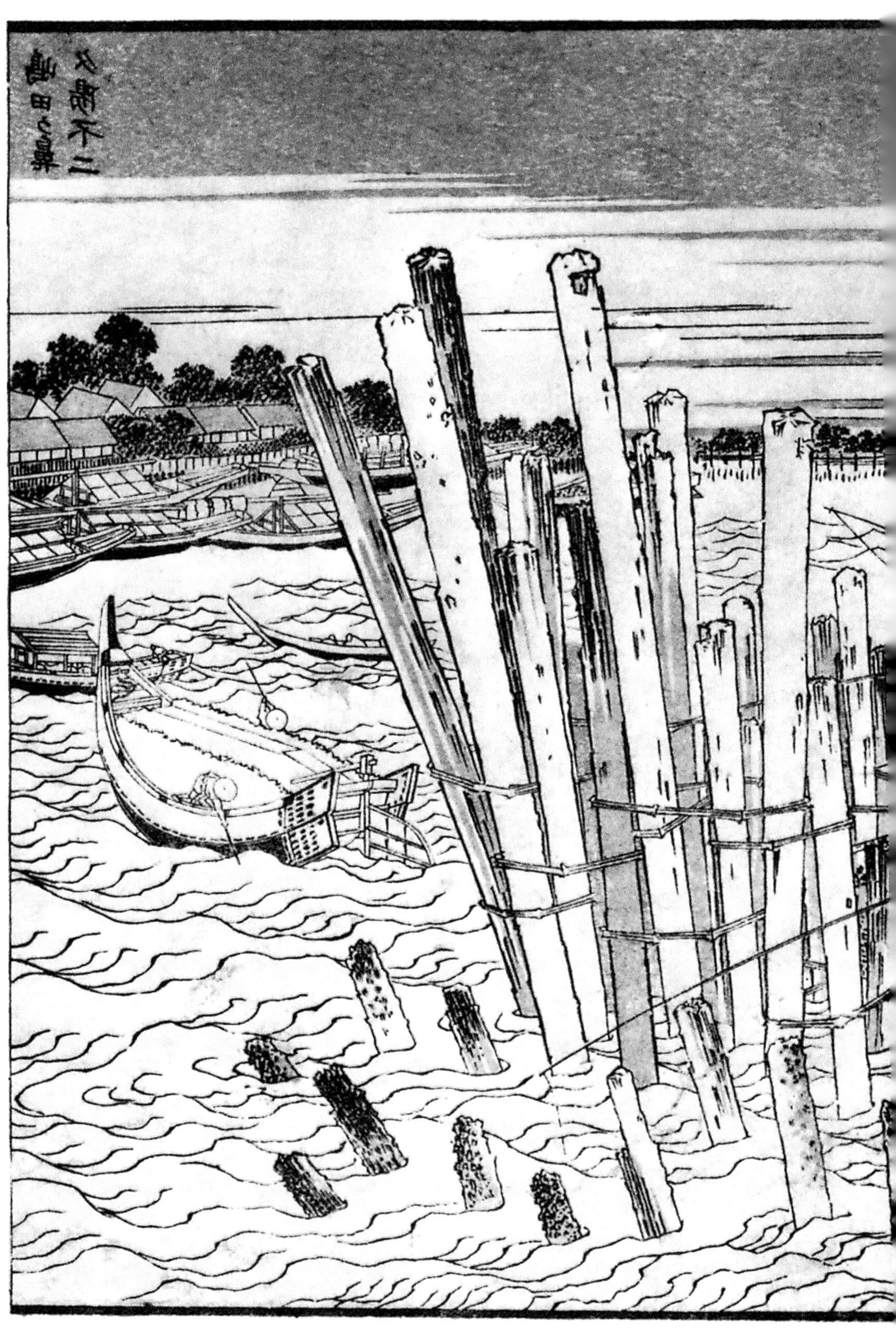
千鳥不二
鶴田ヶ鼻

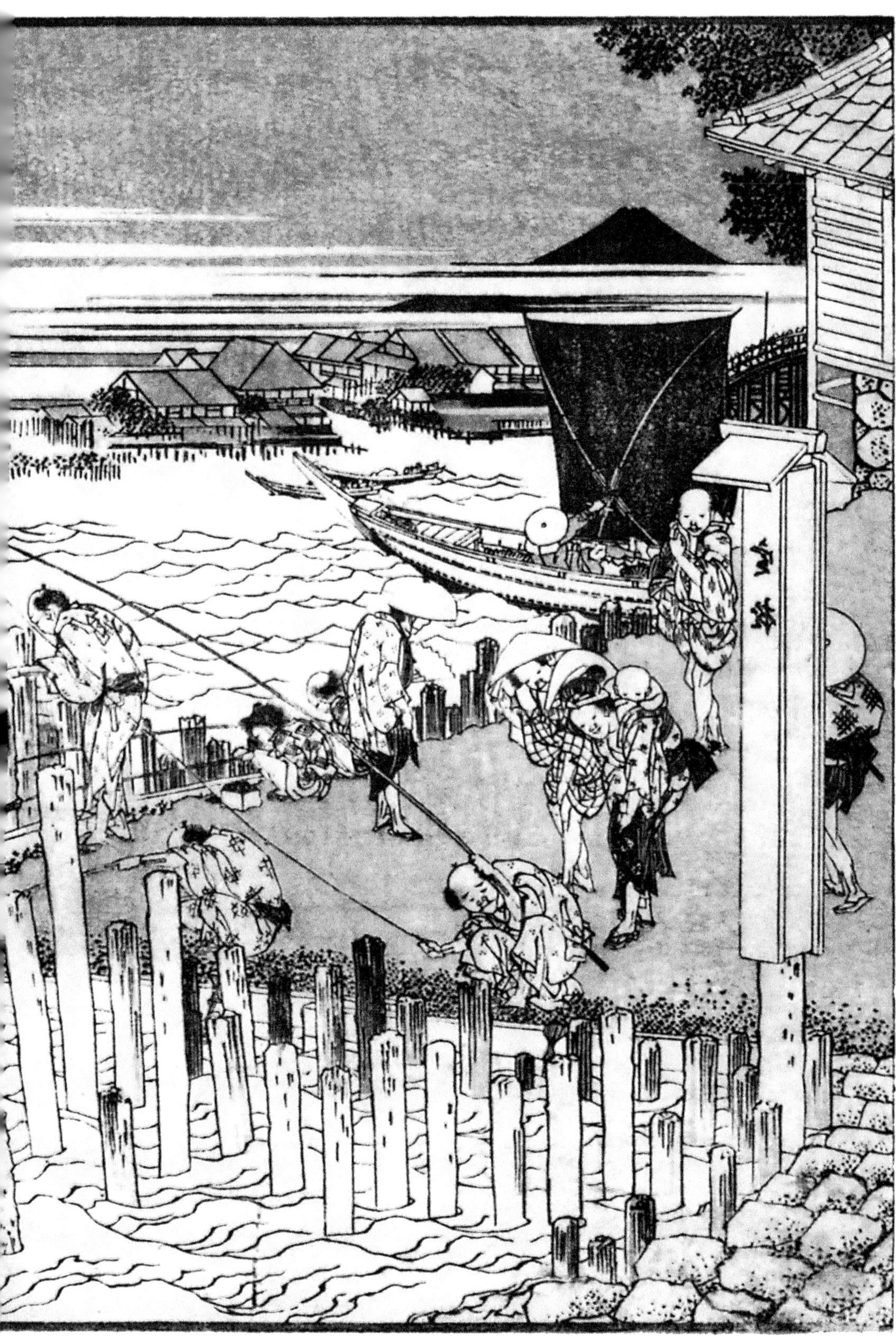

Plate XIX

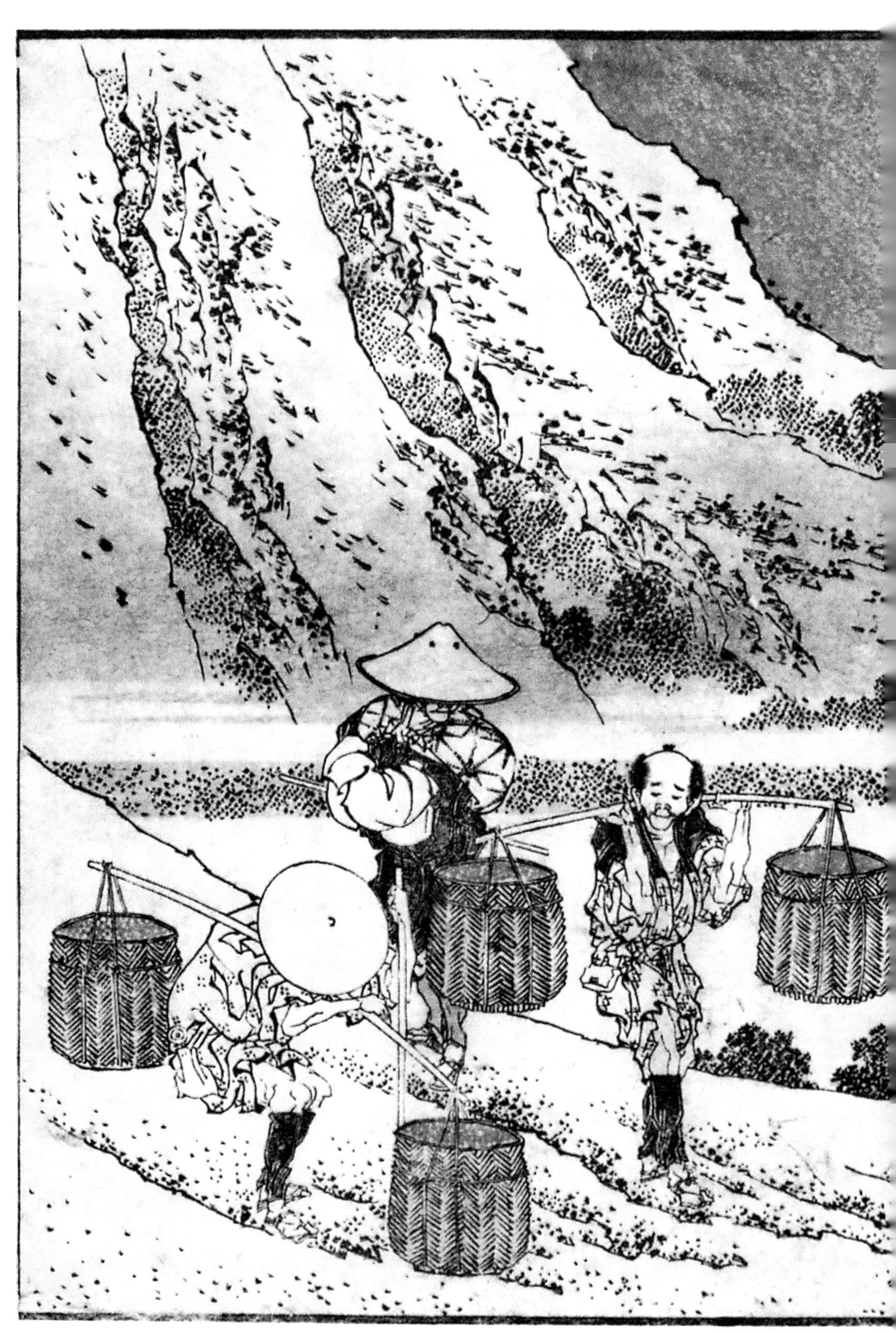

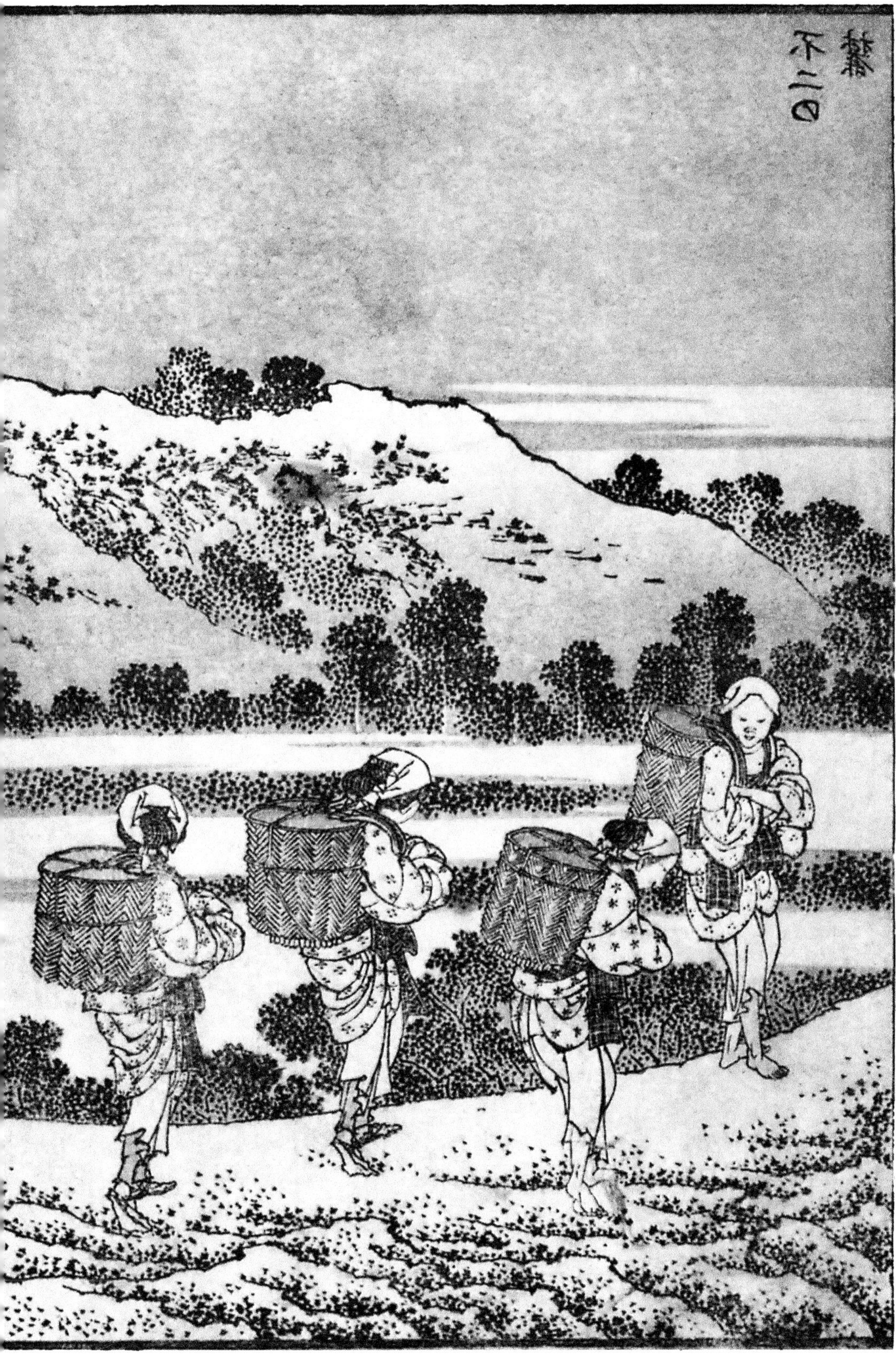

Plate XX

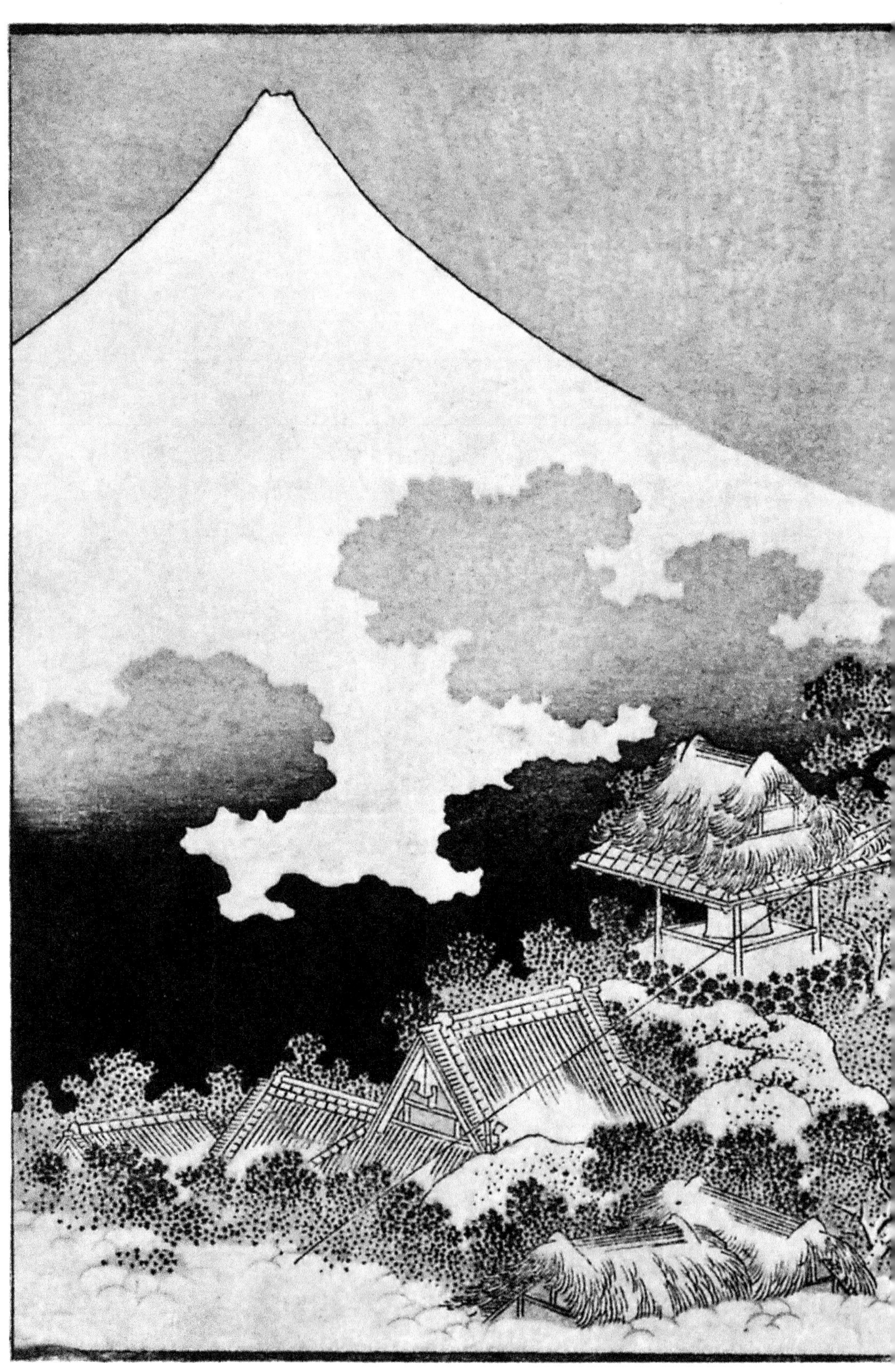

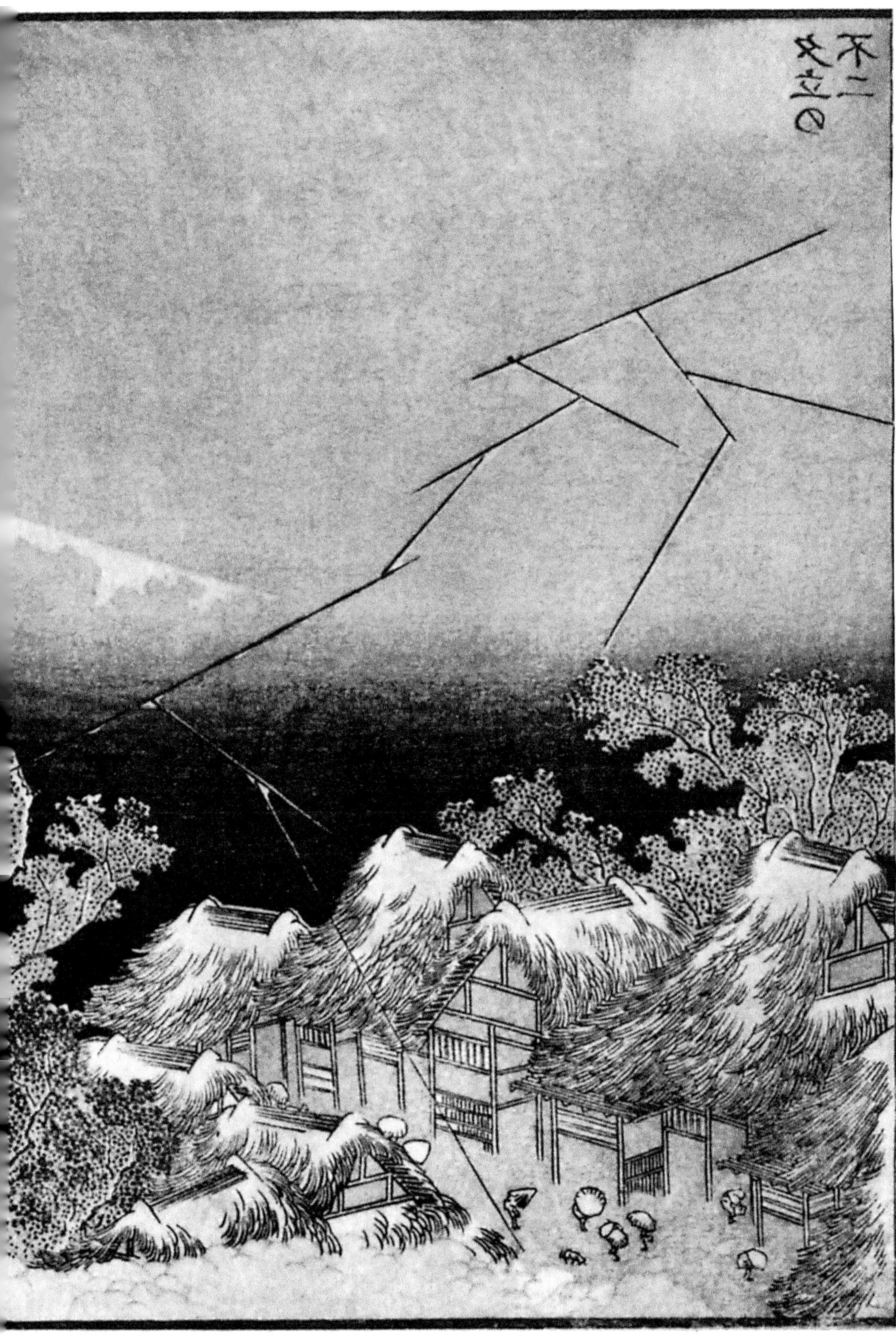

Plate XXI

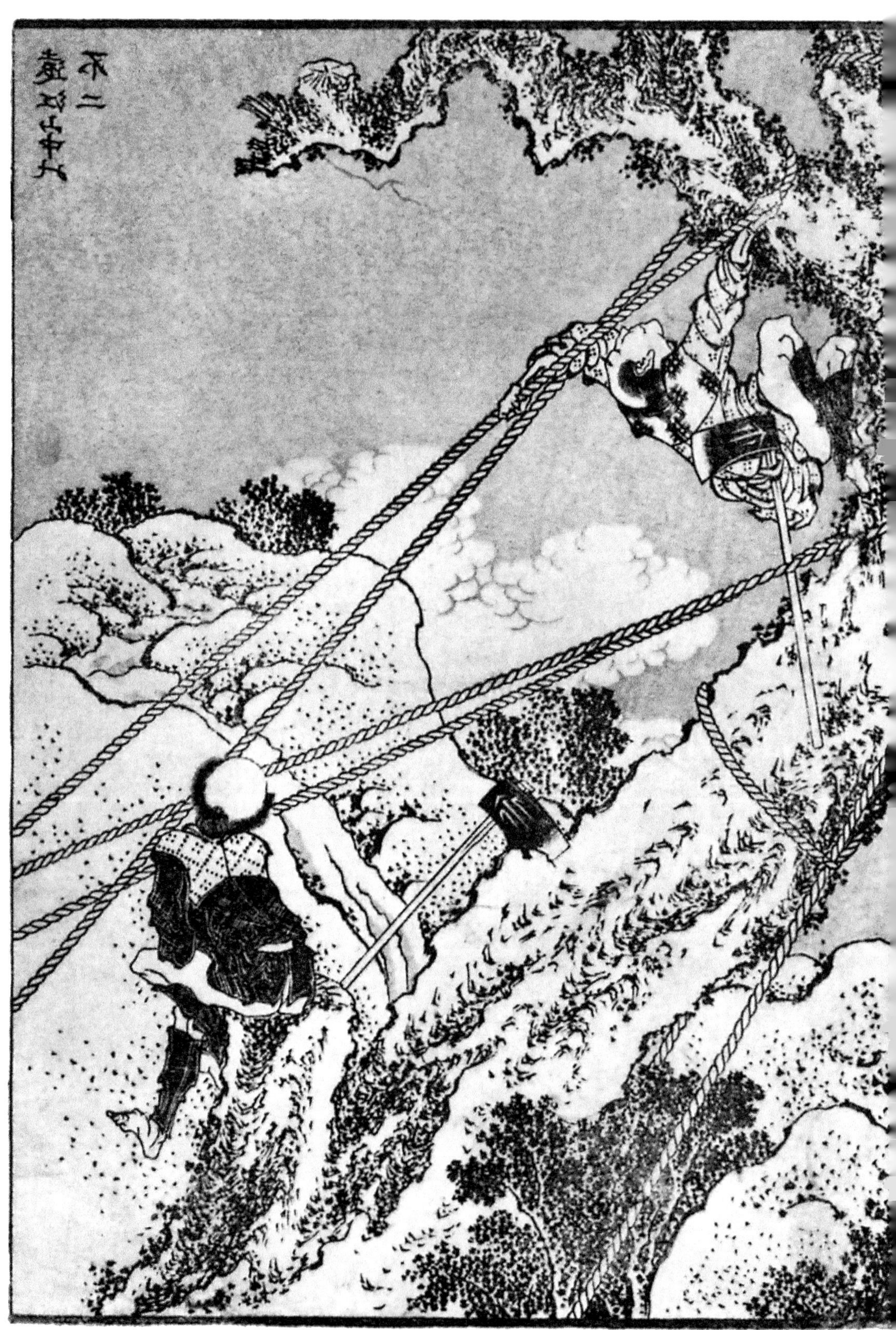

不二
遠ぢかの不二

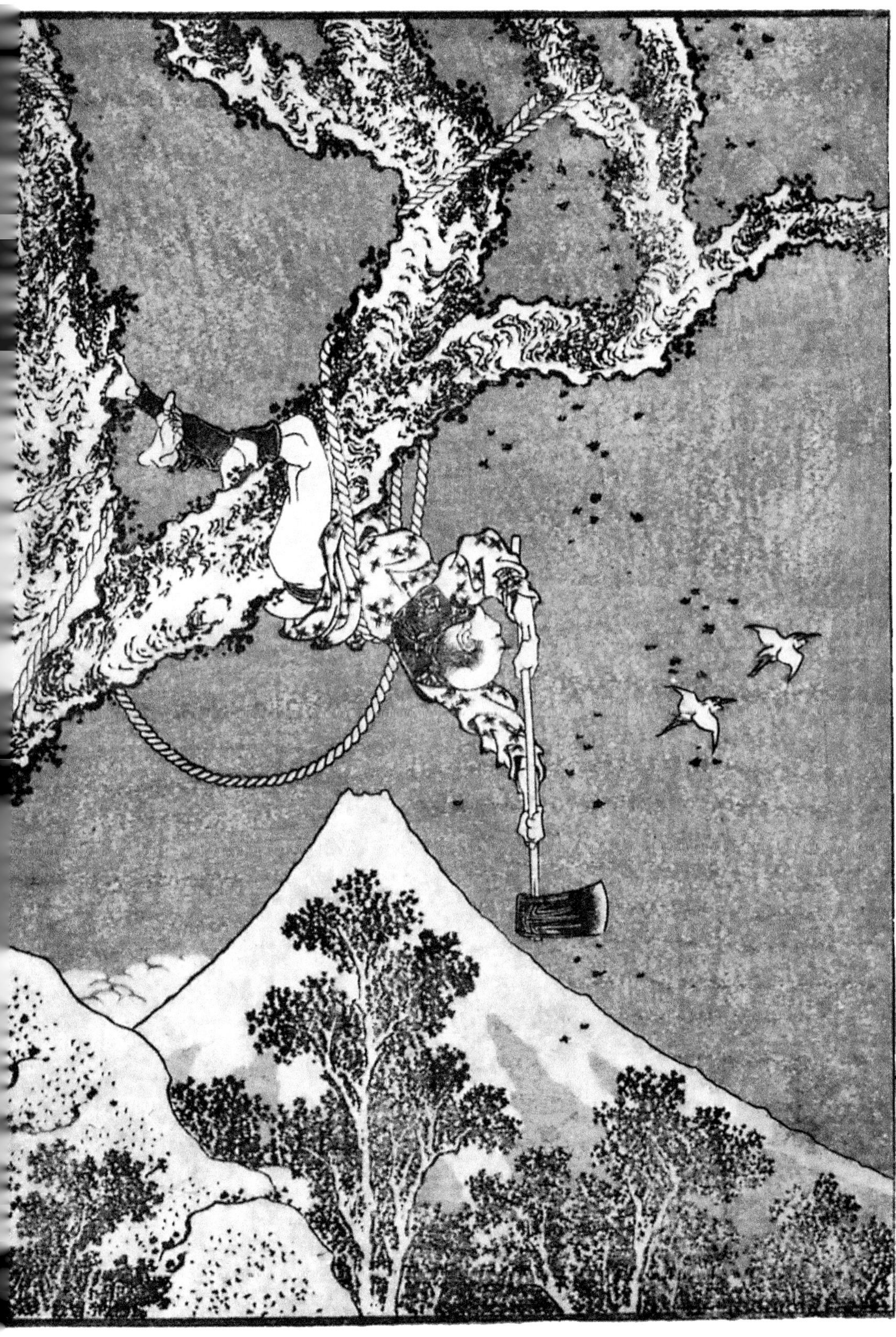

Plate XXII

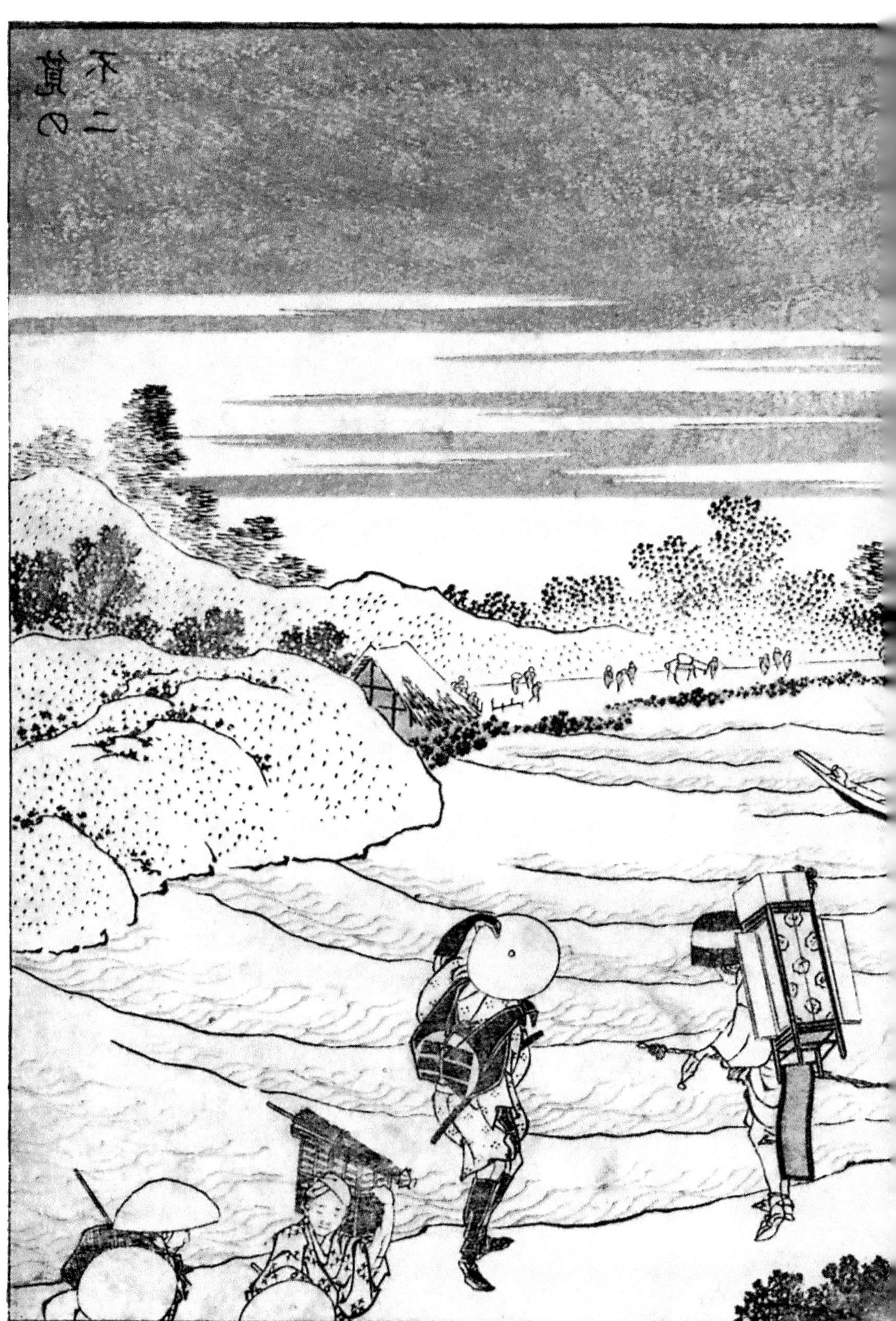

不二
真の

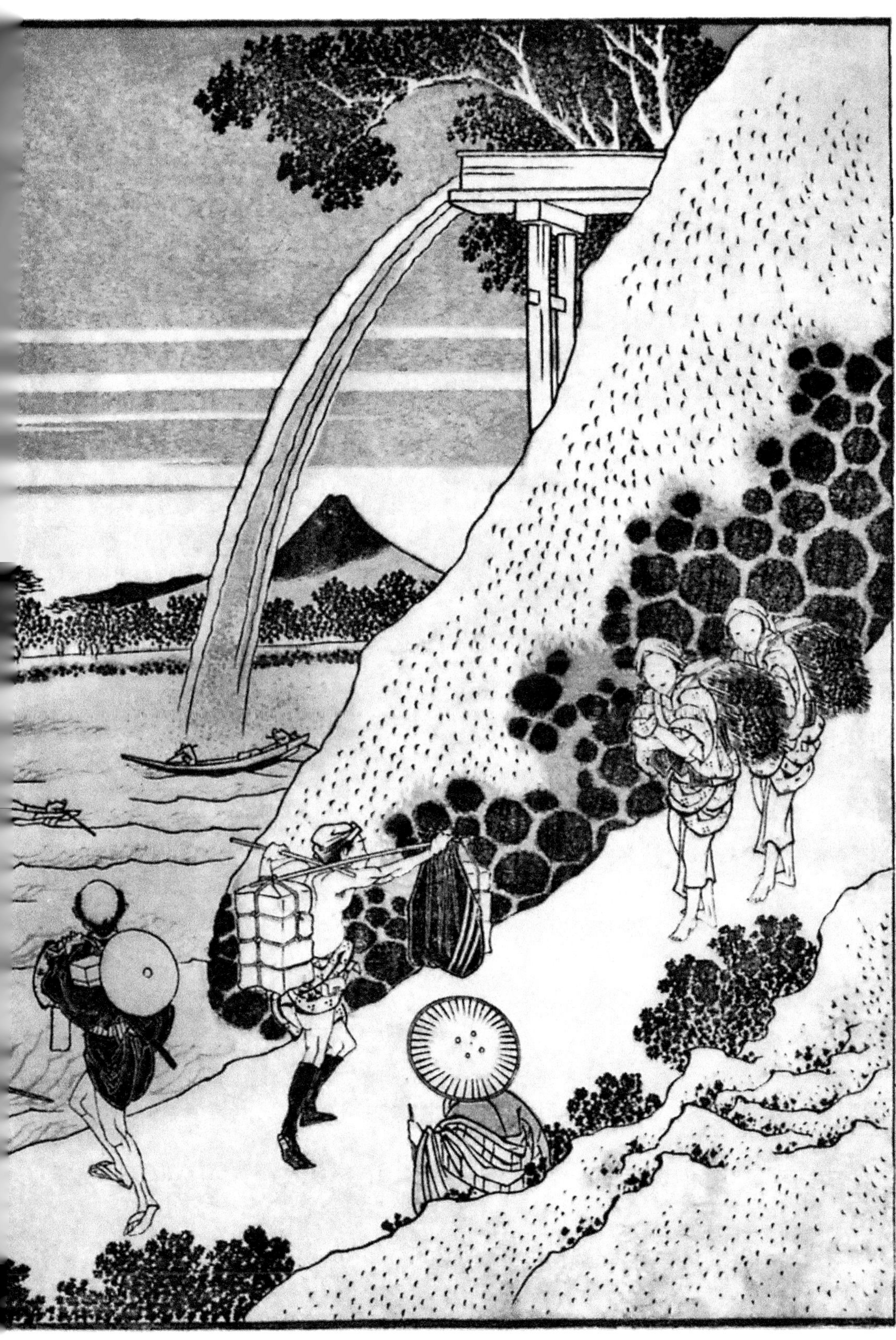

Plate XXIII

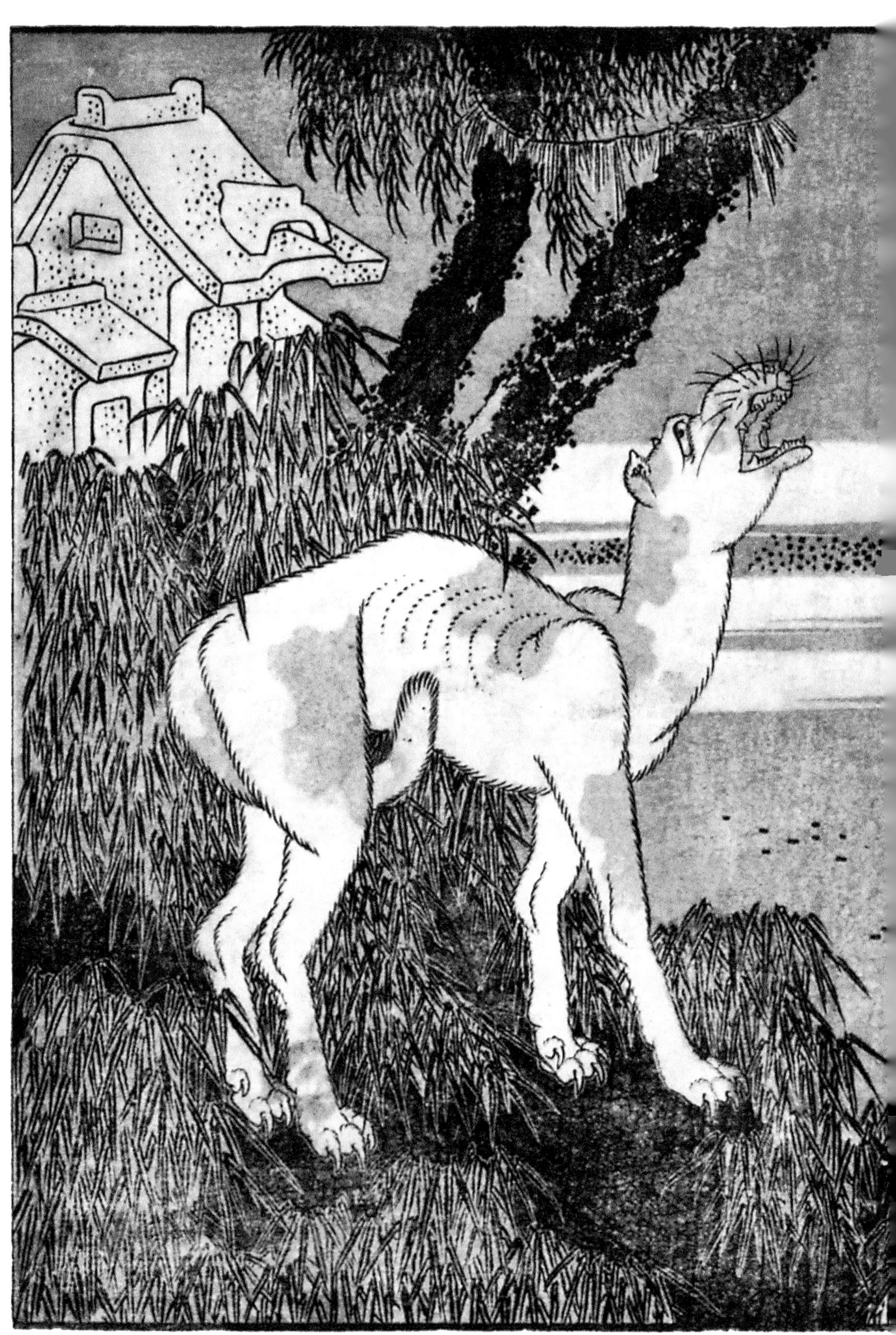

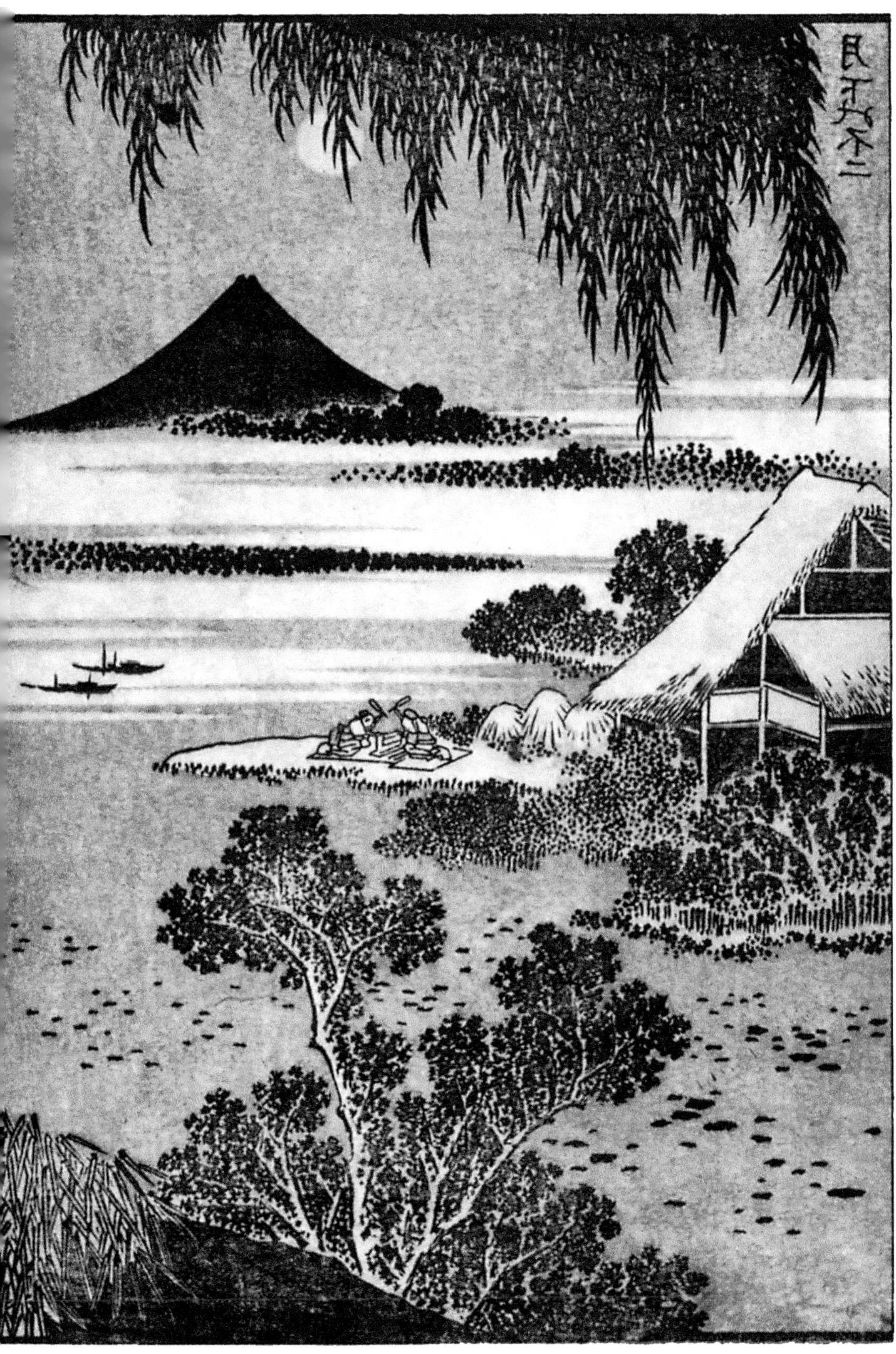

Plate XXIV

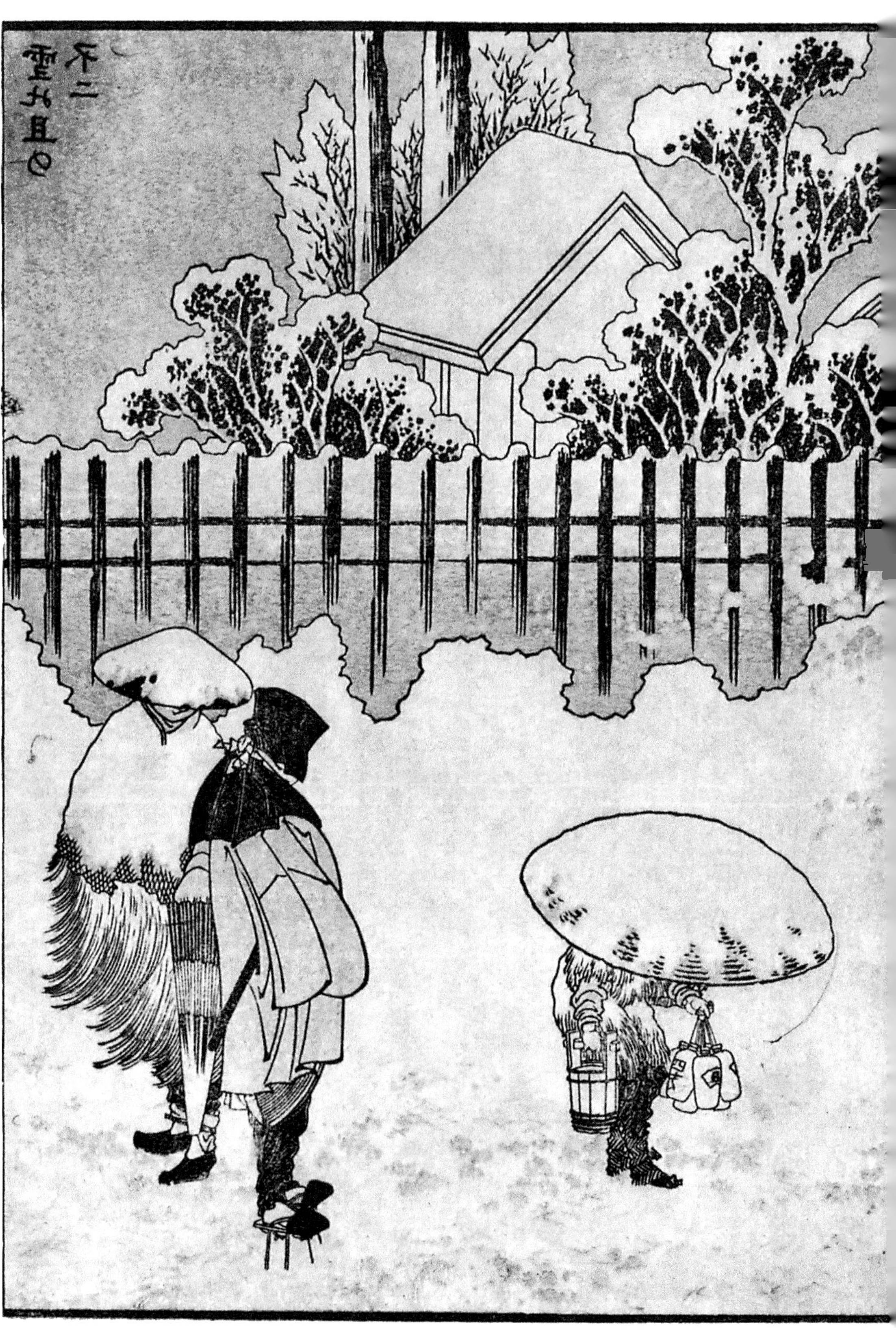

不二
雪竹の旦

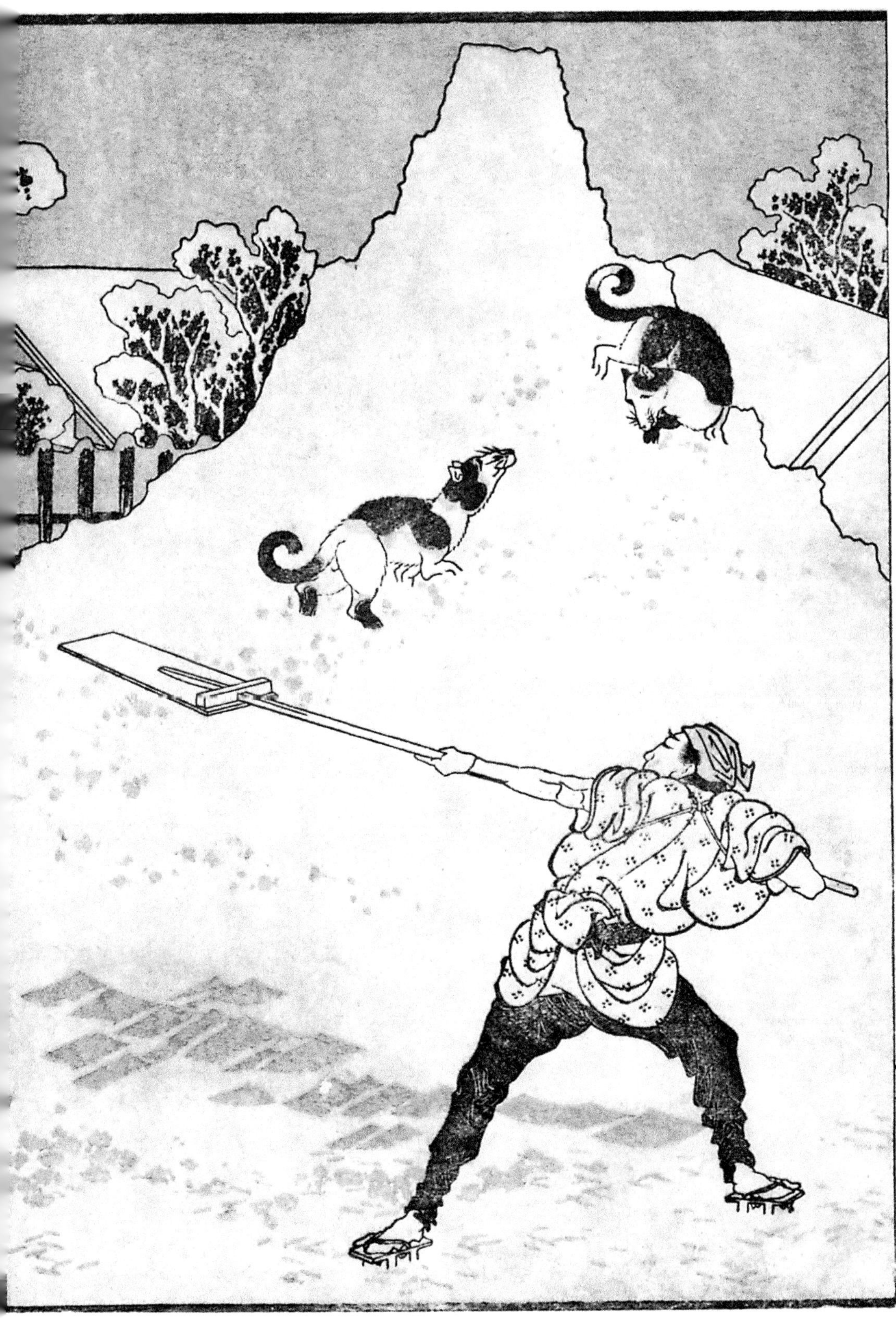

Plate XXV

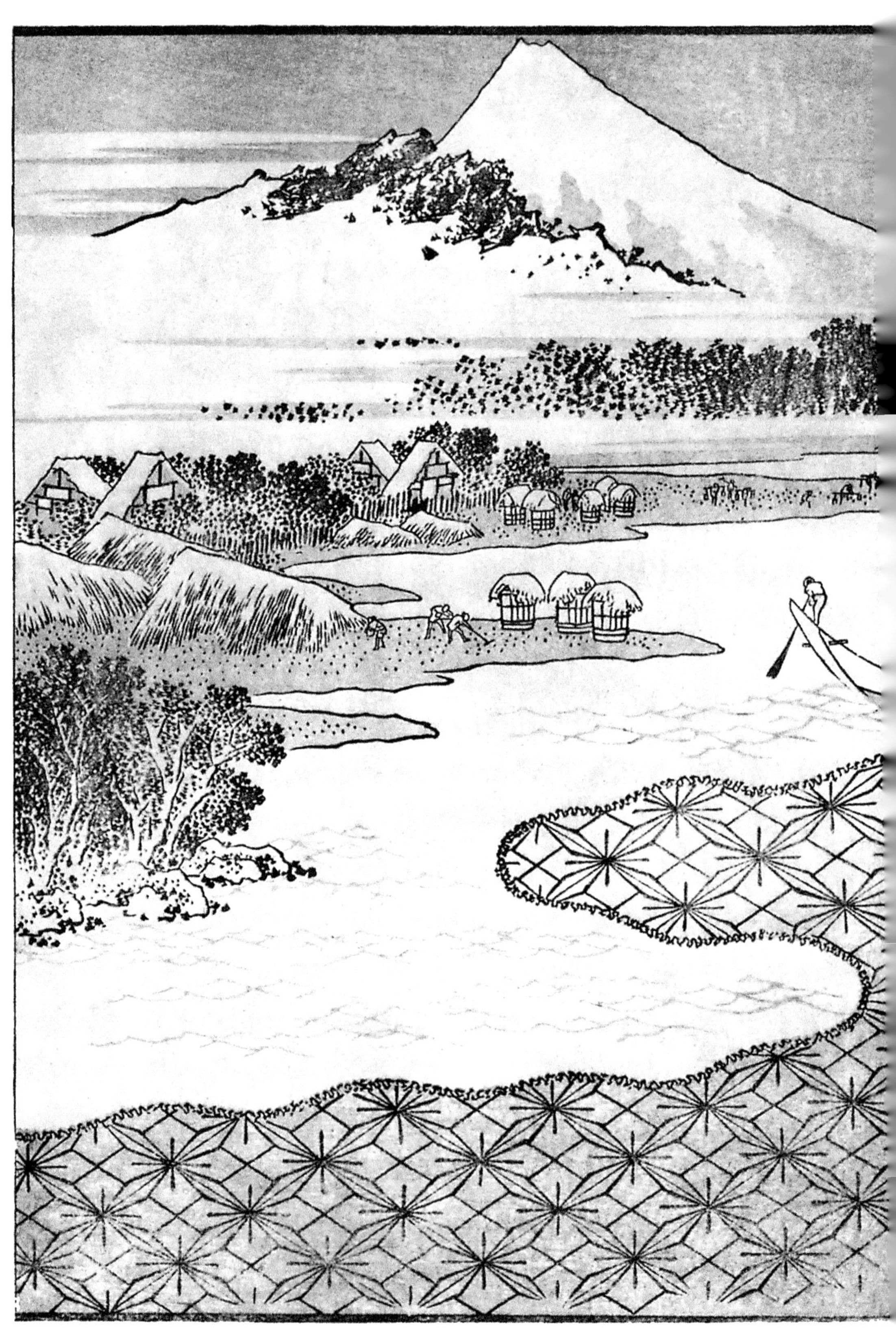

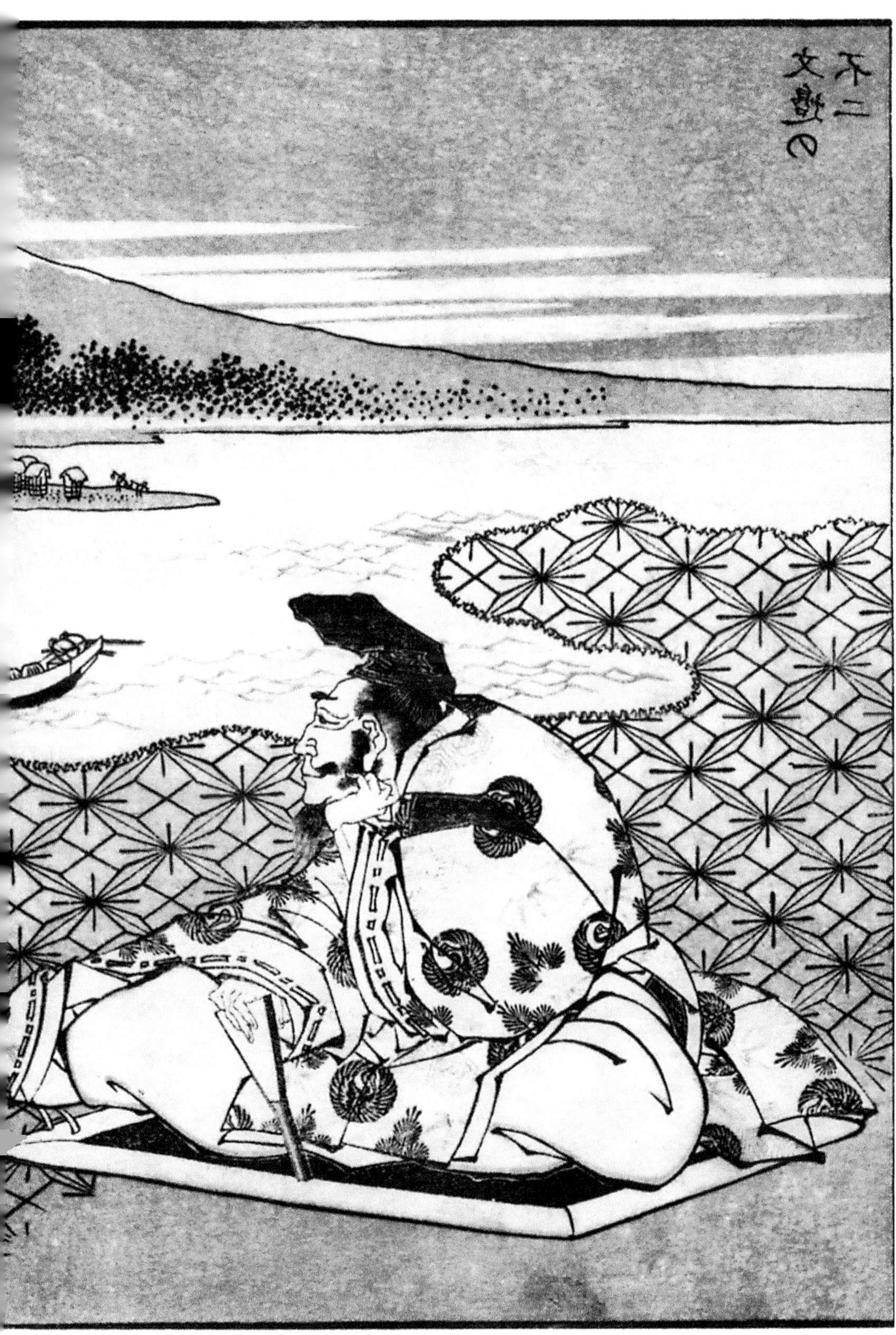

Plate XXVI

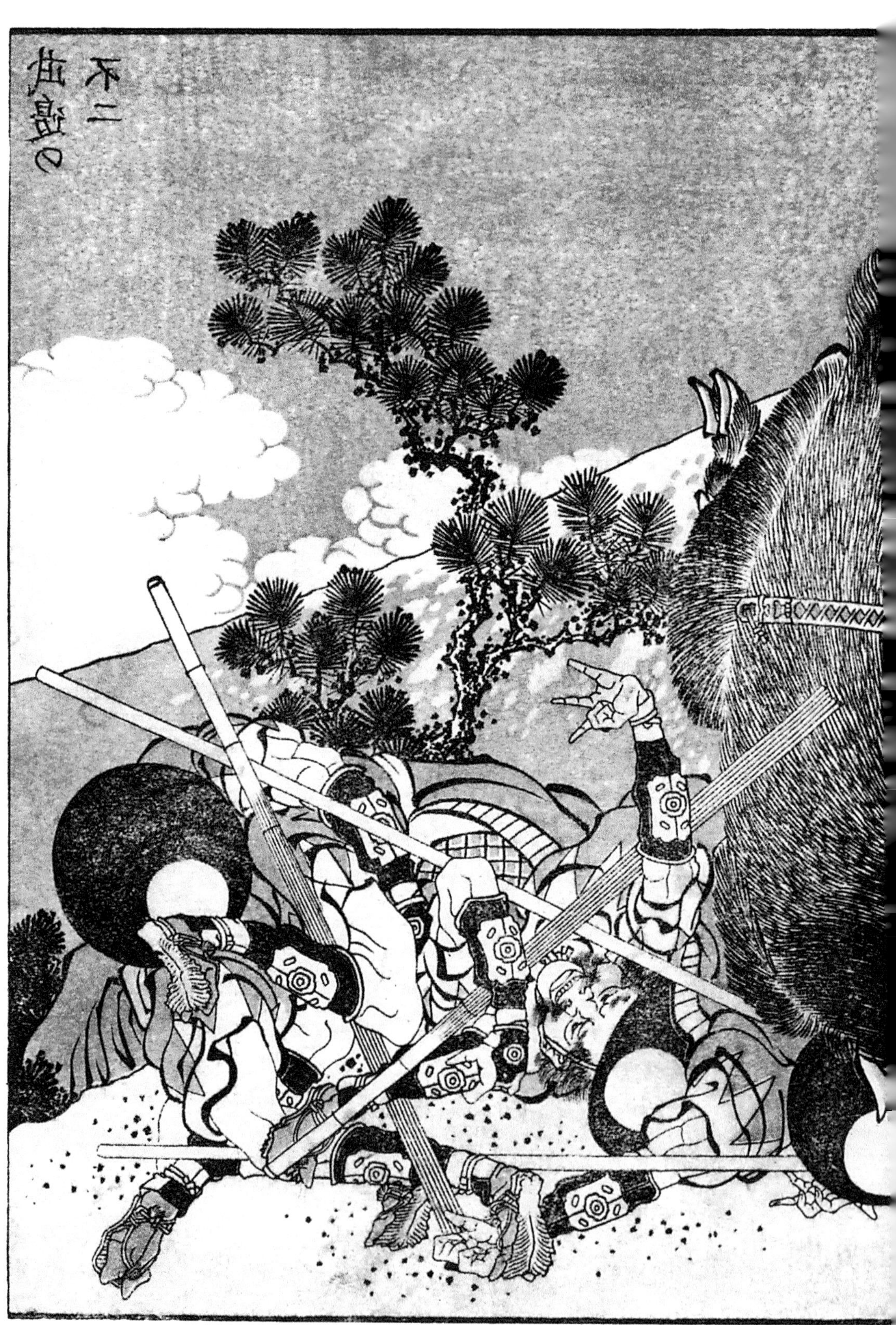

不二
生出の

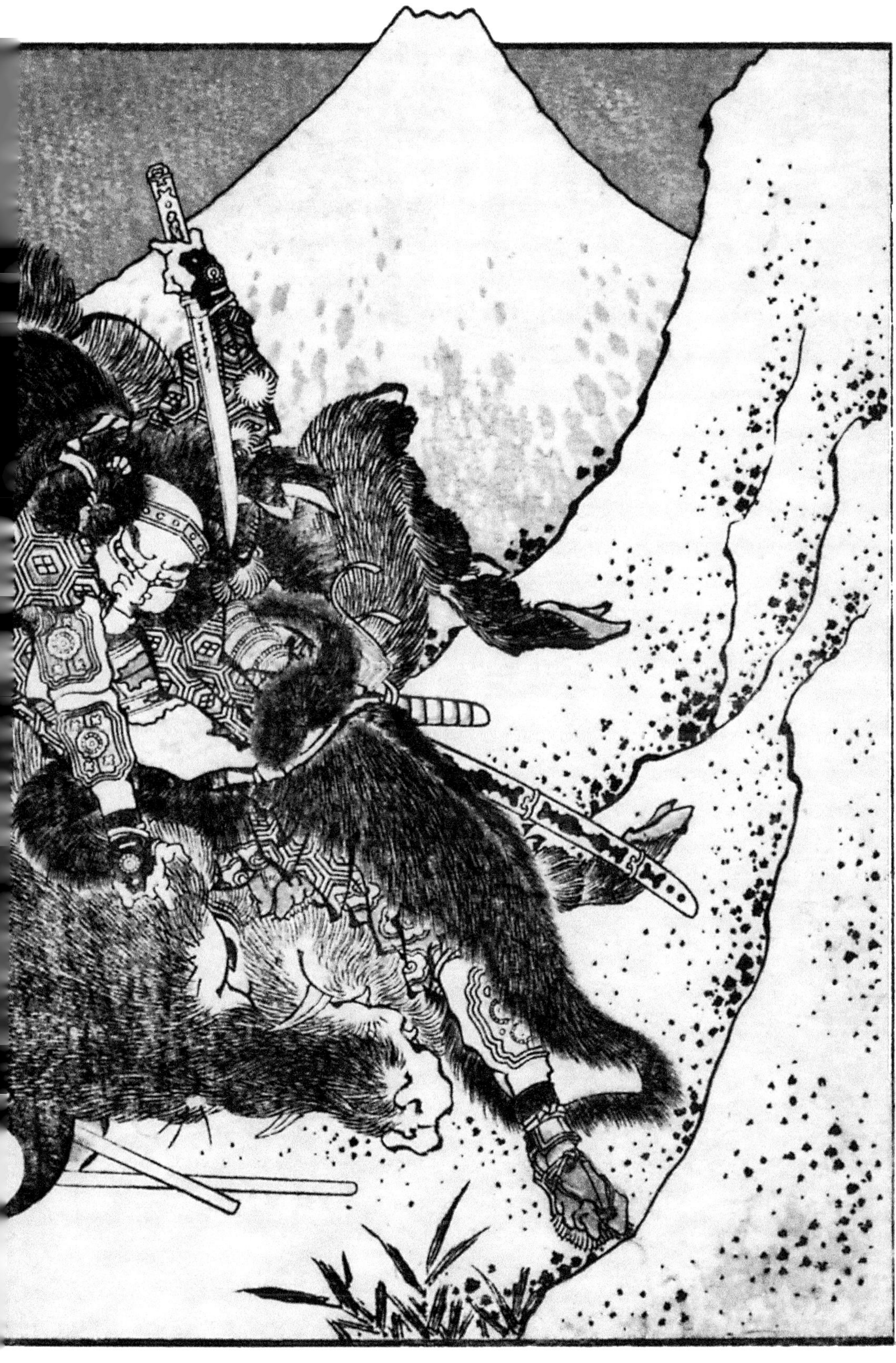

Plate XXVII

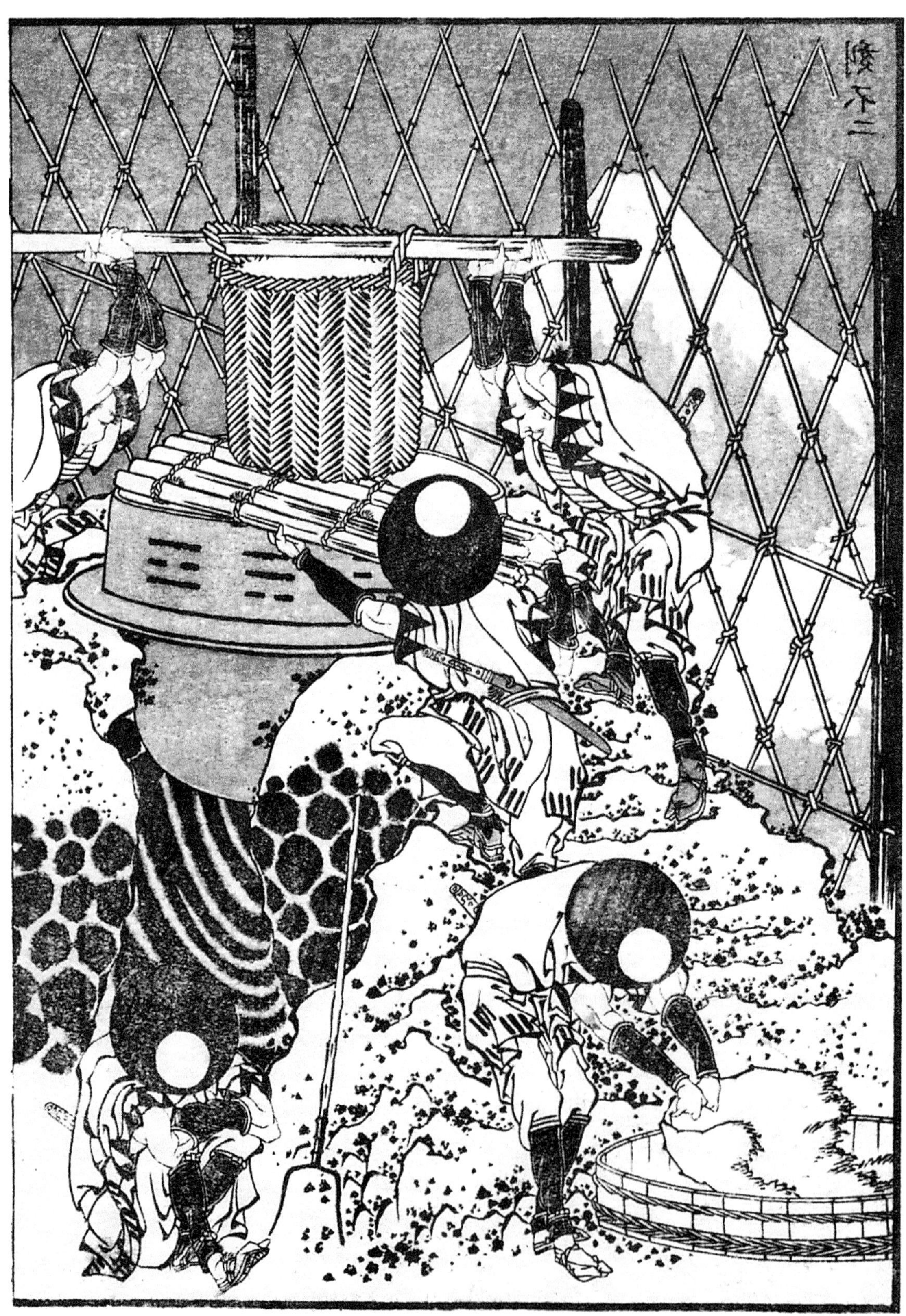

Plate XXVIII

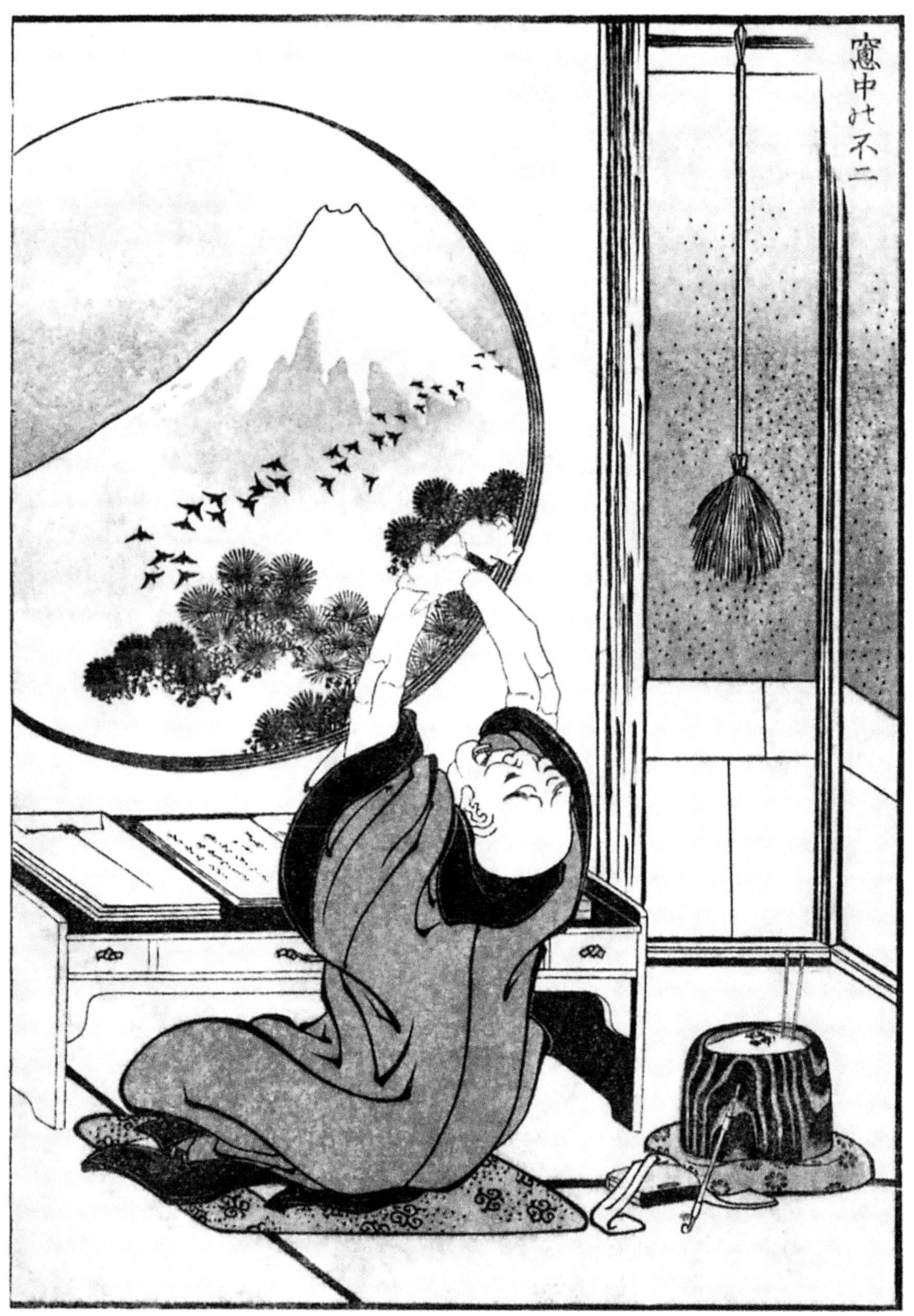

Plate XXIX

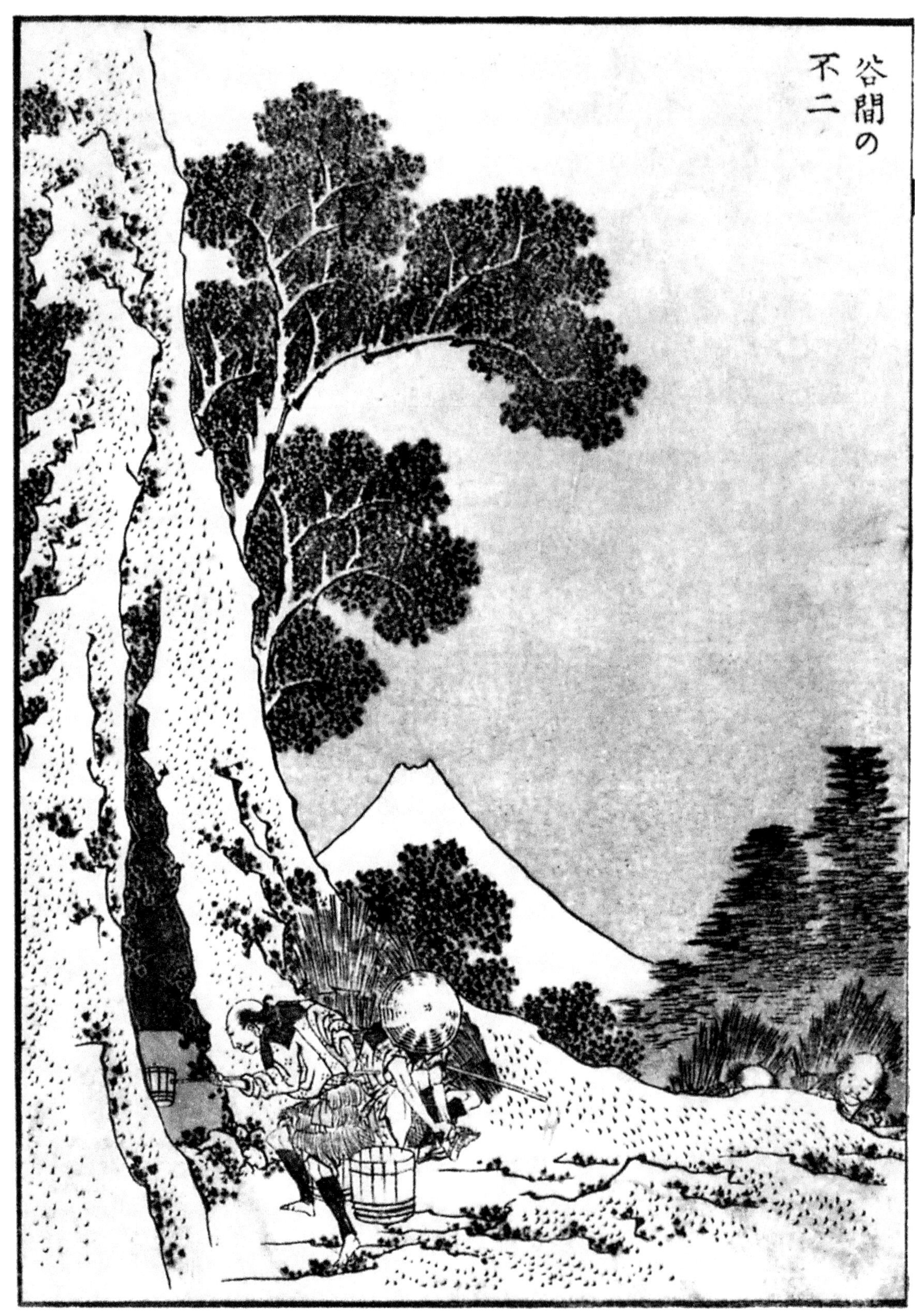

Plate XXX

(Translation.)

WHILE Kunshô in his Hundred Views of Fuji merely aims at a bare delineation of the great Mountain, our venerable Hokusai here presents to us the picturesque aspects of the Peerless Hill, and the following pages show with how sure and bold a brush, with how unrivalled a talent, he has rendered every feature of his subject. Our venerable Master indeed, who, if report be true, has overlived his ninetieth year,* shows all the vigour of youth in his work ; and, indeed, it was on this famous Mountain that of old the Elixir of Life was sought for and found.

When this Third Volume was ready for publication, I was asked to contribute a Preface to it, to which request I acceded without ado.

Written by the old gentleman OGASAWARA, living at the foot of the Mountain of the Seven Treasures (Shichi-hô-zan.)

---

* See Preface to the First Volume.

DESCRIPTION OF PLATES.

PLATE I.

Akasawa no Fuji.

A sort of frontispiece, representing a struggle between two noted wrestlers (sumô-tori), named Matanogoró Kumihisa and Kawadzusaburô Sukeyosu, who dwelt in the quarter or ward of Yedo known as Akasawa.

PLATE II.

Noretsu Henkei no Fuji.

Distant view of the Mountain from the natural bridge formed of the intertwining branches of two ancient and gnarled pines at Noretau, over which pilgrims pass on their way up Nantai-zan, the high Mountain towering over the lake of Chiuzenji, near Nikkô, some ninety miles north of Yedo.

PLATE III.

Shiusetsu no Fuji.

The Mountain in a Snowstorm.

The drear winter aspect is well rendered, and the effect is heightened by the train of wayfarers gathering their snow-laden straw capes closely round them as some protection against the biting cold.

Kika Bessô Sunamura no Fuji.

Fuji from the Garden of a Gentleman's Country Residence in the Suburban Village of Suna.

In the foreground three votaries of rod and line are plying their tranquil task. A slight mist rises from the piece of water, and over the shrubbery the great Mountain lifts high its shapely cone. On the brink of the pond stands a paper-paned wooden lantern, and hard by is seen a portion of an old boat, placed bows upward, so as to form a kind of rustic shrine for the Buddhist god Fudô (the Immovable, *i.e.* in righteousness) represented by a rugged boulder taken out of the sea, as symbolic of the name.

The inscription on the boat—"Suichiu shiutsugen Fudô miyô-ó" —means, "To the illustrious King, Fudô, of whom the manifestation took place in the bosom of the waters." Fudô is commonly represented with a cord in one hand to bind demons, and a sword in the other to punish them with, while flames behind testify to the everlastingness of the deity, and at the same time symbolises the " yô " (yang) or male principle.

PLATE V.

Ichi-naka (Shichiu) no Fuji.

The Peak seen from the roof-tops of the City (lit. from the middle of the busy part of the Town.)

A sort of kite is flying high in the air. The lofty ladders with bells (hanshô) fastened to them are eagerly ascended, whenever a fire occurs, by the watchmen posted for that purpose in different quarters of the town, and the tocsin loudly rung to summon the fire-companies of the ward.

PLATE VI.

Donten no Fuji.—*A Cloud-Fuji.*

At the summit of a "tôge" or pass, two travellers, apparently a substantial trader and his servant, halt a space while the latter takes out some necessary article from one of the "hasami-bako," or travelling-boxes, he has been carrying. The stone bears the inscription "Dô-so-jin" (god of roads). On the horizon the banked clouds have assumed the form of the Mountain. The full signification of the sketch, however, is not very clear.

PLATE VII.

Rai-chô no Fuji.

Fuji on a Court Reception Day.

The cortège consists of Loochooan envoys on their way to the Castle. On the banners, rather Chinese than Japanese in fashion, are inscribed the characters "Rai-chô." Trumpeters, drummers, and "samisen" players bring up the rear of the procession, while "samurai," in their "kamishimo" or ceremonial dress, line the road along which it passes. The envoys are contemplating with mingled awe and admiration the beauty and grandeur of the Peerless Mountain.

PLATE VIII.

Akadzuki no Fuji.—*Fuji before Dawn.*

A post-runner has just handed his letter-box and carrying-pole to a relay at the entrance of a village, close by the Kôsatsu, or public notice-board. The Mountain is not yet illumined by the sun still lingering below the horizon, and the morning mists are yet hanging over the landscape.

PLATE IX.

Matagi Fuji.—*The Mountain bestridden.*

The Mountain bestridden by a cooper, hard at work with his fellow upon a well-tub. A humorous record, doubtless, of some such glimpse of Fuji caught by the Master on one of his sauntering tramps about the suburbs of Yedo.

PLATE X.

Suidô Bashi no Fuji.

The Mountain viewed over the Suidô Bridge.

The spot is looked upon as one of the most picturesque points of view in old Yedo, and at the present day (1878) the character of the locality is pretty much what it was in Hokusai's time.

PLATE XI.

Ami ni Hedataru no Fuji.

The Mountain seen through a spider's web, athwart which a maple leaf is falling, showing the clear-skied autumn is come.

PLATE XII.

Kotsurako no Fuji.—*Fuji from Kotsurako, in Korea.*

So lofty is the Mountain that it was said it could be seen from the coast of Chôsen (Korea). The story of Serutosu, given in the extract from the " Wa-kan-sanzai-dzuye," quoted in the Introduction, is an instance of this tradition. The figures in the foreground are Koreans, not Japanese.

PLATE XIII.

Asumi-mura no Fuji.

The Peak topping the thatched Roofs of the Village of Asumi.

"Asu-mi" means "morrow's view," and in the name of the village the Master has seen an allusion to the sudden upheaval of the Mountain, related in the extract from the "Wa-kan-san-zai-dzuye" just referred to.

PLATE XIV.

Sumida no Fuji.

From the cherry orchards of Mukôjima, on the banks of the broad and rapid Sumida, in the fair spring days when the blossoms are at their freshest on the yet leafless trees. Then the dwellers in towns are glad to sally forth, and catch a glimpse of reviving nature thus giving her earliest sign of renewed life.

PLATE XV.

Yasakai mawari no Fuji.

Circuit of the eight Frontiers on Fuji.

Pilgrims are climbing the rough path that leads round the crater, and in making the whole circuit they will pass, in successive review, the eight encompassing provinces referred to in the above-mentioned extract from the "Wa-kan-sanzai-dzuye." The pilgrims, who have passed the night in the rude huts, roughly built up of blocks of lava, that afford shelter on the summit, are hastening to greet the sun just on the point of rising. The writer has a vivid recollection of the sunrise he once

witnessed in such a company, some years back, from the Peak
of the Peerless Mountain. It would require the happiest
inspiration of a Ruskin fitly to paint in words the majesty,
the glory, and the beauty of the scene. Beyond the massy
hills of Kadzusa, still drowsy with the night's slumber,
a faint light broke, and the outline of the far-off range
grew distinct against the brightening sky, over which the
radiance, always broadening, passed swiftly through splendid
hues of crimson and gold into the full blaze of the risen
sun, that made the pinnacles of the red and rugged peak
glow as with a fiery heat. The white dress of the pilgrims,
huddled together against the sunward face of the seared
and riven cliffs that overhung the deep black crater, shone
fair under the level beams, while their earnest and
watching faces were illumined by a more than earthly glory,
as their lips murmured the invocation—strange words from a
strange land—"Namu amida Butsu" (Hail thou Light of the
World, O Buddha !) Far on the western horizon, the shadow
of Fuji, thrown across the immense plain, repeated the form
of the Peerless Mountain against the whitening cloud-bank.
Twelve thousand feet below lay the variegated landscape, spread
out as a feast for those who would take any joy in the magnificent
awakening of Nature. Then soft vapoury veils crept slowly
over the scene, floating their filmy borders up the slope of the
Mountain, till we who stood on its summit could see but sky
and sun above, and the bare, cindery, lurid cone beneath,
rising out of a boundless waste of shining billowy mist, through
the changing rifts and rents of which could be caught glimpses
of the world below — patches of green and brown, and steely
watery glints.

The accompanying plate, taken from the native Guide Book,

"Fujisan michi shirube," pictures us faithfully the sheer-walled pit of the deep crater, with its fantastically jagged and rugged rampart of honey-combed lava, of which the lurid ruddiness seems yet to tell of the fiery birth of the great Mountain.

DESCRIPTION OF CRATER VIEW.

1. Pinnacle of Yakushi, with stone-built shrine, huts, embankments and wind-walls.
2. Kimmei-sui, Golden Well.
3. Pinnacle of Shaka.
4. Riven Rock of Shaka.
5. Sword-Pinnacle.
6. Talus, or Slide.
7. Konoshiro Pool.
8. Dainichi.
9. Gimmei-sui, Silver Well.
10. Hollow of Seishi.
11. Pinnacle of Kuwan-on.
12. Portal of Yoshida and Subashiri.
13. Crater.

The following description is epitomised from the Guide :—
"The circumference is about one 'ri' (two-and-a-half miles*); around the crater stand eight pinnacles of rock, say the Buddhists, but there are not really so many. Various Buddhist images are set up here from the opening on the first of the sixth month, up to the closing on the twenty-seventh of the seventh month, when they are taken down and buried under loose cinders, to preserve them from the action of rain and snow. The most important of these image-seats, beginning from the North where the path from Yoshida and Subashiri emerges on the top, is that of Yakushi Nyorai,† to whom a shrine has been erected. Here are various 'muro,' (stone huts), and a wall to keep off the violence of the wind. Following the path eastwards one passes under the Pinnacle of Kuwan-on (the Buddhist Venus), where stands an

---

* The length of the path, leading more or less sinuously round the crater, is probably meant.

† Nyorai, *tathâgata*, is a sublime epithet of a Buddha.

iron statue of the goddess with eleven faces, erected in the second year of Mei-ô (A.D. 1493), according to the inscription on it, and close by the bronze-headed, iron-bodied image of Dainichi Niyorai (a Buddhist deity), set up by the men of Owari in the second year of Daiyei (A. D. 1522), with a bronze flower-vase inscribed eighth year of Kuwanbun (A.D. 1669). More towards the south is a hollow—Seishi ga kubo—whence a view may be had over the provinces of Suruga and Idzu, with the adjoining islands. Now is reached the Ginmei-sui or Silver Well, at the top of the ascent from Suyama. In the Danichi shrine it should be mentioned is a statue of the 'giyôja' (devotee) Yen no Shôkaku,* and it is here that the white dress of the pilgrims is stamped with the characters 'Fu-ji.' Follows a pool called the Pool of Konoshiro (a kind of freshwater fish, which are not, however, mentioned as found in it), dry except in damp weather. Various images are set up along this portion of the path. About midway between the southern and western points is the highest of the pinnacles, called the Sword pinnacle, from a fancied likeness to a 'ken,' or Chinese sword, at the foot of which is a slide or talus of loose cinders running down to the bottom o the crater, and known as Oyashiradzu-Koshiradzu (lit. "unknown to parent, unknown to child," probably after a place similarly named, for what reason the translator has not been able to discover, on the Tôkaidô). From the top of the Sword-pinnacle Fuji appears to rise sheer out of the sea. Stones must not be taken hence, lest the gods should be angry. Westwards of it the path divides into an outer-verge and an inner-verge path. Facing the setting sun rises the Pinnacle of Shaka (Buddha) under a huge overhanging portion of which, called the Riven Rock of Shaka, the path leads,—so narrow is it that only one

---

* *Vide* Plate III. Volume I.

person can pass along it at a time. Here snow is always to be found throughout the year, icicles hang down from the rock-roof, and water drips from it. Coming back to the starting-point, a little northwards of it, is the Kinmei-sui, or Golden Well, the water of which is known as the August Water. The diameter of the crater (nai-in) is about 1500 yards,* the depth of it about 500 feet; from it issue clouds, mists, and winds. The pilgrims throw in offerings of cash, and thus obtain health and strength through the grace of the Daibosatsu (Buddhist Saint) Sengen or Asama. There are four principal ascents up the Mountain; from Murayama on the South; Suyama on the South-East; Subashiri on the East; and Yoshida on the North.

PLATE XVI.

FUUZEI OMOSHIROKI FUJI.

The delightfulness of the Mountain on a clear fresh day.

This is a strange sketch, in which the humour of the Master passes all due limits.

Two priests and a layman — perhaps a guest—are giving vent, each after his own fashion, to the rapturous joy the view of Fuji has awakened in their hearts. One of the servants of Buddha stands on a stone-faced embankment close to the porch of his temple or monastery; the other, below, lies on his back kicking up a football into the air with his feet, while the guest, with a somewhat astonished expression, regards the gambols of his reverend host.

---

* Thirteen "chô," but this seems an exaggeration. The greatest diameter does not probably exceed 800 or 900 yards at the most.

PLATE XVII.

Kai no Fuji koi otoko.

The Northern slope of Fuji seen from the Province of Kai.

In the foreground a farmer is directing a couple of labourers, who are drawing out of the pond bags of seed-rice prepared by maceration for sowing. Behind, the newly-sown fields are protected by coarse netting from the ravages of birds, while on the horizon towers the lofty cone of the Mountain. The snow yet crowns the top, and marks out—say some—on the dark slope, the shapes of a youth and maid a-courting. There seems to be a sort of pun intended in the title—" Koi-otoko," meaning " lovers;" but " Koi " has also the sense of " fertilising,"—the allusion being to the maceration of the rice-seed, without which it will not germinate after being sown.

PLATE XVIII.

Inage-riyô no Fuji.

Fuji from Inage on a Summer's Day.

A pretty country resort in the neighbourhood of Yedo. The sun is near setting, and long lines of cloud are beginning to veil the distant Peak. A picnic party are enjoying themselves in the cool of the evening, the ladies, with their elaborate coiffures protected from the dust and heat by a dexterously folded head-dress, of blue and white cotton cloth, or, perhaps, silk crape.

PLATE XIX.

Torigoye no Fuji.

The Mountain from the Observatory at Torigoye, within the Castle-Moat.

169

PLATE XX.

TAKIGOYE NO FUJI.

Fuji intercepted by a Waterfall.

PLATE XXI.

MURASAKAI NO FUJI.

Fuji from the Boundary of a Village District.

The straw-rope and bamboo hung with strips of paper (gohei) are supposed to ward off evil influences, and to propitiate and attract the local deities. In such spots images of the Daishi (Great Teacher) Kôbô, the inventor of one of the Japanese Syllabaries—the " Katakana "—and boulders or blocks of stone set upright in the ground, and having various significations, are often found. The " gohei " symbolize the ornaments attached to a slip of *Cleyera,* which aided in inducing the Sun-goddess to sally from the cavern into which, disgusted by the rudeness of her brother Sosa, the god of the sea, she had retired, and so left the world in darkness.

PLATE XXII.

AOYAMA NO FUJI.

From an Umbrella-maker's Yard at Aoyama in Yedo.

The conical form of the umbrellas waiting to be oiled and varnished probably suggested this quaint sketch to the Master.

PLATE XXIII.

AMI-URA NO FUJI.

The Peak veiled by a Fisherman's Net

Which has been stretched out to dry on crossed bamboo poles—a sight common enough round the shores of the Gulf of Yedo.

PLATE XXIV.

Hashishita no Fuji.—*View of Fuji under a Bridge.*
Perhaps the famous Saru-hashi.*

PLATE XXV.

Ashiro no Fuji.

The Mountain, with a Scaffolding in the foreground.

Plasterers are at work daubing with mud, taken out of the river-bottom, the walls of a "dozô" or fire-proof godown (store-house). The exaggerated attitudes of the figures are characteristically humorous.

PLATE XXVI.

Murasame no Fuji.—*Through a Summer Downpour.*

The sketch recalls vividly the wearisome drip-drip and the steamy closeness of the rainy season in Japan.

PLATE XXVII.

Rôyen no Fuji.—*Fuji and the Rocket-signal.*

In the foreground a couple of fishermen are charring the bottom of their boat. The view is from the East shore, across the Gulf of Yedo; to the right of Fuji may be dimly seen the outline of the Ôyama range. Up to the very edge of the slightly overhanging, stone-faced embankment, are crowded the village dwellings. Here and there are nets hung tent-wise on bamboo poles, to dry in the sun, not long risen over the horizon. Rôyen may also mean dragon-smoke, and the appearance of the rocket is by this play upon words supposed to resemble that of the dragon that haunts the Mountain.

* See translation of preface to seventh volume of the "Manguwa," given at the end of the Preface to this work.

PLATE XXVIII.

One of the Seven Gods of Happiness or Prosperity,

Symbolised by the very ill-drawn deer in the foreground,
supposed to be specially favoured by the deity, who is often
represented as riding upon the animal. A capital account of
the Seven Gods, drawn from Japanese sources, has been given
by Carlo Puini, in a little book of some fifty pages, entitled
" I Sette Genii della Felicità," from which, in view of the
frequency with which they are represented in Japanese bronze,
lacquer, and pictorial work, the following brief notice has been
taken :—

The Seven Gods of Prosperity are

1. Yebisu, the only one purely of Japanese origin. He
was the offspring of Izanagi and Izanami, the last pair of the
generations of the primeval gods, who, standing upon the Bridge
of Heaven (the Milky Way) stirred up the waters beneath
with a spear, the drops falling from which congealed, and formed
the first of the Islands of the Japanese Archipelago. He is
commonly represented as a fisherman with rod and line, often
as having just caught a "tai" or sea-perch; sometimes humorously,
as dismayed at finding on his hook not "fuku" (happiness),
but a " fugu," or kind of poisonous fish.

2. Dai-koku-ten, a Buddhist deity of Brahmanic origin, one
of the forms of Siva. He is commonly represented as a dwarf
wearing a round cap, standing on two straw rice-bags, holding
in his right hand a mallet, and in his left a wallet slung over
his shoulder, and which becomes filled with treasure at each
blow of his mallet.

3. Bishamon or Tamonten, also of Brahmanic origin. He is a form of Vaisravana, one of the Four Kings who rule the world from the mythical Mount Meru. In his left hand he grasps a spear, the point of which is thrust into the ground, in the right a small pagoda. His adoration is specially useful for the attainment of "nirvana."

4. Benzaiiten, a goddess also of Brahmanic origin. On her head she wears a crown surmounted by a white snake, which is a woman who was condemned to pass a thousand years under that form by Buddha on account of her sins. She has eight arms, in which she carries various weapons, &c.

5. Hotei, a god of Chinese origin, originally a monk. Usually represented with a jovial countenance and a fat paunch.

6. Jiurôjiu, a god of Chinese origin, supposed to have first appeared upon earth as an incarnation of the Star of Long Life (near the South Polar circle), usually represented as a dwarfish old man with an elongated head, and probably identical with

7. Fukurokujiu, a god of Chinese origin, doubtless a synonym of the last. He is often accompanied by a stag, a tortoise, and a stork, the two latter symbolising longevity—on the former he is frequently represented as riding.

These Seven Gods form a strange company, and must be regarded as examples of the Buddhist proclivity to adopt the existing mythologies of the countries of its origin and apostleship, and incorporate them into its own system.

PLATE XXIX.

ÔIGAWA OKEGOYE NO FUJI.

Fuji from the Tub-ferry over the Ôi river.

The travellers are humorously depicted as being ferried across the broad and rapid river of the province of Tôtomi, in

a tub, in lieu of a boat. In not a few Japanese sketches this
kind of tub-voyage is depicted, but the allusion involved in it is
unknown to the present writer.

PLATE XXX.

MI-KIRI NO FUJI.

Intercepted View of Fuji,

Through the unpapered panes of the lower portion of a "shôji,"
or sliding window, turned upside down.   On the wall of the
house, probably a boatman's cottage on the Sumida river, are
advertised pleasure boats, fishing boats, and covered boats for
hire. The man with the brush is engaged in writing on a sort
of large paper lantern, the name or sign of the house—Fuji-ya.
He is just making the turn of the " ya."

Or, as the inscription on the other side of the lantern or
paper-paned case seems to show, it may be a portion of a
pedlar's travelling gear.

PLATE XXXI.

MUSASHI-NO FUJI.

*The Mountain over the Moor of Musashino, in the Province
of Sagami.*

The sun is on the point of setting in a clear autumn sky,
behind the great cone.

PLATE XXXII.

KAYANOWA NO FUJI.

*The Mountain framed, so to speak, in a hoop or circle of Kaya,
or thatch-rush, depending from a Tori-i, or Sacred Portal.*

These "tori-i," sometimes in wood, sometimes in bronze or
granite, betoken the approach to a Shintô shrine (and in that
case are commonly of wood painted red), or to a Buddhist
temple. They are of Shintô origin, and were intended as
perches for the sacred cocks, who, heralding the dawn with their
crow, woke up the gods of the shrine to their daily round of
duty.

PLATE XXXIII.

FUTO-MI NO FUJI.

A sudden Glimpse of the Mountain

Through the gap in a broken wall, built up of flat mud tiles
and mortar, on a foundation of rough blocks of basalt, and
finished with a tile coping.

PLATE XXXIV.

SANKI FUKAKU KATACHI WO KEDZUSU NO FUJI.

*The Mountain with its Shape blotted from view by the thick
Mists rising among the Hills.*

'Tis autumn time ; the day's work is over ; a peasant wending
homewards gives a light to a tired wayfarer making for the next
hamlet, there to find a night's lodging. The evening vapours
curl upwards from the valley-bottoms, and creep slowly up the
slopes of the great Mountain, purply-black against the steely sky.

PLATE XXXV.

KAK'KÔ NO FUJI.

A lover of nature, seated on the jetty of some river-side "chaya"
or tea-house, in the cool of an evening in early summer, watches
a "hototogisu" or Japanese cuckoo, flying between him and the
still snow-clad slope, and remembers the legend of the Chinese
prince Kak-kô, whose soul was changed into a "hototogisu."

PLATE XXXVI.

RAKAN-JI NO FUJI.

Fuji from the Roof of the Rakan Temple.

The Rakan are the 500 disciples of Buddha (ar-hân) who
will one day be again born, each as a future Buddha.

PLATE XXXVII.

CHIDZUKA NO FUJI.

*Fuji from Chidzuka, on the Ôshiu-kaidô or main road
to the North.*

PLATE XXXVIII.

MAMI-ANA NO FUJI.

*An unexpected Reflection of Fuji on the Paper-paned upper
portion of a Shôji.**

The admiration of the spectators outside is well contrasted
with the apathy of the servant sweeping the floor of the verandah,
who of course sees nothing of the prodigy. In the word
Mamiana—the name of a district in Yedo—a faint pun seems
to be intended, by no means however worth the trouble of a
tedious explanation.

---

* *Vide supra*, Plate XXX.

PLATE XXXIX.

Kai-hin no Fuji.

*From the Sea-shore, through a natural Rock Arch on the Beach
at Yenoshima.*

The shadow on the slope is, perhaps, intended to be that of
the high rocky mass of the island of Yenoshima itself, thrown by
an artist's license, at earliest sunrise, across the waters of the bay
of Odahara, at the foot of the ascent to Hakone.

PLATE XL.

Ja-oi numa no Fuji.

The Mountain mirrored in the Marshes of Ja-oi.

Ja-oi signifies the pursuit of the "ja"-dragon.

PLATE XLI.

Taibi hitofude no Fuji.

Adieu !—A last Flourish of the Brush.

A rapid sketch of the Mountain with clouds about its base,
made, so to speak, at one stroke, without refilling the brush with
ink, for each of the two tints used.

End of Volume III.

富嶽百景

君錫子の百富士を畫乃正たるか
北齋翁の富嶽百景八
畫乃帚うる者なり翁雄健く
筆をにて一富峰をよく椿墨の
間は鼓舞す八面向皆寫し得く
きハめて妙絶まり閒翁の齡
今九十を踰て視聽な弐少年

而此すそ空豈曾て仙丹を此名

山を求得きる歌三編　刻成ふ及て

東辟主人五蝶子序を可ま需

一関三數もそ之を記

七寳山下老人小笠

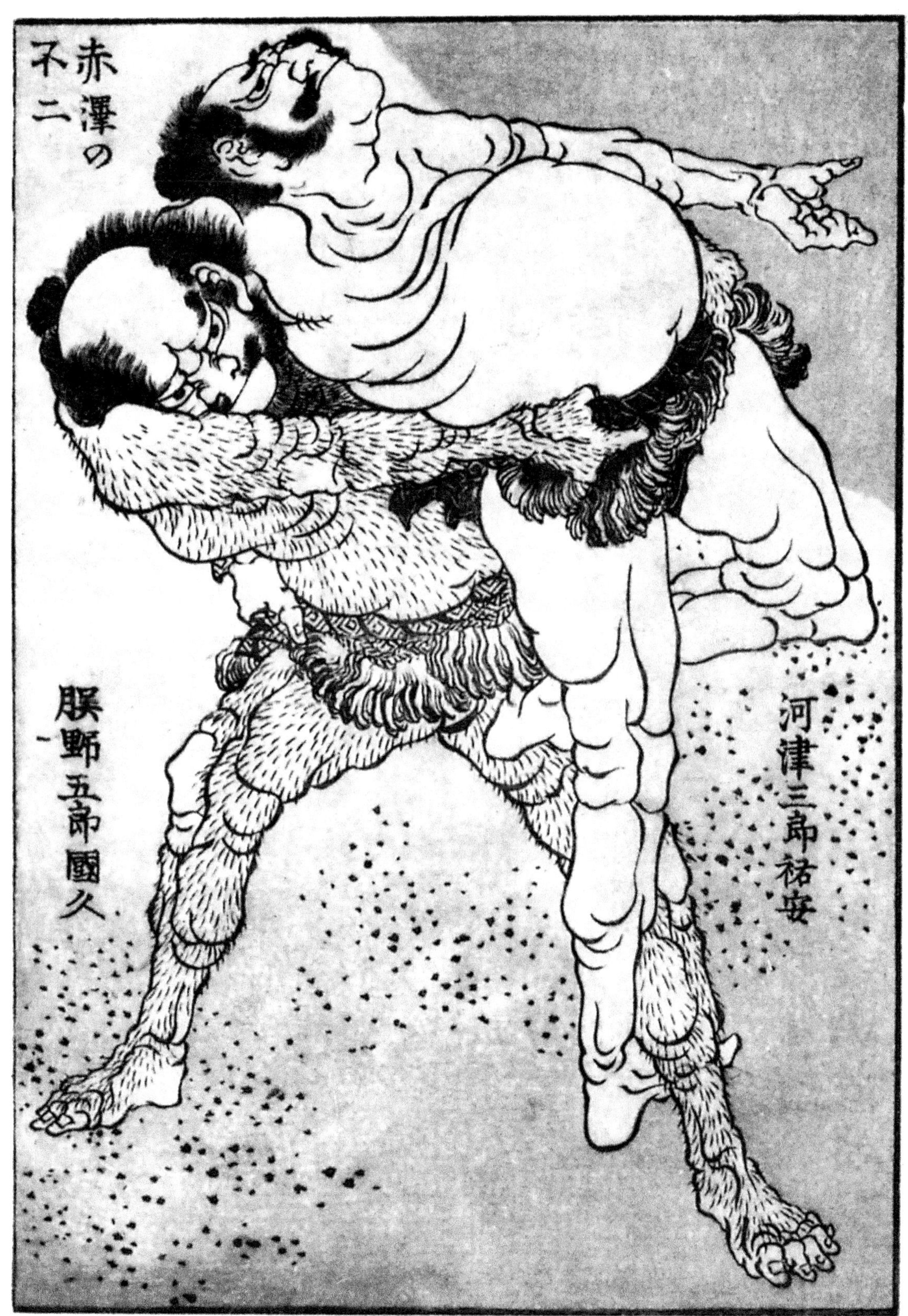

Plate I

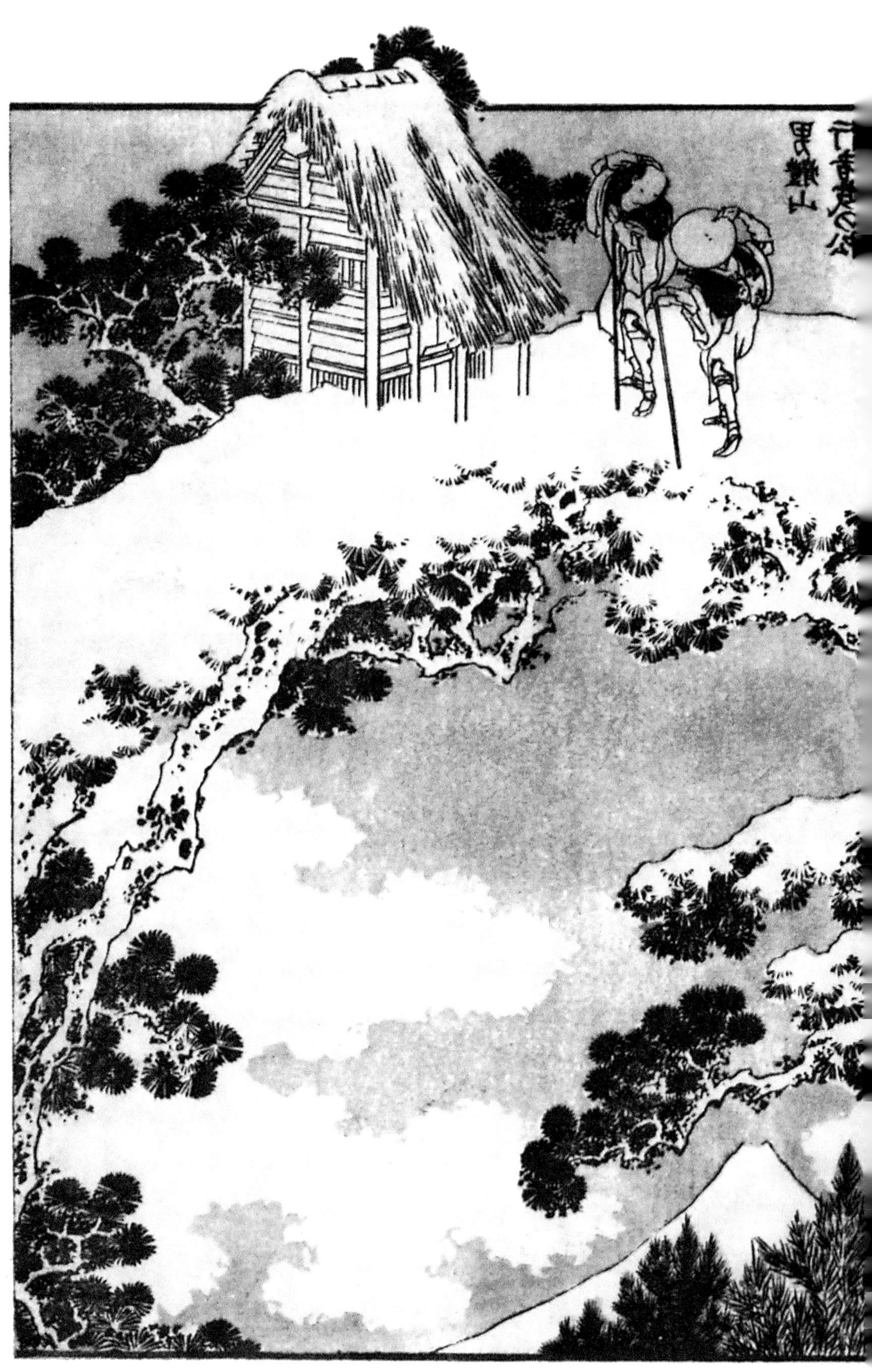

裏嶽不二

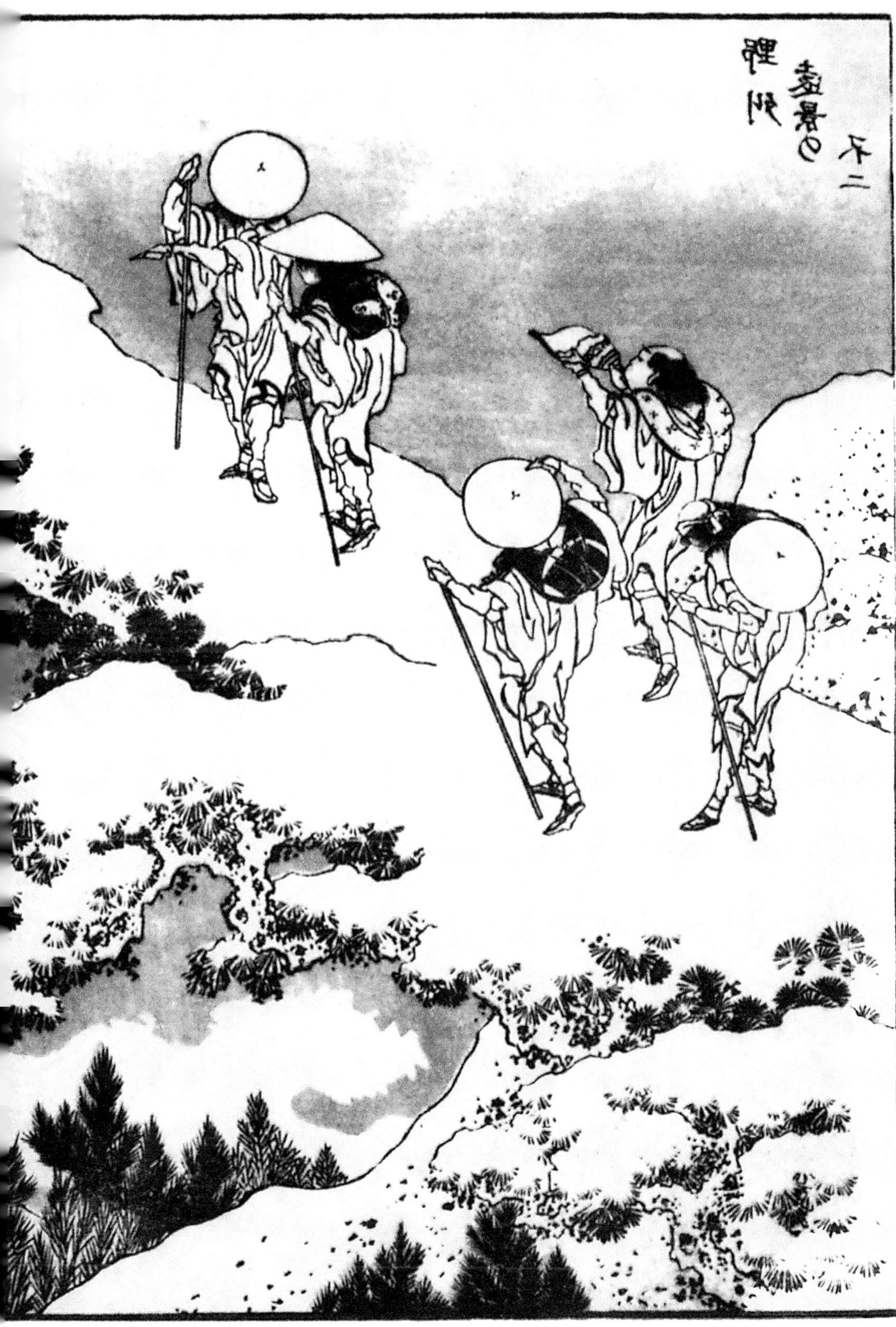

Plate II

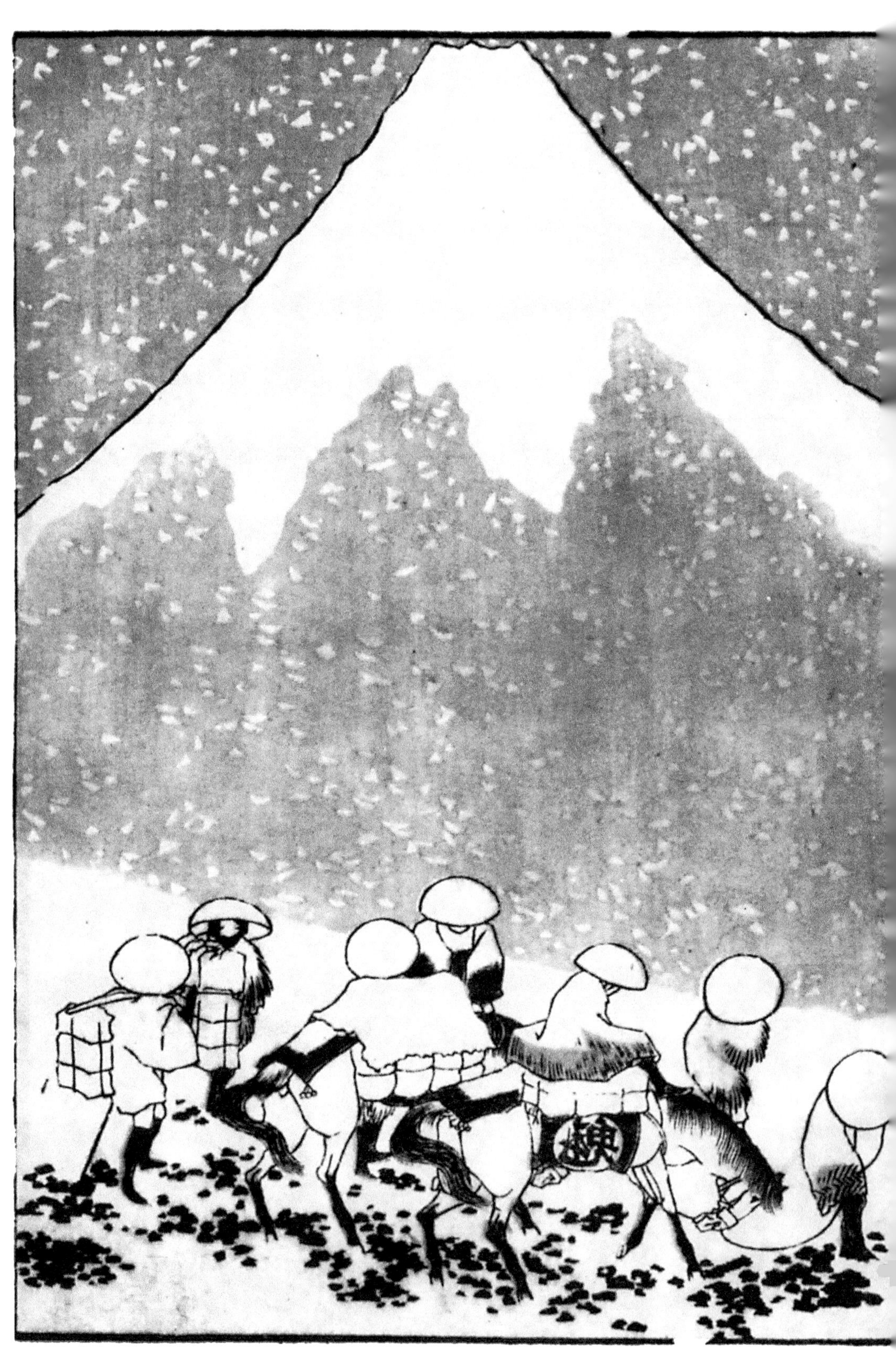

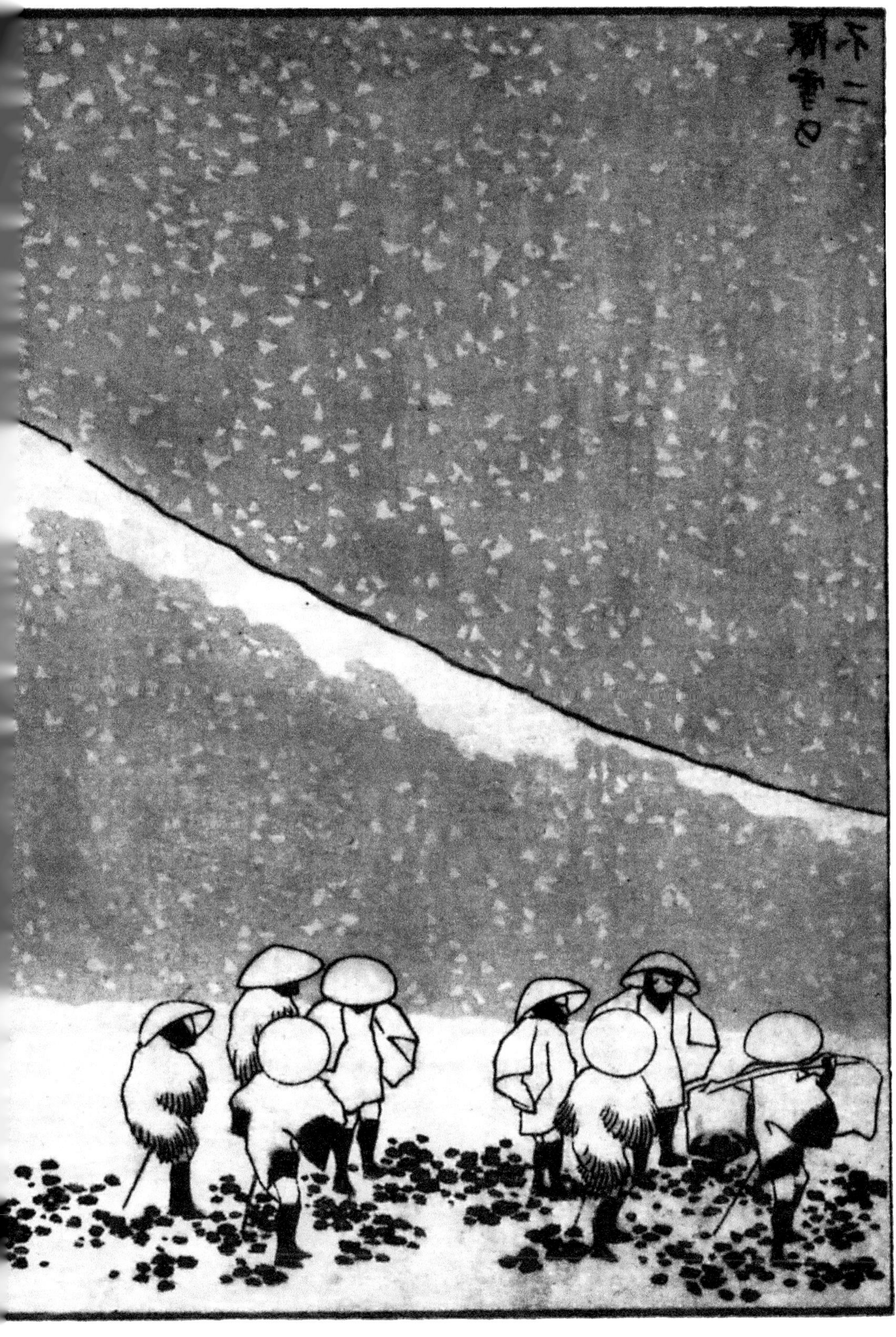

Plate III

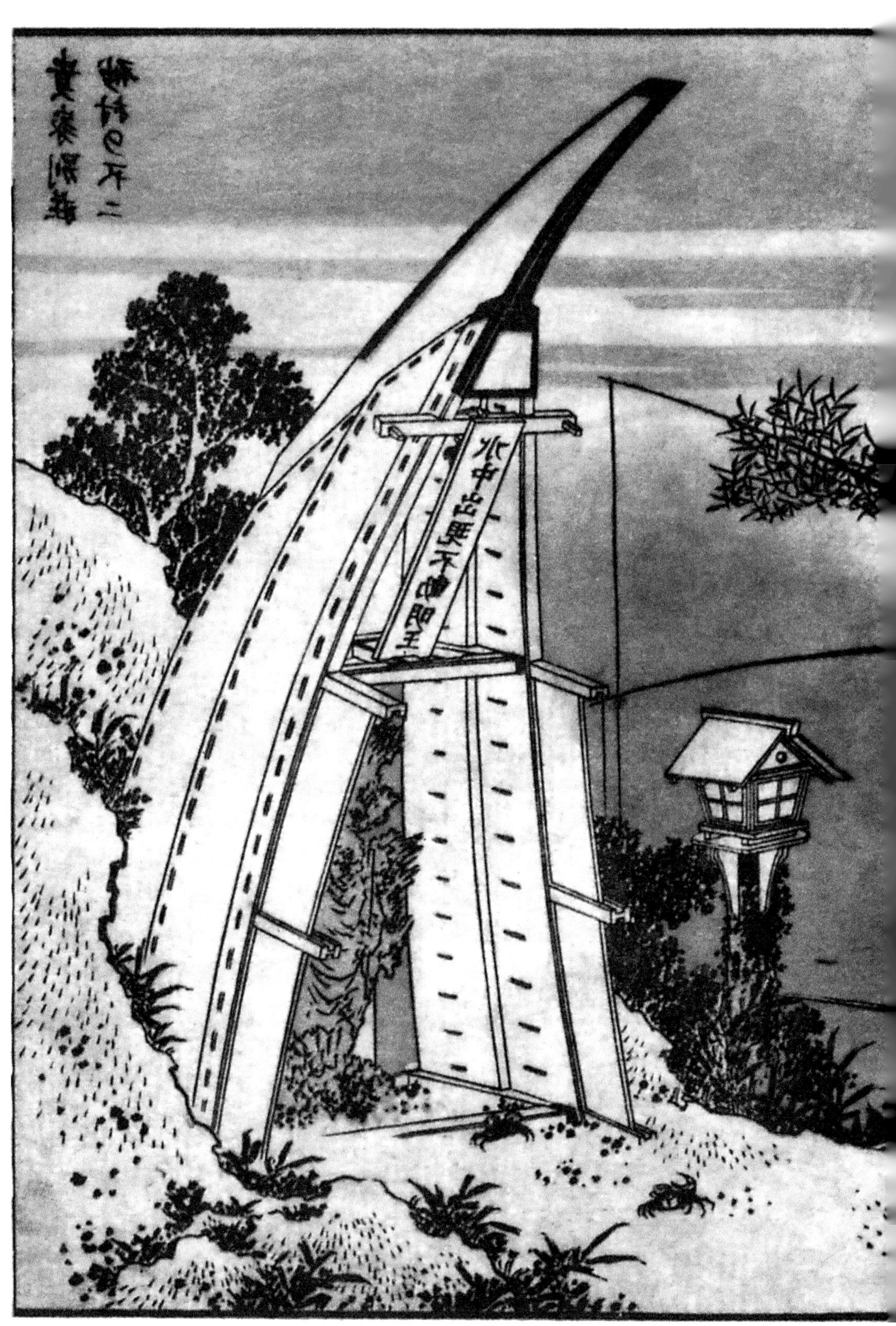

水中出現不動明王

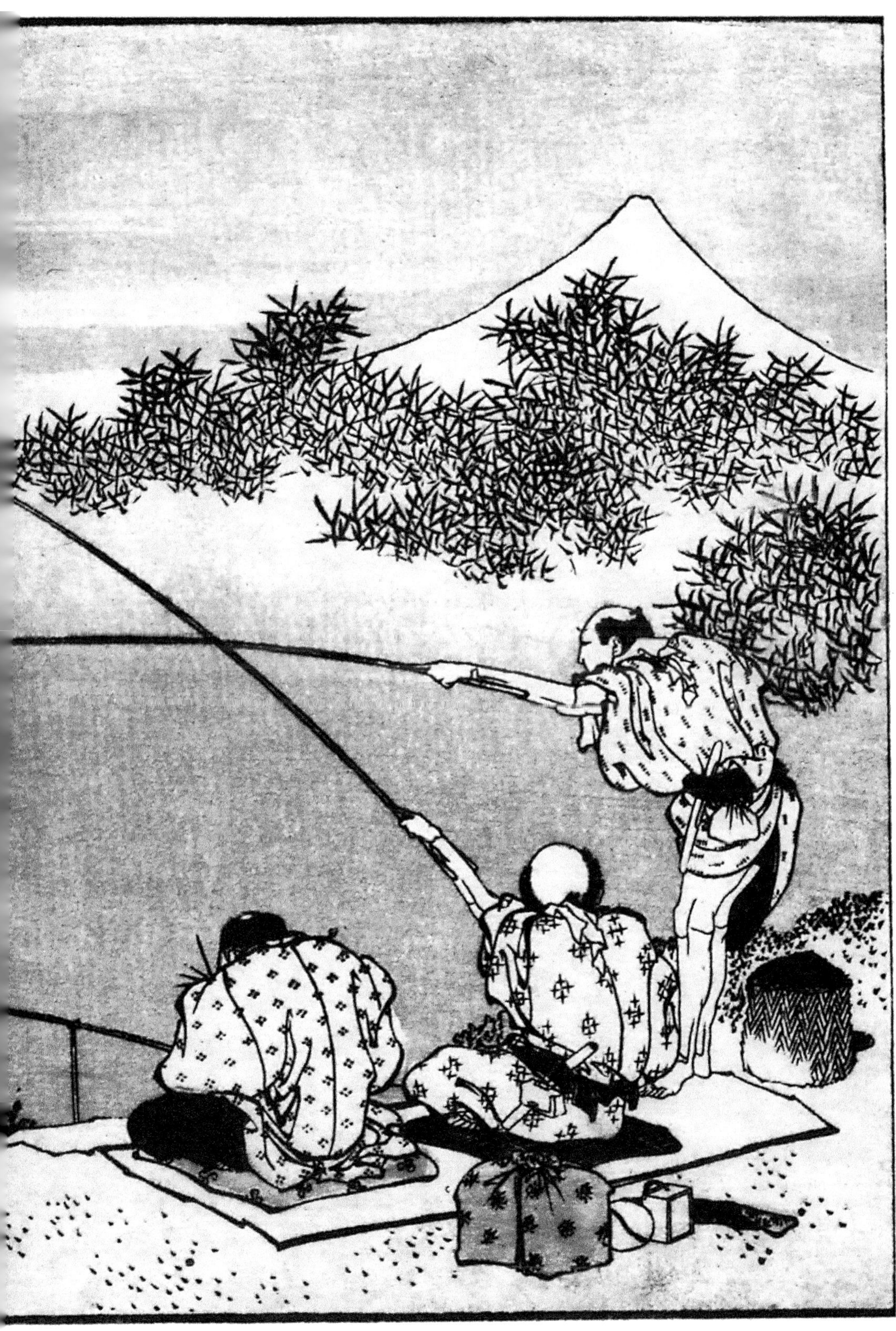

Plate IV

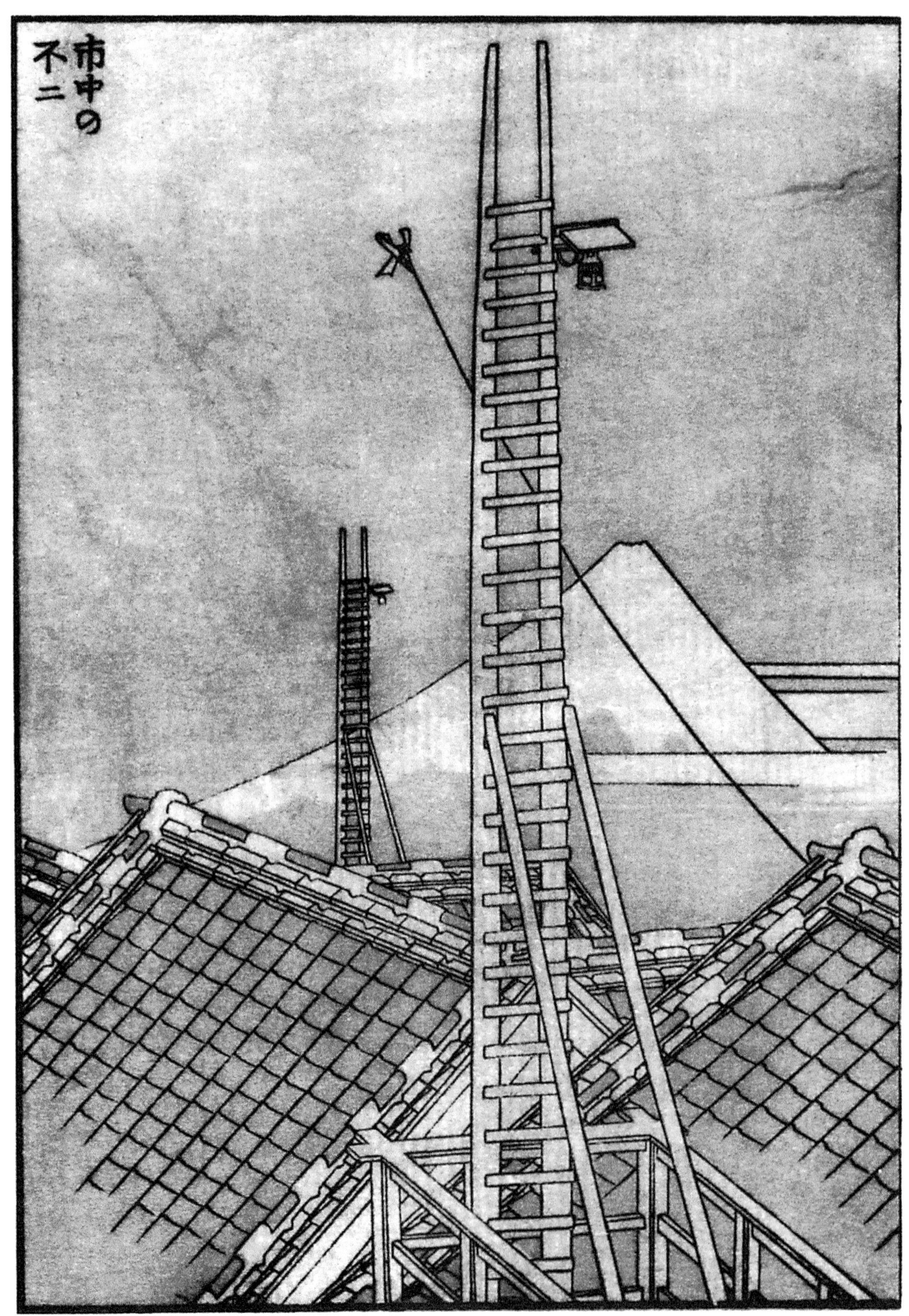

Plate V

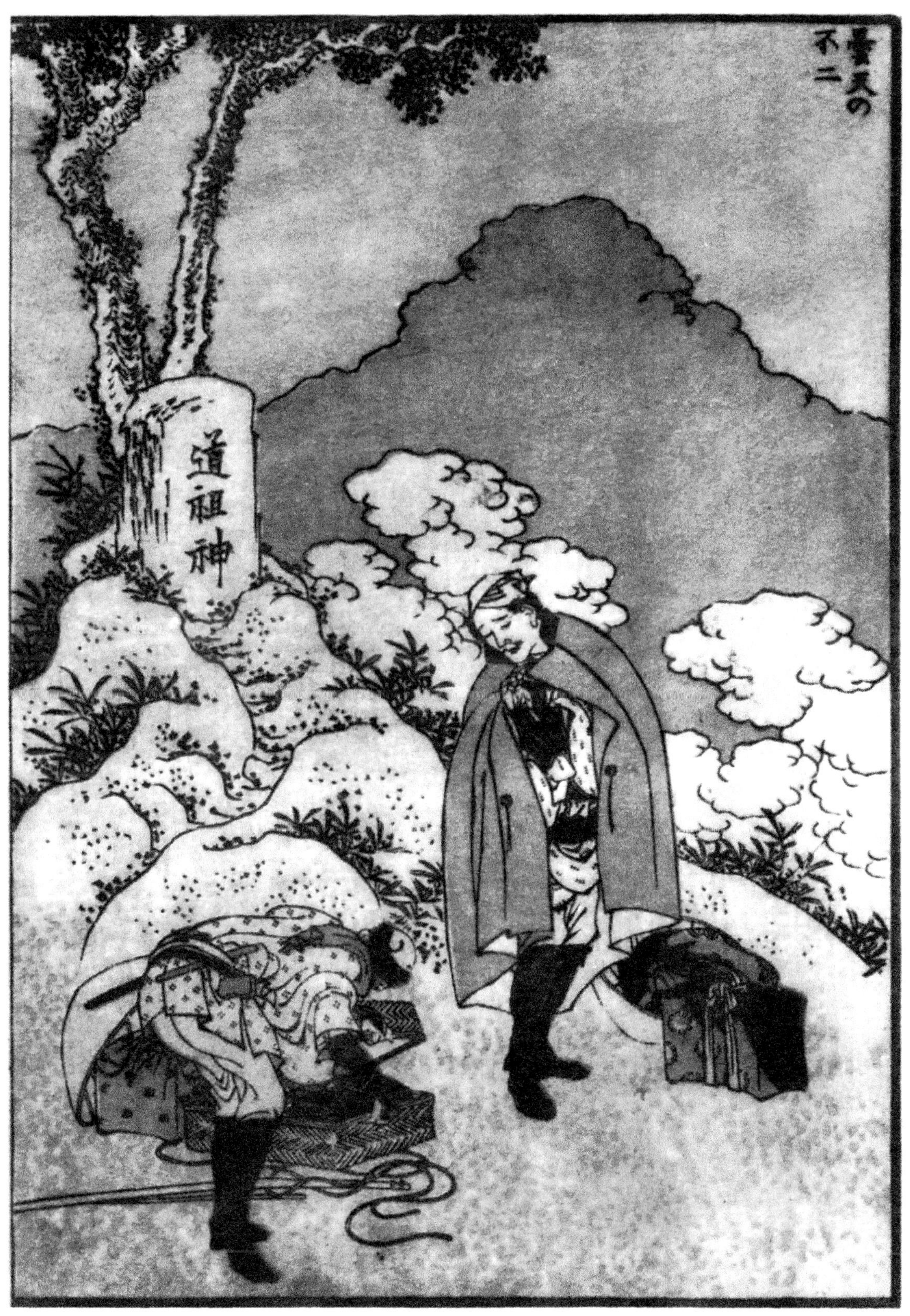

Plate VI

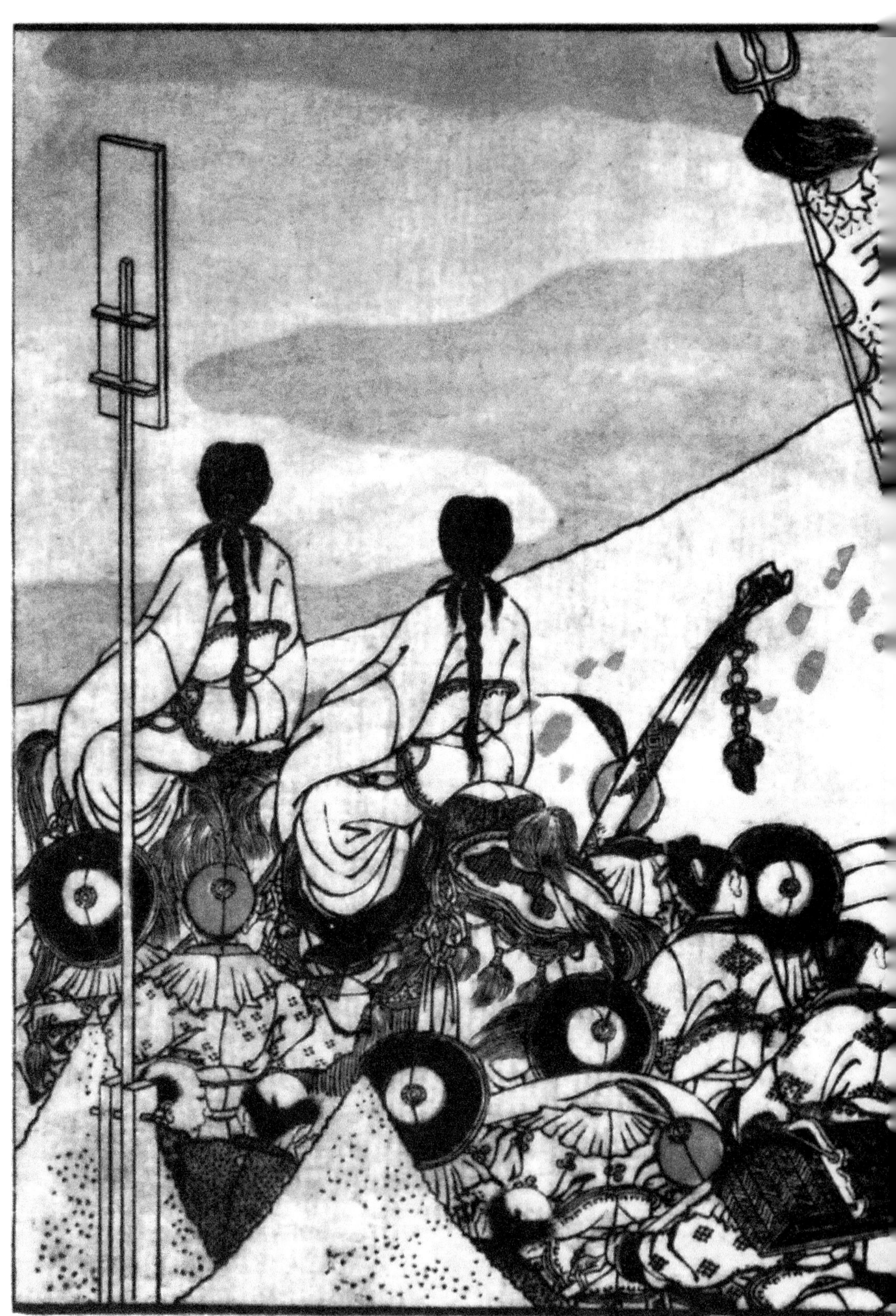

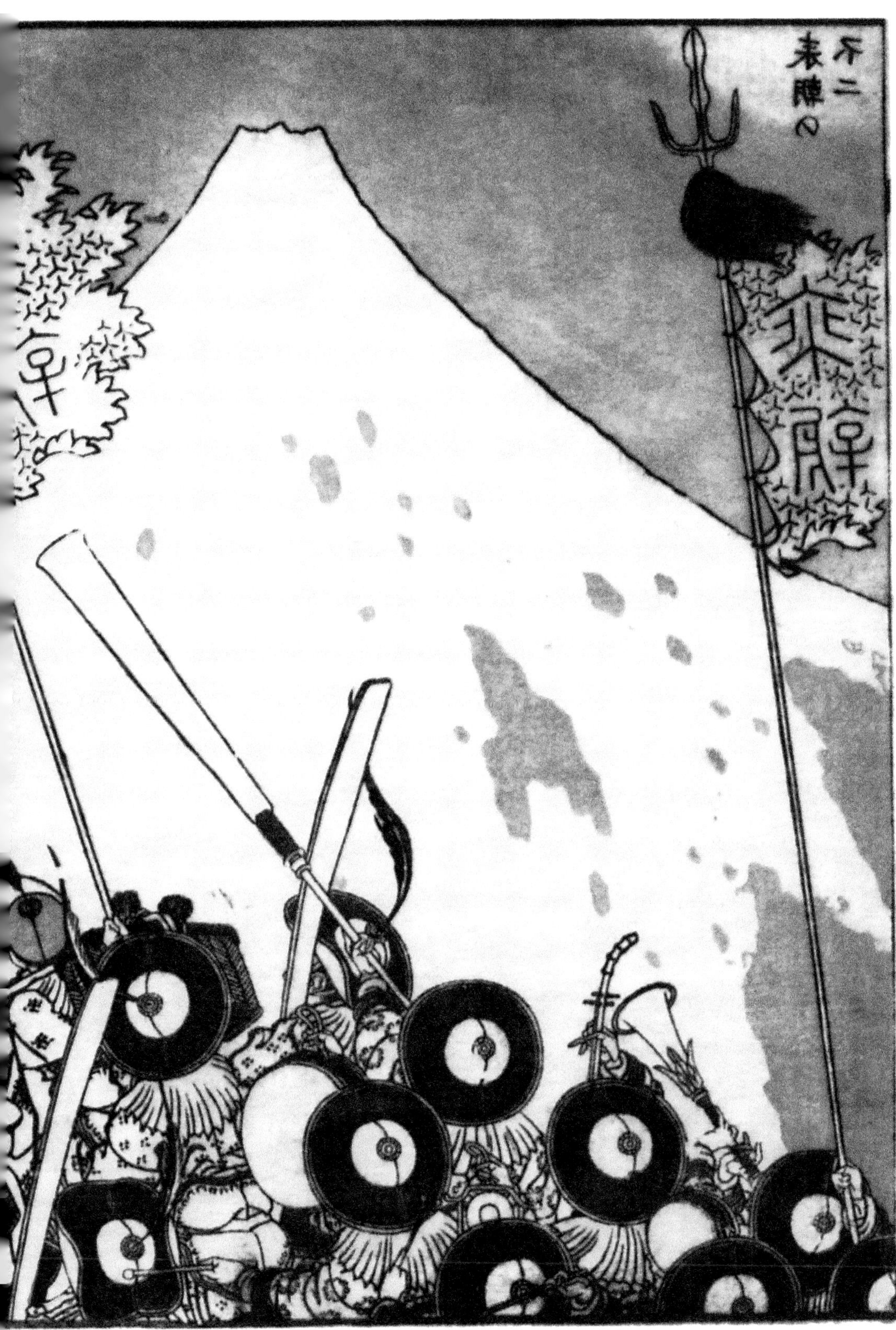

Plate VII

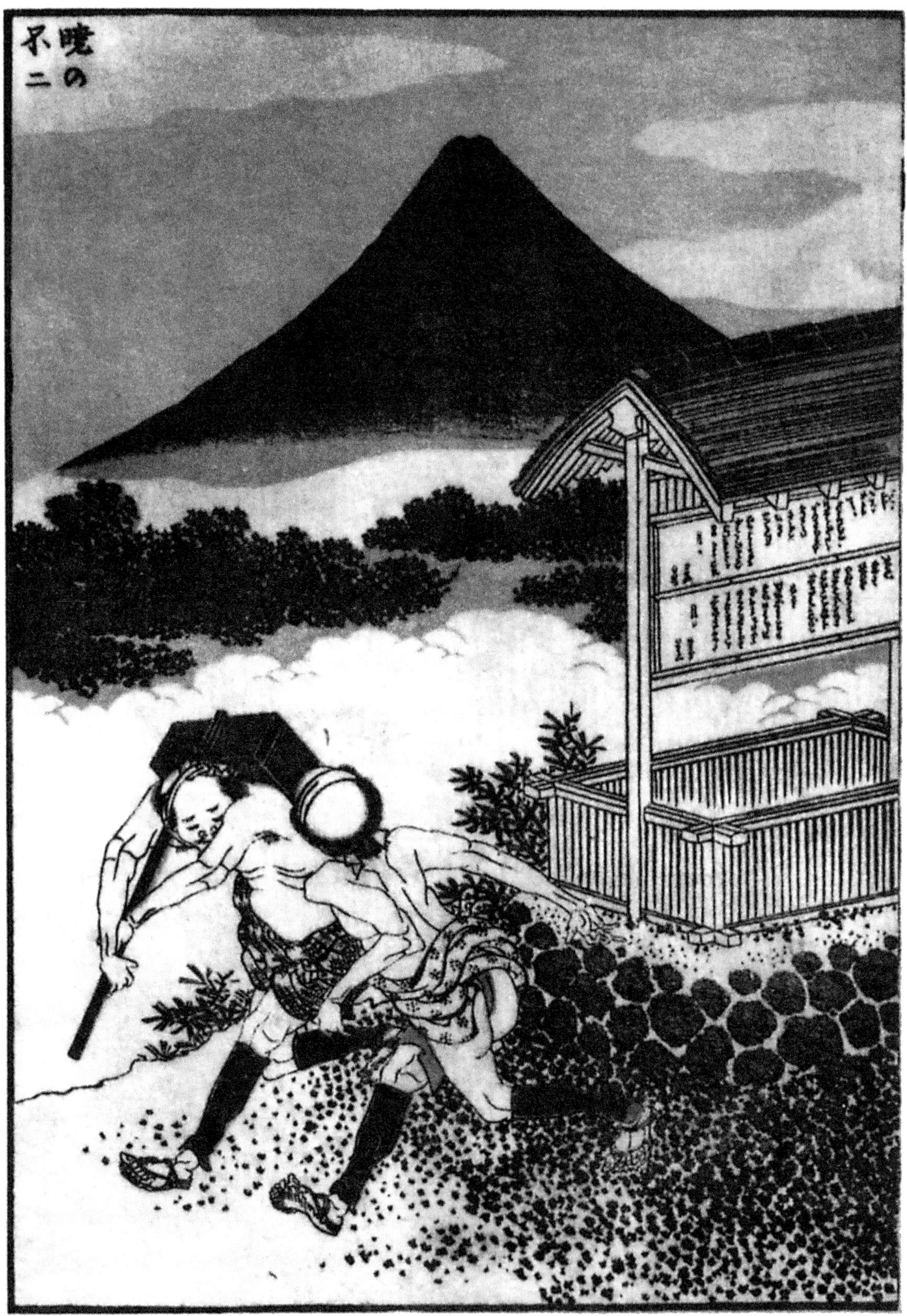

Plate VIII

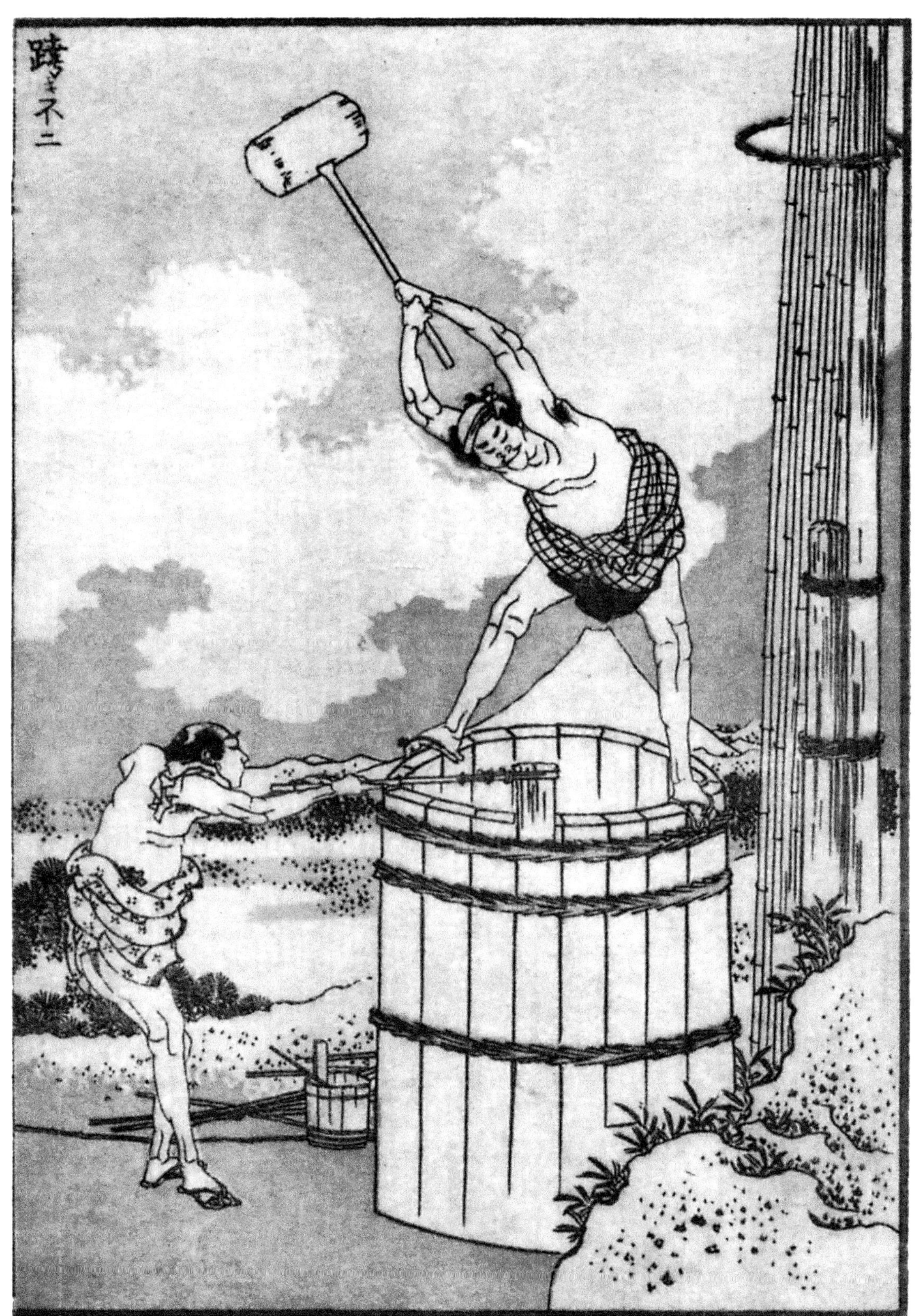

Plate IX

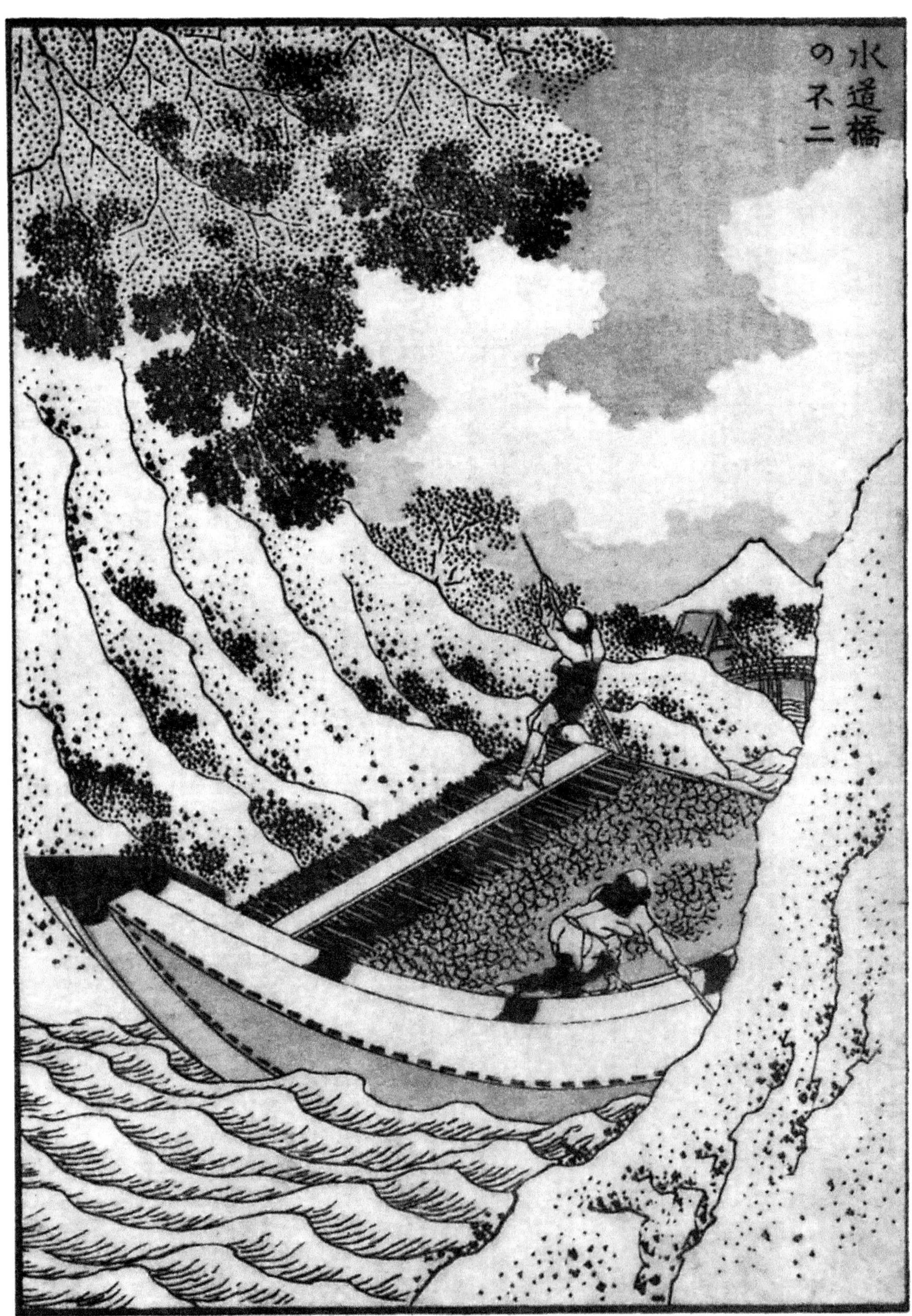

Plate X

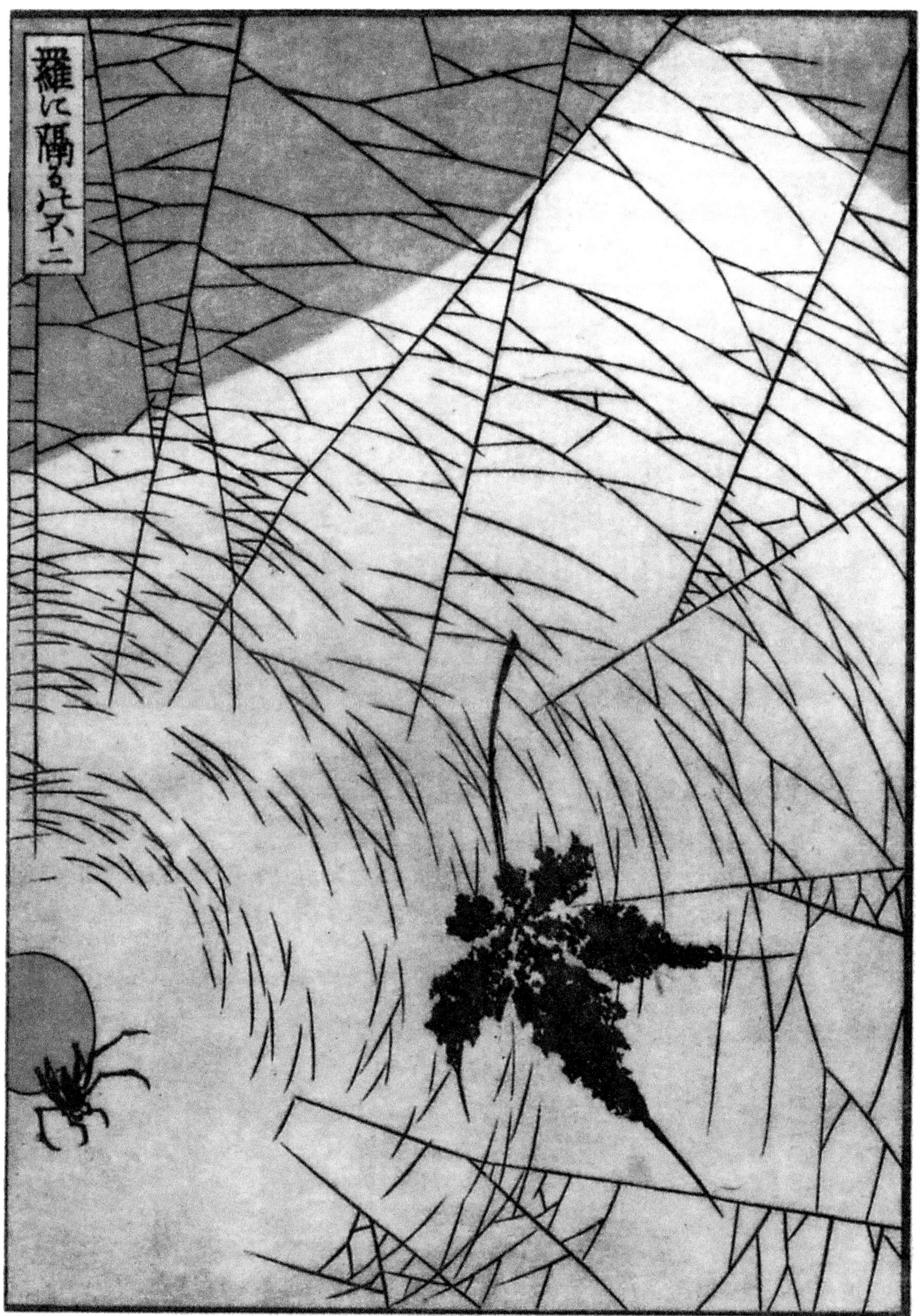

Plate XI

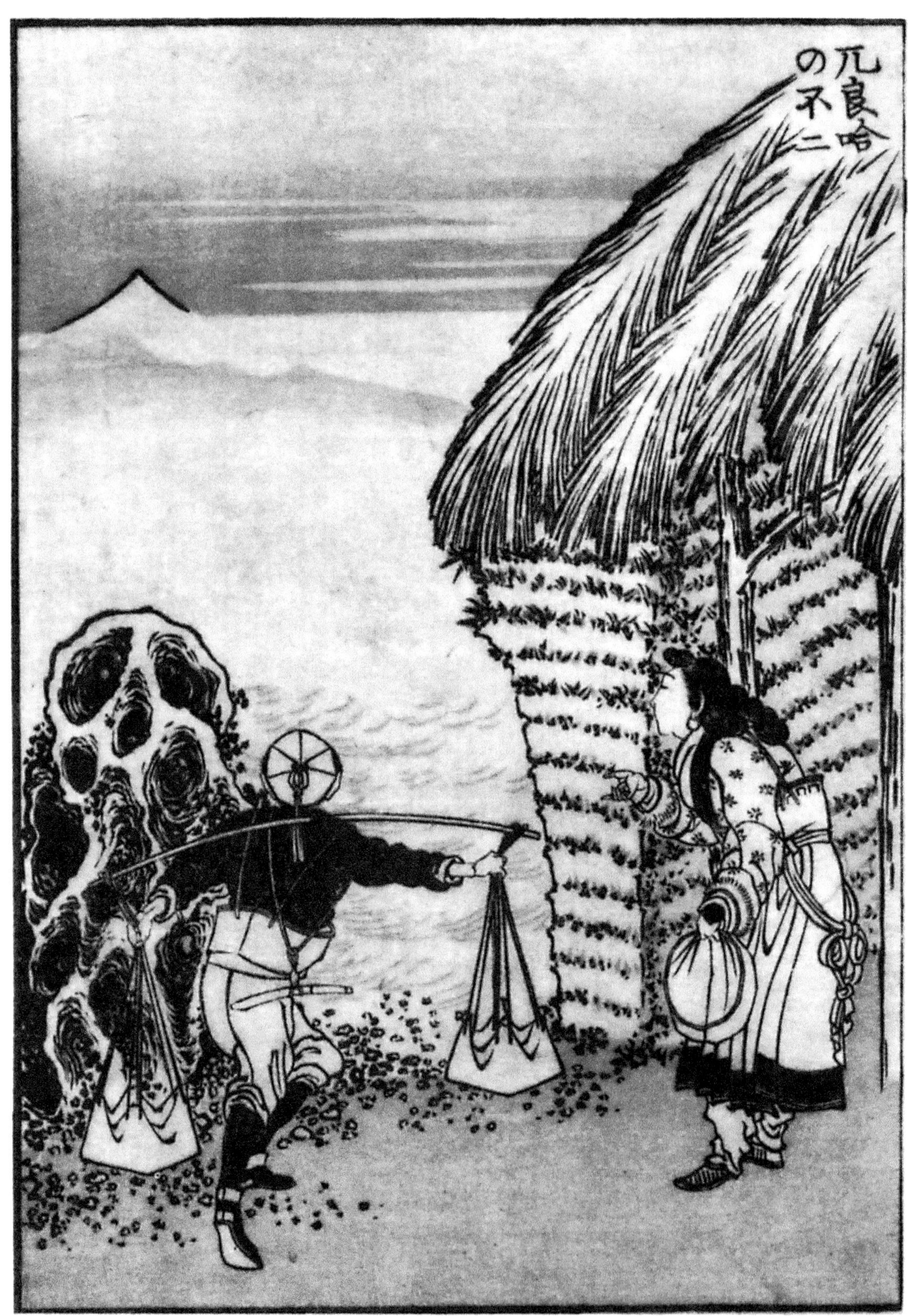

Plate XII

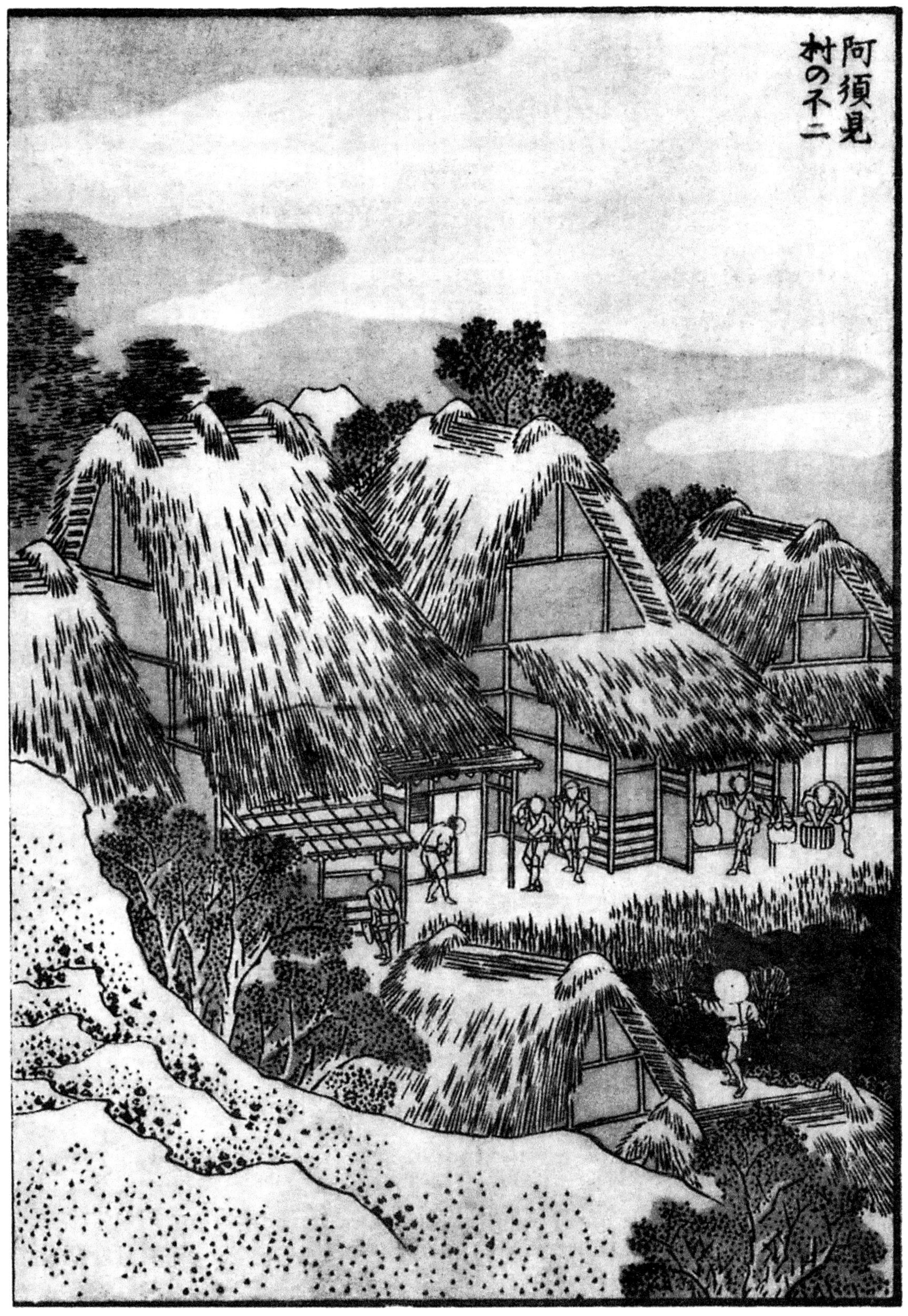

Plate XIII

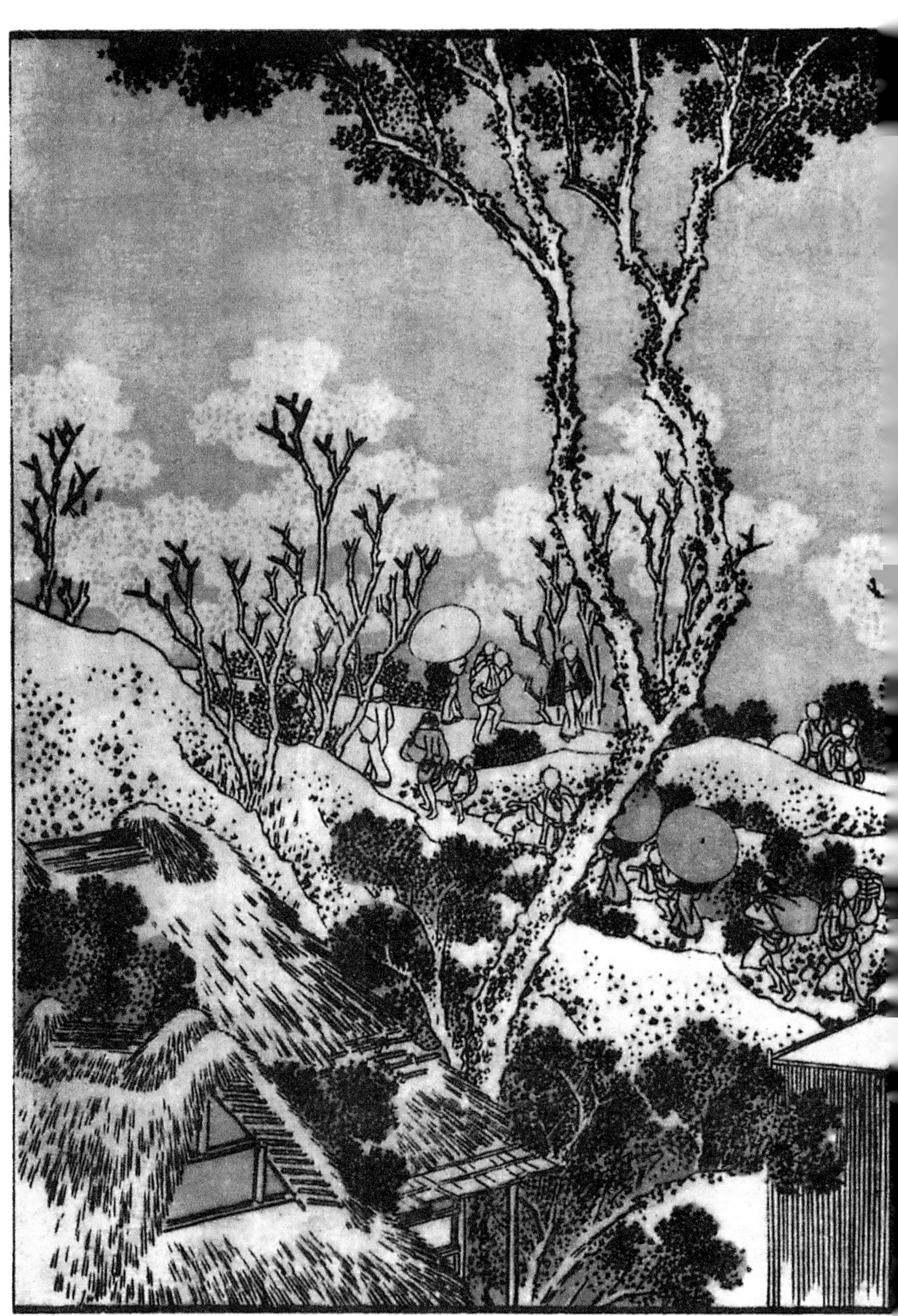

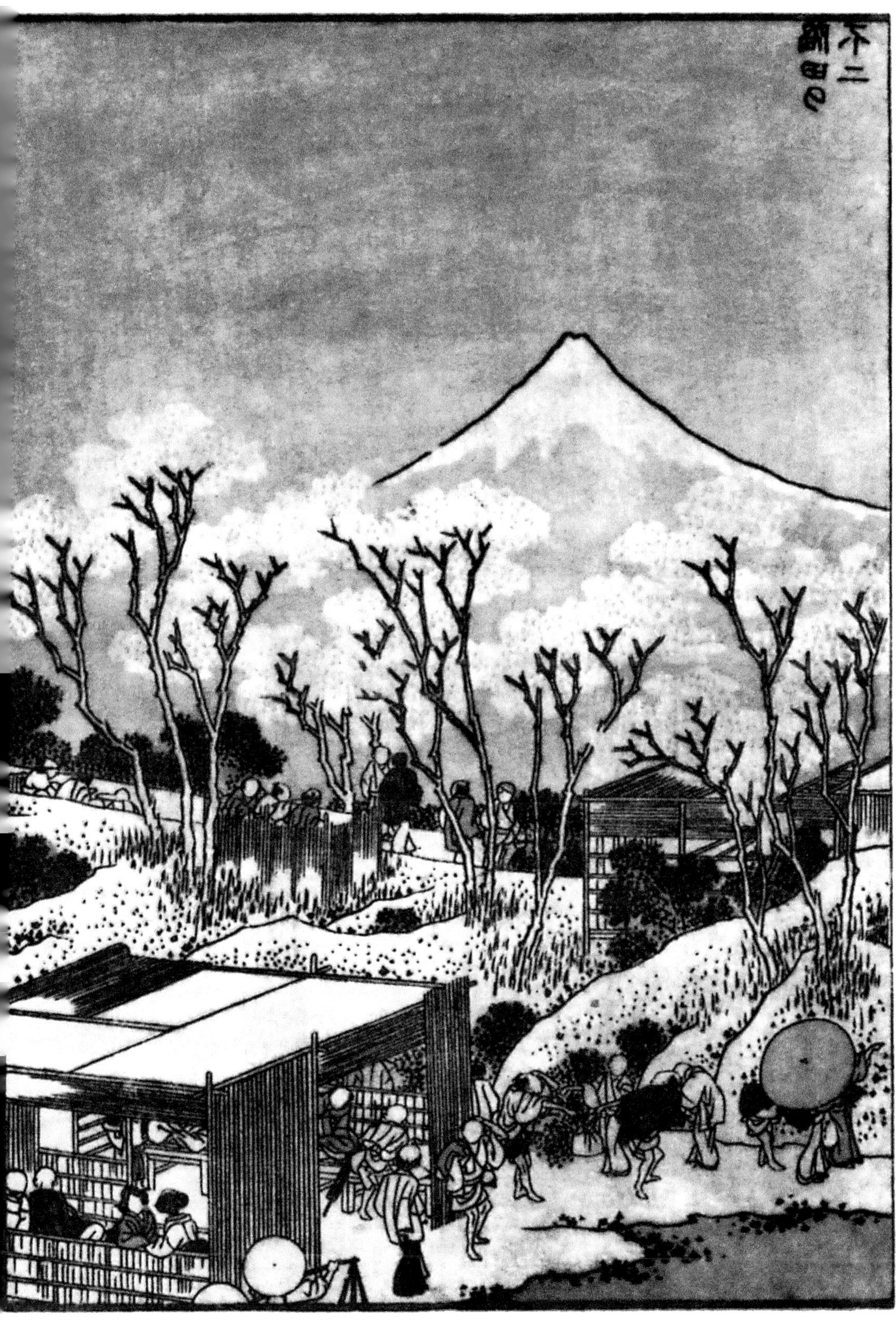

Plate XIV

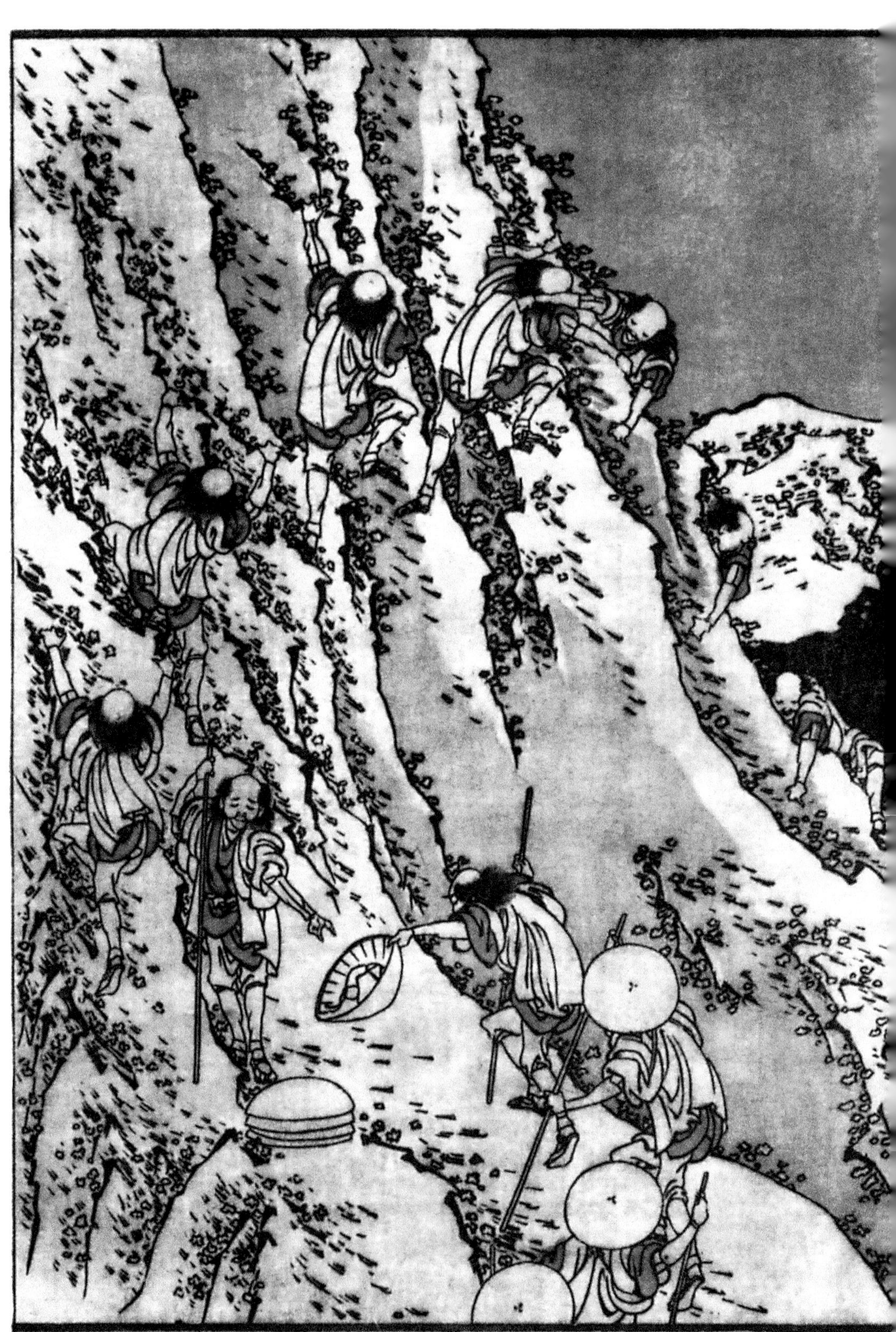

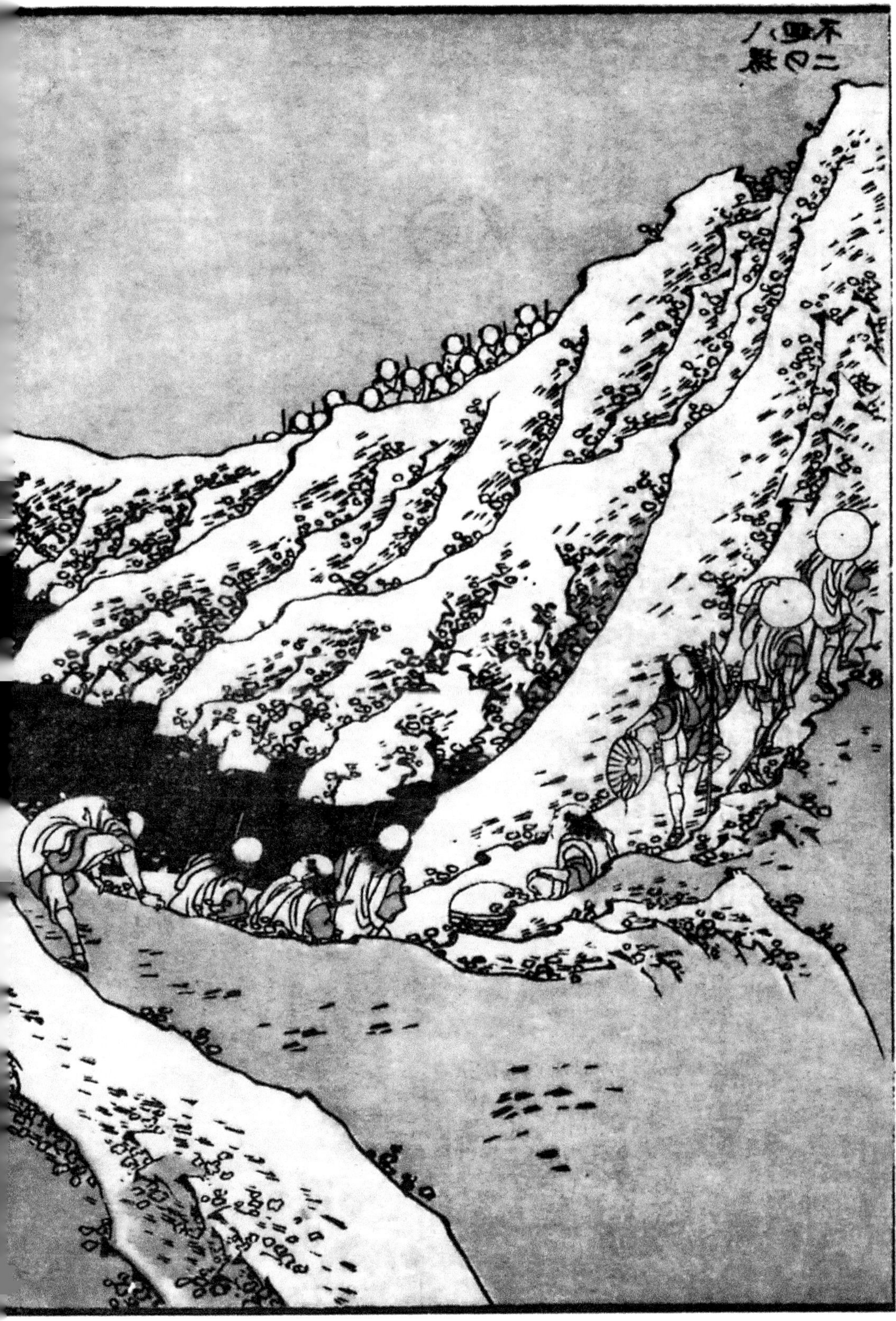

Plate XV

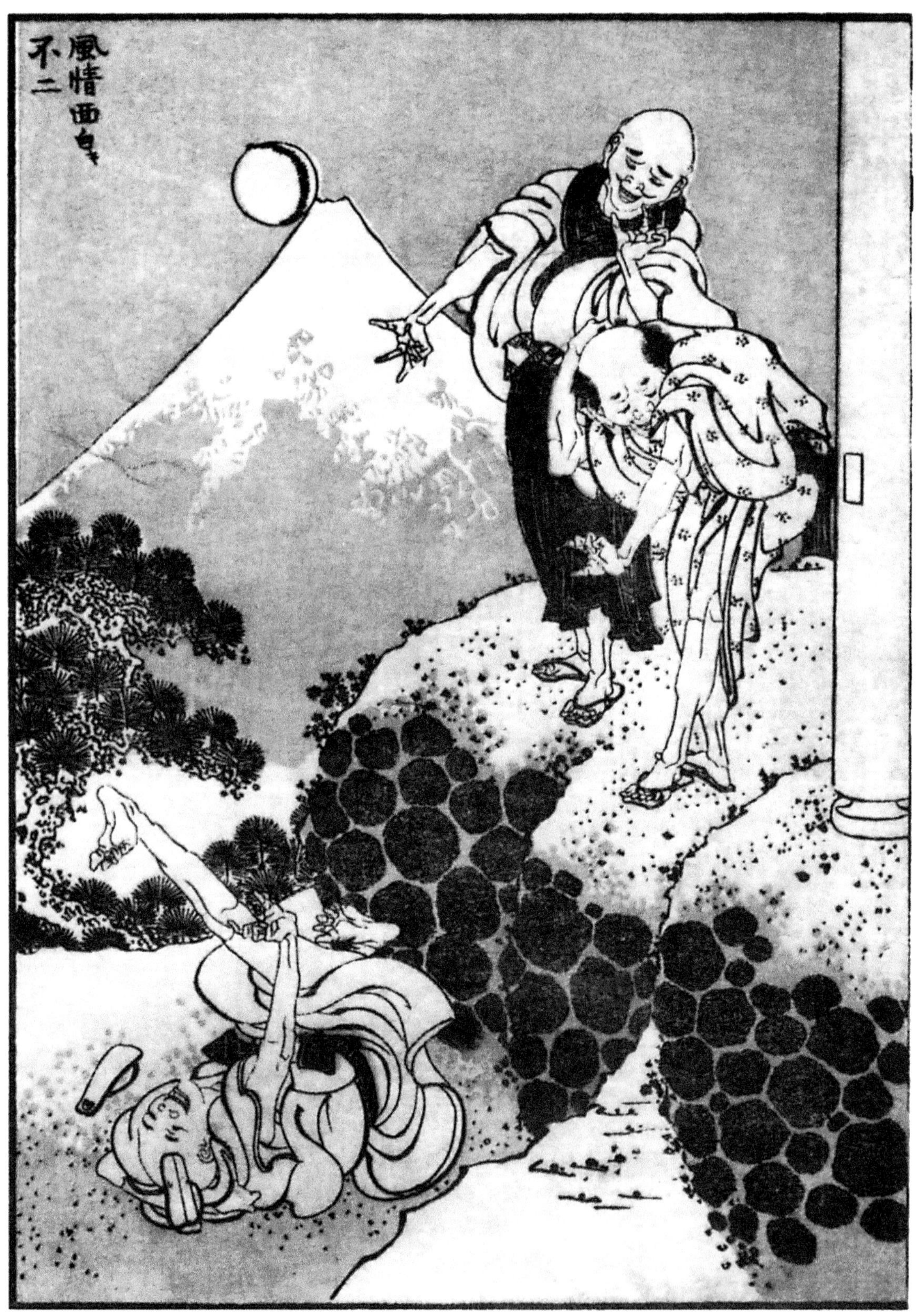

Plate XVI

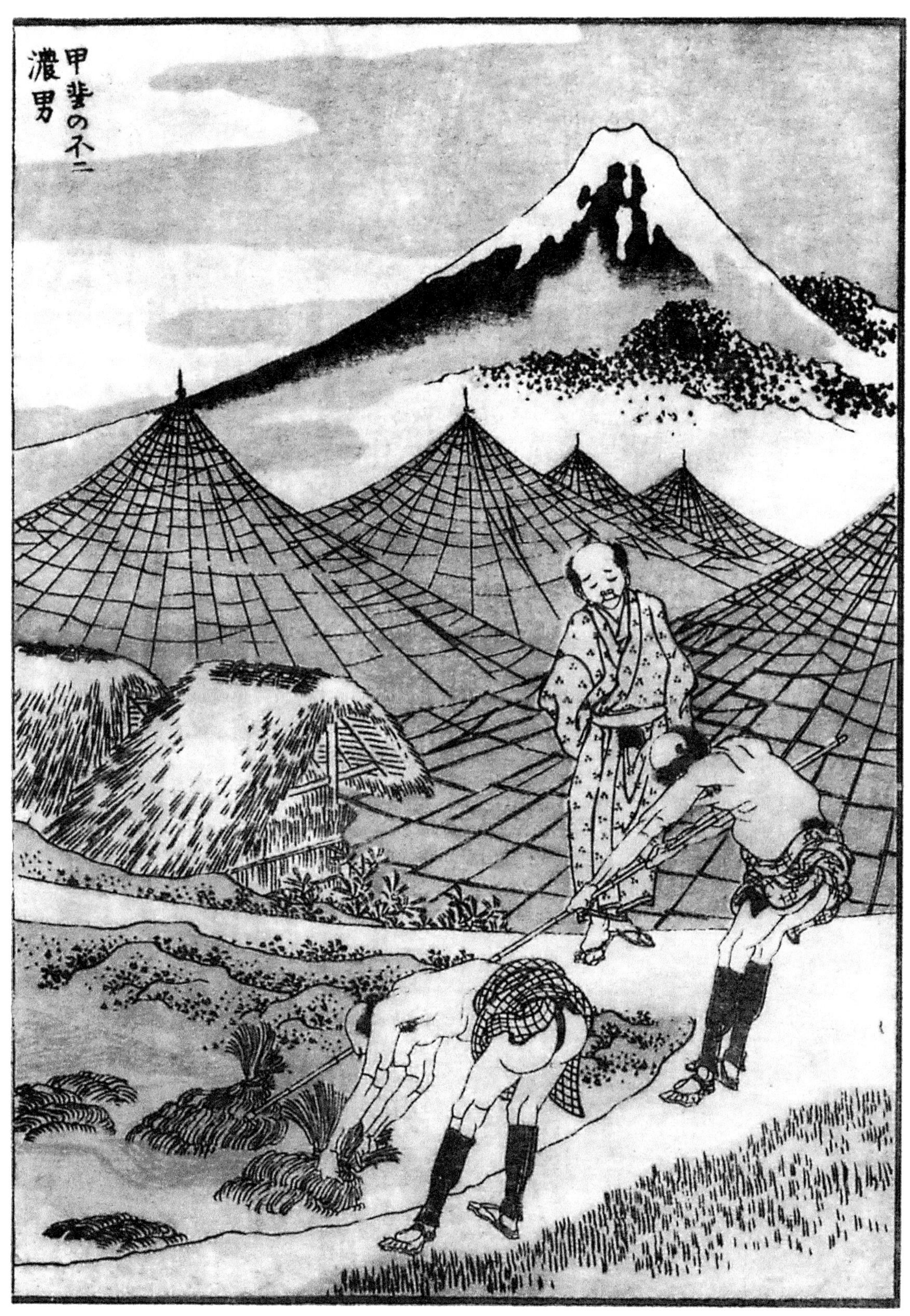

Plate XVII

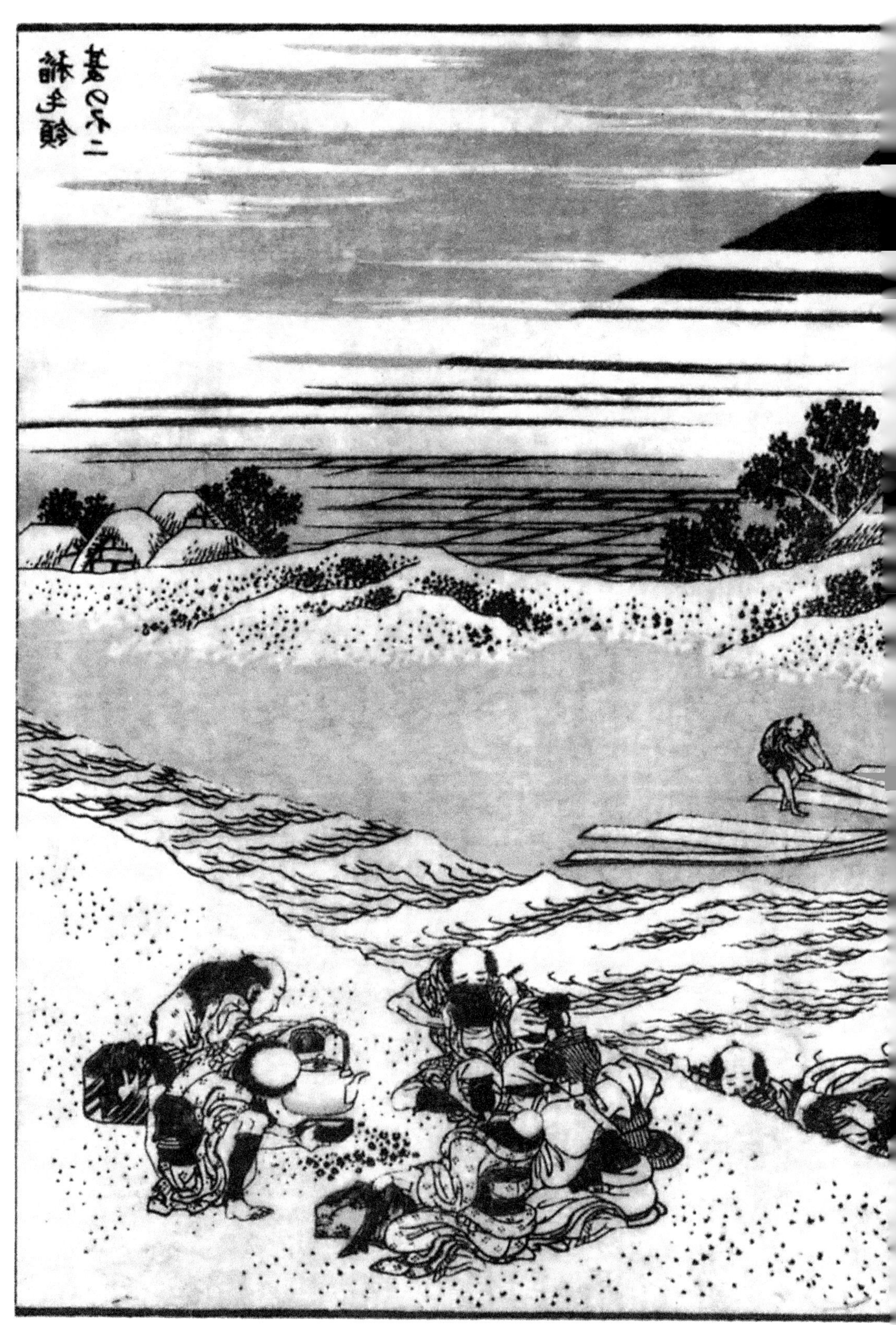

其の十二
詠手齢

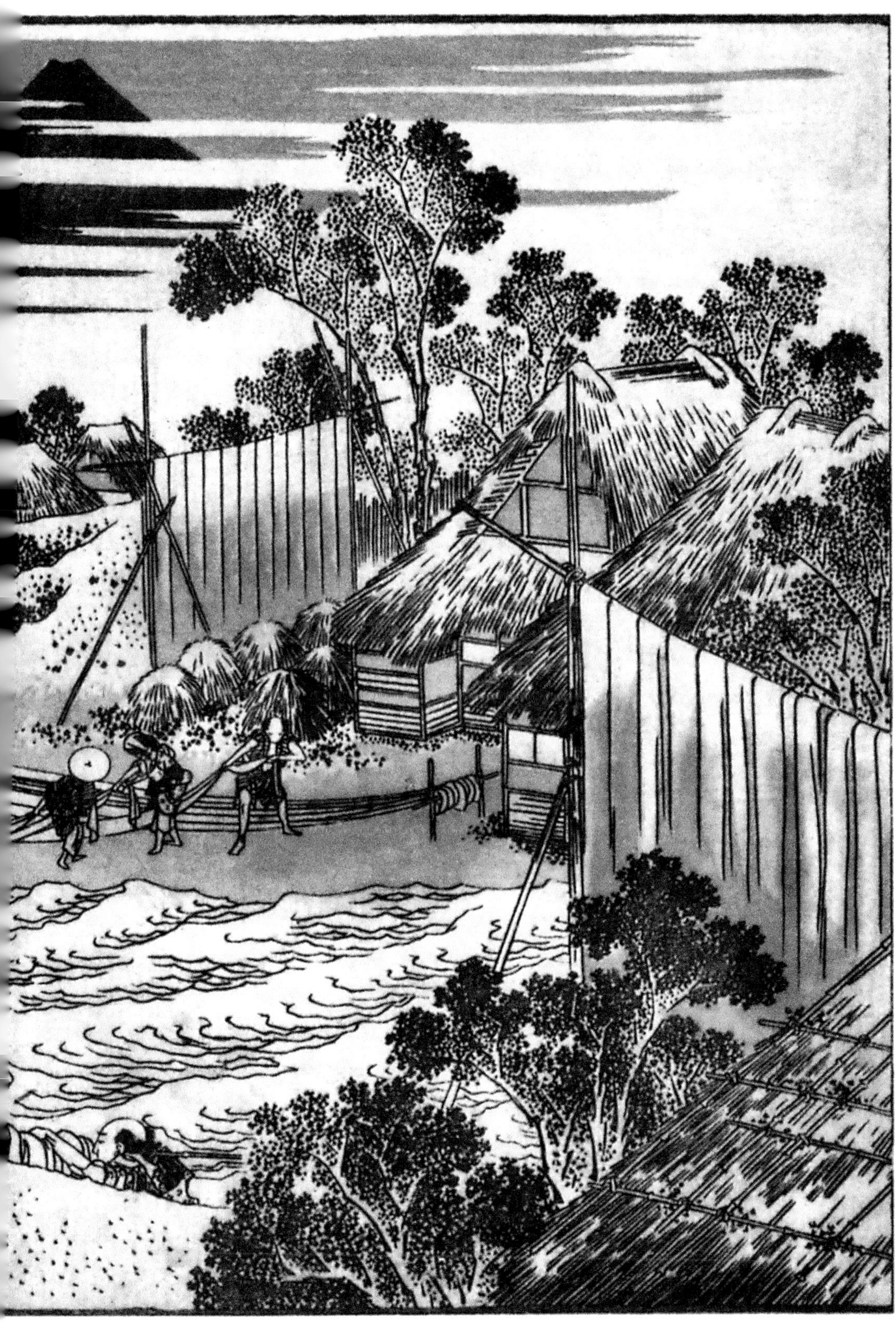

Plate XVIII

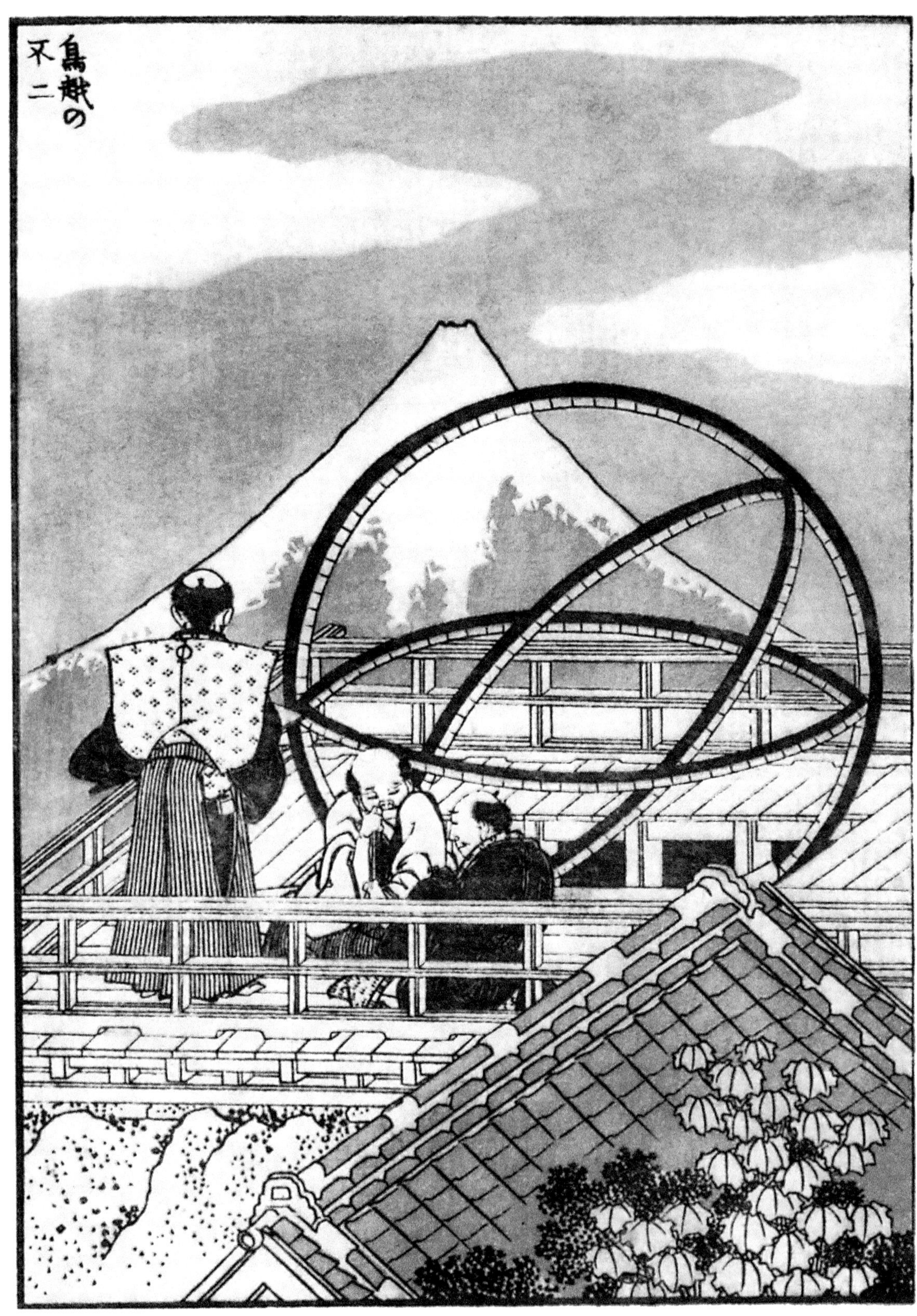

Plate XIX

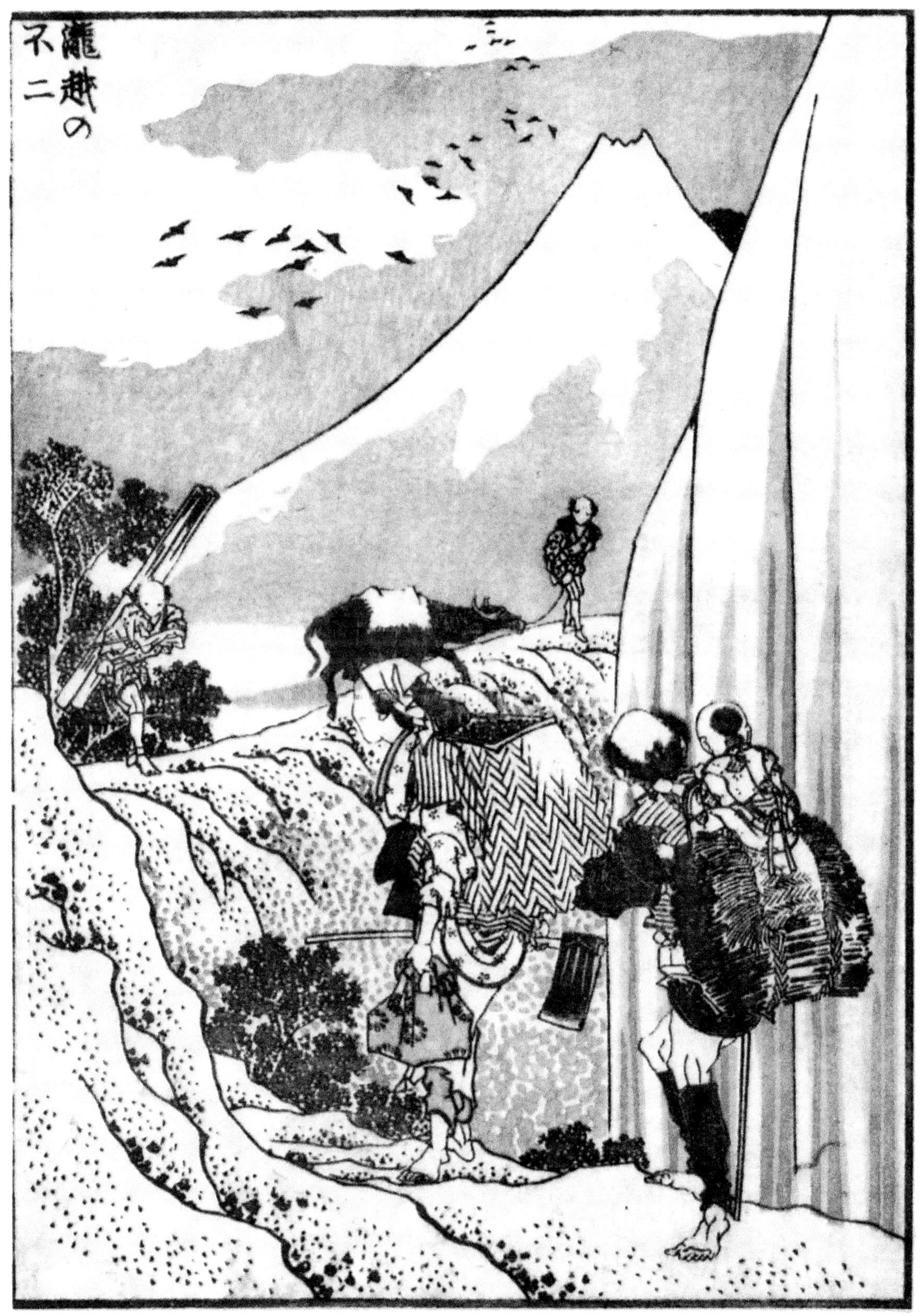

Plate XX

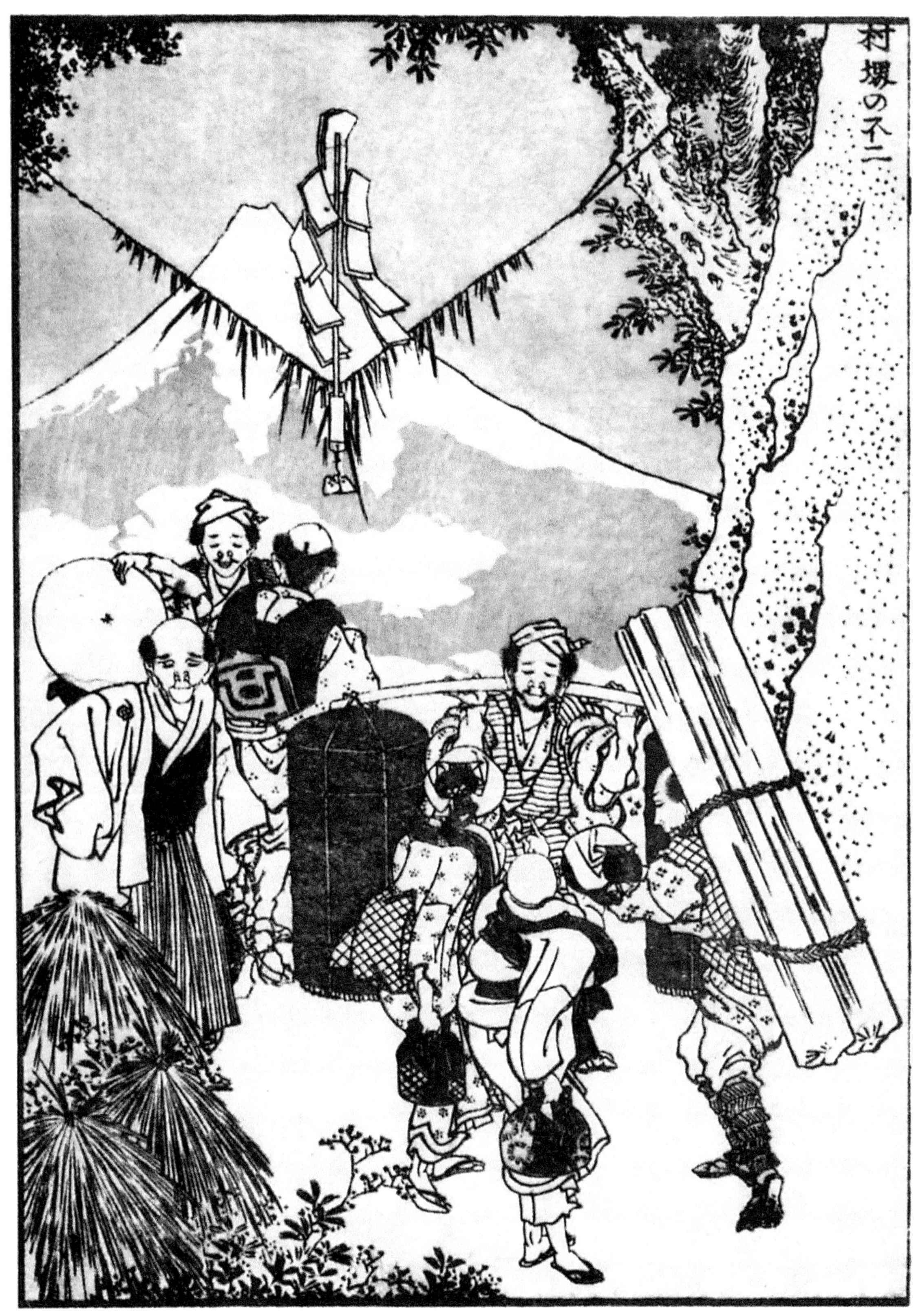

Plate XXI

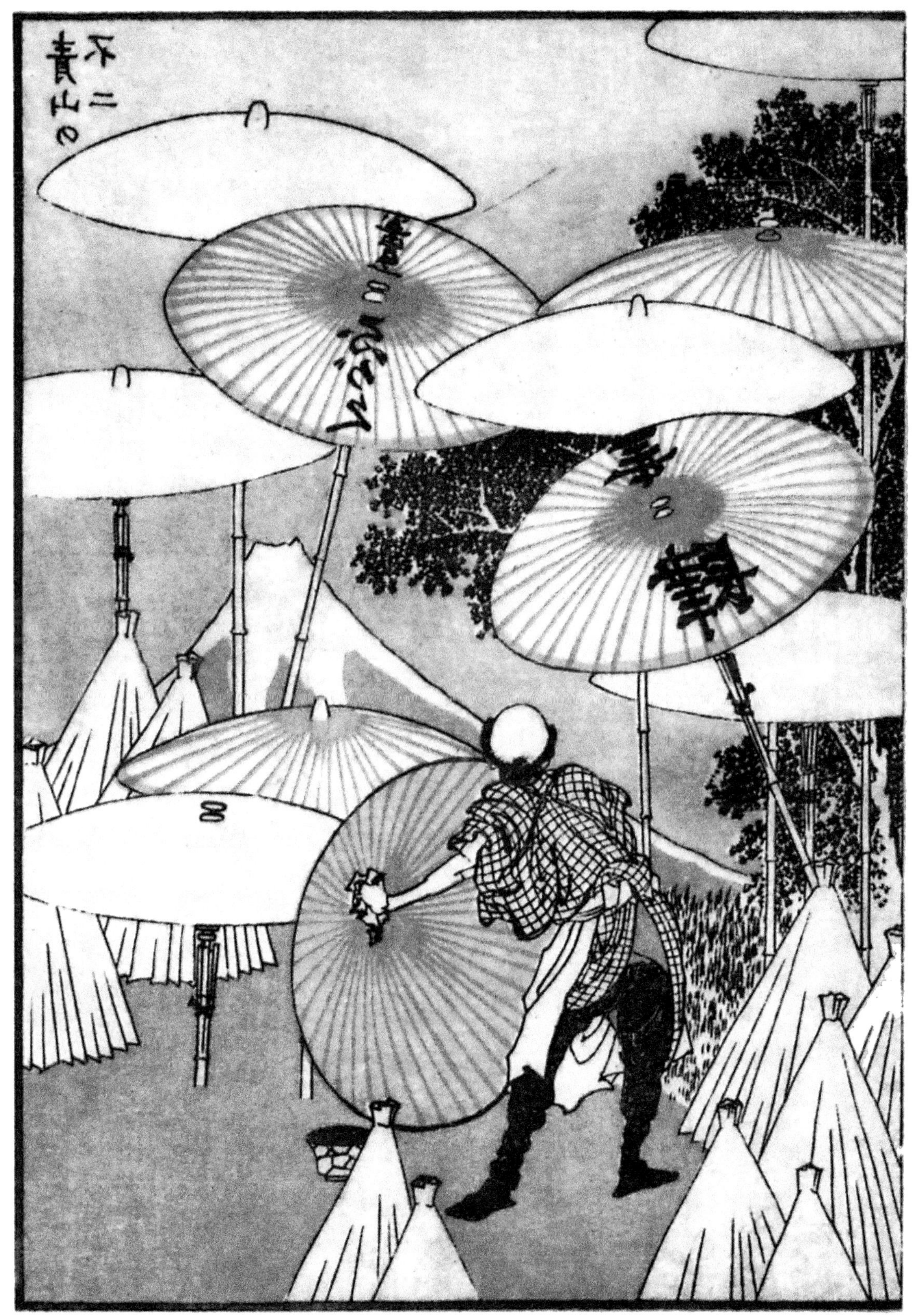

Plate XXII

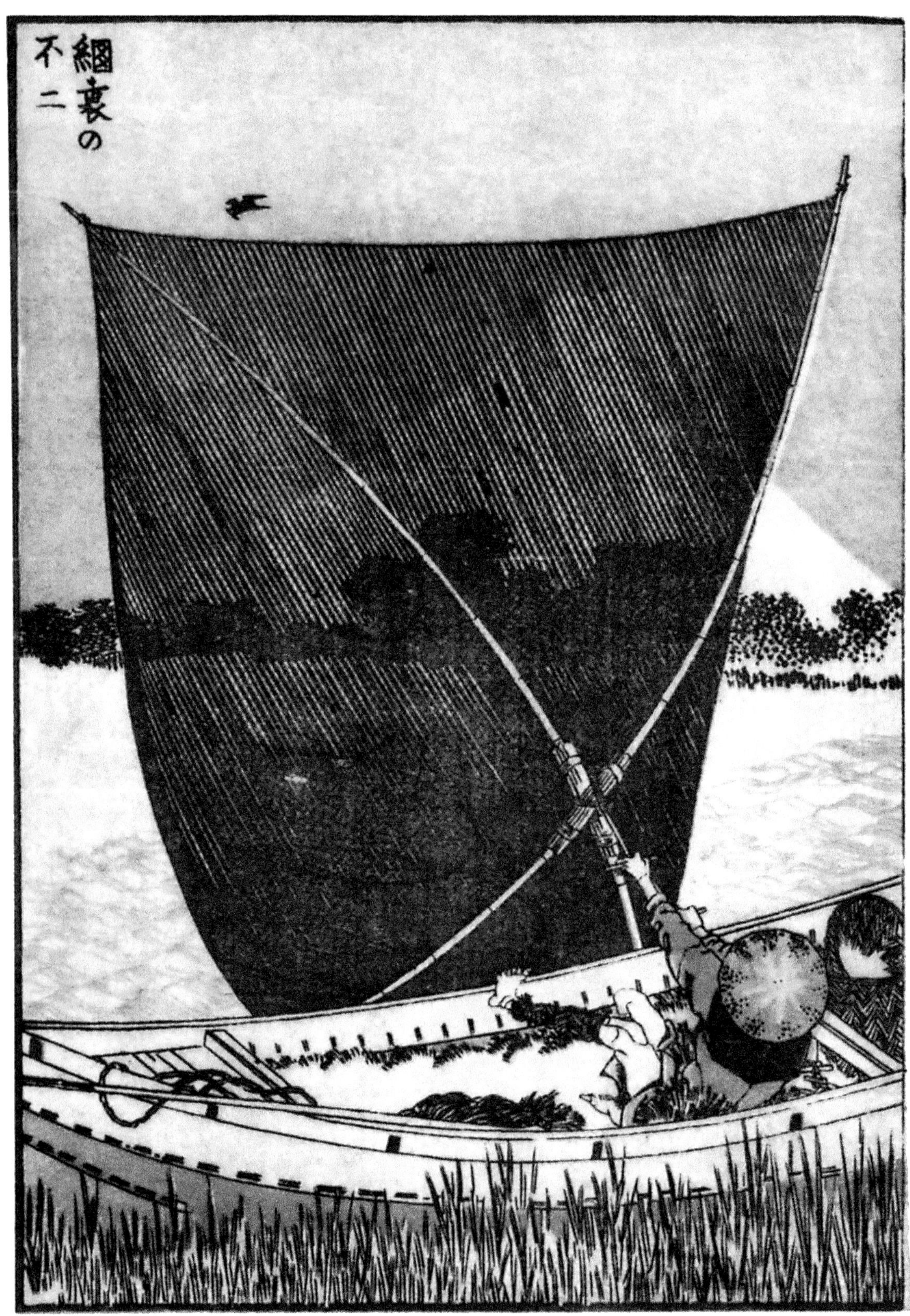

Plate XXIII

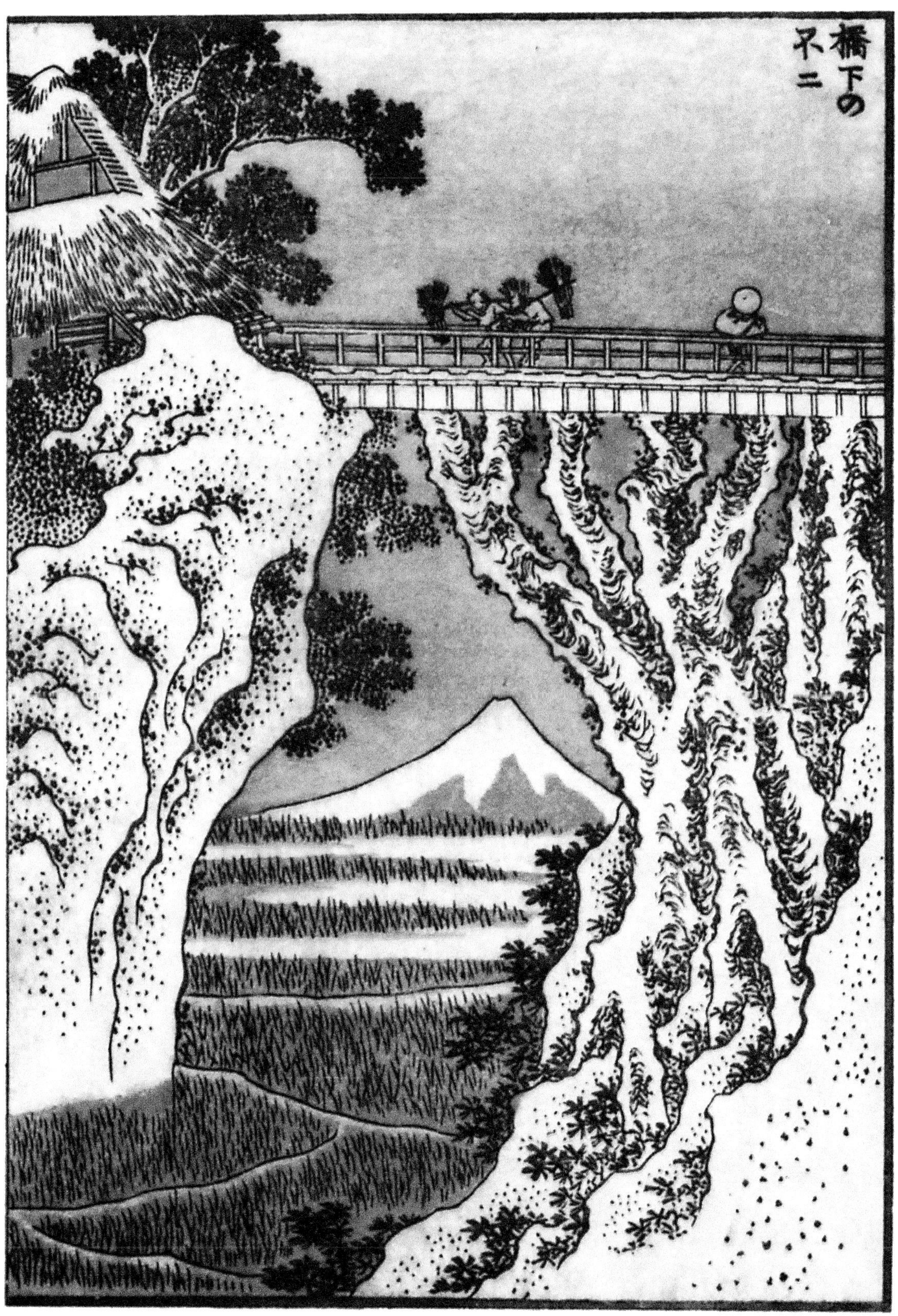

Plate XXIV

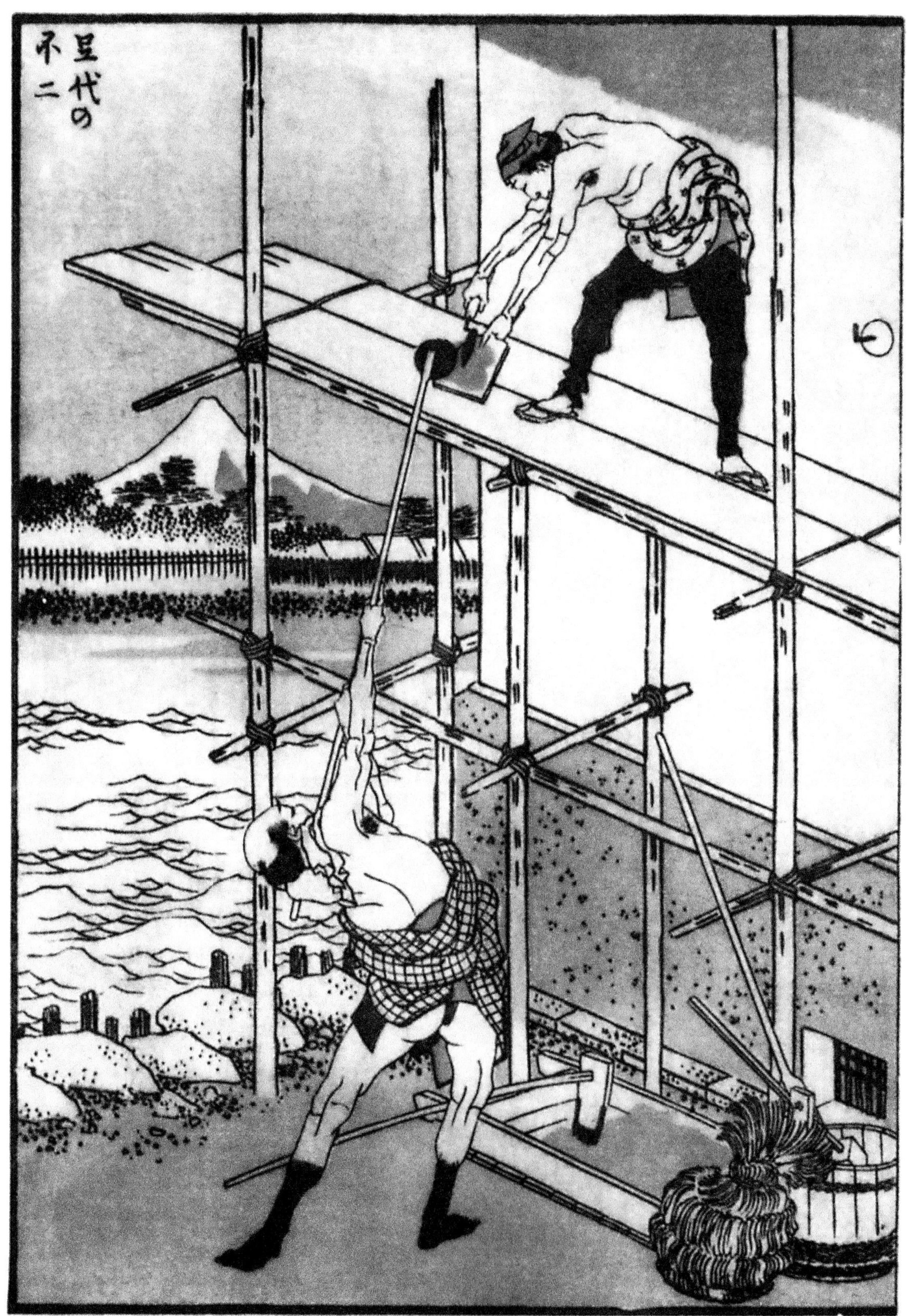

Plate XXV

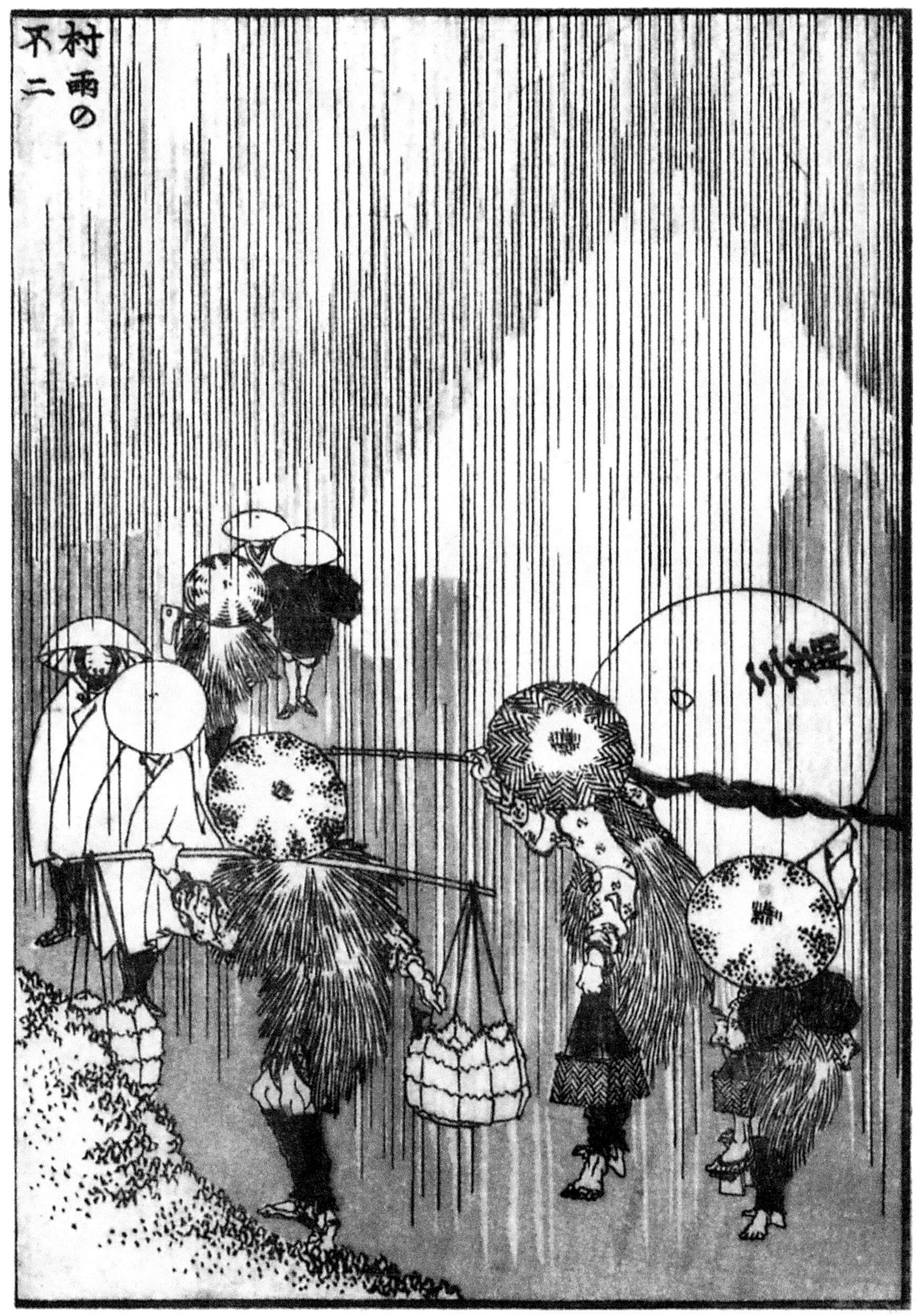

Plate XXVI

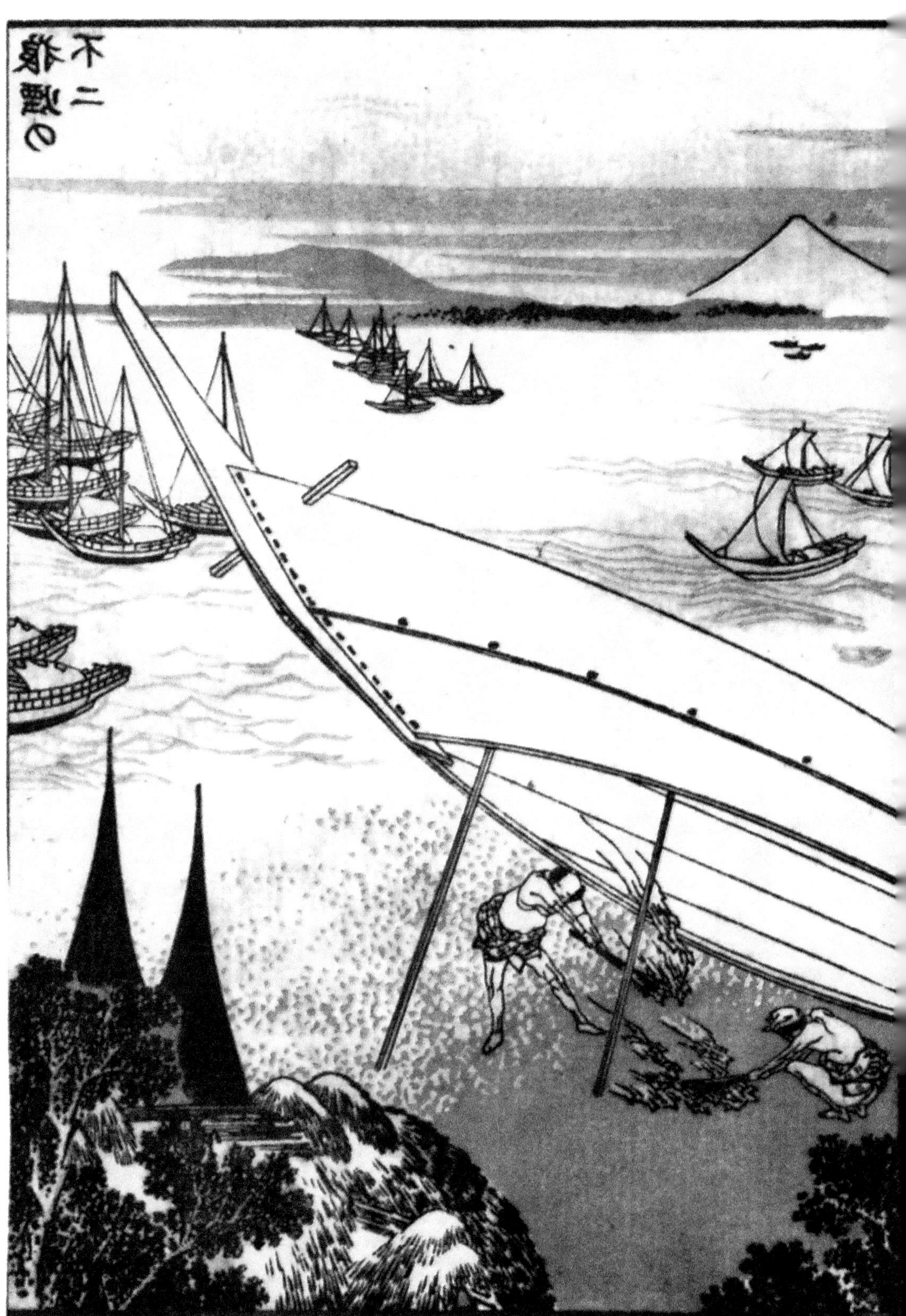

不二
東都の

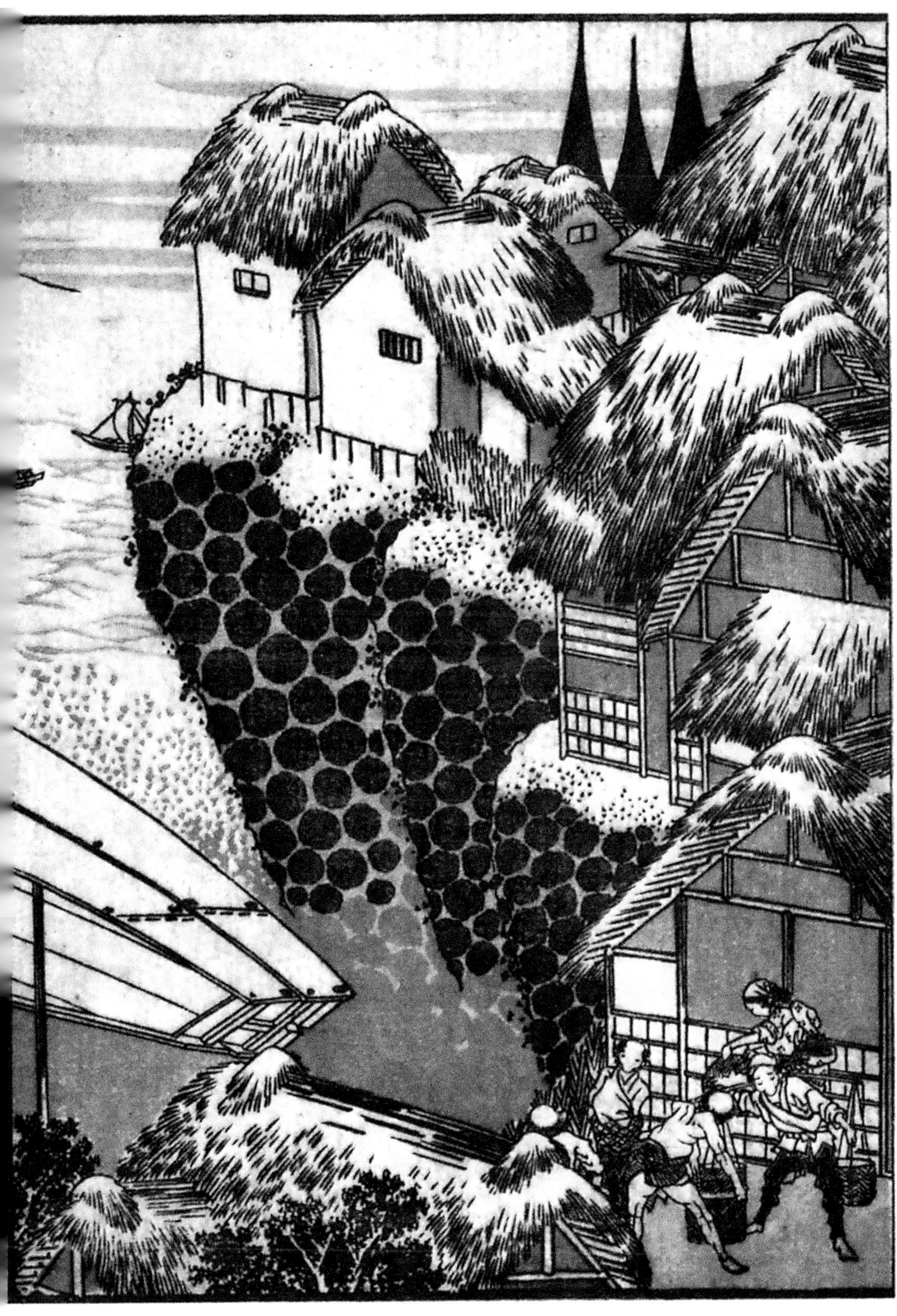

Plate XXVII

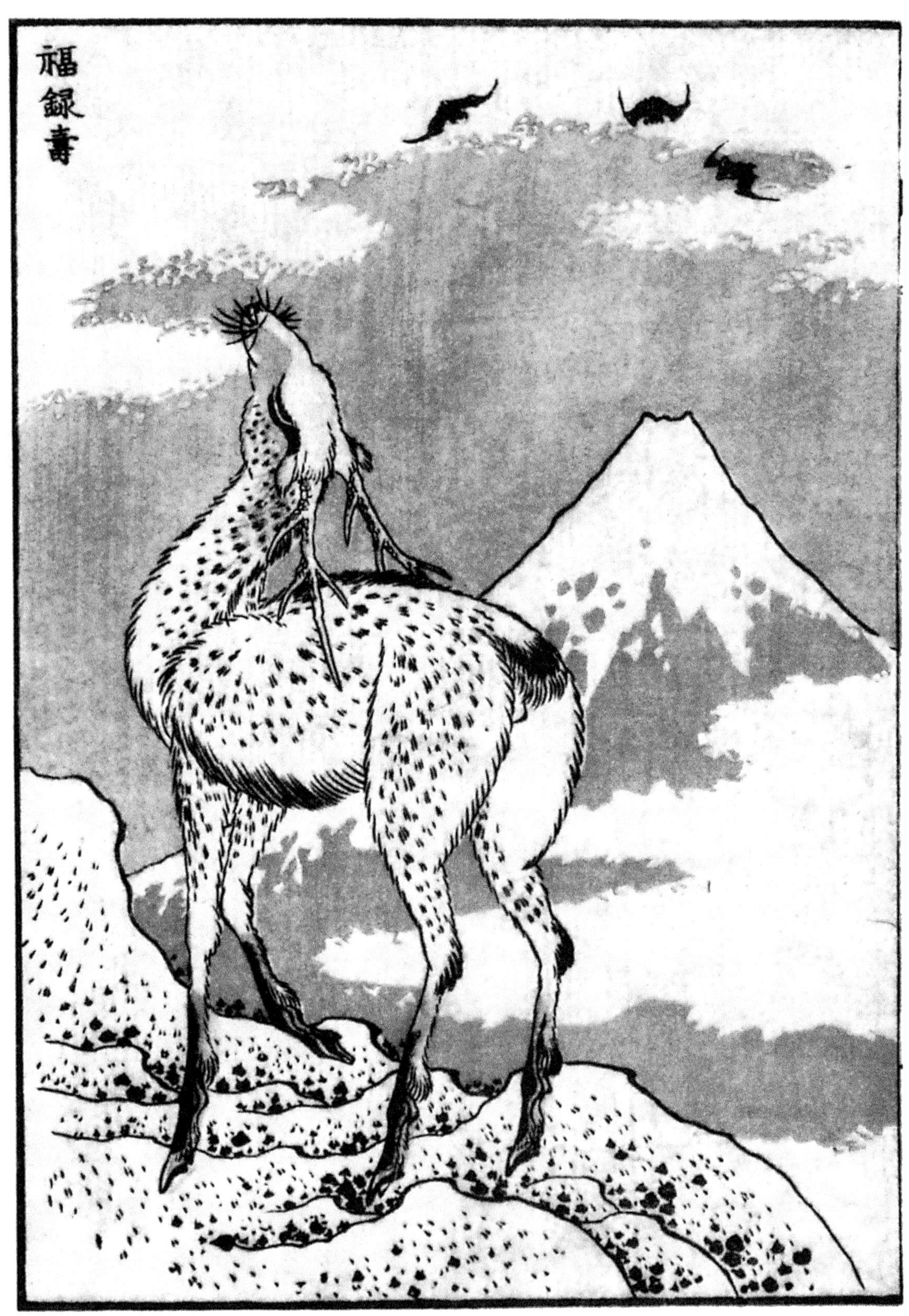

Plate XXVIII

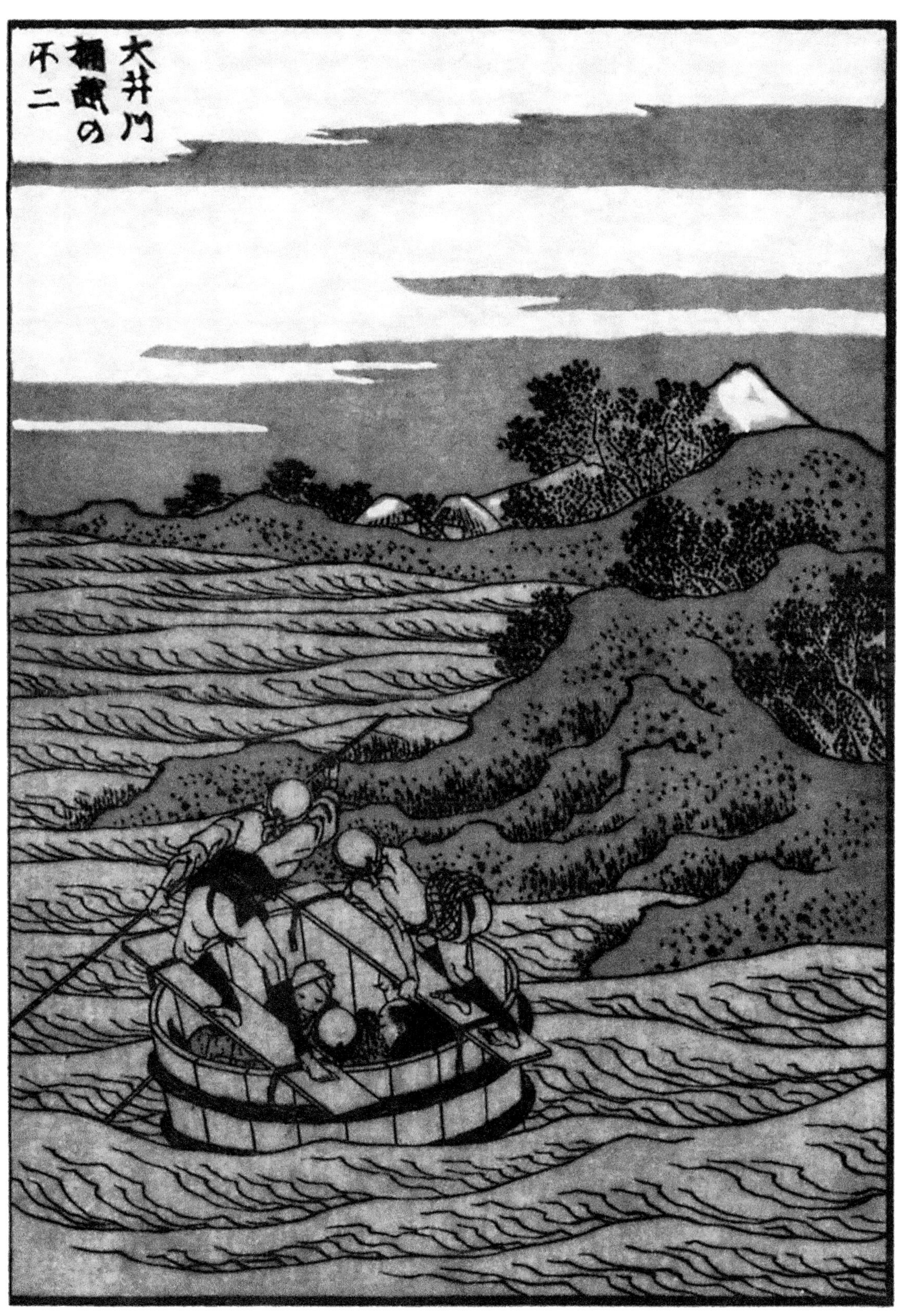

Plate XXIX

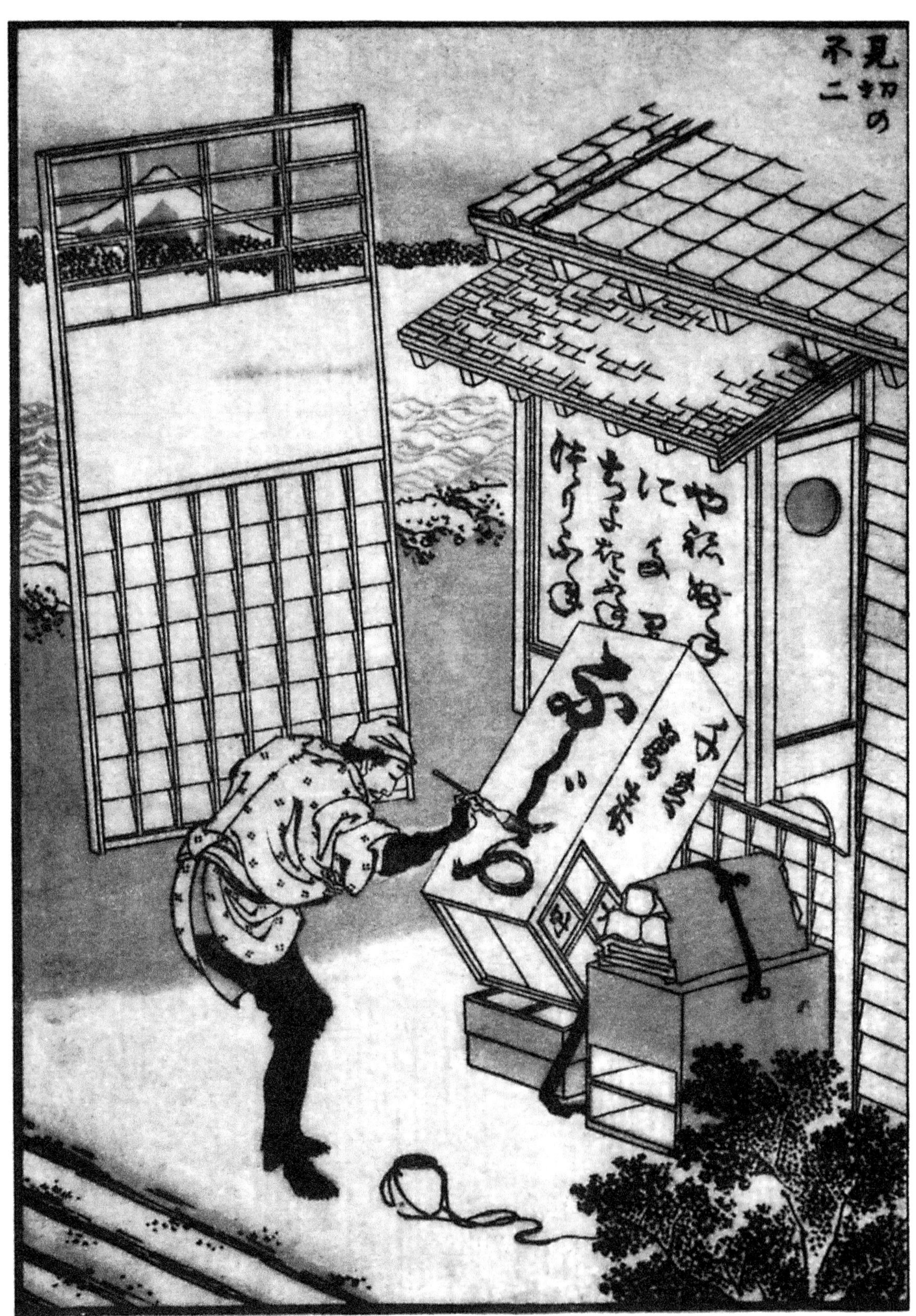

Plate XXX

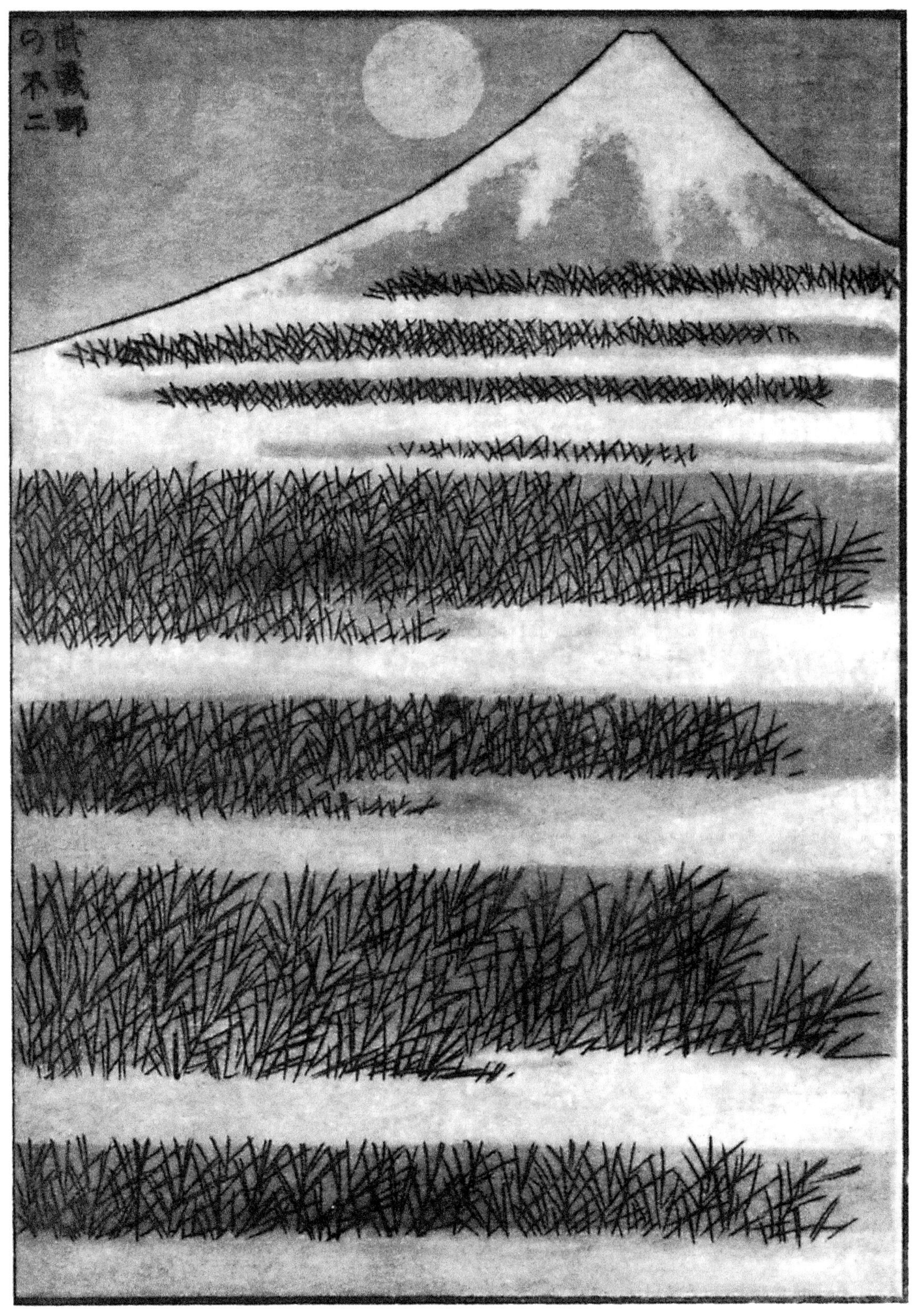

Plate XXXI

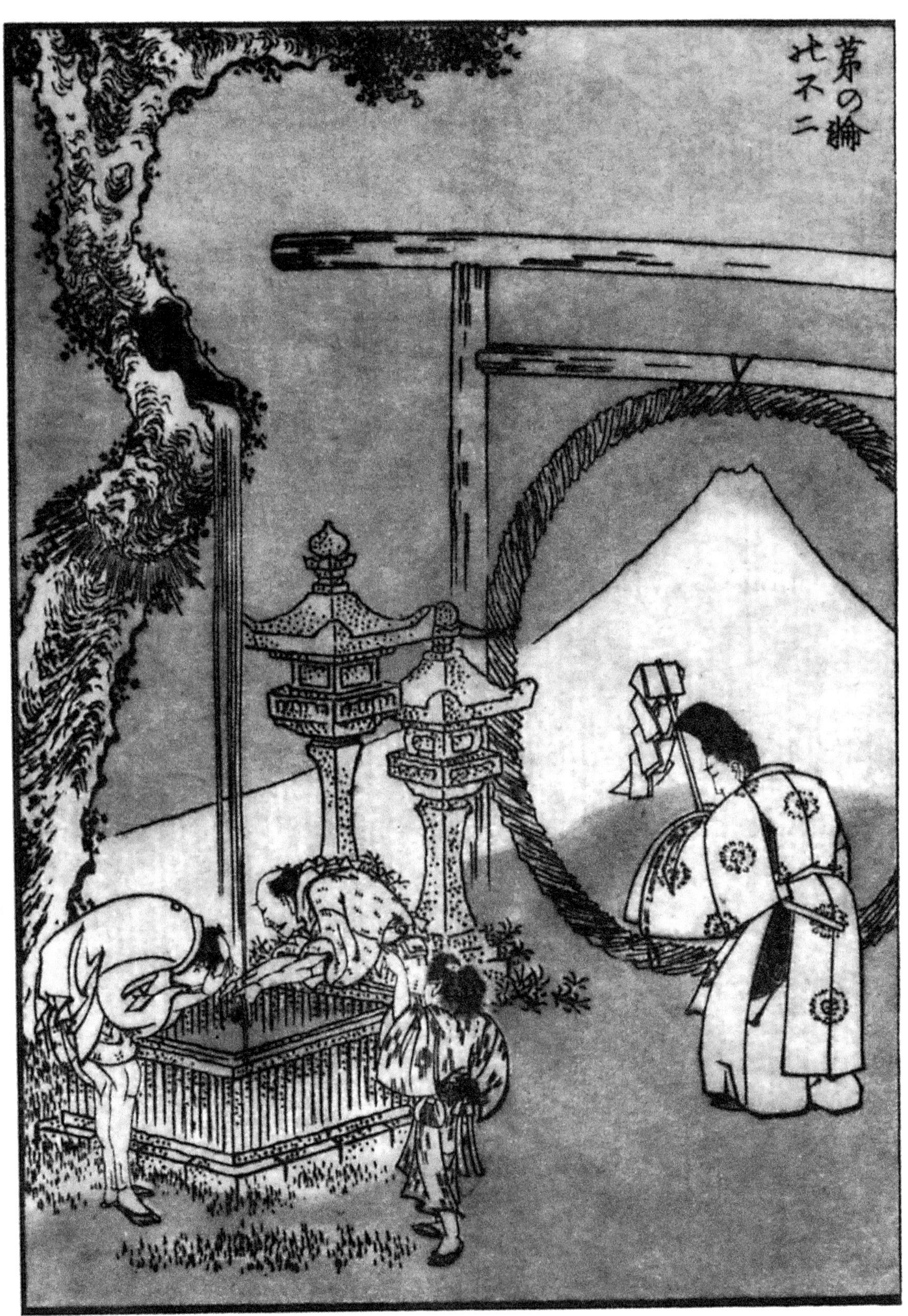

Plate XXXII

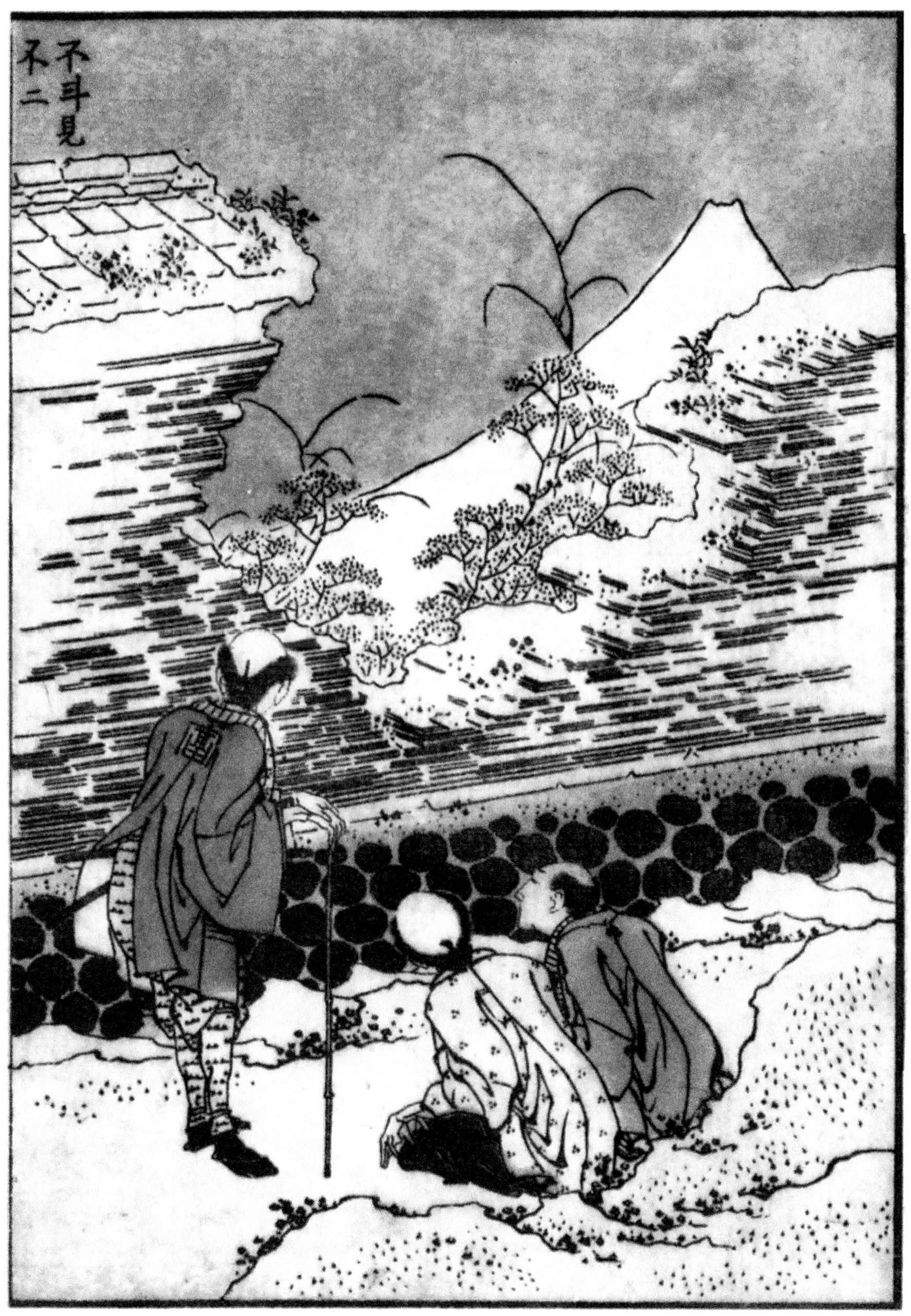

Plate XXXIII

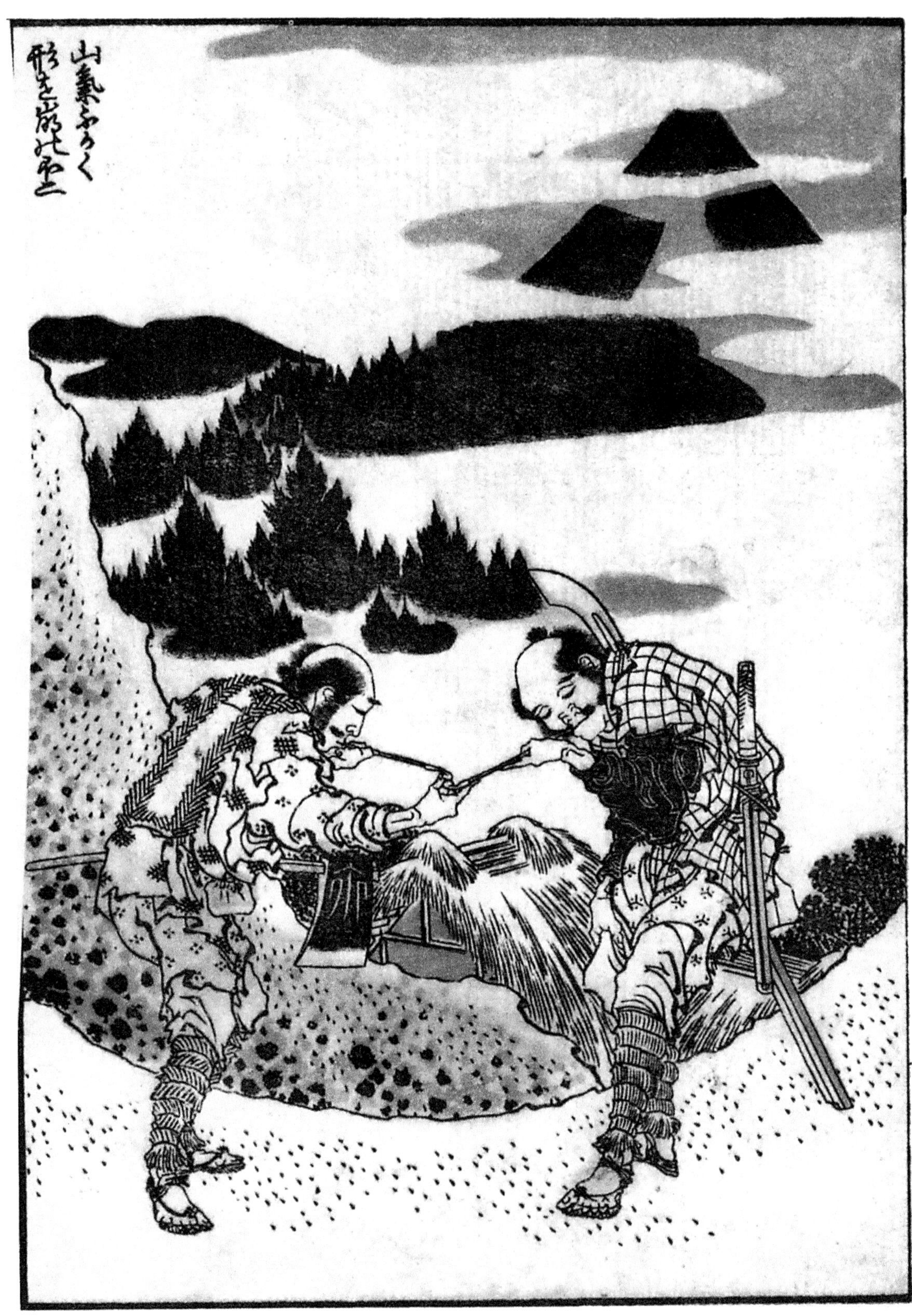

Plate XXXIV

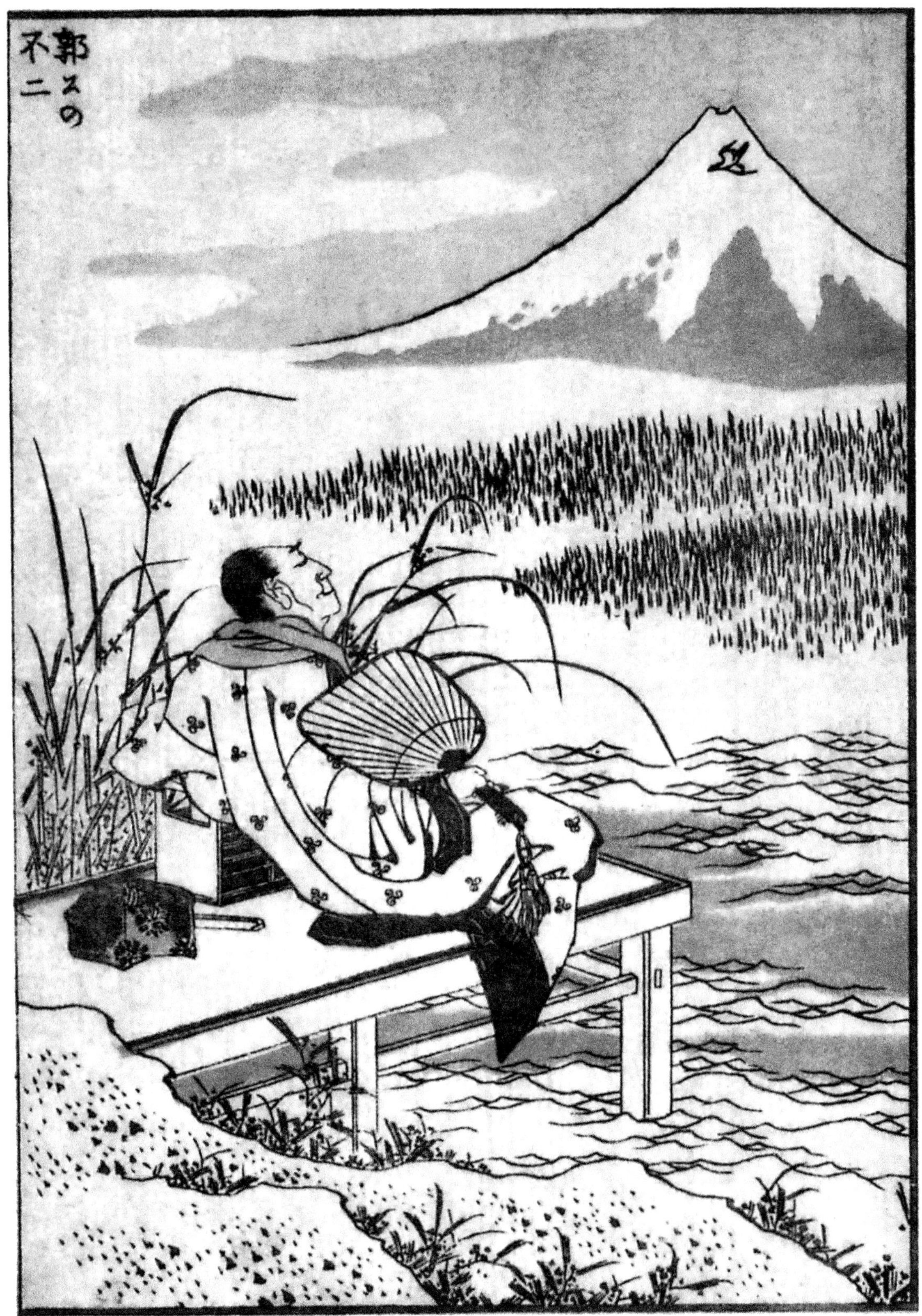

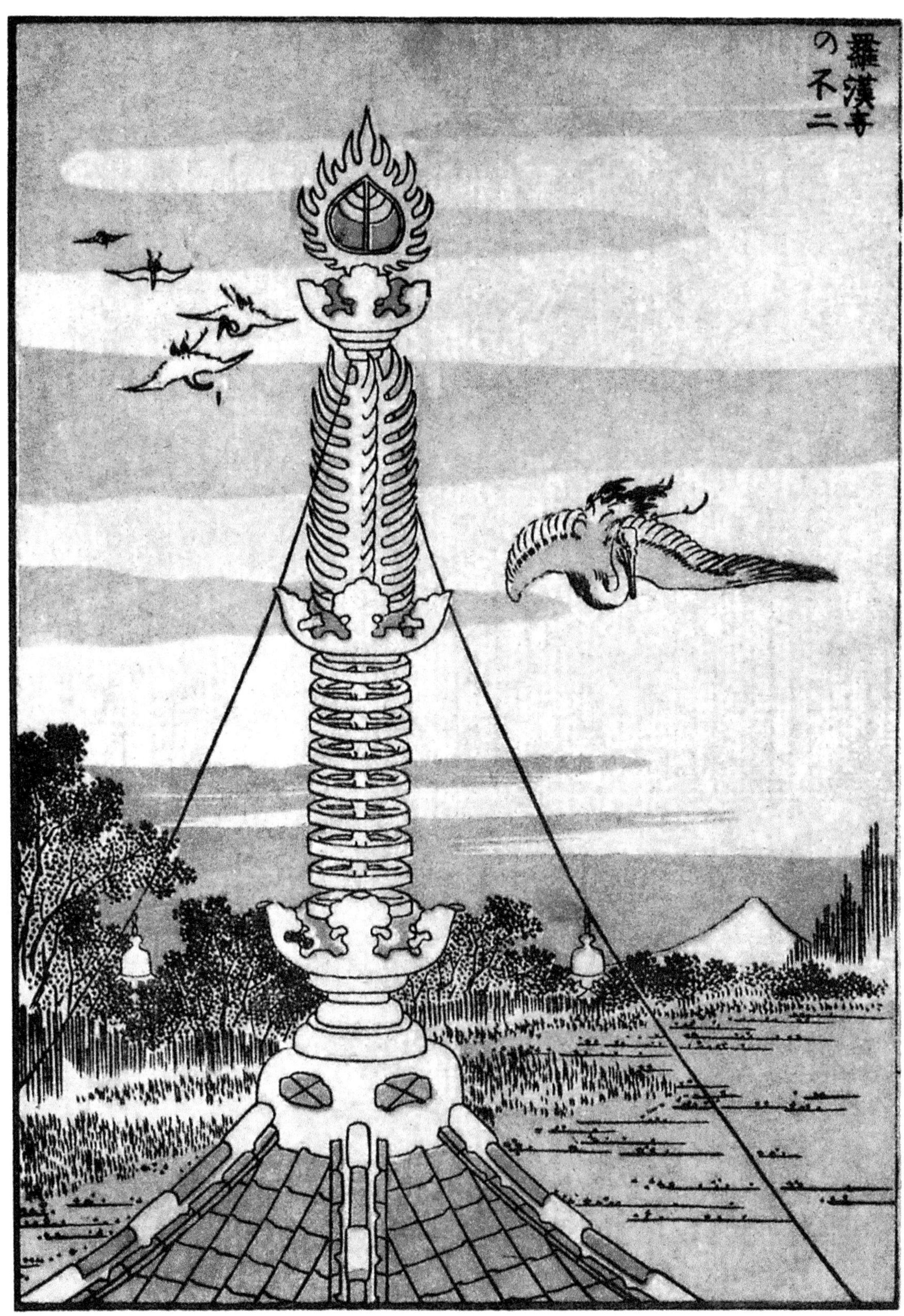

Plate XXXVI

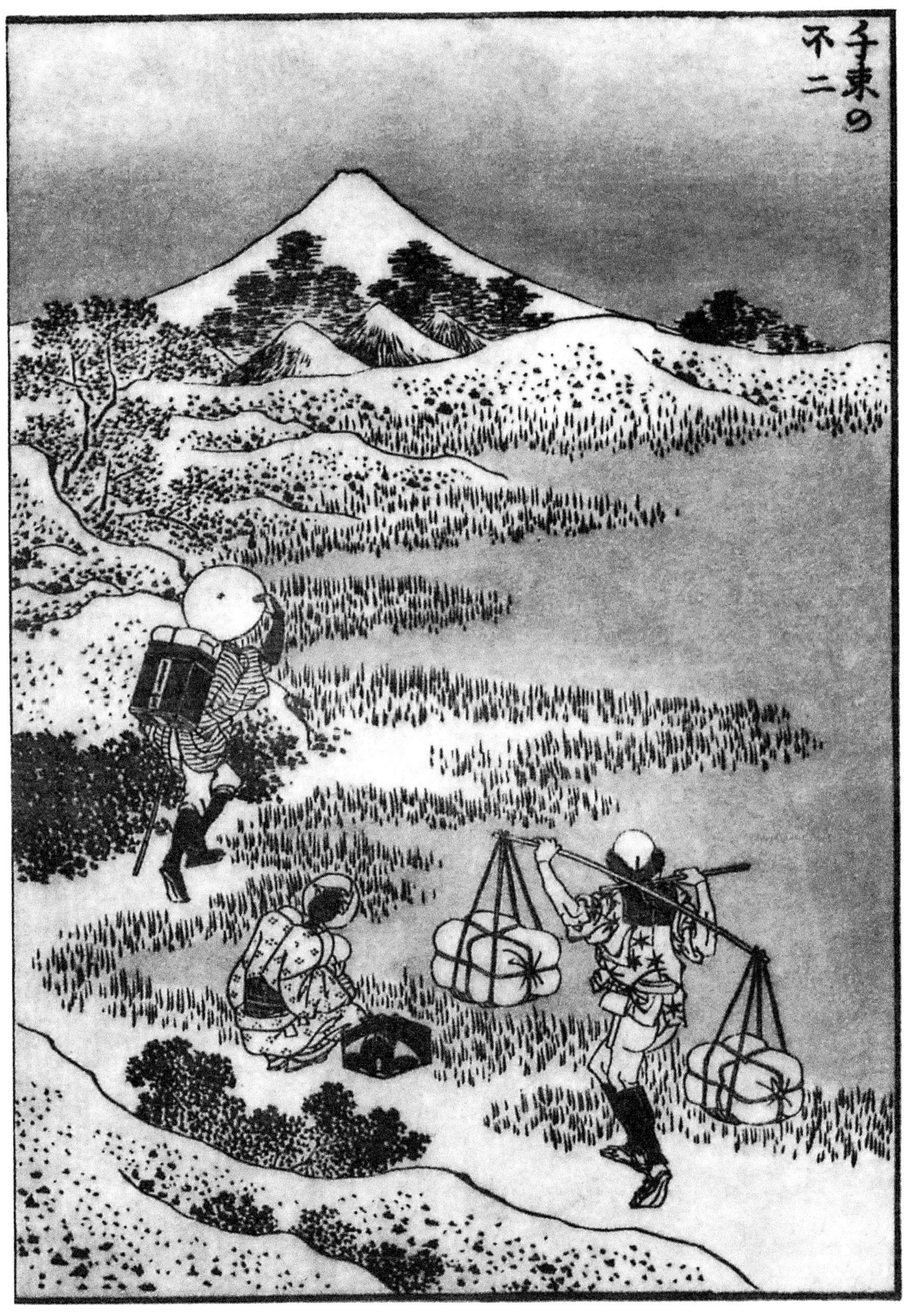

Plate XXXVII

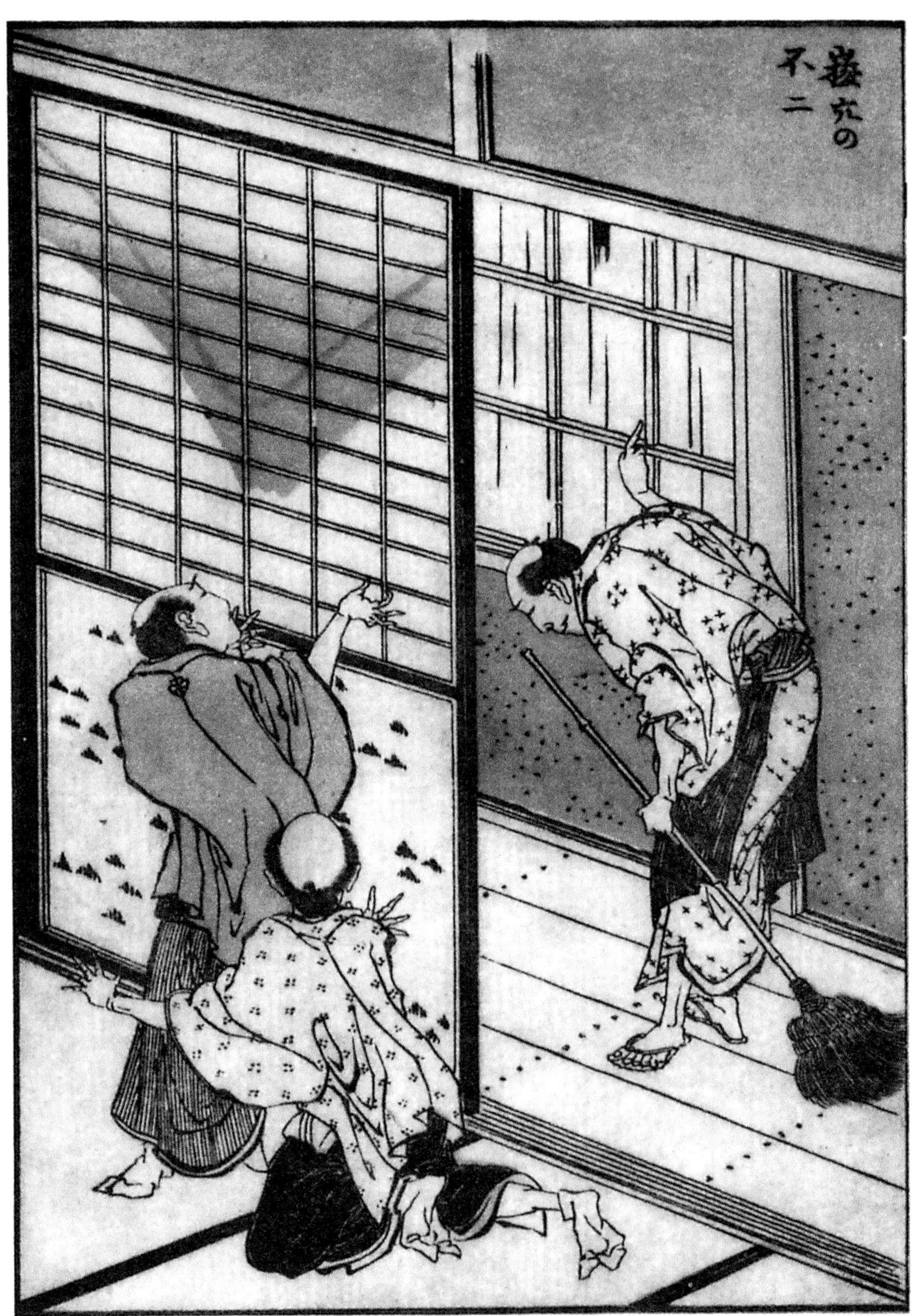

Plate XXXVIII

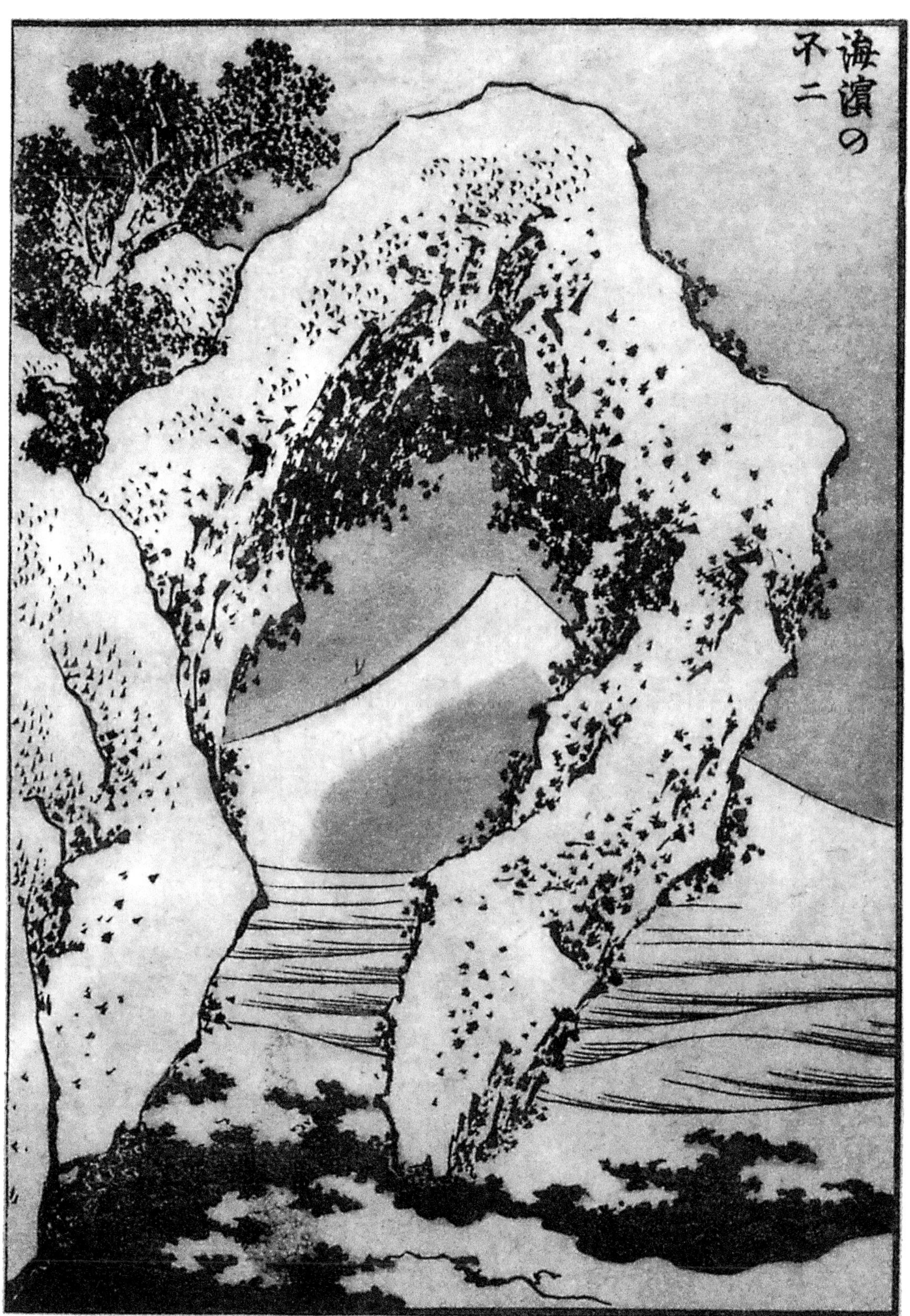

Plate XXXIX

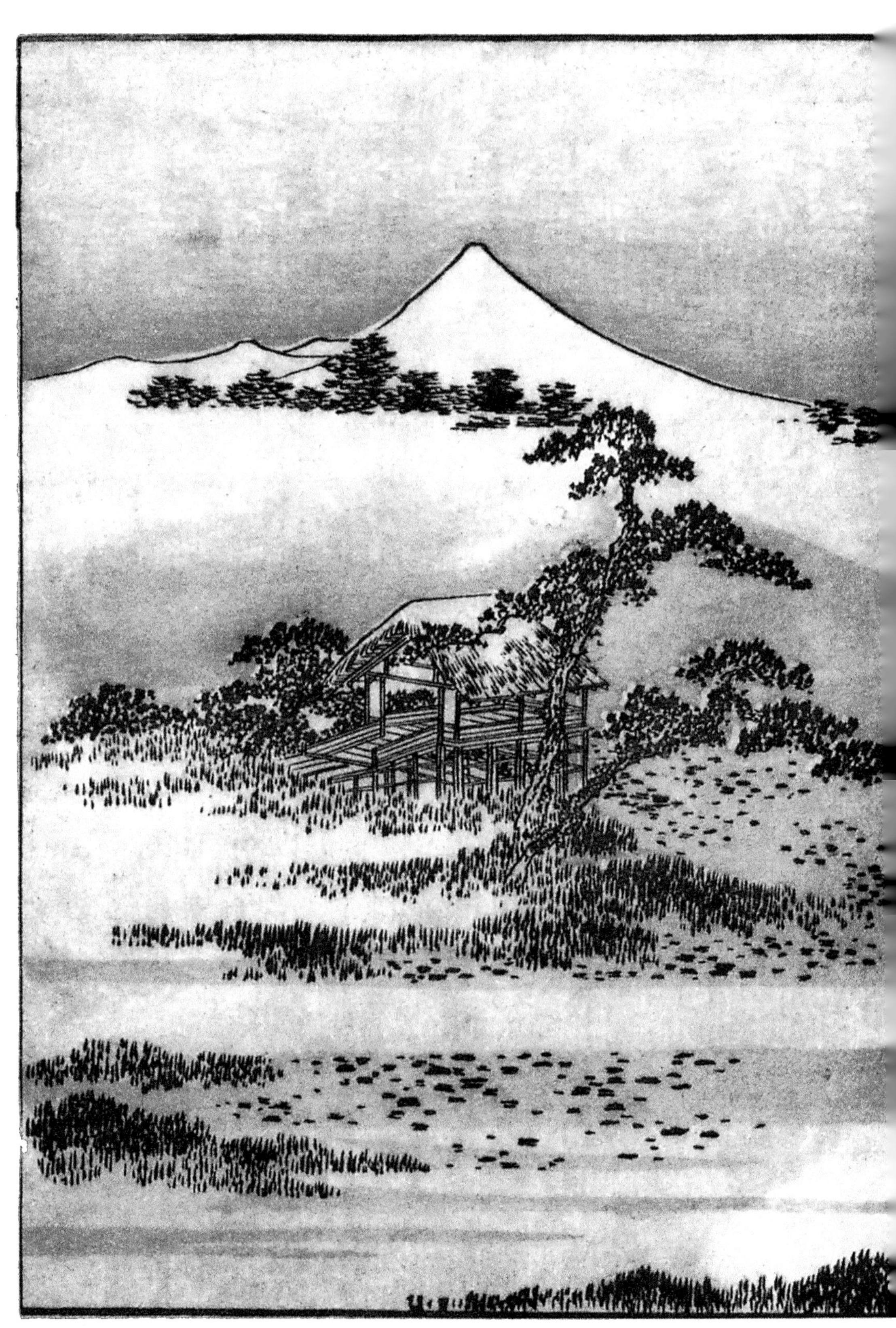

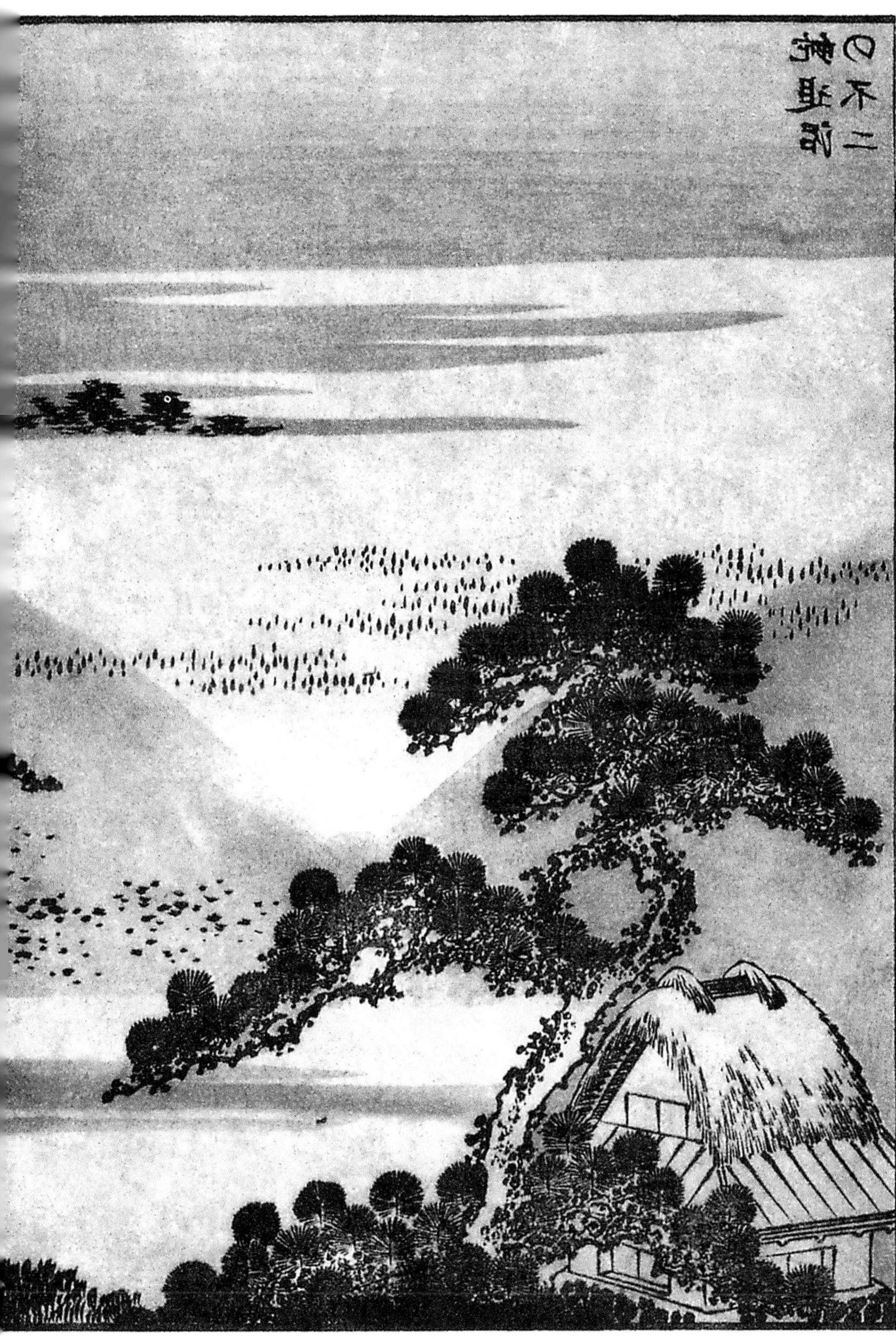

Plate XL

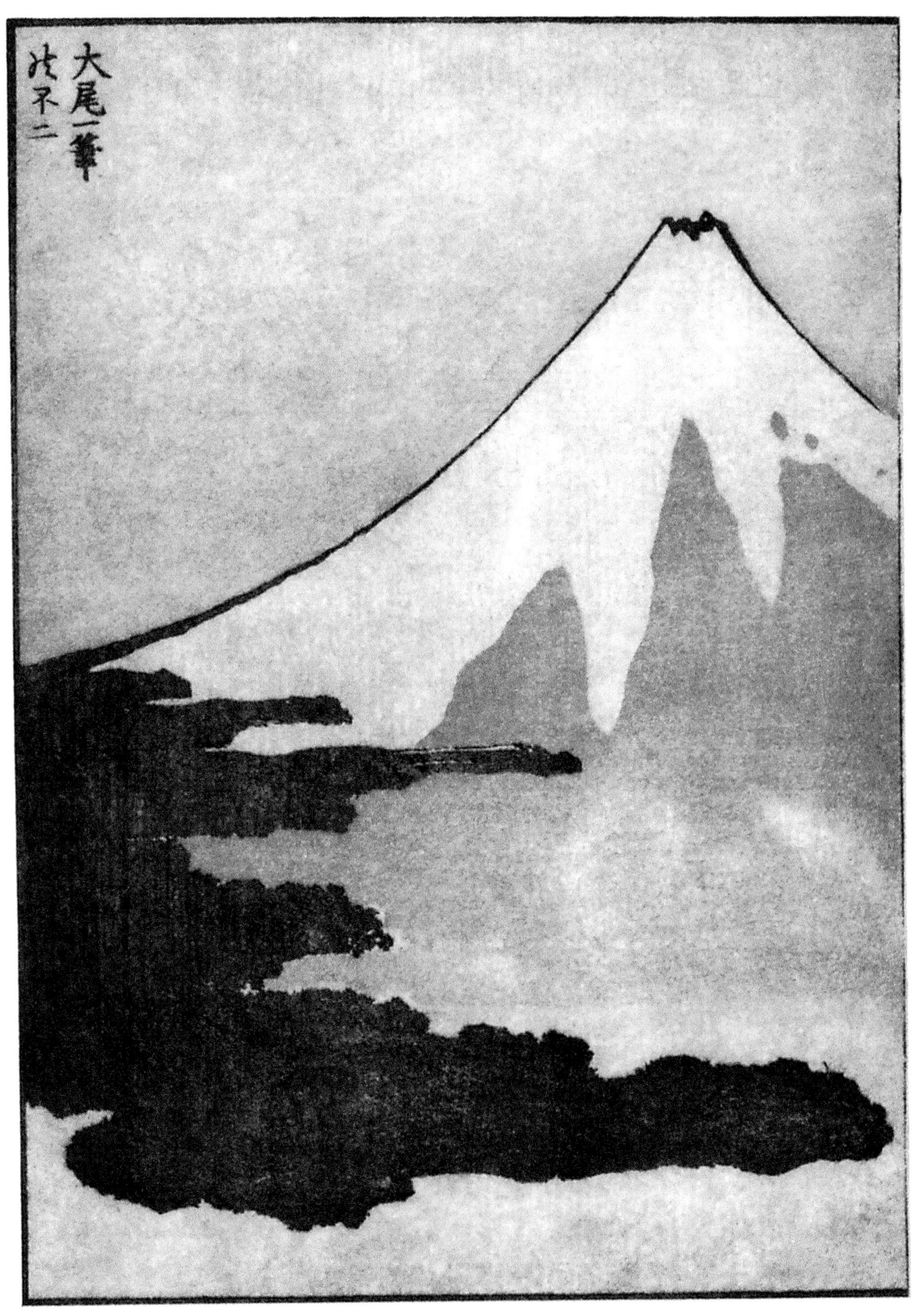

Plate XLI

DESCRIPTION OF FUJISAN.

*(From the 56th Volume of the "Wa-kan-sanzai-dzuye.")**

TO the South the Mountain looks towards the province of Suruga, Eastwards over the province of Sagami, to the North and West over that of Kai, to the North and East in the direction of Idsu. The fame of it is unequalled throughout the three realms (Japan, China, and India). Viewed from any of the surrounding eight provinces it presents the same appearance, its summit reminding the beholder of the eight-petaled "renge" (lotus flower, commonly known in Japan as "hachisu-bana," or "hasu-nohana"—*Nelumbo nucifera Gaert*). But viewed from front the peak is seen to be trifid. If you want to have an exact notion of the form of the Mountain, take a ten-ribbed fan, roll this conewise, and draw out one rib, so as to leave nine remaining, then place the fan with the truncated apex upwards, and you have the Mountain before you. I should here remark that from Hakone the peak looks five-pointed, from Hara four-pointed, from Yejiri trifid.

Tradition tells us that the manifestation of Fuji took place in the fifth year of the reign of the Emperor Kôrei (B.C. 285). In one night it was formed. The earth gaped in the province of Ômi, and Lake Biwa or Ômi was thus produced, the soil thrown

* Chinese and Japanese Pictorial Encyclopædia of the Three Powers, *i.e.* Heaven, Earth, and Man, an illustrated work in about 80 volumes, published A.D. 1714, and founded upon the Chinese "San ts'ai t'ó hwui."

up becoming the Mountain in Suruga. [The histories, however, say nothing about this event, and in my opinion—that of the author of the Sanzai—the whole story is little worthy of belief.]

Throughout the four seasons snow lies upon Fuji; from the hollow summit smoke constantly issues. In shape Mikami-yama in Ômi is like to it, but is on a smaller scale, as if indeed it had been made by the hand of man.

Jofuku (Sü Fuh)* of Shin in China is said to have discovered a mountain in the reign of the Emperor Kôrei, which was Fujisan. Afterwards, Yen no Shôkaku was the first to open up the Mountain to men. [Although the Mountain is said to be situate in Suruga, the " tori-i " of the principal approach is on the Northern slope in the province of Kai.]

The first shrine on the Mountain was erected by the Emperor Heijô, or Heizei, in the first year of the period Daidô (A.D. 806). Every year from the sixth month (July-August), crowds of pilgrims make the ascent, having first refrained from fish and flesh, and used ablutions for a hundred days. The people of the province of Ômi, however, need only fast for seven days, the reason of this privilege being the fact that the mass of Fuji consists of the soil of that province, from old time a favourite abode of the gods. The slopes of the Mountain are covered

* Sü Fuh or Sü She was a magician of Ts'i (Shantung) in China, in the reign of She Hwang ti, the founder of the Chinese Empire. He was sent, accompanied by a number of youths and maidens, on an expedition in search of the Three Isles of the Genii, which were supposed to exist in the Eastern Ocean. One of these was the Péng-lai-shan, in Japanese Hôraisan, concerning which so many legends are told. Another is known as Ying Chow, on which are found the fairy "che " plant, whereof the manifestation is said to betoken the advent of a wise ruler, and a vast mass of jade, whence trickles a fount of sweet wine, a draught of which bestows immortality upon the drinker. The three isles are inhabited by genii, who nourish themselves upon the seeds ot the " che," and upon the gems with which the islands aie plentifully strewn, while their beverage is drawn from the jade-spring (See Mayer's Chinese Reader's Manual).

with loose stones, which roll down under the feet of the pilgrims during the day, but slip up again in the night-time, so that the Mountain remains unchanged in size and form. Keyaki trees (a kind of elm, *Zelkowa Keyaki*) are plentiful on Fuji.

" Fuji no ne ni
  furi-tsumoru yuki wa,
  minadzuki no,
  nochi ni kiyete wa ;
  sono yo furitsutsu."

" On the Peak of Fuji
  falls the snow in heaps,
  past the godless month,*
  vanishes the snow away,
  and the same night falls again."

Yoshika of the Capital tells us in his Chronicles that Fuji is situate in Suruga, and forms a truncated cone, rising high into the sky, of immeasurable loftiness, the like of which is not to be found described in any book. The exalted peak seems to touch Heaven: for the broad and deep foundations we must search the abysses of the ocean. Many days are needed to travel round it, and learn all its beauty and splendour. So huge is Fujisan that the receding traveller, as he looks back upon it from time to time, imagines that he is still in the near neighbourhood of the Great Mountain, which genii have made their haunt.

"Ame tsuchi no
  wakareshi toki ni,
  kami† sabite,
  takaku tôtoki
  Suruga naru
  Fuji no takane wo !
  Ama no hara
  furisake mireba,
  wataru hi no
  kage mo kakuroi,
  teru tsuki no
  hiikari mo miyedzu,

" Heaven above from earth below
  when of yore the god did part,
  lonely in his majesty,
  Fuji loftily sublime,
  o'er Suruga's land uprose!
  O the tow'ring peak of Fuji !
  All the vasty plain of heaven,
  when with upturn'd glance men scan it,
  and of sun on daily path
  all the lustrous light is hidden,
  and of nightly radiant moon
  not a shimmer may be seen,

---

* The eleventh month, when the gods are supposed to be absent in council settling the affairs of men for the ensuing year.

† So in the " Wa-kan-zansai-dzuye." In the Riyaku-ge edition of the "Manyôshiu," in the first part of the third volume of which the ode will be found, the text is in this place slightly different, but the variation seems to be merely in the direction of a more archaic form of language.

shira-kumo mo	still round thee shall white clouds hover,
i-yuki habakari,	scarcely daring stay or go;
tokijiku zo	still the snow shall fall upon thee,
yuki wa furikeru,	ever falling ceaselessly;
katari-tsugi,	still shall men the story tell,
iitsugi yukan,	ever men the tale shall tell,
Fuji no takane wa ! "	lofty peak of Fujisan ! " *

In the "Six Sections" of Gisho (a Chinese miscellany) we read: " There is a Mountain to the east-north of the capital of Japan, some thousand 'li'† away, which people call Fuji, also Hôrai. It is very steep, three sides thereof rising sheer out of the sea, and flames and smoke are belched forth from its lofty summit. At noontide various treasures are manifested to the climber under his feet ; after nightfall music may be heard on the Mountain. Here came of old Jofuku, and gave to the Mountain the name Hôrai.   To the descendants of this sage it has been permitted to use the surname Hata."

When Hideyoshi (Taikôsama) overran Chôsen (Korea), one of his warriors, by name Katô Kiyomasa, took prisoner in Orankai (a district of Korea) a man named Serutôsu, a Japanese of Matsumaye in Yezo, who some twenty years previously

---

* The above ode is from "Manyôshiu" (lit. The Myriad Leaves), the oldest collection of Japanese poetry extant, compiled in the early part of the ninth century of our era.   The argument of the ode, of the quaint beauty of which the above version gives but a faint idea, seems to be that, even though the sun and moon should pass away, the white peak of Fuji shall never cease to gladden the eyes of men.   The archaic language of the "Manyôshiu," and the frequency of wordplay—a defect, it must be acknowledged, rather than a beauty—in the odes contained in it, render their successful translation a matter both of difficulty and uncertainty.   As a kind of antistrophe there follows in the "Manyôshiu" the following "tanka :"—

"Tago no ura ni,	"Tago's famous strand I seek,
uchi-dete mireba	now my eyes let wander round,
mashiro no zo	O ! the dazzling of the whiteness—
Fuji no takane ni,	on the lofty peak of Fuji
yuki wa furitsutsu."	gleams the newly-fallen snow."

† The Chinese " li " is here meant, not the Japanese " ri," which is much longer.

had been cast by a storm upon the Korean coast. On being brought back by his capturer to his own country, he assumed the name of Gotôjirô. According to his statements Fuji was as visible from the Korean shores on a clear day as if it were in close neighbourhood to them.

In my opinion [that of the author of the "Wa-kan-sanzai"] the common tradition that Fuji is composed of the earth ejected when Lake Biwa was formed, is pure nonsense. A hundred "ri" lie between the lake and the mountain, and how could such a mass of earth be projected so far? Whether the Mountain was suddenly thrown up, or the lake suddenly bubbled into being, neither event is an out-of-the-way one calling for Divine interference. Such take place in various countries. Thus, we read in the "Tôkoku tsugan" (Mirror of Countries to the East, *i.e.* of China) that in the tenth year of Bokuso in Korea, which is the fourth year of Keitoku (A.D. 1008?) in So (Sung in China), a mountain was suddenly thrown up in the sea near Shinra (southern portion of Korea) in manner following :—First, thick mists and clouds appeared, causing an intense darkness, then the ground began to rock, there were noises as of thunder, and there were flashes as of lightning. After a time the mists and clouds cleared away, and revealed a Mountain rising more than a hundred fathoms above the sea level, having a contour of about forty "li," with neither herb nor tree upon it, and its summit was capped by wreaths of smoke. It looked liked a mass of reeking sulphur. A learned man, named Denkiyoshi, was sent to report upon the occurrence, and he visited the Mountain accordingly, and submitted a map of it.

In the reign of the Emperor Kwammu, from the fourteenth of the third month to the eighteenth of the fourth month of the eighteenth year of the period Yenreki or Yenriyaku (A.D. 800), the crater of Fuji belched forth flames, which reddened the sky at night-time. There was a noise as of thunder, the showers of ashes and cinders sounded like rain, and the streams and waters around the mountain were tinged red.

In the reign of the Emperor Seiwa, in the sixth month of the fifth year of the period Jôguwan (A.D. 865), Fuji was again in eruption, the flames rising twenty fathoms high, and illuminating the country for two "ri" (five miles) round; thunderous rumblings and earthquakes were repeatedly heard and felt at the same time. This state of things lasted for more than ten days, and still the fury of the outburst was not lessened, the sides of the crater were torn and riven, sand and stones were showered down like rain; a lake to the west-north was choked up by the cinders and ashes ejected from the crater—the lake was thirty "ri" (seventy-five miles) long and about four "ri" wide (ten miles). The flaming matter penetrated into the province of Kai, and burnt up the hills and rocks; the waters of a lake in the district of Yashiu were made so hot by the burning stones that fell into it that all the fish in it died, and finally the lake itself became dried up, while hundreds of peasants' dwellings were destroyed.

On the twenty-third day of the eleventh month of the fourth year of the period Hôyei (A.D. 1707), in the night time occurred a terrible shock of earthquake, twice repeated; flames and smoke burst forth from Fuji, and cinders and ashes were showered down upon the country for tens of "ri" around, from Okabe as far as Kurihashi. The next day the violence of the eruption abated somewhat; but on the twenty-fifth and twenty-sixth of the same month the eruption was again in full fury; rocks and stones were thrown out of the crater, earth, sand, and slag were showered around in all directions, while cinders and dust covered the country about Hara and Yoshihara to the depth of five or six

feet—even about Yedo five or six inches of fine dust fell upon
the ground.   At the point where the eruption took place, a vast
hole was blown out upon the flank of the mountain, around
which a hump was formed now known as Hôyei-san.

How Jofuku of Shun came to Japan, and visited Hôrai-Zan.

In the Shiki (Chinese Annals) we read that the ruler of Shin
(Ts'in) sent Jofuku (Sü-she or Sü-fuh*) over the sea in quest of a
divine medicine.   He wandered about for several years without
finding the object of his search.   Much money was thus
uselessly expended, and, fearing punishment, he told a lie.
" Your vassal," he said, " saw the god of the sea, and he spoke
thus unto me : ' Thou comest from the Emperor of the West,
what wantest thou ? '   And I answered, ' For years have I sought,
but sought in vain, the elixir of life.'   The god replied, ' The
gifts thou bringest show but scant piety in thy master ; even
shouldest thou behold the elixir thou canst not obtain it.'   I then
fared on to the south and east, and came to the mountain of
Hôrai.   There saw I a shrine and a watch-house, wherein was a
being of brazen hue, and shaped like a dragon.   From him there
went forth a radiance that illumined the heavens.   I bowed with
reverence, and asked, ' What gifts shall I lay at thy feet ? '   And
the answer was, ' Bring noble youths and maidens, and artisans
of the hundred arts, and then shall thy prayer be heard.' "
The ruler of Shin,† overjoyed at this report, assembled a

* See above, and also next page.

† Shi-Hwang-ti, B.C. 259-210, sovereign of the state of Ts'in.   He
gradually brought under his sway the feudal states into which China was at
that time divided, and founded the Chinese empire.   He subdued the Huns,

troop of youths and maidens, three thousand in number, and gave them artisans of the hundred arts, and a provision of the five esculent grains (hemp, millet, rice, corn, pulse), and they embarked under the guidance of Jofuku.   In the reign of the Emperor Kôrei they landed in our country near the base of Fujisan.*

and built the Great Wall. But the glory of his reign is much diminished by the ruthless destruction of the ancient literary records, which he effected in the vain hope that after-ages would not look elsewhere than to his own times for the starting-point of Chinese history.

* According to the story of Wasôbiyôye, the Japanese Gulliver (part translated by Mr. Chamberlain, Trans. Asiat. Soc. of Japan, vol. vii. part iv.), Jofuku did not obey his sovereign's behests, but in the course of his voyage in search of the elixir, coming across the Land of Perennial Youth and Life, some sixty or seventy thousand leagues from the shores of the Middle Flowery Realm, chose to remain there. Fuji is sometimes written—as Mr. Chamberlain remarks—with two Chinese characters, signifying " deathless."

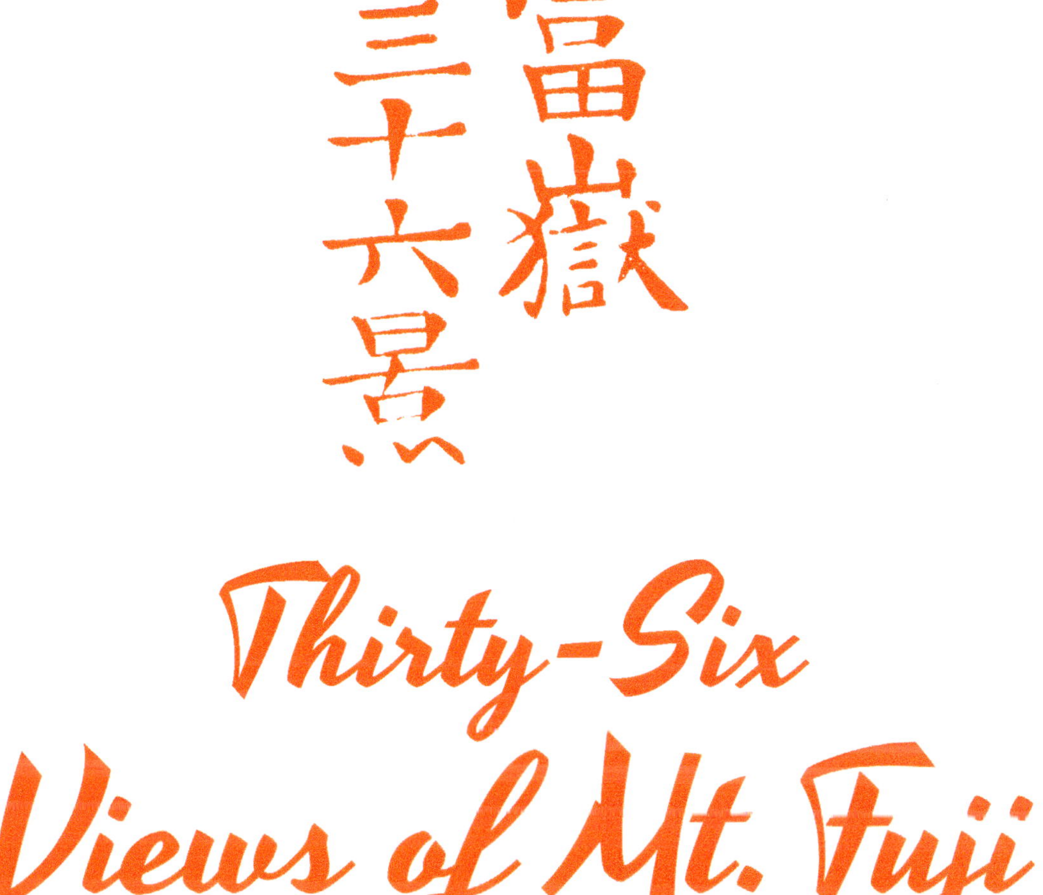

Thirty-Six Views of Mt. Fuji

Katsushika Hokusai

INTRODUCTION

LIKE MOST other print artists of Tokugawa Japan, the man whose greatest work is reproduced in this book was largely ignored by contemporary chroniclers and diarists. A few of his letters and scribblings have been preserved, and he is mentioned in a number of fairly reliable documents, but most of our knowledge concerning him is based on his works and on a remarkable series of semi-apocryphal anecdotes.

His real name was Kawamura Tokitaro, but he is never called this today. During his lifetime he used at least thirty pseudonyms, often employing two or more concurrently. Nowadays, he is most often called Katsushika Hokusai, Katsushika being the name of the district near Edo where he was born, and Hokusai being the pen name under which he first became famous. Sometime around 1816, he gave the name Hokusai to a disciple, possibly in return for a sum of money, and afterward for a number of years he called himself Taito, but his earlier name was so well known that he continued throughout his life to write "the former Hokusai" on many of his prints. During later years, he most frequently called himself Iitsu, Manji, or Gakyo Rojin. The last name, which means "Old Man Crazy about Painting," is perhaps the most meaningful of all his self-chosen epithets.

Hokusai was born in 1760, and since he later referred to himself as the "farmer of Katsushika," it may be assumed that he was of peasant stock. At the age of five or six, he was apprenticed to an engraver, who no doubt taught him much that was of use to him in later life. Beyond this, little is known of his childhood, except that, as he himself later put it, "from the age of six I developed the habit of drawing the shape and appearance of things."

At eighteen, he became a pupil of Katsukawa Shunsho (1726-1792), a leading print designer, who like so many of his confrères, specialized in portraits of Kabuki actors and scenes from the Kabuki stage. Hokusai obviously pleased Shunsho, for after no more than a year of study, he was allowed to take the name Katsukawa Shunro, which indicated that he had been adopted into the master's artistic lineage.

Hokusai continued to belong to Shunsho's school until around 1786, when, according to most accounts, he quarreled with his teacher and was forced to leave. Later he seems to have been connected in some tenuous way with Kano Yusen, who belonged to the government-supported Chinese school of painting, and with Tawaraya Sori, who painted in the decorative style of Ogata Korin (1658-1716). Presumably he learned at least the rudiments of the traditional styles of painting, but their effect upon his own style can easily be exaggerated. It is fairly common for Japanese admirers to attempt to make Hokusai "respectable" by associating him with the great painting schools of the past, but whatever he may have absorbed from the Kano and Korin styles, he was through and through a painter of *ukiyoe*, "pictures of the floating world," that exquisitely plebeian form of painting created to please the common townspeople of Edo.

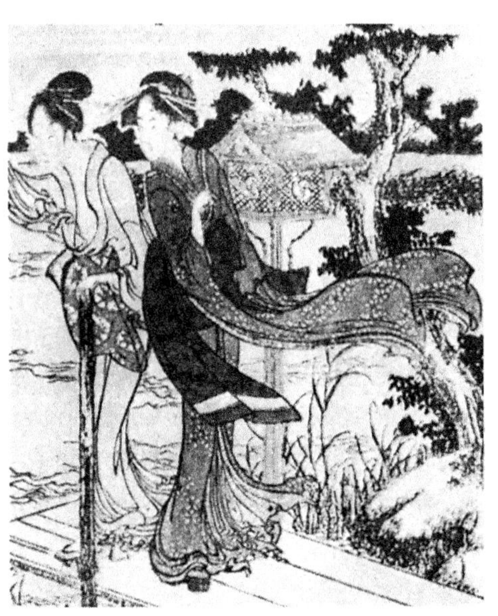

Fig. 1   Page from A View of Famous Places in Edo, *published by Hokusai around 1800.*

242

In general, the works produced by Hokusai before his fortieth year have little to distinguish them from the usual woodblock print of this period. A certain stylistic development is recognizable, but had Hokusai died at forty, he would have been classed among the miscellaneous artists working in the shadow of Kiyonaga, Utamaro, and Shunsho. Though he turned out perfectly competent pictures of beautiful ladies (*see Figure 1*), little of the genius he later displayed is to be found in them.

After 1800, however, his illustrations for novels by the renowned writer Bakin brought him a measure of fame, and with the publication of the *Hokusai Manga,* a series of heterogeneous printed sketches which eventually ran to fifteen volumes, he began to display that fiery originality that led to his later success.

Success, it seems, was what Hokusai wanted. He was given to spectacular displays of his powers—great public performances in which he drew pictures 120 feet high, using a broom for a brush. In a more private gathering, it is said, he astonished the shogun by painting a piece of paper blue, allowing a rooster whose feet had been coated with red paint to scamper across it, and presenting the result as a painting entitled "Maple Leaves on the Tatta River." During his long lifetime, he is thought to have produced no less than 30,000 designs or paintings, in what must have been one of the most colossal one-man attempts to curry public favor ever known.

The stories about Hokusai reveal a proud, independent nature, restless and eccentric, prone to iconoclasm. He is supposed to have rejected the blandishments of high-ranking feudatories, insulted prospective patrons, and refused all gifts in order to avoid the obligations they entailed. In a period when peasants, at least, were supposed to be bound to the land, he changed residences ninety-three times—he is quoted, in fact, as having said it was easier to move than to do the house-cleaning. Not all of these stories are true, of course, but to have inspired them Hokusai must have had the same willful, volatile temperament that is so often found in other artistic geniuses.

Coupled with his native ability was a constant urge to find some-

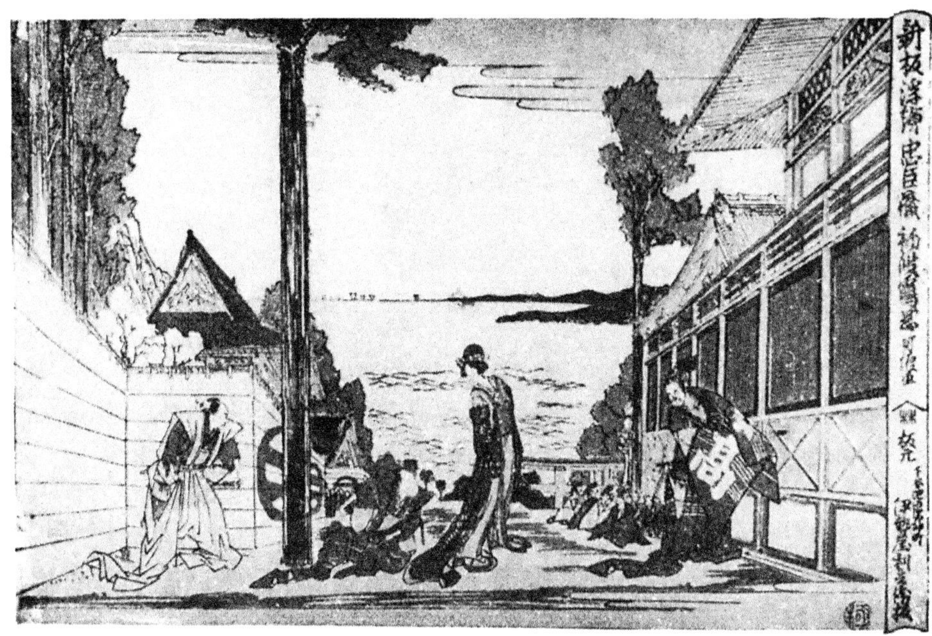

Fig. 2   Section from Chushingura, published in 1798.

thing new.   Throughout his life he continued to shift from style to style.   The most important change in this respect was doubtless his desertion of Kabuki scenes and portraits of women for landscapes.   This transition began when he was in his late thirties and continued for many years afterward.   Not until Hokusai was sixty did he become what one could legitimately describe as a landscape artist.

He was not the first Japanese print designer to produce landscapes, but his achievements in this field are so much more outstanding than those of earlier artists that he is usually given credit for having invented the landscape print.   It should be observed, however, that he painted relatively few pure landscapes.   Almost always his medium was the "landscape-with-people" form inherited from the art of China.   The same, incidentally, is true of Hokusai's greatest rival, Hiroshige.

Hokusai's landscapes were in part a logical outgrowth of his earlier work.   This can be seen from an early series of prints based on the celebrated Kabuki drama *Chushingura (see Figure 2)*, in several of

244

which the actors are all but obscured by the landscape in the background. In part, however, Hokusai's adoption of the landscape was dictated by circumstances. The fact was that the traditional subjects for woodblock prints had already been practically exhausted, and there was little that a spirited artist could do but abandon them and search for new material.

Another factor was that Hokusai was exposed on the one hand to a contemporary Japanese trend toward naturalism and on the other to actual examples of Western landscape art. Writers often speak of the Tokugawa period as an age of airtight isolation, but, in fact, throughout the epoch the Japanese maintained contact with the Dutch, the Chinese, and, through them, the rest of the outside world. By the early nineteenth century, Japanese scholars, many of them rockribbed Confucianists, had amassed a fairly large body of information about the Occident, and some of it had filtered down to the urban masses to which Hokusai belonged. This fact is extremely significant in any consideration of Hokusai's art, for it is doubtful that his art could ever have come into being had he not felt the force of what is usually called "Western influence." By this it is meant that he knew something of Western realism and the techniques of perspective associated with it.

How he came by his knowledge is uncertain, but one may assume that he was acquainted with experimental imitations of Western art made by Shiba Kokan (1738-1818) and his followers, and he certainly saw Dutch copper-plate prints introduced to Japan by way of Nagasaki. The title page to a

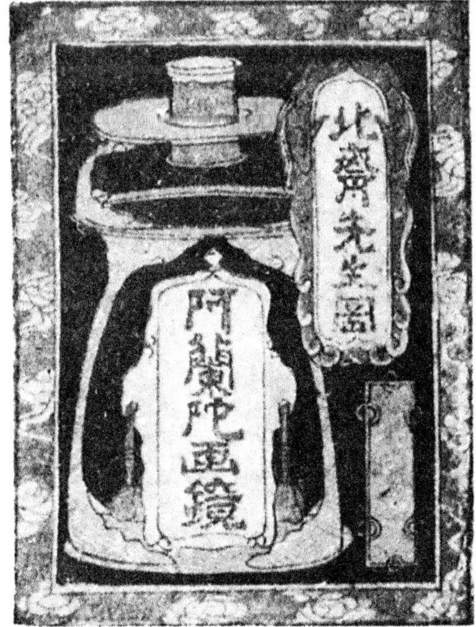

Fig. 3 *Picture on wrapping for* Eight Views of Edo, *with title reading* Oranda Gakyo (Collection of Dutch Paintings).

series entitled *Eight Views of Omi,* which Hokusai made around 1800, states that the prints were made from copper plates, though in fact they were simply woodblock prints in the copper-plate style.

In *Eight Views of Edo,* published around the same time, Hokusai not only attempted to achieve an Occidental effect of distance, but even went so far as to put frame-like edges around the borders, and on the wrapper of the series he printed a title which,

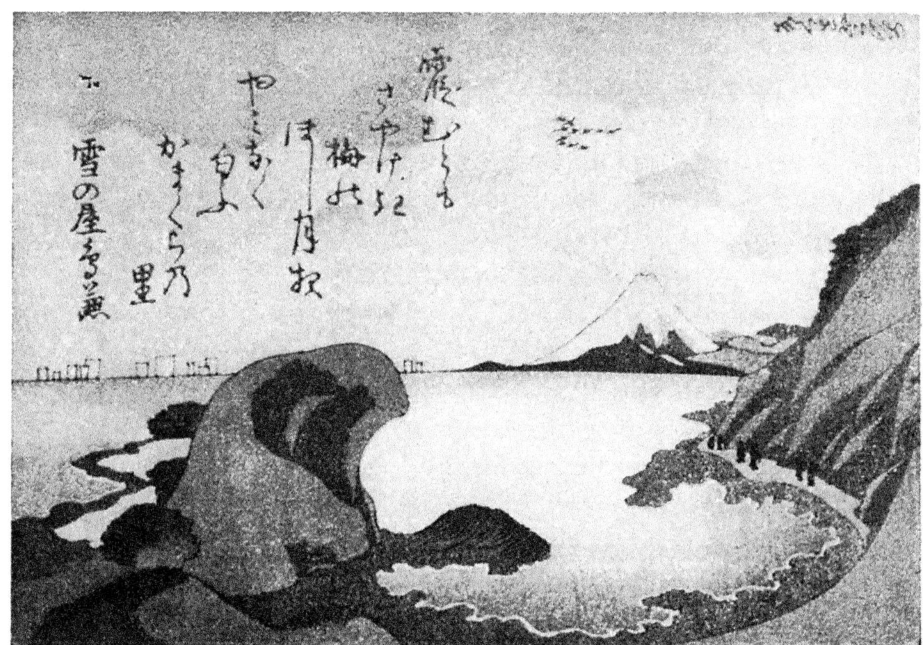

Fig. 4   *Scene at Kamakura, printed around 1800, with signature written sideways at upper right.*

translated freely, means "Collection of Dutch Pictures" (*see Figure 3*). In several other prints he signed his name sidewise, so that the appearance was much the same as that of Occidental writing (*Figure 4*).

A glance at these prints reveals that Hokusai's attempt to use the Western style was none too successful. It remained for him to digest realism, to learn to employ its tenets where they aided his over-all composition and discard them when they did not. For at his best,

Hokusai, though more realistic than most earlier Japanese painters or print designers, would never allow accuracy with regard to size, timbre, or location to interfere with the composition of his prints. His point of view is implicit in his oft-quoted dictum to the effect that everything in the world can be reduced to combinations of angles and curves. This, it will be noted, is the view of a designer, not a realist. Everyone who has ever thought about it knows it is a great over-simplification, but it is nevertheless an entirely valid point of departure for a painter who wishes to arrange three-dimensional fact into a two-dimensional design.

The date of the *Thirty-six Views of Mt. Fuji* is not completely certain. The series was apparently published print by print over a period of several years. One key to the problem lies in the three signatures Hokusai affixed to the various prints. These are "Hokusai Iitsu," "Hokusai changed to Iitsu," and "Iitsu, the former Hoku-sai" (Japanese: *Hokusai Iitsu, Hokusai aratamete Iitsu, Saki no Hokusai Iitsu;* see *Figure 5*). Since Hokusai first began calling himself Iitsu around 1822, it seems logical to suppose that "Hokusai changed to Iitsu" dates from about this time. Later the word for "changed to" was probably dropped as a matter of course, though as noted above, "the former Hokusai" appeared together with the newer name. This would mean that the prints signed "Hokusai changed to Iitsu" were made around 1822 and were the earliest of the series.

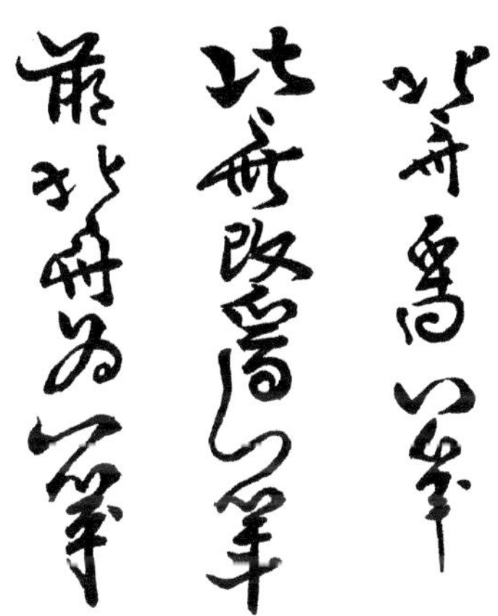

Fig. 5   *The three signatures used by Hokusai in the Fuji series. Right to left:* Hokusai Iitsu, Hokusai aratamete Iitsu, Saki no Hokusai Iitsu.

As it happens, the three greatest prints, "The Red Fuji" (*Plate 1*), "The Great Wave off Kanagawa" (*Plate 24*), and "Fuji in a Storm" (*Plate 38*), all belong to this group. It is therefore tempting to assume that in using the word for "changed to," Hokusai meant to imply that he was a new man, not only in name, but in style. The scope and grandeur of these new prints do indeed mark them off from even the best of his previous works, and they would make an auspicious debut piece for any new name. To be sure, the prints signed "Hokusai changed to Iitsu" also include six others, not all of which could be classed as breathtaking, but still it seems more than coincidental that the "big three" are all signed in this way.

Around 1814, Hokusai made a trip to Nagoya, and it was probably then that he made the sketches for the prints in the Fuji series which deal with points along the Tokaido, or Eastern Coast Route, a

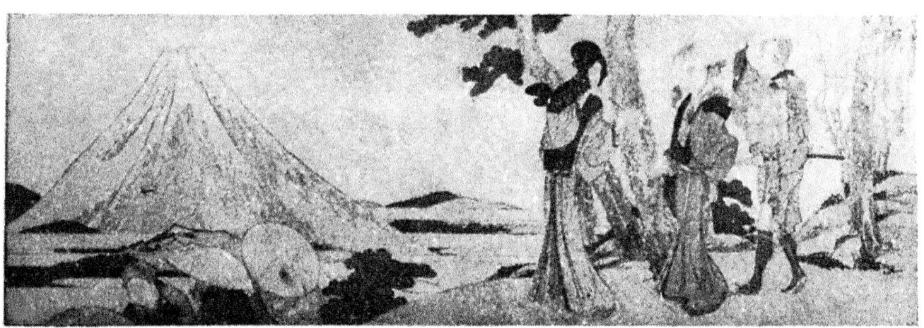

Fig. 6 "Hara" from Hokusai's View of Famous Places on the Tokaido, *published in 1818.*

highway leading from Edo to Kyoto. Around the same time he produced a series called *View of Famous Places on the Tokaido*, in which a number of prints hint at the scope of the *Thirty-six Views*, but are nevertheless still closely related to Hokusai's earlier style (*see Figure 6*).

It has often been recorded that the Fuji prints include an original thirty-six, plus ten later ones showing the "back" (western) side of the mountain. As it happens, however, only seven of the prints are actually designated as being on the western side, and though there are three others with no indication of the location, two of them are among the "big three," which were certainly not later supplements. An important clew to the date of the series is found in an advertisement put out in 1831 by Nishimuraya Yohachi, the publisher of the

248

Thirty-six Views as well as of many other landscape prints by Hokusai:

THIRTY-SIX VIEWS OF MT. FUJI

by Old Man Iitsu, the former Hokusai (One indigo print)
These pictures show Mt. Fuji as it appears from the Coast
of Seven Leagues, from Tsukuda Island and from many
other points. The pictures are all different, and they therefore
serve as a convenient guide for those who are studying the
art of landscape. They are being engraved one by one, a
new scene in each print. The series is not limited to thir-
ty-six, but will eventually extend to one hundred.

This statement, which was actually written in 1830, shows that thirty-six color prints and one print in indigo (*Plate 19?*) were on sale at that time. Furthermore, it appears that Hokusai intended to carry the series on until he reached a hundred prints. Presumably, then, the ten prints not included in the title of the series were simply a continuation, not necessarily distinguished geographically from the earlier ones.

Why, one will ask, did the title continue to carry the number thirty-six? There is no definite explanation, but the most probable supposition is that the number is an allusion to the "Thirty-six Immortal Poets," a numerical category of long standing, which referred to the most famous poets of the Heian period. Any number of scrolls containing thirty-six pictures and poems—one each for each of the Immortal Poets—had been produced, and so far as ancient poets were concerned, the numeral thirty-six meant "all." Consequently, the application of this title to Hokusai's series might well have been intended to mean that the prints included all possible views of the mountain.

If in Japanese thought patterns "thirty-six" meant complete, however, the figure of one hundred meant even more complete, and it will be observed that in 1834 Hokusai published a black-and-white series in book form entitled *One Hundred Views of Mt. Fuji.* Having started out to make a hundred color prints, then, he stopped midway and started all over again on a black-and-white series. It is obvious that either he or his publisher lost interest in the original project, but there remains the question of why. There was probably a combination of several factors. For one thing, it is possible that the cost of a hundred prints in color would have been prohibitive. For another, it may well be that there was no public demand for further additions to the same series. The public of this age, as of any other, was on the whole fickle in matters of this sort, and Hokusai or Nishimuraya may have felt that a brand new series would be more successful. Finally, a noted Japanese expert, Ichitaro Kondo, has suggested that the success of Hiroshige's *Fifty-three Stages of the Tokaido,* which began coming out in 1832, may have moved Hokusai to drop the old series and begin a new one. At any rate, Hokusai did not make any additions to the *Thirty-six Views* after 1831.

All in all, the 1820's were the high point of Hokusai's career, and the rest of his life was by and large a series of disappointments. After 1832 he began to be eclipsed by Hiroshige. He made valiant attempts to keep his fame from slipping away (*e.g.,* not thirty-six, not fifty-three, but a *hundred* views of Mt. Fuji), but to little avail. He turned out picture after picture, some of them excellent, but he could not stave off the stagnation of age. Finally, in 1849, he died, praying, pleading at the time for ten more years to live.

Ninety years, 30,000 drawings, thirty-odd names, ninety-three houses, and he wanted ten years more! Clearly the man knew neither fatigue nor boredom nor contentment. Herein lay his greatness. His was an ever-changing talent, undisciplined perhaps, but enormous in its scope, irrepressible in its enthusiasm, unquenchable in its thirst for recognition. Whatever he did, he did in the grand manner. When he was vulgar, he was vulgar almost beyond belief, but when he was at his best, he was sublime.

He was at his very best in the *Thirty-six Views of Mt. Fuji.*

CHARLES S. TERRY

250

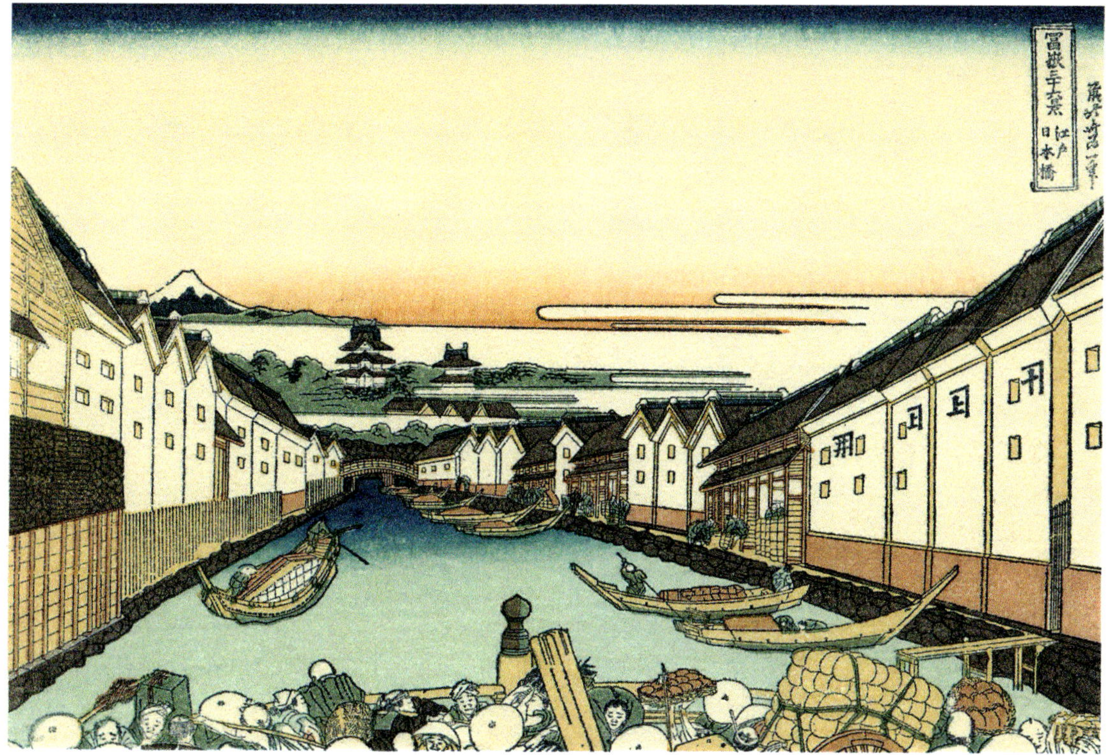

1. *Nihonbashi, Tokyo*

Center of Edo (Tokyo), starting and ending point of all highways leading to and from Tokyo.
Western style perspective is employed in this drawing.

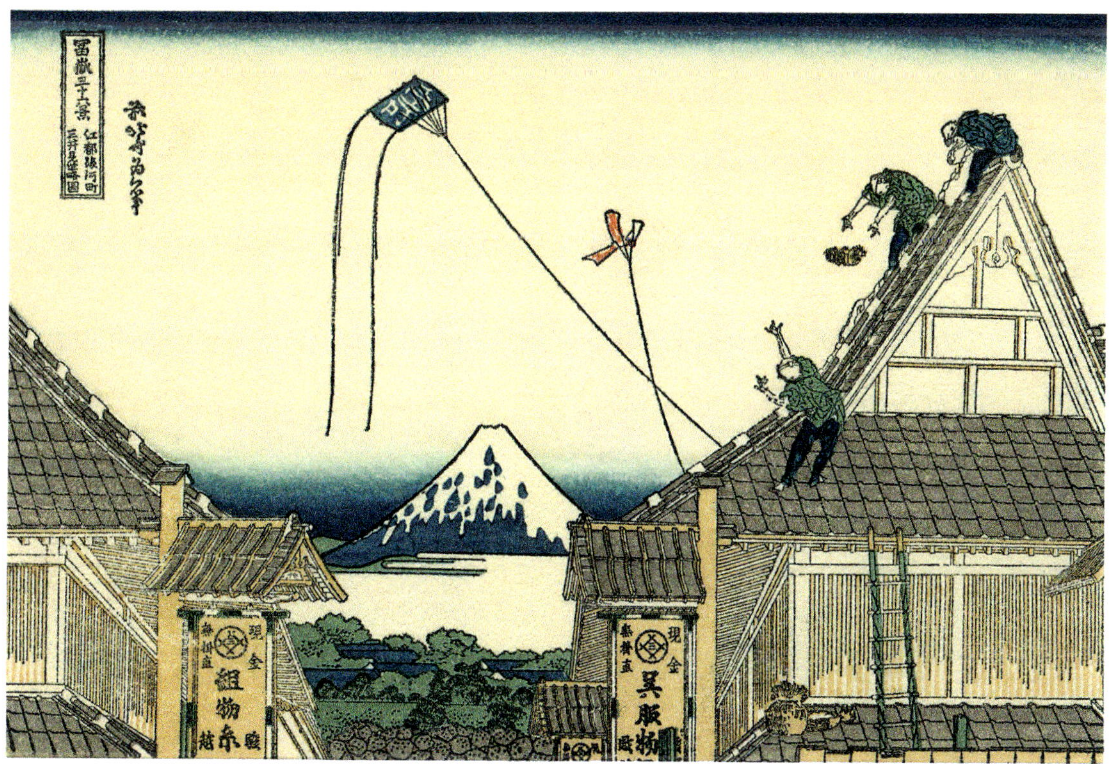

2. *Fuji at New Year's in Tokyo*

Most of the thirty-six views of Mt. Fuji portray the common people busy at their daily tasks.
Hokusai was extremely skillful in catching and depicting actions and movements.

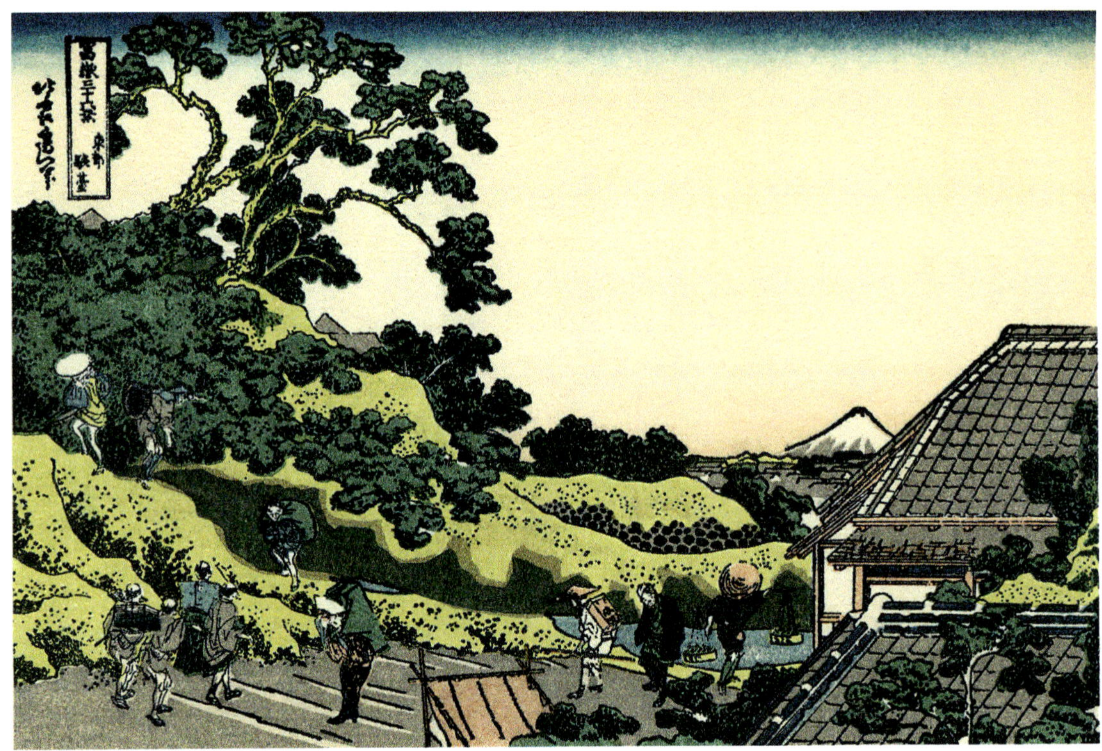

3. *Suruga Hill, Tokyo*

The ascending road where Mt. Fuji can be seen in the glowing sunset,
and the trees in the back and foreground have been done with great care.

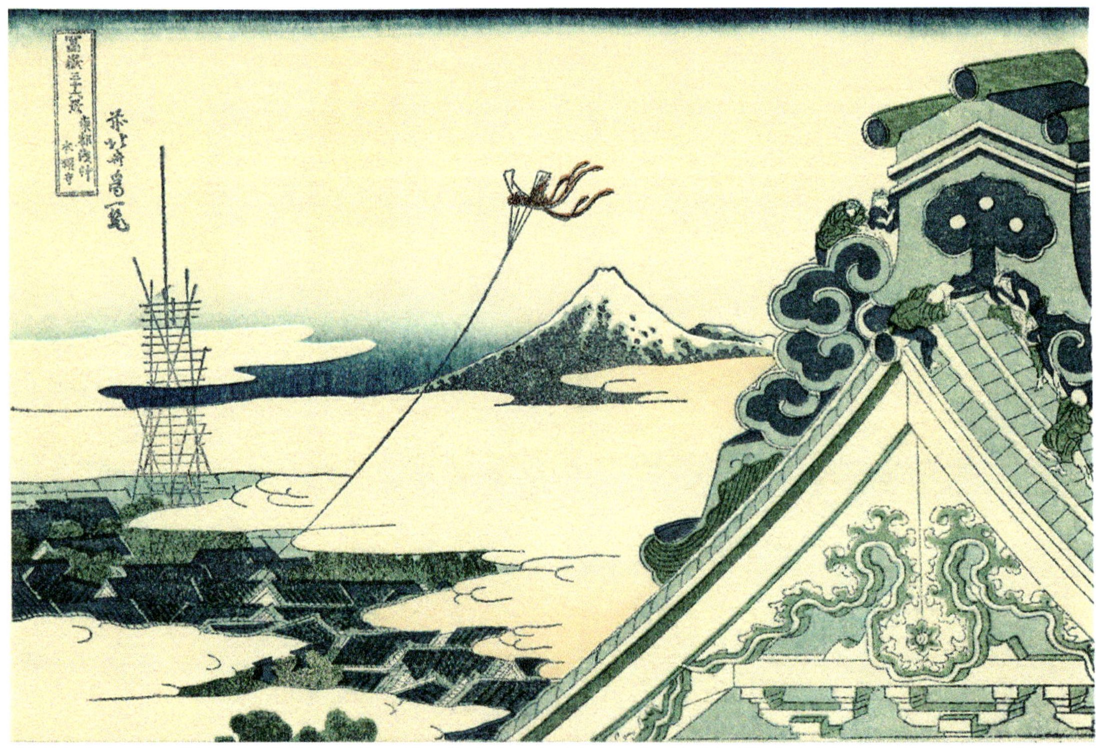

4. *Honganji Temple in Asakusa, Tokyo*

Fuji at New Year's from the largest temple in Tokyo. Fuji here is viewed from a very high point.

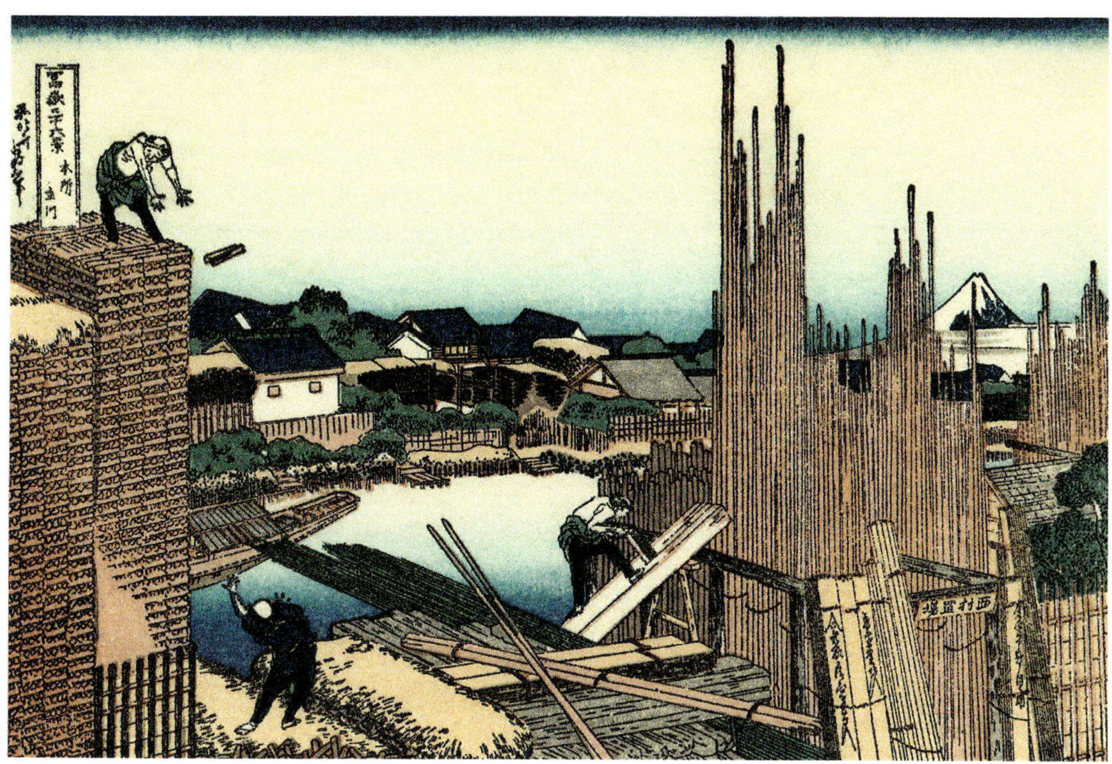

5. *Lumber Yard in Honjo, Tokyo*

Hokusai's clever composition and the carvers' delicate work can be observed in this drawing
of a lumber yard. This composition is very interesting. The vertical lines of lumber,
horizontal lines of the far away houses, and Fuji between the lumber.

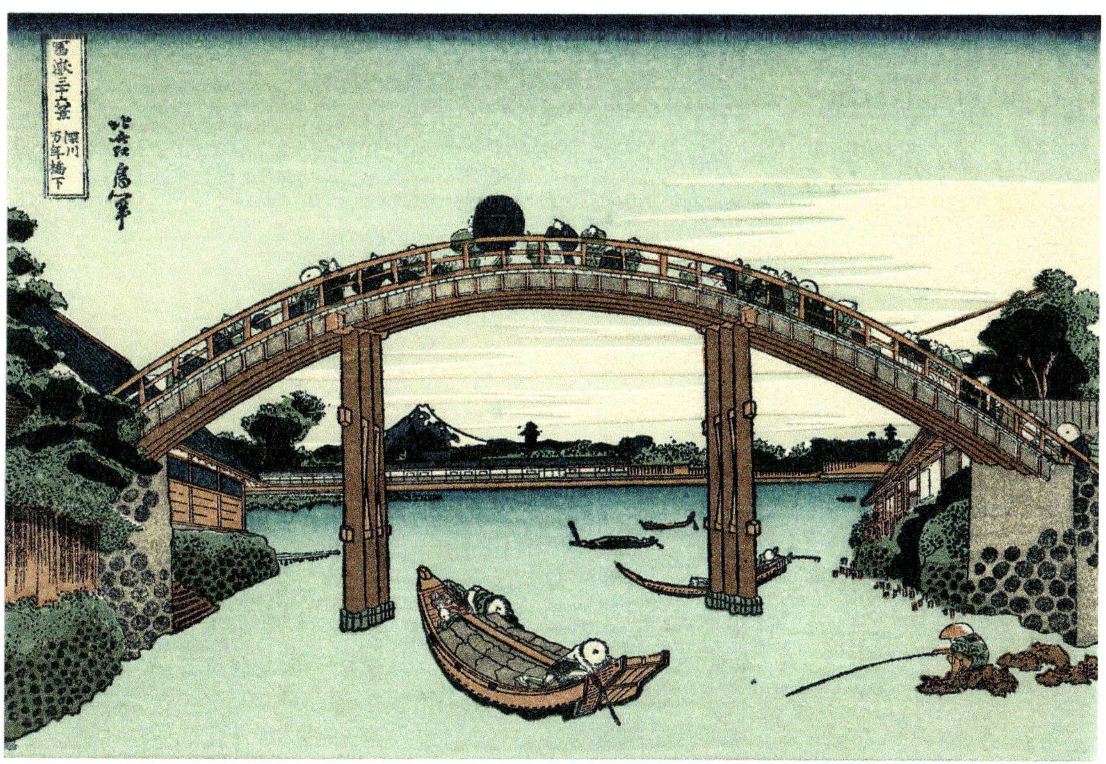

6. *Under Mannen Bridge in Fukagawa, Tokyo*

A bold drawing of the arc-shaped bridge with a slightly exaggerated perspective.

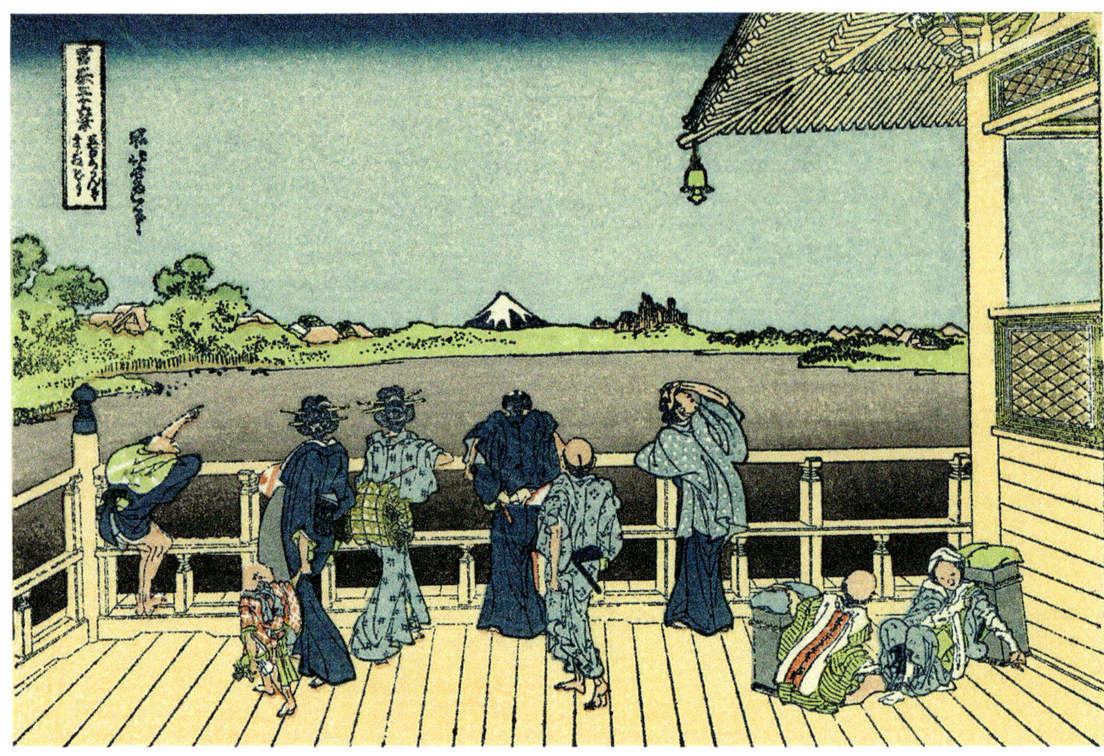

7. *The Temple of Gohyaku Rakan*

The manners and ways of those days can be imagined by this drawing of the people
viewing Fuji from the temple in Tokyo.

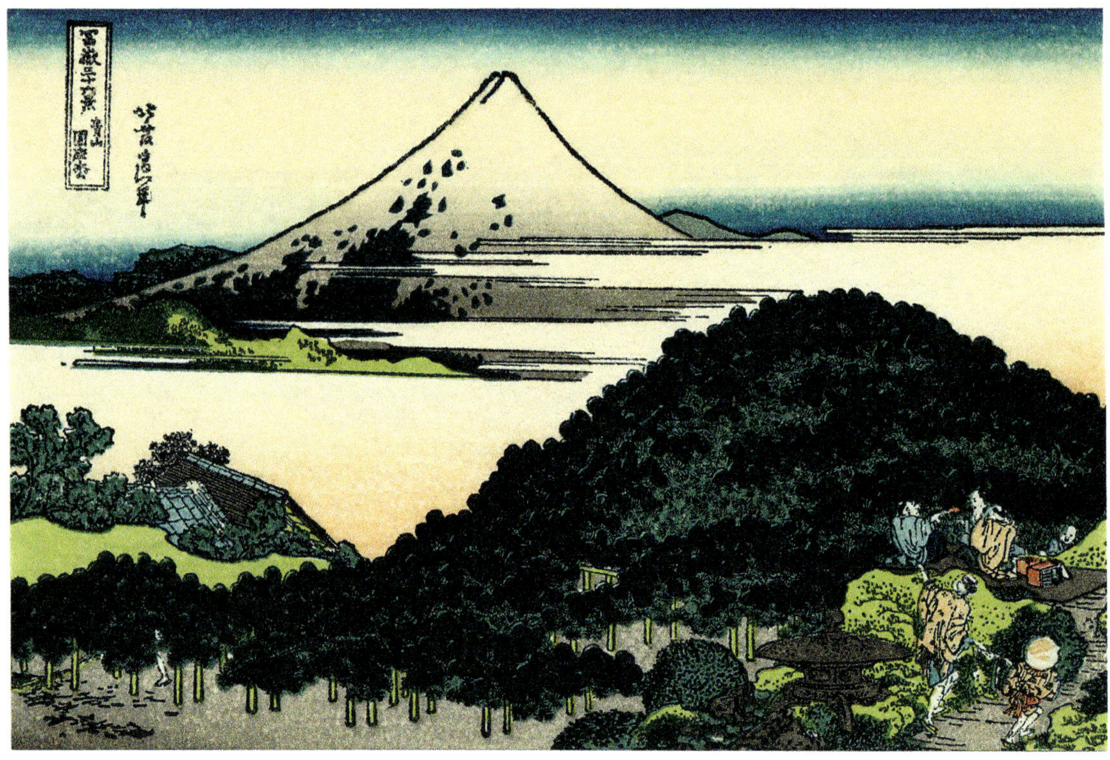

8. *The Old Pine Tree in Aoyama, Tokyo*

This probably refers to an old pine tree in the grounds of a temple in Aoyama, Tokyo.
The density of the leaves has been done with great care.

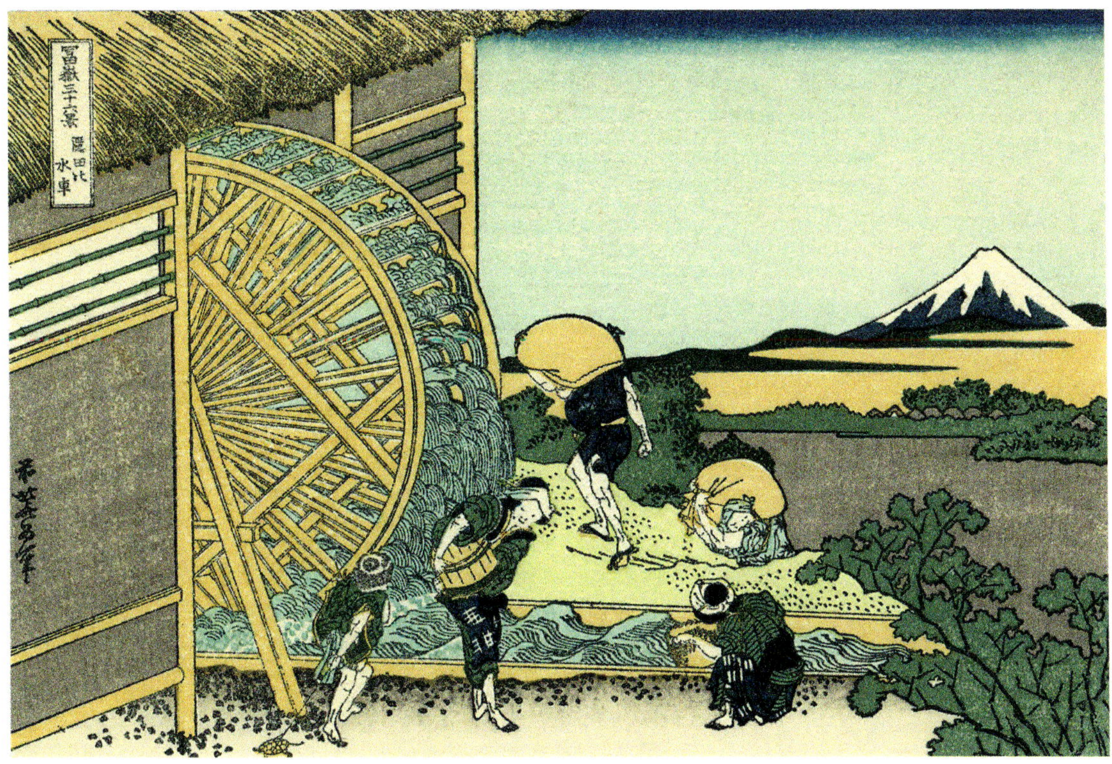

9. *Waterwheel at Onden*

The waterwheel and toiling peasants, the moving water falling from the wheel and flowing on,
are all very well depicted.

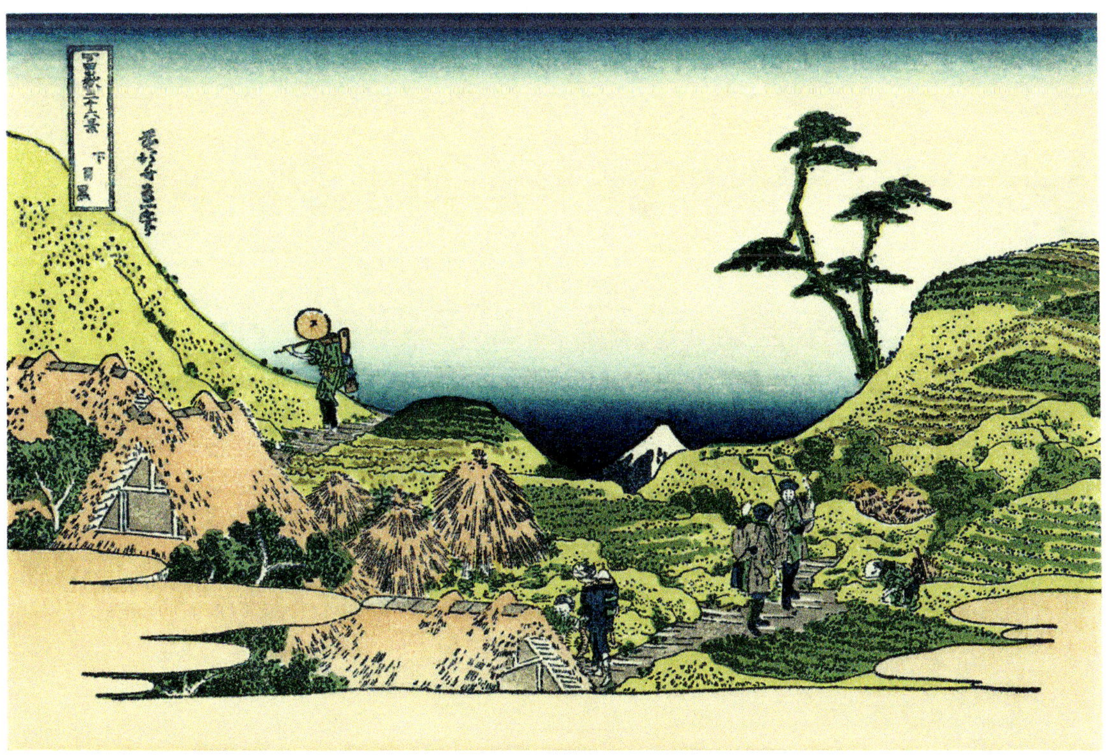

10. *Shimo-Meguro, Tokyo*

A peasant on the slope, resting for a moment, turns to see the beautiful Fuji.
A pastoral by Hokusai.

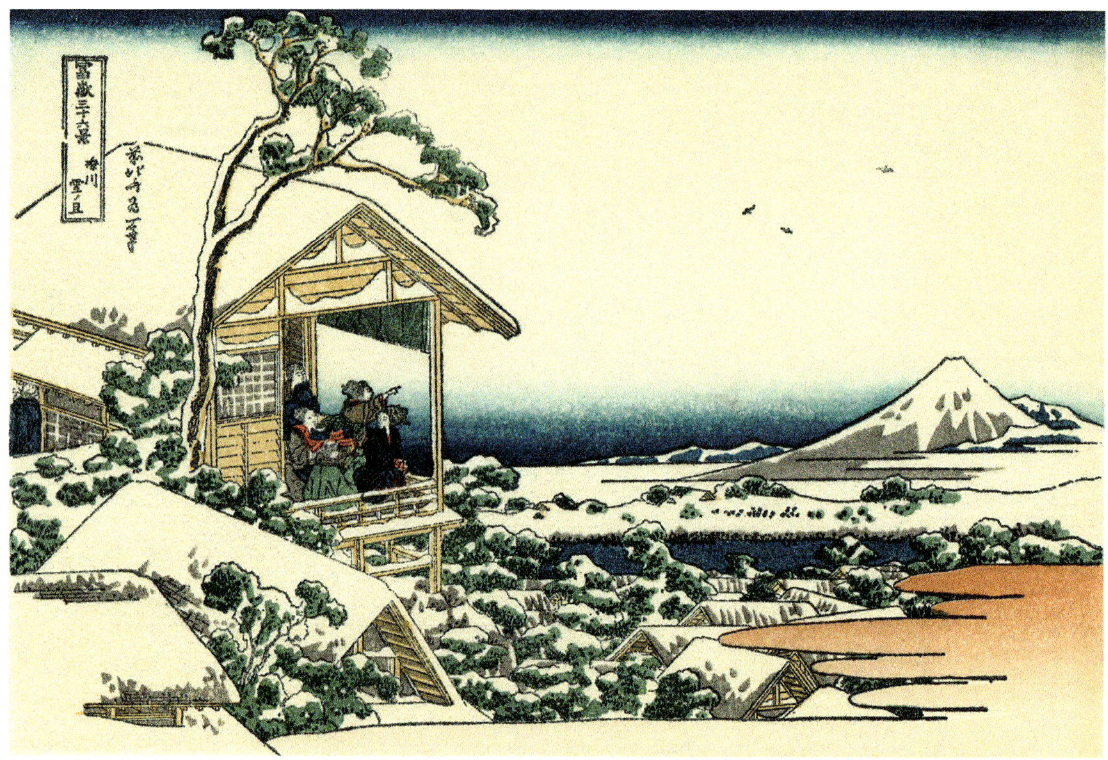

11. *A Snowy Morning in Koishikawa, Tokyo*

Of the thirty-six views of Mt. Fuji, this is the only snow scene. Beautiful Musashino (Musashino Plains) covered with snow, as in this drawing, cannot be seen from today's Tokyo.

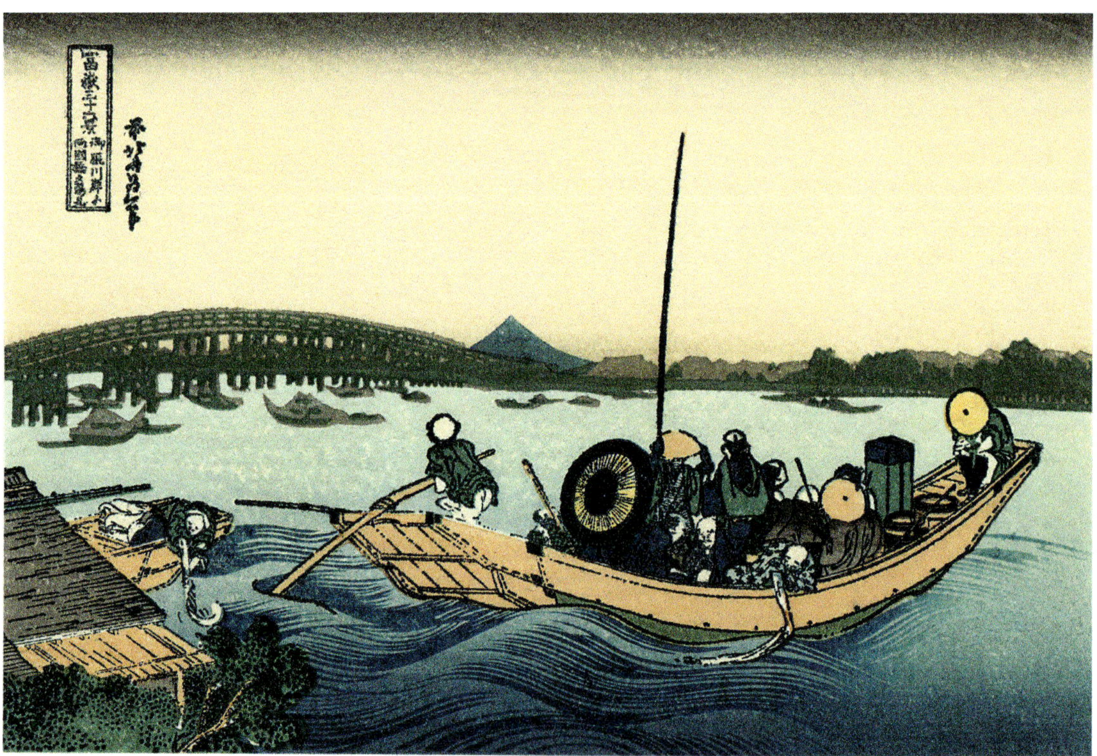

12. *Sunset Over the Ryogoku Bridge*

A scene of the Sumida River crossing with Fuji in blue and clear against the sunset sky. The boatman is admiring its beauty. The ferry is shown carrying people of all classes.

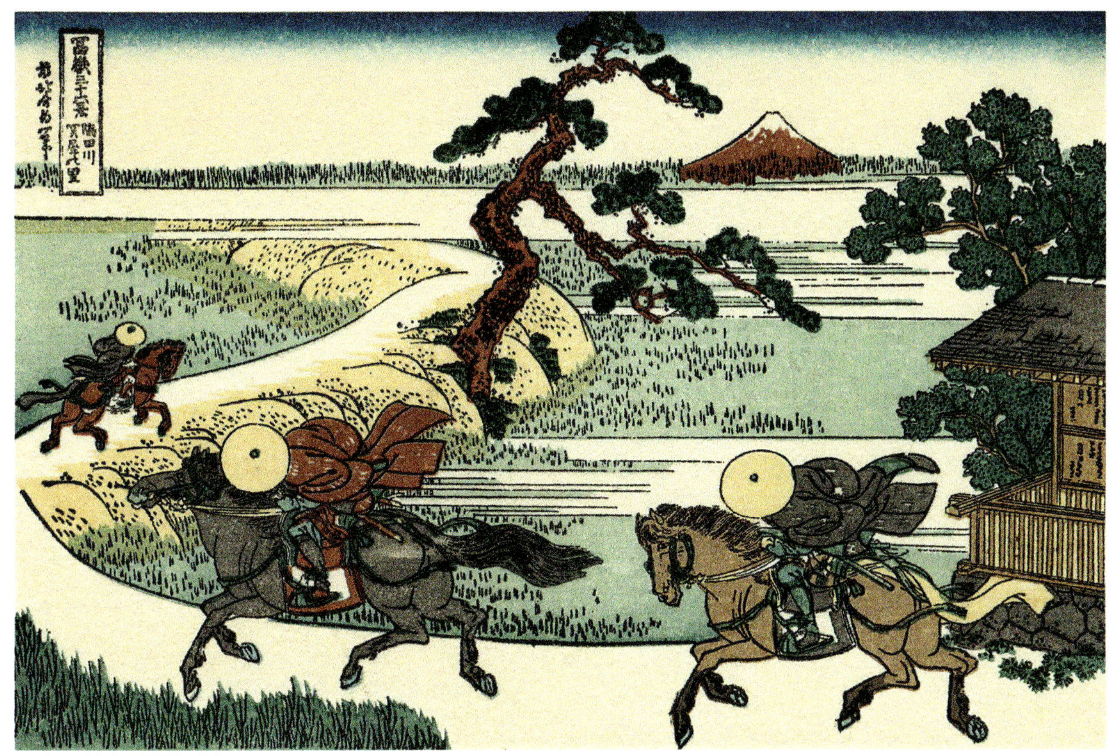

13. *Barrier Town in the Sumida River*

A scenic spot in the upper reaches of the Sumida River.
Three samurai horsemen, apparently on an urgent mission, gallop through the town.

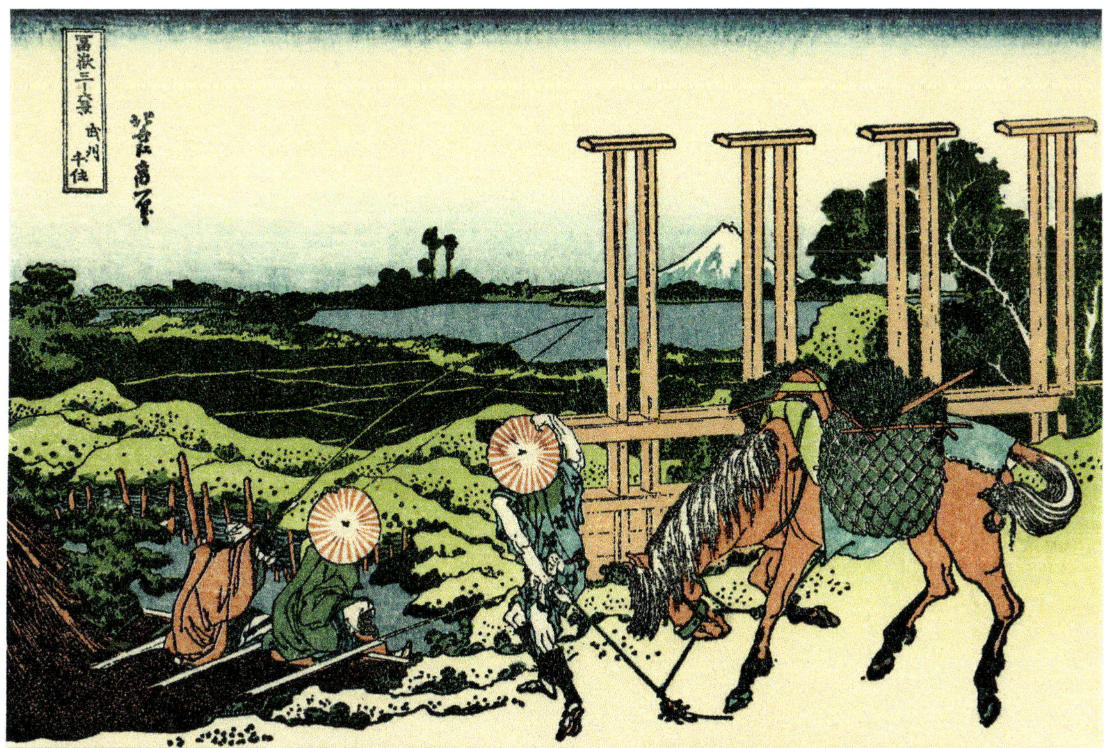

14. *Sunju in Musashi Province*

One of the men fishing, and the horse driver, lose themselves and gaze intently at the beautiful Fuji.
A very peaceful riverside scene.

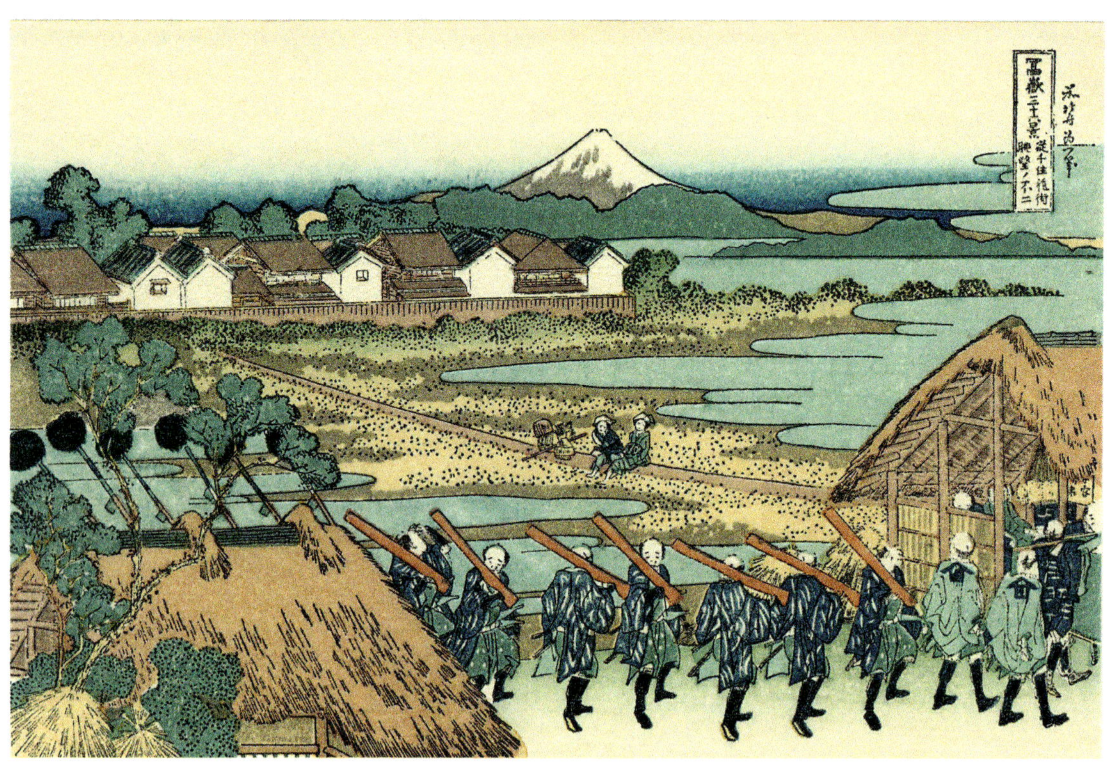

15. *Fuji from the Gay Quarters in Senju*

The scene shows a group of gun bearers, a portion of the procession of a lord, passing by.
The houses in the distance are the gay quarters of Senju.

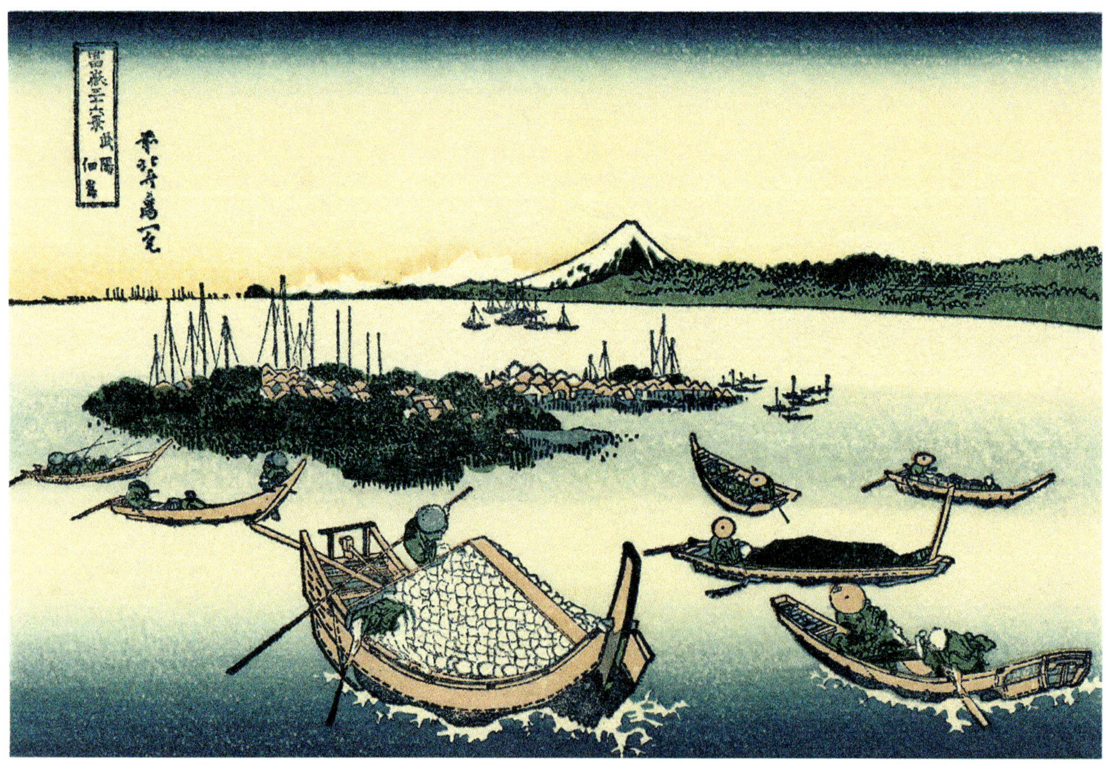

16. *Tsukuda Island*

Tsukuda Island, a fishing village, is the island in the center of this drawing and is famous
for large catches of white bait.

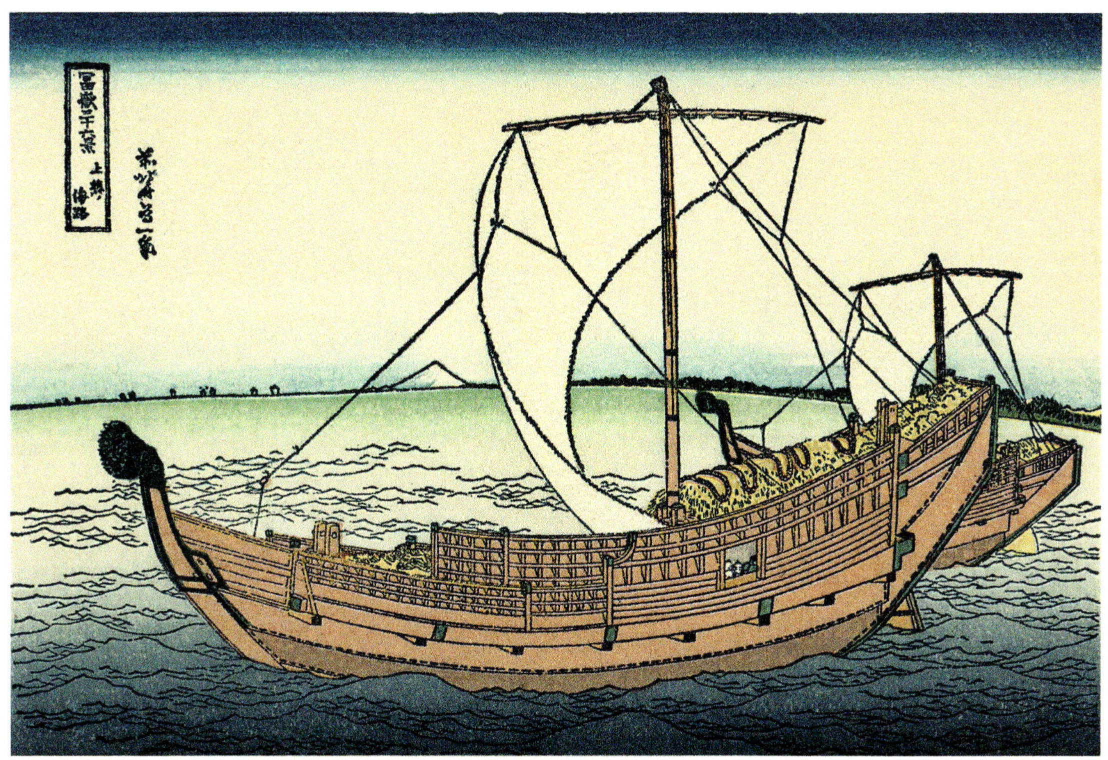

17. *Kazusa Sea Route*

Off the coast of Chiba Prefecture, two boats with spread sails pass by and Fuji can be seen far away.
The horizon has been curved, this being based on the Western theory that the earth is round.

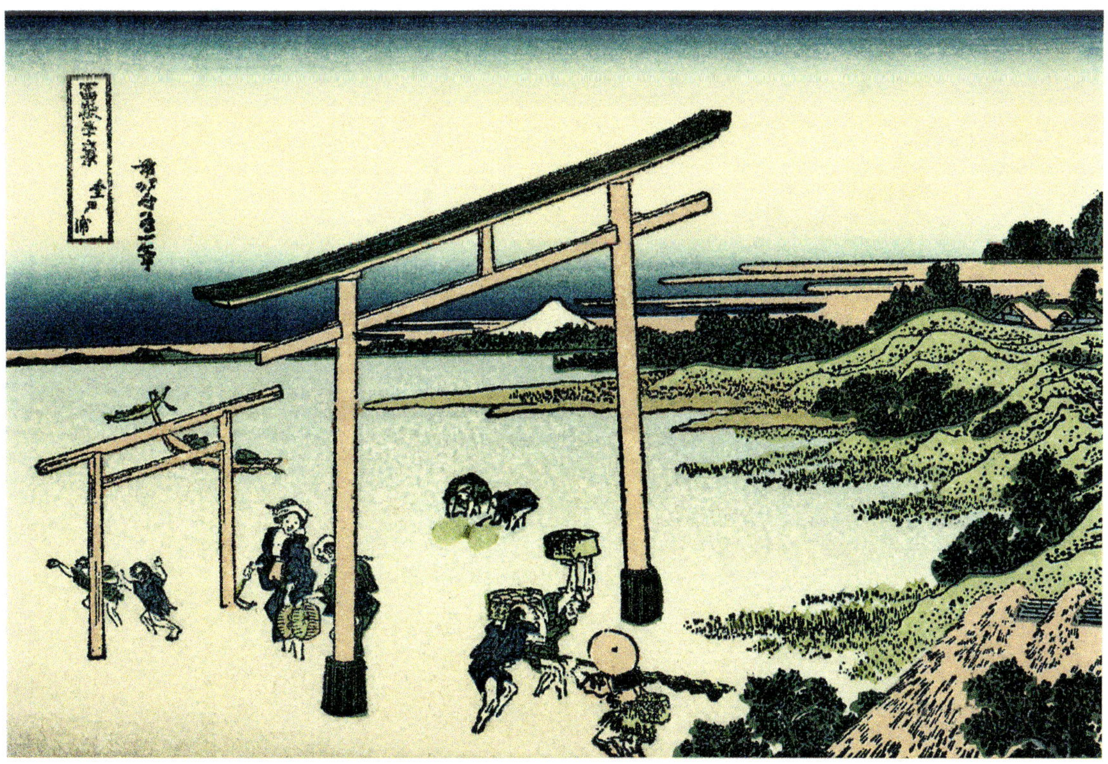

18. *Nobuto Beach, Chiba Prefecture*

This drawing shows people gathering sea shells around the two torii built off the beach.

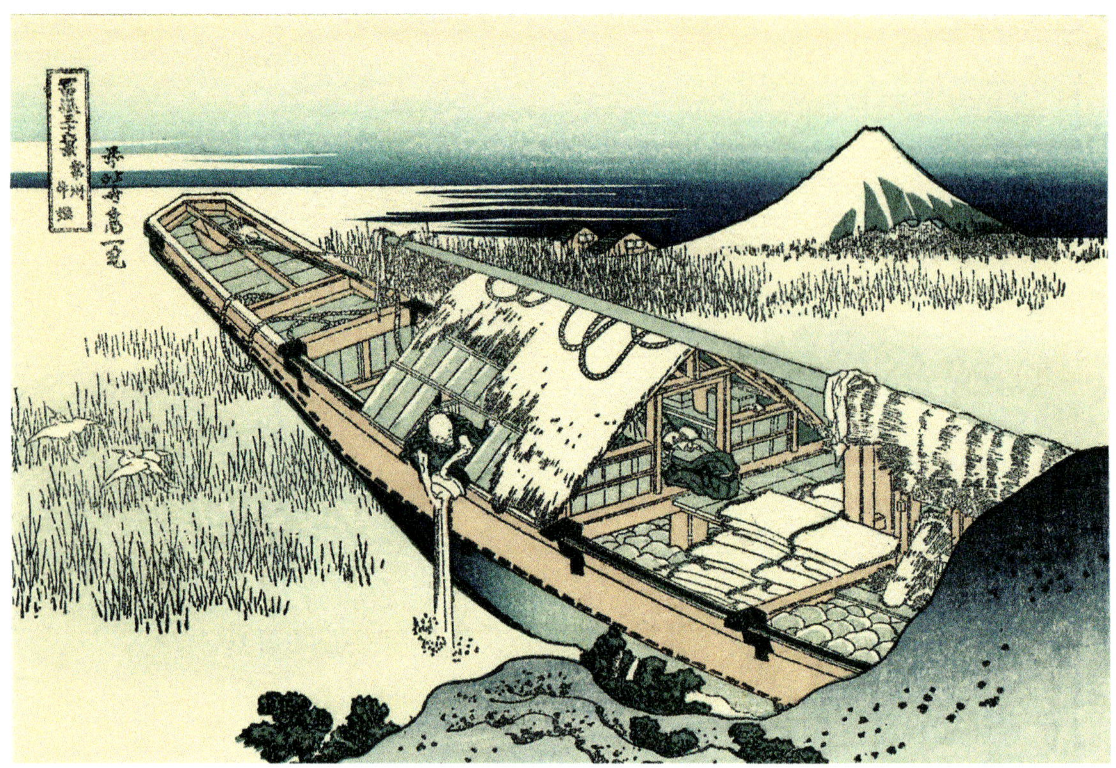

19. *Ushibori, Ibaragi Prefecture*

Fuji from the swamps in Ibaragi Prefecture, done in refreshing shades of blue. The only movements
to break the silence are two herons flying off and the boatman washing rice.

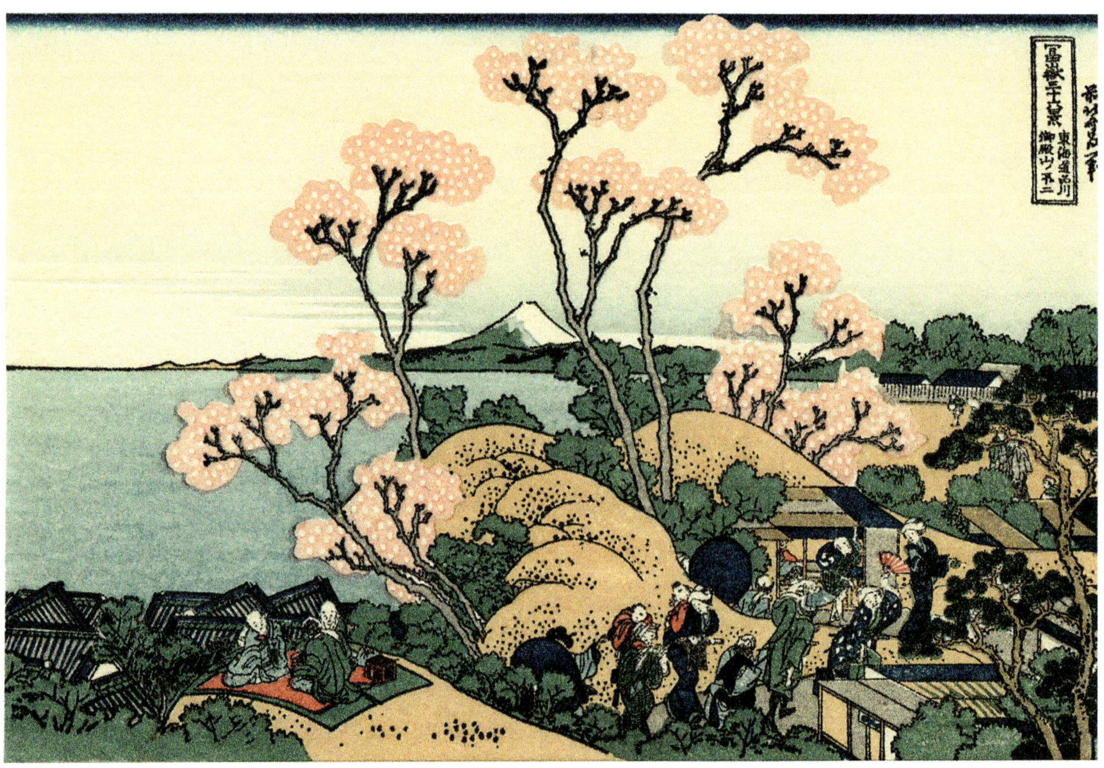

20. *Cherry Blossoms at Gotenyama, Tokyo*

Pictured are people that came to picnic here to see the famous cherry blossoms
of this hill near the bay.

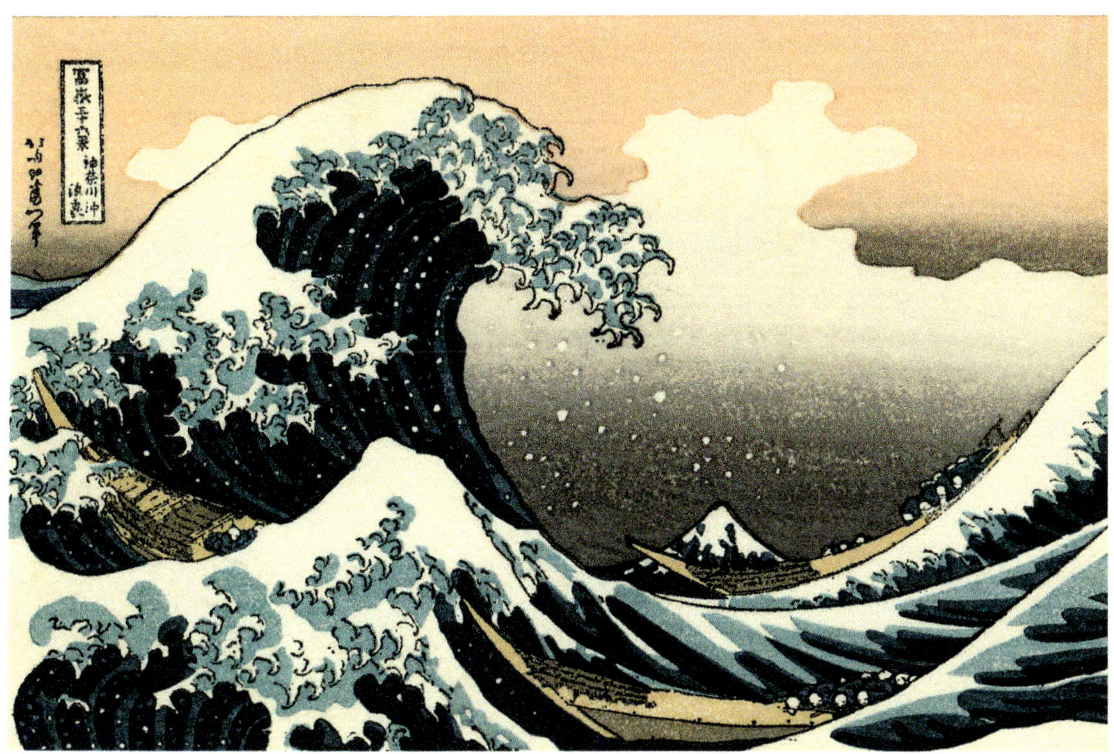

21. *The Great Wave off Kanagawa*

Quiet Fuji can be seen from below the high wave that is bearing down on the small craft.
A remarkable contrast of dynamic violence and serenity. (One of Hokusai's masterpieces).

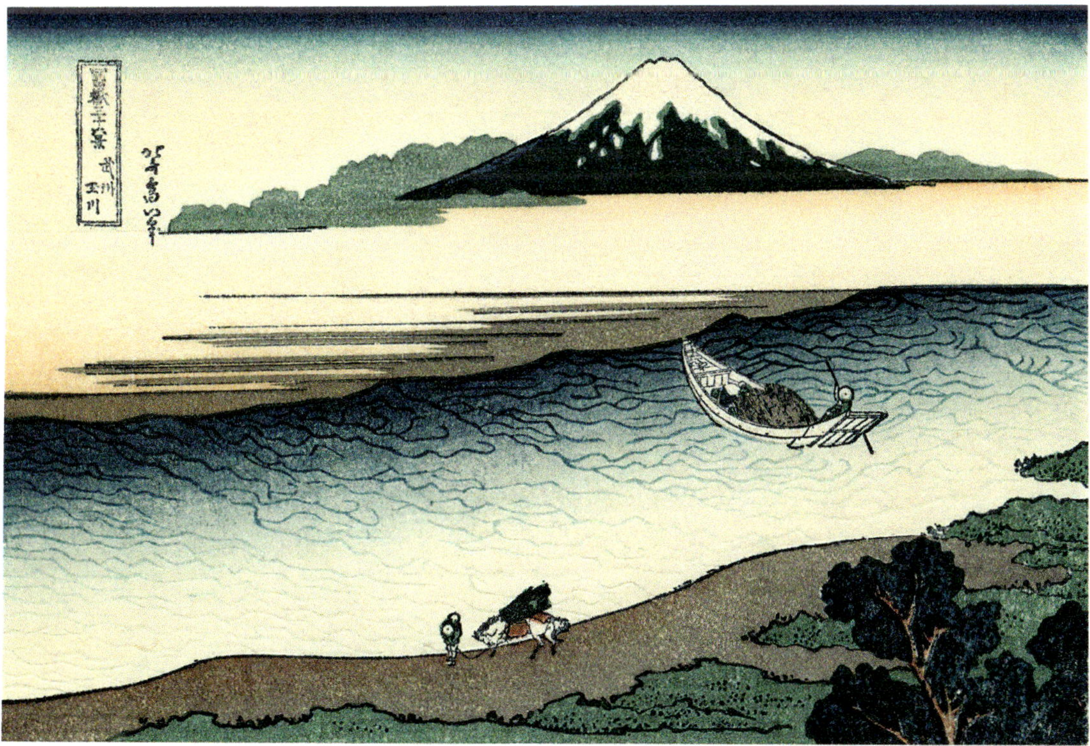

22. *Tama River, Tokyo*

A bridge 198 meters long spanned this river, but after it was washed away, ferry service was begun.
Note the excellent depiction of moving water.

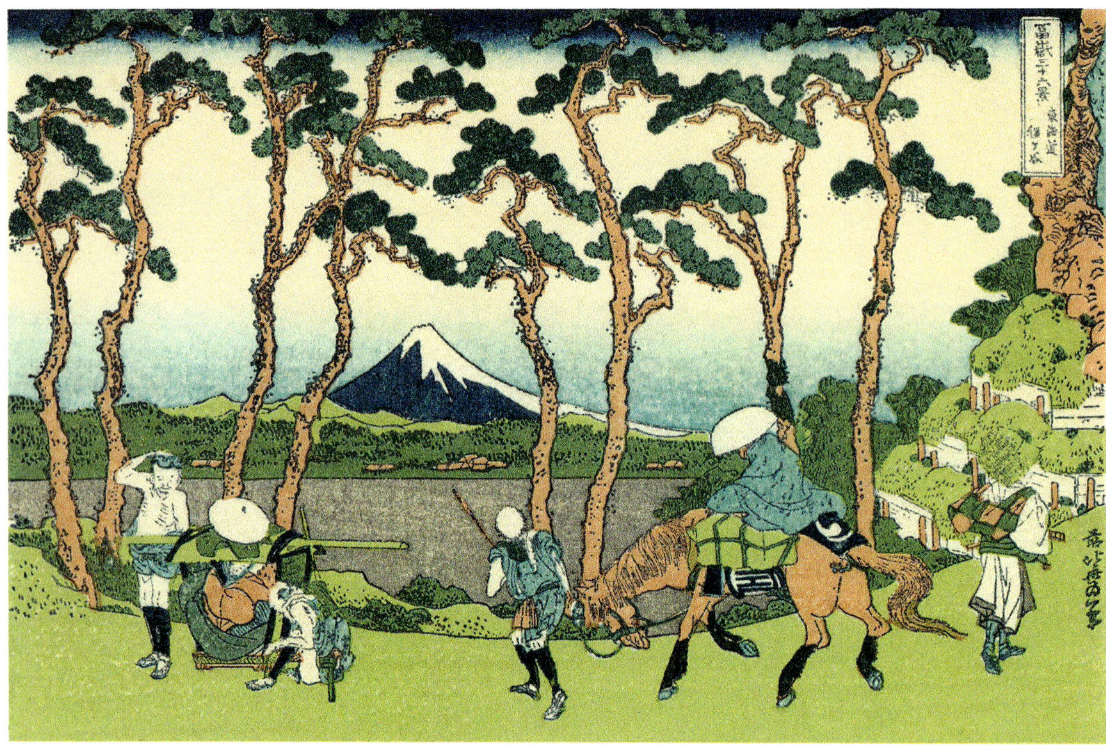

23. *Hodogaya on Tokaido Highway*

The trees shown here are pine trees, however, formerly it is said that fruit trees lined this highway to offer fruit to travelers. These trees also served as barricades in times of battle.

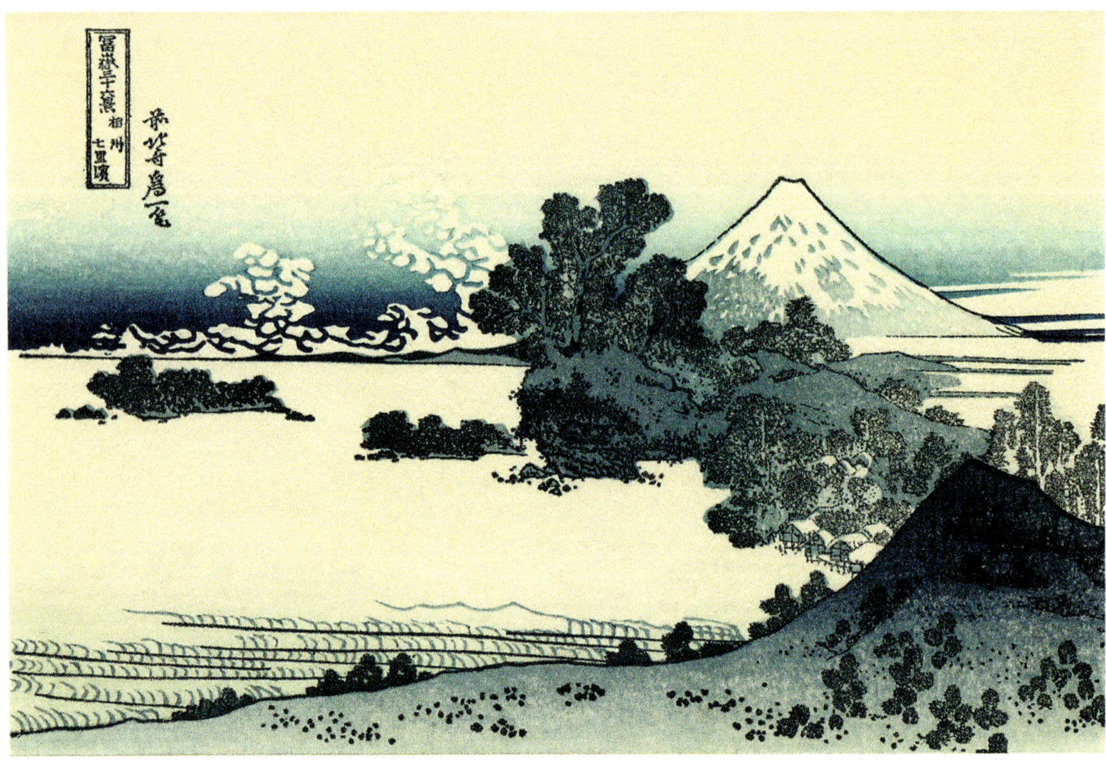

24. *The Coast of Seven Leagues*

Fuji from Kamakura. Cumulus clouds rise from the horizon. On the left is Enoshima.
This drawing is also mostly in shades of blue.

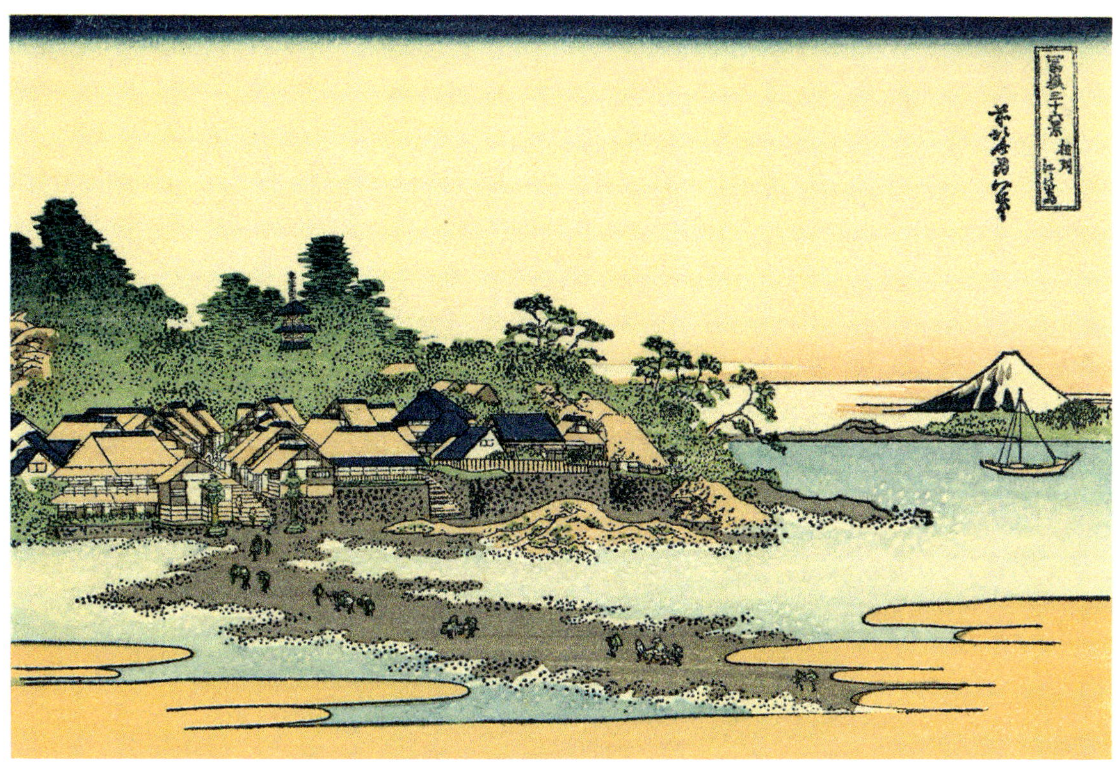

25. *Enoshima*

The temple at Enoshima is famous for a nude sculpture of the Goddess of Fortune.
People thronged this island when festivals were held. They were able to walk the island on low tide,
but went by boats when the tide was high.

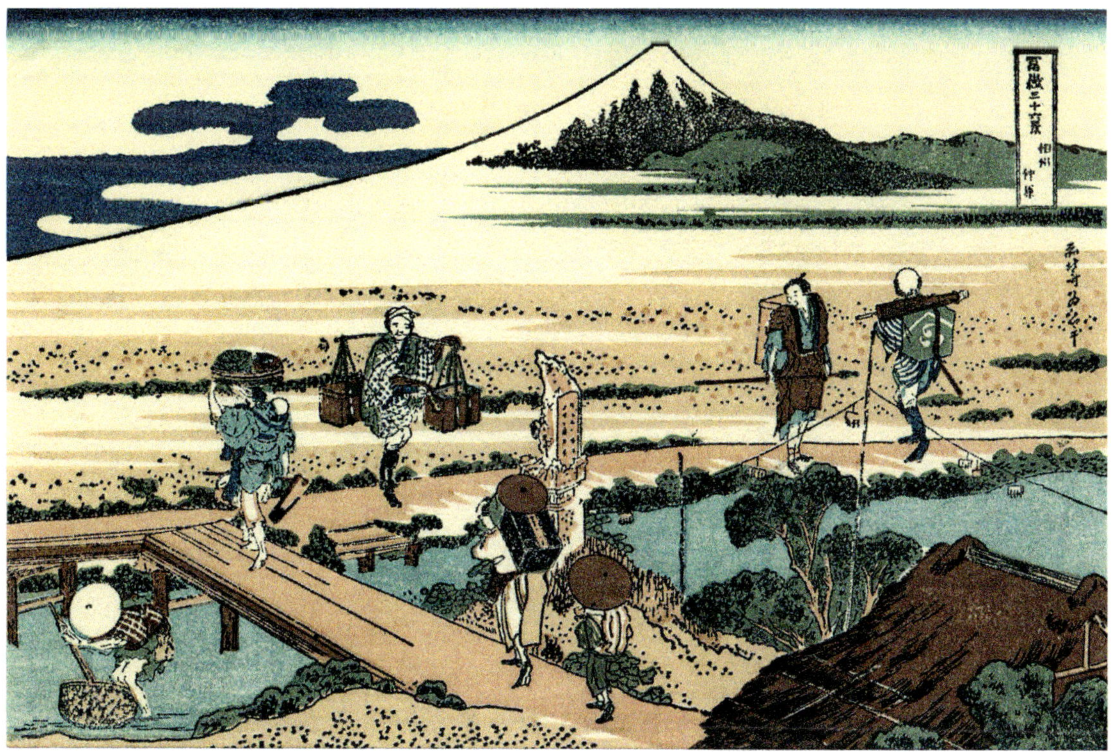

26. *Nakahara, Hiratsuka City*

This drawing is featureless in composition and not too attractive in coloring, however, this is an
actual view of Fuji and in this respect Hokusai's seriousness should be appreciated.

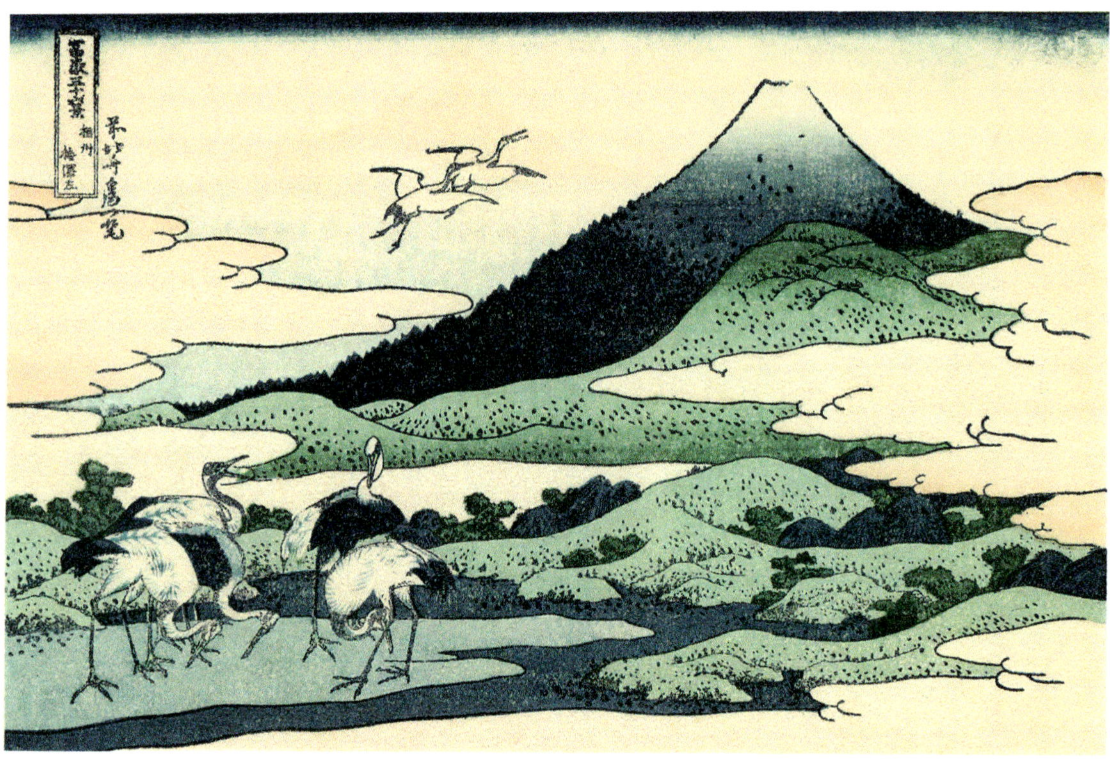

27. *Umezawa Near Oiso*

Apart from a portion of the clouds with a slight reddish tint suggesting dawn,
the entire drawing is in refreshing blue and green.

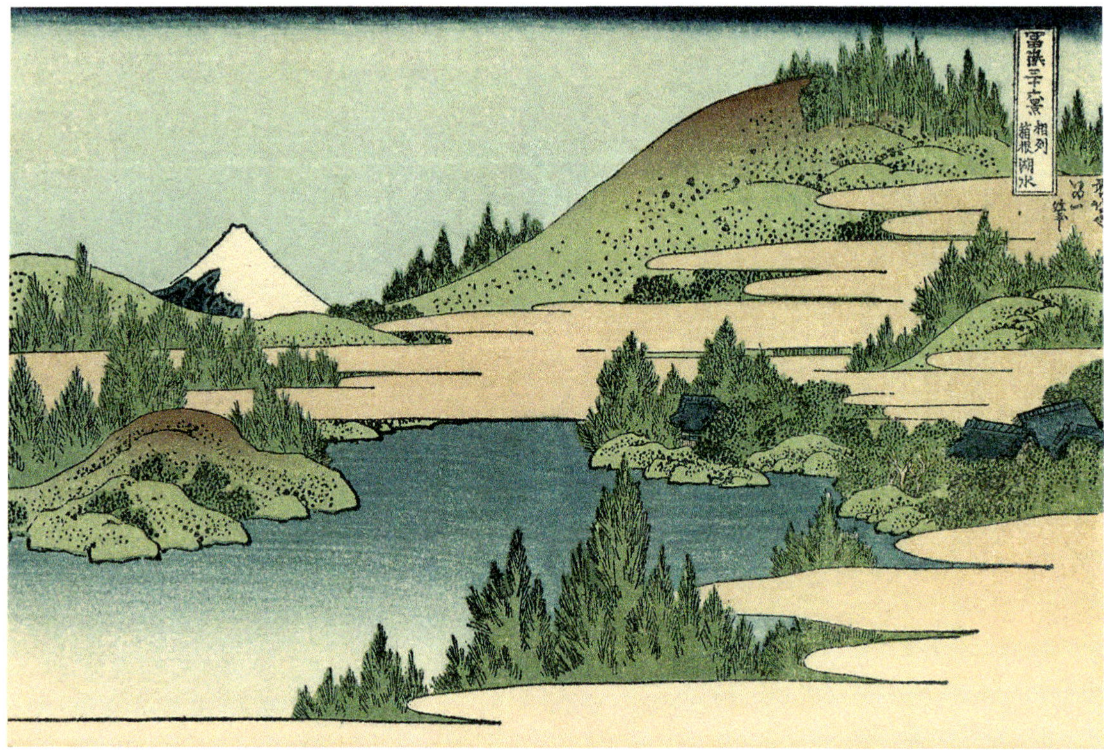

28. *Lake Hakone*

The first thing that a traveler sees upon arriving at the summit, after climbing steep mountain paths
and constantly threatened by thieves, is the beautiful view of the Lake and Fuji.

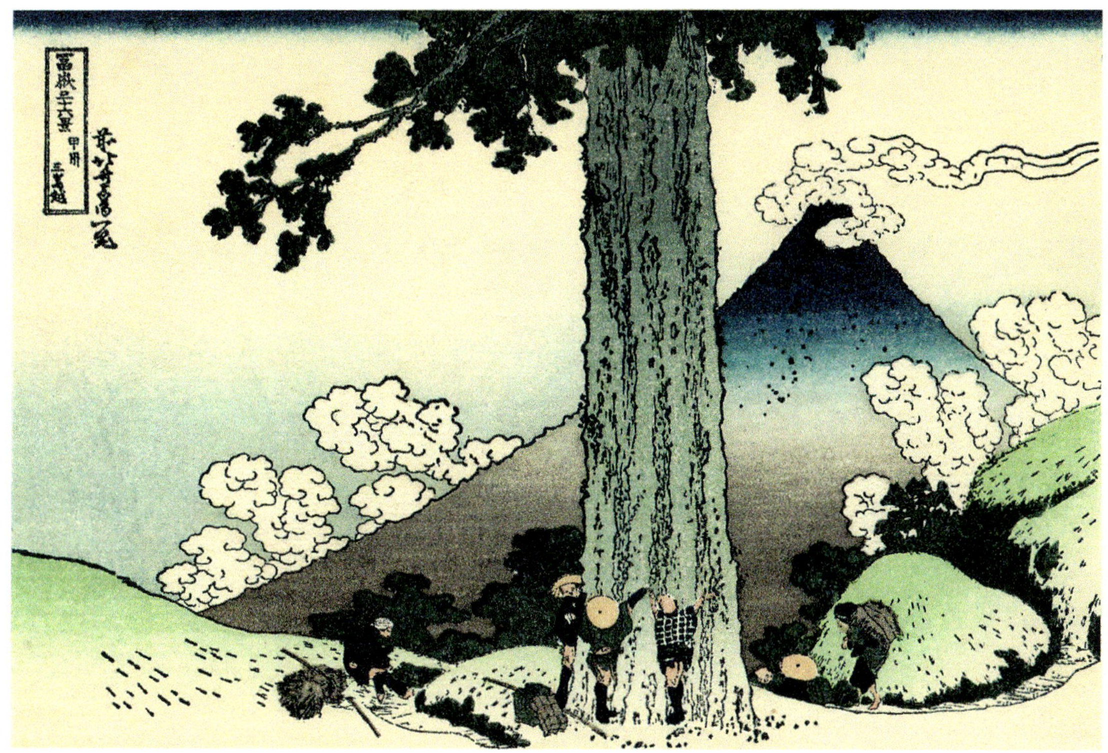

29. *Mishima Pass, Hakone*

Travelers measuring a giant tree while others are seen resting and smoking is a typical mountain
pass scene. This drawing is famous for its remarkable composition.

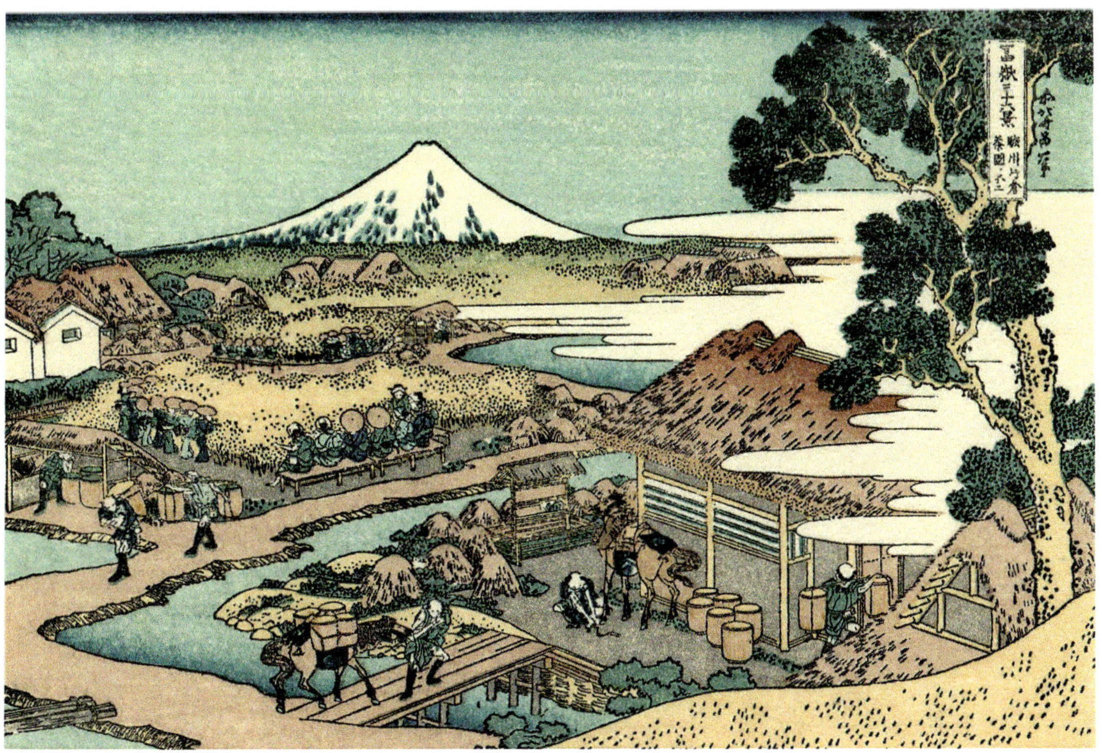

30. *Fuji From a Tea Plantation at Katakura*

A scene showing tea-pickers in Shizuoka Prefecture, apparently singing the
"Tea-Pickers" folk song while working.

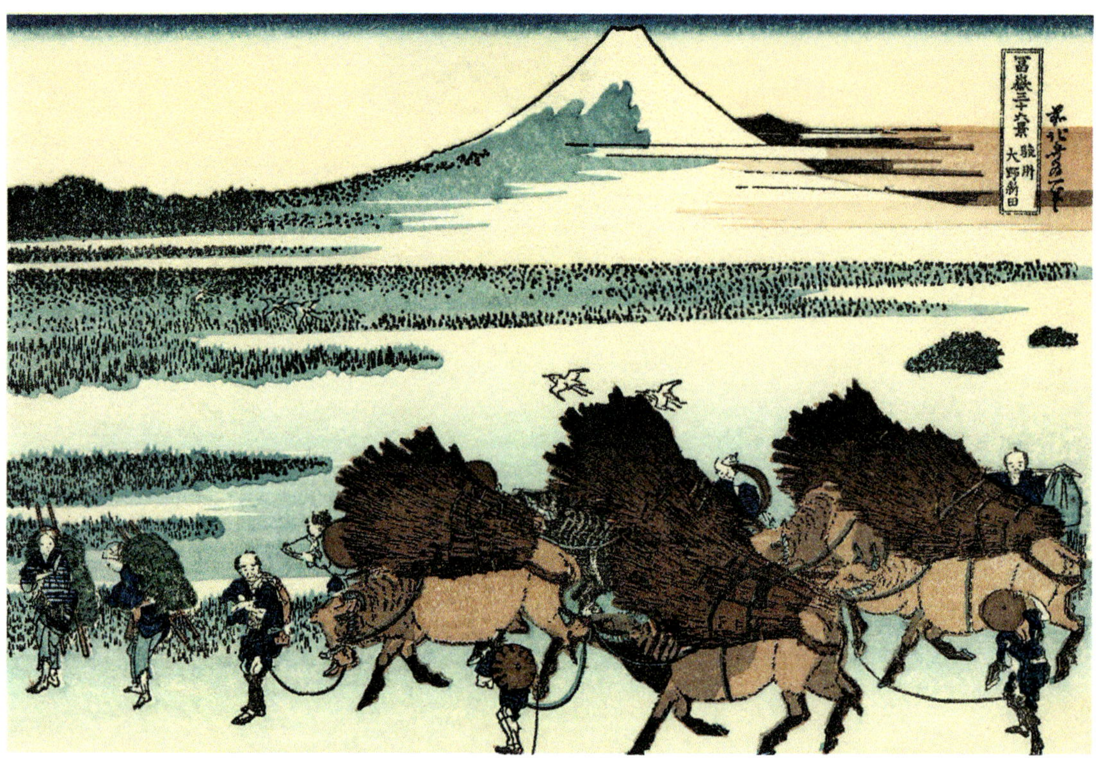

31. *Ono-Shinden, Near Yoshiwara City*

The peasants, early in the morning, cut reeds that grow in this vicinity and haul the reeds
on the backs of oxen. Women are also shown carrying loads on their backs.
These peasants are on their way home, leaving behind them the beautiful Fuji.

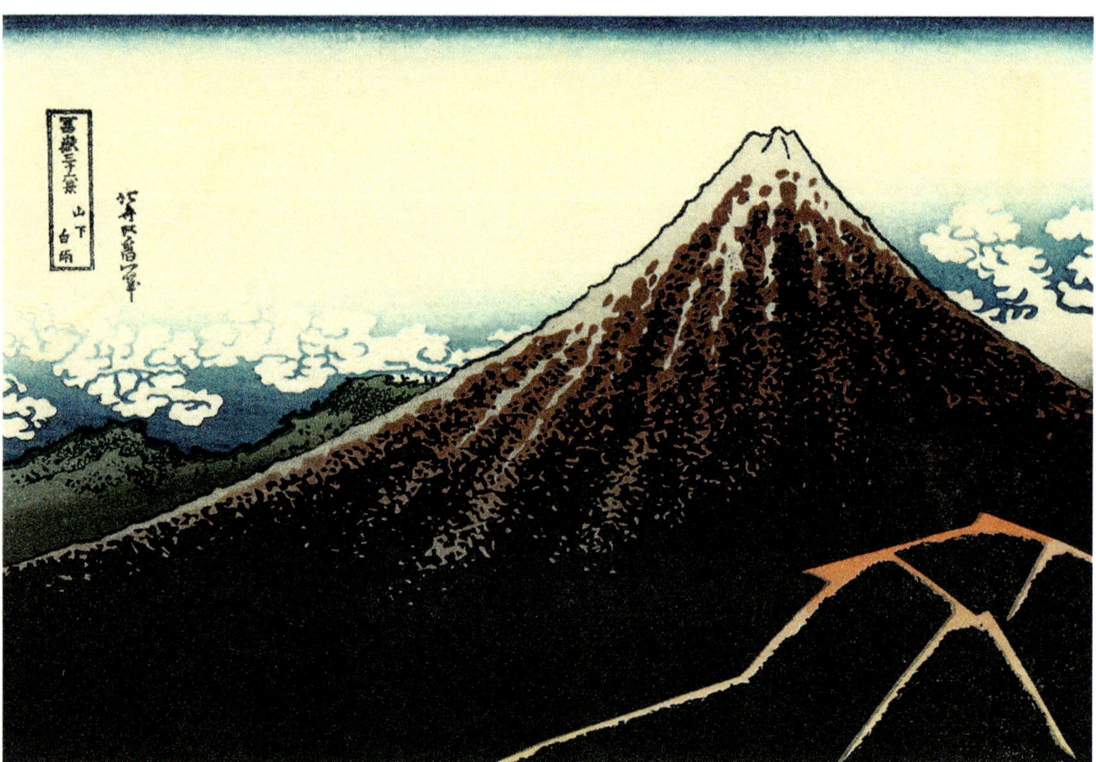

32. *Showers on the Foot of Fuji (Black Fuji)*

If Gaifu Kaisei (No. 33) is the serene Fuji, this is the dynamic Fuji.
A violent flash of lightning suggests rain down at the foot of Fuji.

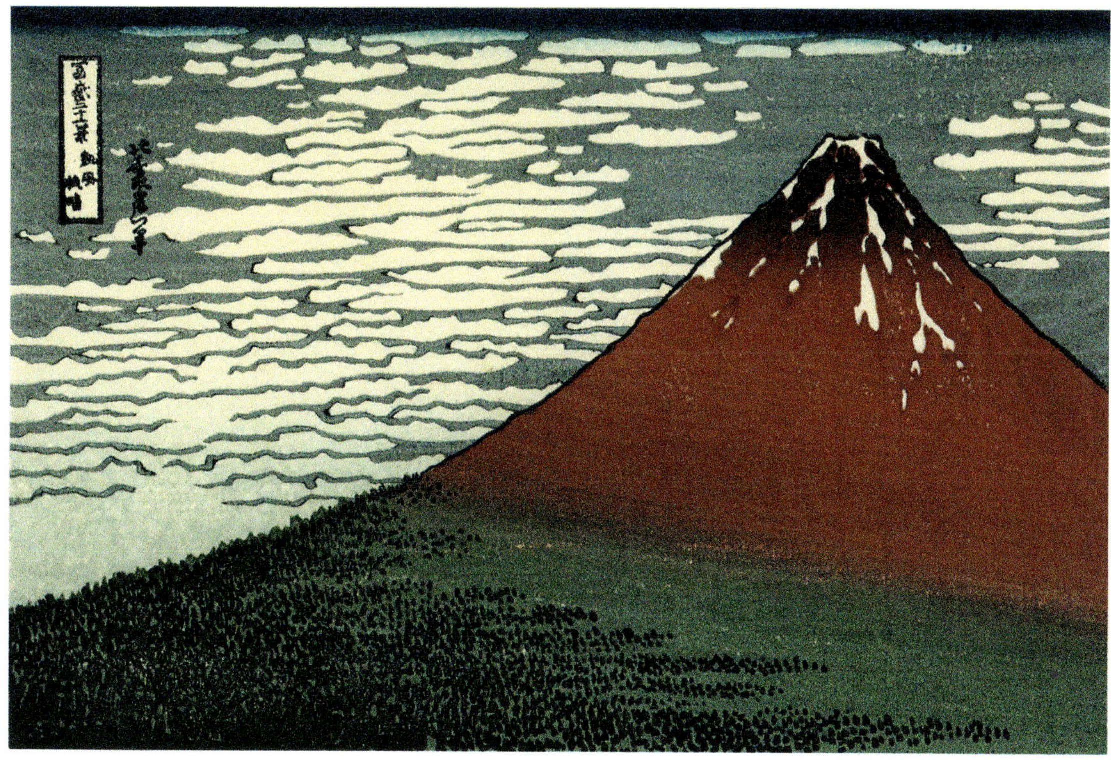

33. *The Red Fuji*

Red Fuji is the result of Mother Nature's tricks and can be seen at dawn or sunset.
Note the clear depiction of the height of Fuji and the broad and endless sky done in blue.
(The best of Hokusai's masterpieces).

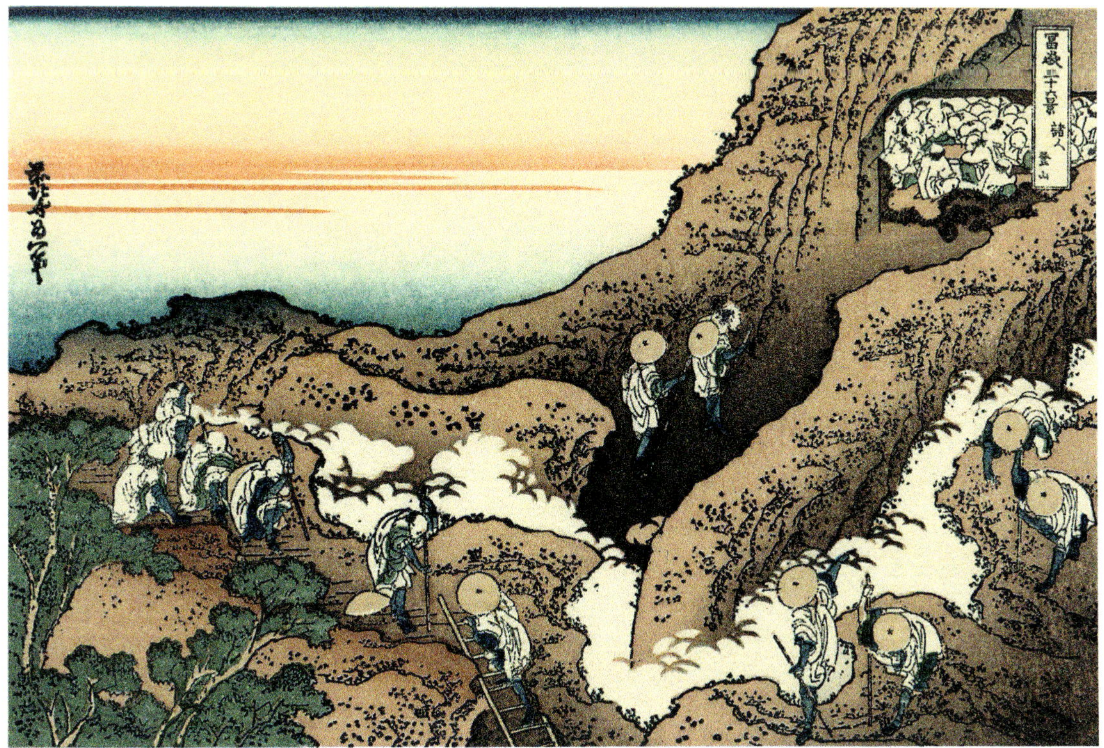

34. *Climbing Fuji*

Today, climbing Mt. Fuji is considered as sport, but in the olden days the purpose was a religious
one. This is the only drawing in the entire series that does not show a complete view of Mt. Fuji.

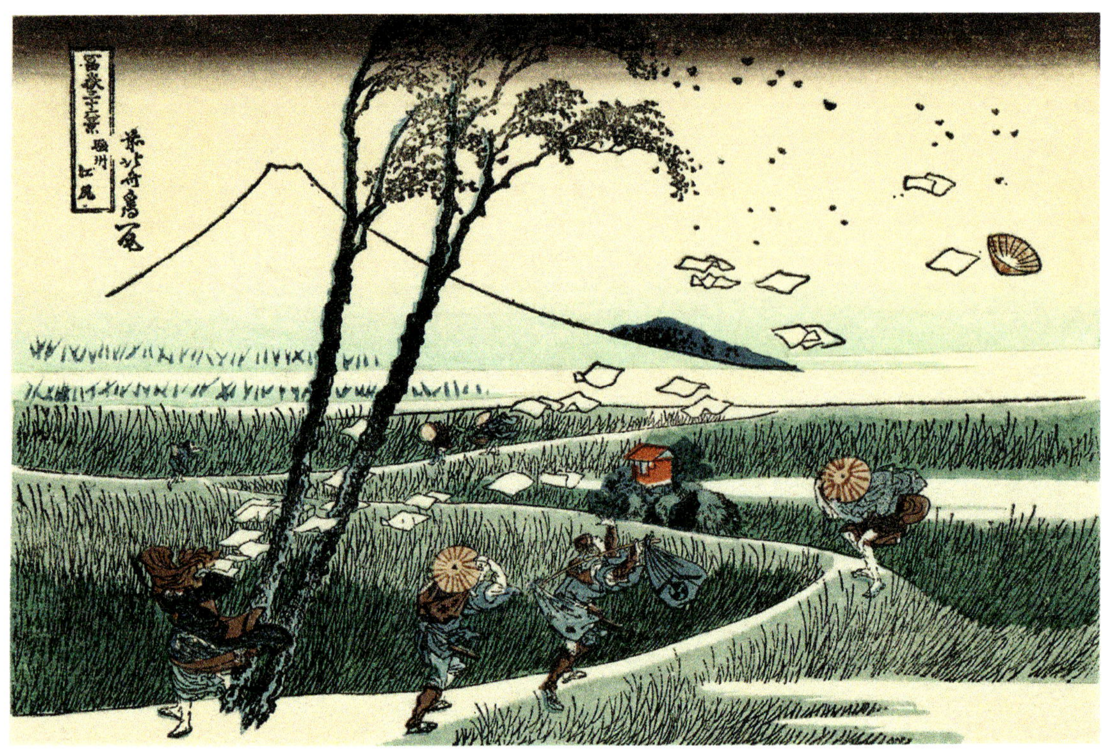

35. *Ejiri Near Shimizu City*

A woman loses some tissue and a man loses his hat to a sudden gust of wind.
Only the outline of Fuji is drawn, calm and high in the distance.

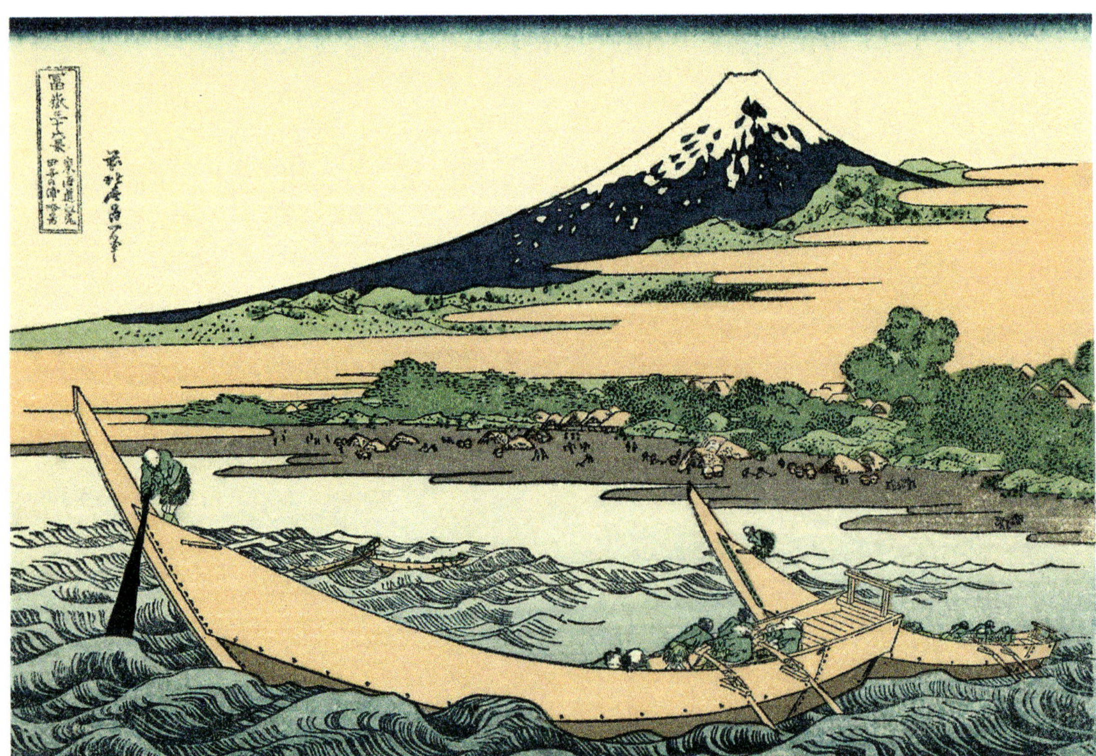

36. *Tagonoura Near Ejiri, Tokaido Highway*

In the center, in the distance, are people working in a salt field.
In the foreground, fishermen work hard on the oars to cut through the high waves.

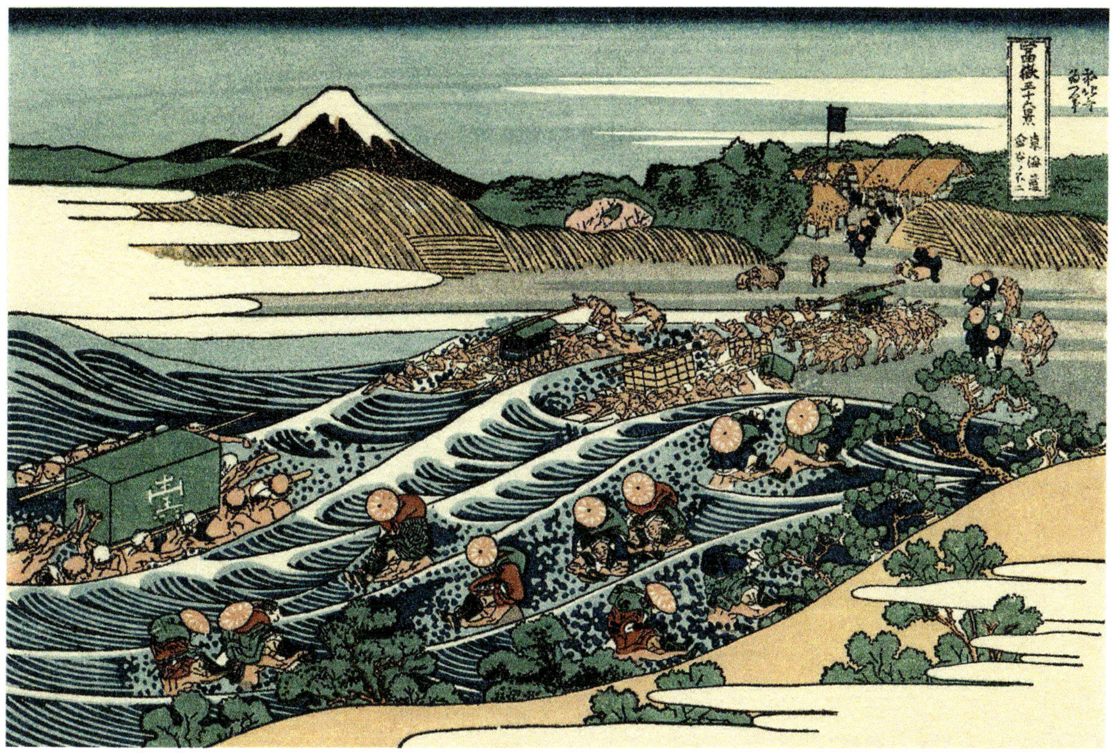

37. *Fuji From Kanaya, Tokaido*

Travelers crossing Oi River rapids. Wealthy people cross the river in their own palanquins carried by numerous porters. Some are shown on porter's backs. The poor had to cross the river on their own.

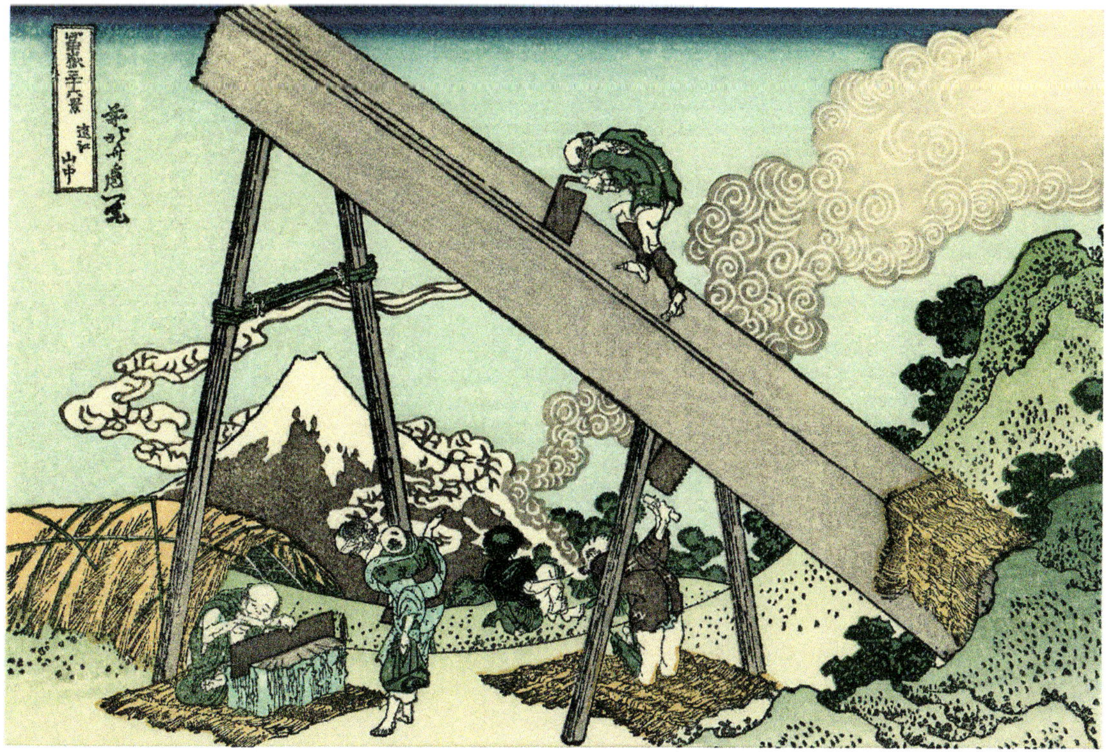

38. *In the Mountains of Totomi*

In this drawing is shown a sawyer and his family in the mountains from where Fuji can be seen. Fuji can be seen from below the huge timber set at a diagonal position. Note the remarkable combination of triangles from different angles.

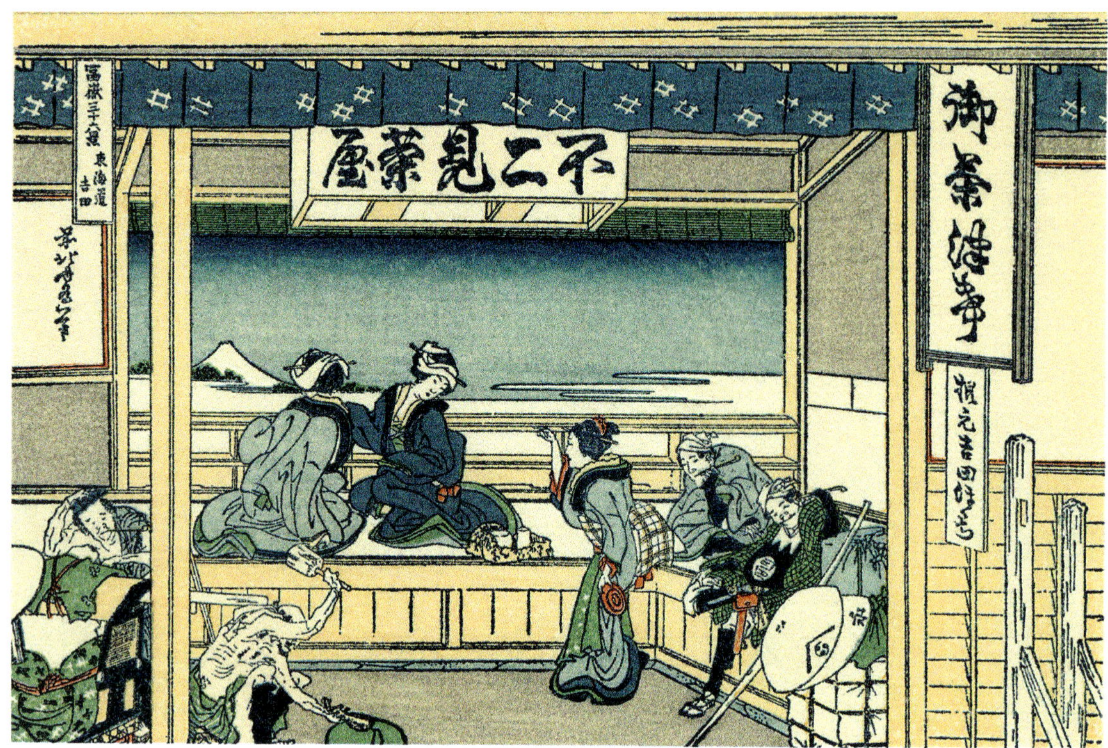

39. *The Tea-House at Yoshida*

In a tea house along the highway tired travelers rest while a maid points to Fuji, apparently explaining something. Another traveler smokes, while a man uses a mallet to soften straw slippers. Hokusai was extremely clever in portraying people.

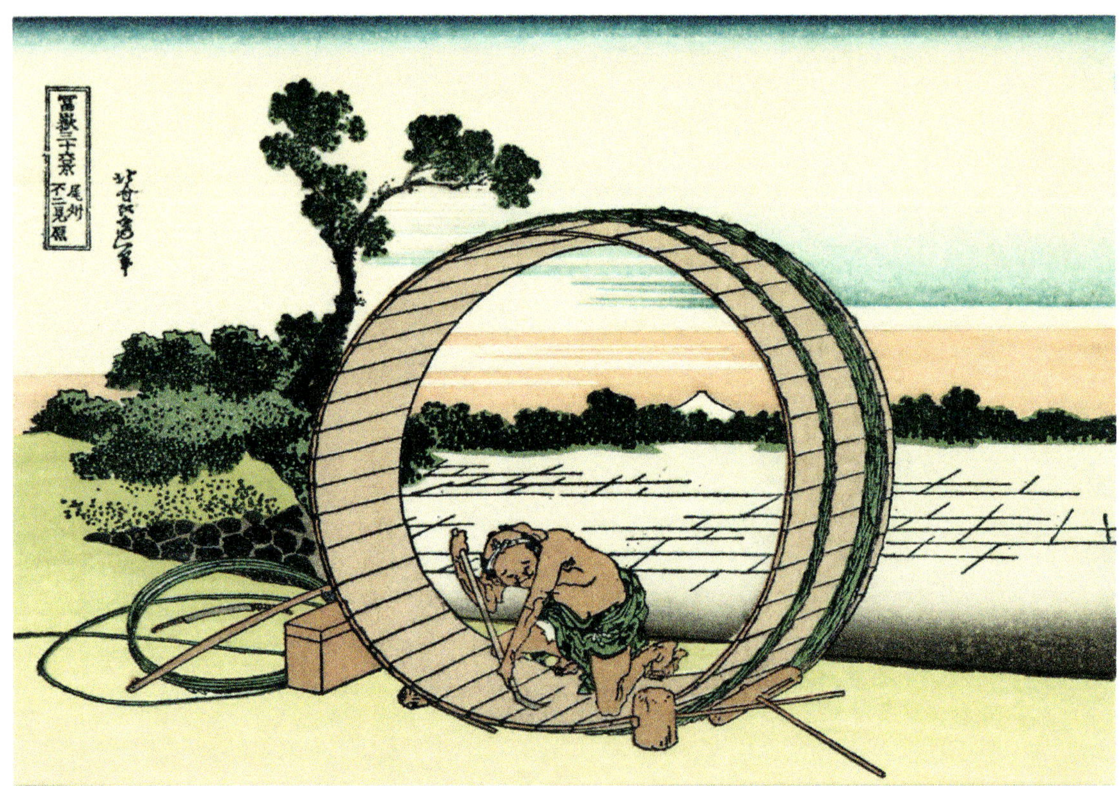

40. *Fujimihara, Aichi Prefecture*

Fuji, small in the distance, seen through a huge wooden tub.
This drawing is famous for its novel composition.

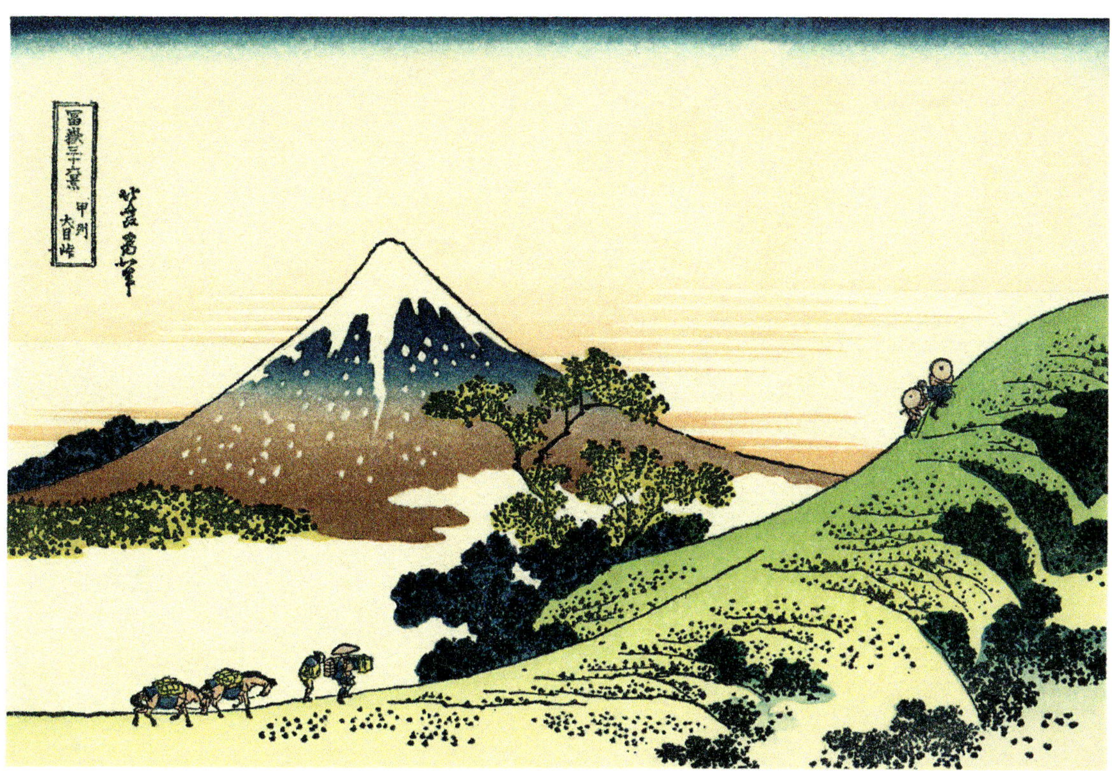

41. *Inume Pass, Yamanashi Prefecture*

Climbing the gradual slope of a beautiful hill are some travelers.
The travelers and horses are dwarfed by Mother Nature.

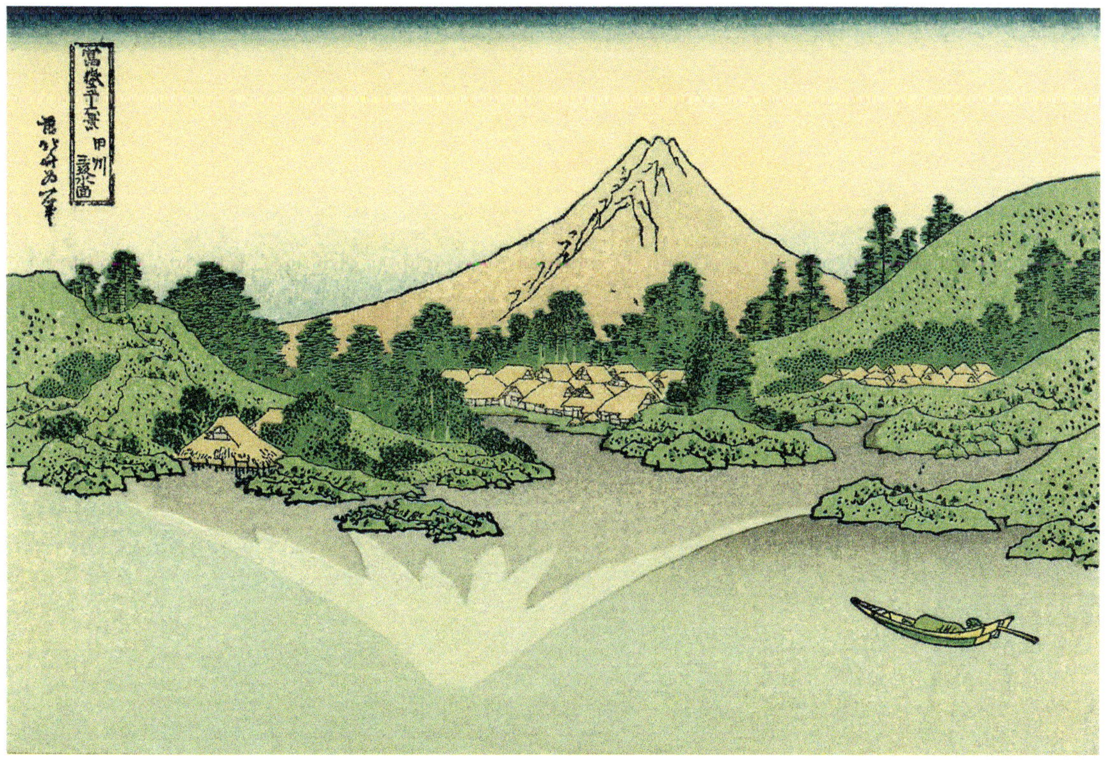

42. *The Reflection of Fuji in the Lake*

A reflection of Fuji on Lake Kawaguchi, seen early in the morning.
The jagged and precipitous "back Fuji" is remarkably drawn.

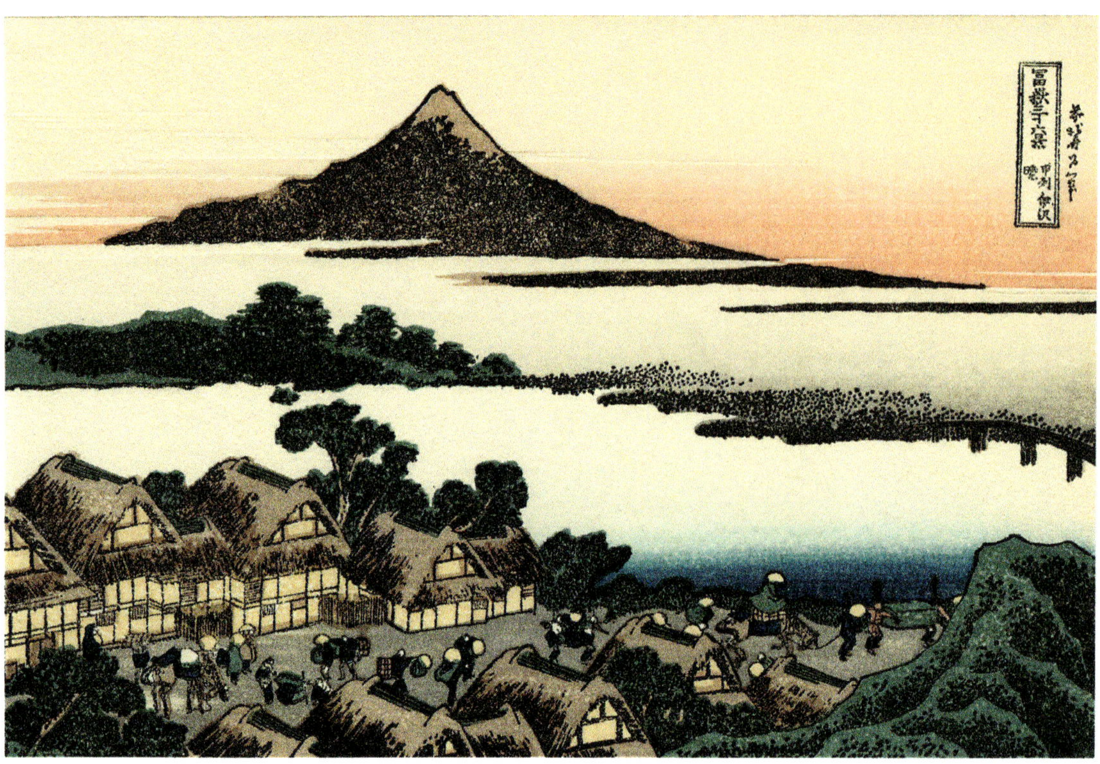

43. *Dawn in Izawa, Yamanashi Prefecture*

From inns near the river, travelers leave early in the morning to continue on their journey.
The color of the sky, the roofs of the houses cleverly depicts daybreak.

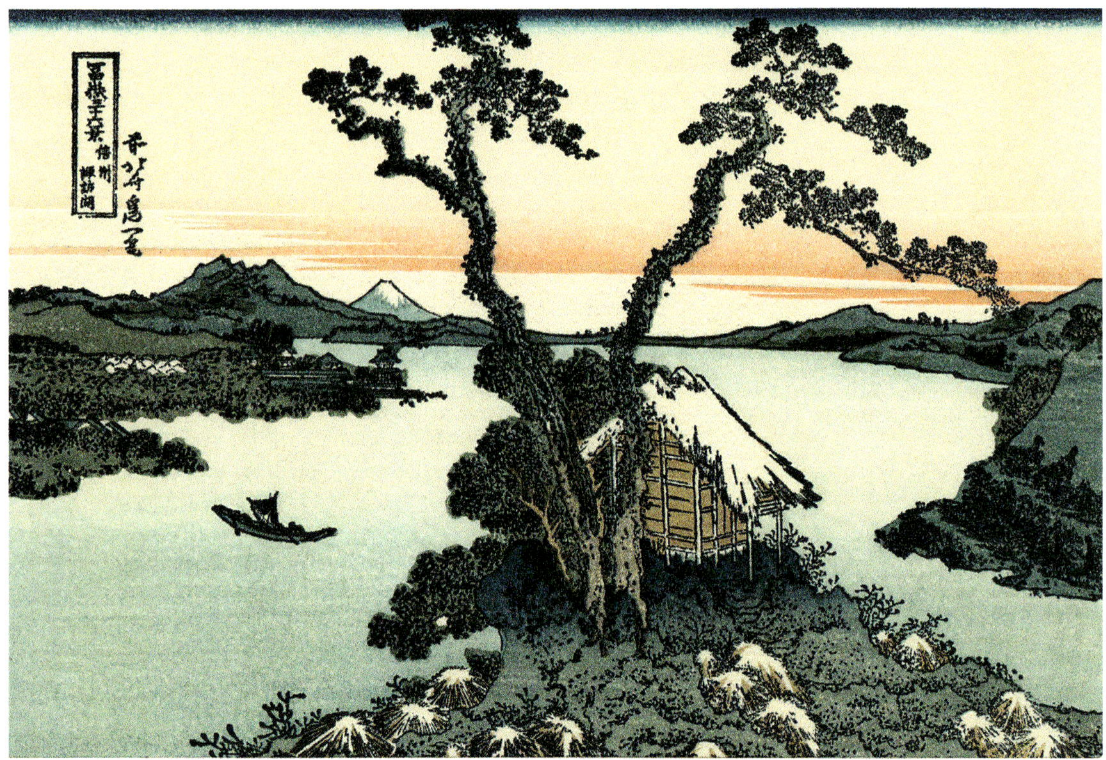

44. *Lake Suwa, Nagano Prefecture*

The castle standing near the shore of this lake is Takashima Castle.
The only remains of this castle today are part of the stone walls and moat.

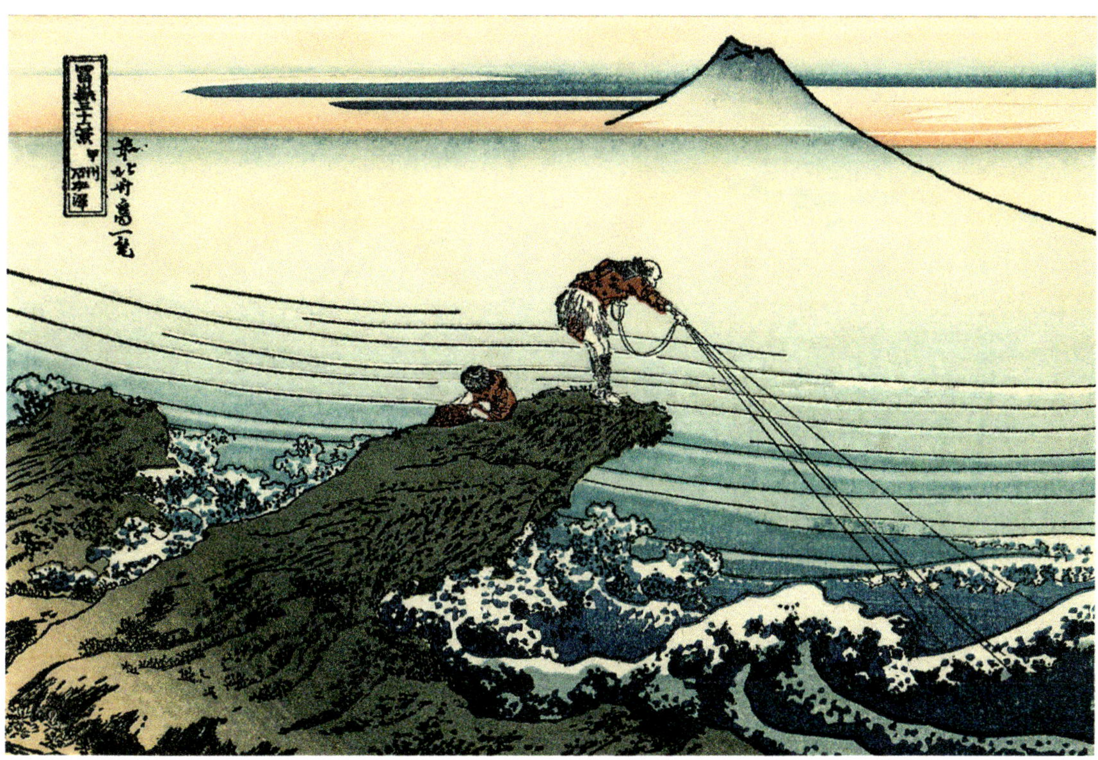

45. *Kajikazawa, Yamanashi Prefecture*

A fisherman and his son seen on a huge rock with the fisherman fishing with a net.
The river rapids breaking against the rock is similar to high waves of the sea.

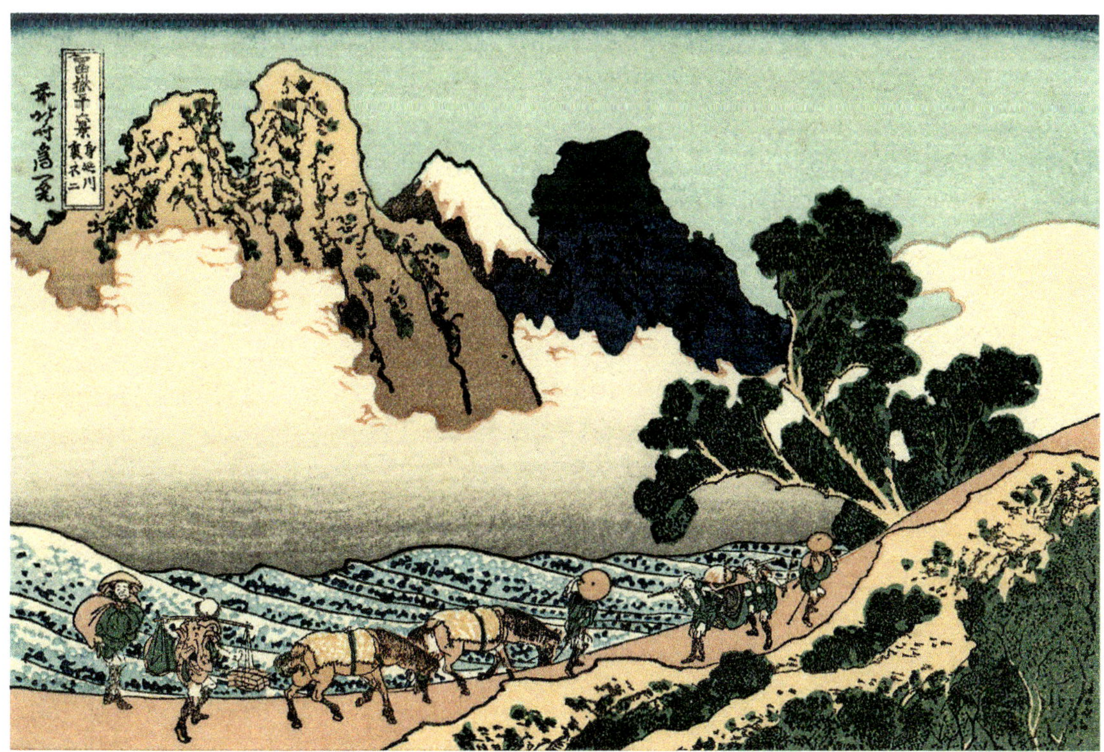

46. *Back of Fuji from Minobu River*

The jagged precipitous mountains and rising clouds give the impression
of a scene deep in the high mountains.

A CATALOG OF SELECTED

DOVER BOOKS

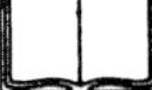

Art and Design from Many Cultures

JAPANESE EMBLEMS AND DESIGNS, Walter Amstutz. Almost 800 *mon* (emblems or crests) combine natural and geometric forms for striking effects. Ideal for design, jewelry, mosaics, and more. 160pp. 8 1/4 x 9 1/4. 0-486-28184-1

TRADITIONAL CHINESE DESIGNS, Edited by Stanley Appelbaum. Over 200 royalty-free motifs: dragons, peonies, plum blossoms, tigers, clouds, geometrics, and other favorites. 48pp. 8 1/4 x 11. 0-486-25347-3

AMERICAN INDIAN DESIGN & DECORATION, Le Roy H. Appleton. Full text, plus more than 700 precise drawings of basketry, sculpture, painting, pottery, sand paintings, metal, much more. 4 plates in color. Text gives lore and tradition behind the designs. 279pp. 8 3/8 x 11. 0-486-22704-9

THE ORNAMENTAL ARTS OF JAPAN: 60 Full-Color Plates, George Ashdown Audsley. Assembled by a renowned art historian, these vivid illustrations offer spectacular examples of Japanese painting, printing, embroidery, lacquer work, and cloisonné, as well as masterpieces in ivory and porcelain. 64pp. 8 3/8 x 11. 0-486-46549-7

ANIMAL MOTIFS IN ASIAN ART: An Illustrated Guide to Their Meanings and Aesthetics, Katherine M. Ball. Highly readable authoritative reference, rich with sidelights from literature and legend, explains animal symbolism in art of the Far East. The 673 black-and-white illustrations depict dragons, tigers, bats, butterflies, elephants, and other creatures. 320pp. 9 x 12. 0-486-43338-2

JAPANESE WARRIORS, ROGUES AND BEAUTIES: Woodblocks from Adventure Stories, Edited and with a Preface by Kendall H. Brown. Selected from woodblock-printed book covers and frontispieces from 1898 to 1903, this original compilation features 64 dramatic images from the Japanese equivalent of dime-store novels. An expert in Asian art contributes captions and an informative Introduction. 128pp. 11 x 8 1/4. 0-486-47640-5

A GRAMMAR OF JAPANESE ORNAMENT AND DESIGN, Thomas W. Cutler. From one of the most comprehensive surveys of mid-19th-century Japanese art and ornamentation: graceful details from landscapes, floral motifs, abstracts, images of sea life, and others. Over 300 figures on 65 plates. 112pp. 9 3/8 x 12 1/4. 0-486-42976-8

TREASURY OF CHINESE DESIGN MOTIFS, Joseph D'Addetta. 284 Chinese motifs — flowers and plants, animal life, and more. 100 plates. 112pp. 8 3/8 x 11 1/4. 0-486-24167-X

TRADITIONAL JAPANESE DESIGN MOTIFS, Joseph D'Addetta. Over 250 readily usable, royalty-free, authentic Japanese designs — from ceramics, textiles, more. Includes florals, demons, animals, geometrics, more. 96pp. 8 3/8 x 11 1/4. 0-486-24629-9

CHINESE BRUSHWORK IN CALLIGRAPHY AND PAINTING: Its History, Aesthetics, and Techniques, Kwo Da-Wei. Comprehensive volume traces historical development of techniques and styles, analyzes aesthetic concepts, and provides information on materials, technical principles, and brush strokes. 224pp. 8 3/8 x 11 1/4. 0-486-26481-5

100 JAPANESE STENCIL DESIGNS, Edited by Friedrich Deneken. The natural Japanese affinity for decorative art is apparent in this striking collection of 104 exquisite stencil designs, reproduced from a rare 19th-century publication. 96pp. 8 3/8 x 11. 0-486-44724-3

THE CODEX BORGIA: A Full-Color Restoration of the Ancient Mexican Manuscript, Gisele Díaz and Alan Rodgers. First republication of remarkable repainting of great Mexican codex, dated to ca. AD 1400. 76 large full-color plates show gods, kings, warriors, mythical creatures, and abstract designs. Introduction. 96pp. 9 x 12. 0-486-27569-8

CHINESE CUT-PAPER ANIMAL DESIGNS, Dover. This bold assortment features an original selection of 125 rare black-and-white cuts of animal motifs, with unusual renderings of fish, dragons, butterflies, horses, cranes, and other creatures. 64pp. 8 3/8 x 11. 0-486-45225-5

FULL-COLOR JAPANESE DESIGNS AND MOTIFS, Dover. Dragons, tigers, cranes, peacocks, and peonies abound in this collection of 130 authentic Japanese motifs. So do flowers, plants, and animals. Geometric, abstract, and allover patterns are also included. 64pp. 8 3/8 x 11. 0-486-44891-6

Art and Design from Many Cultures

A MIRROR OF JAPANESE ORNAMENT: 600 Traditional Designs, Dover. This magnificent treasury of 100 full-color plates — many with multiple images — ranges from ornate florals, elegant cranes, and fierce dragons to Silk Road imports and Edo-era textile patterns. 128pp. 8 3/8 x 11.   0-486-47318-X

EGYPTIAN MOTIFS IN THE ART DECO STYLE, Dover. Drawn from a 20th-century French collection, hundreds of images include serpents, scarabs, and mythological creatures as well as a profusion of flowers, each rendered in authentic Art Deco style. 80pp. 9 x 12.   0-486-48446-7

JAPANESE WOODBLOCK KIMONO DESIGNS IN FULL COLOR, Dover. Japanese art at its most subtly elegant, these luminous 19th-century kimono designs include allover patterns, nature scenes, magnificent floral sprays, and other finely detailed full-color motifs. 62 illustrations. 64pp. 8 3/8 x 11.
0-486-45602-1

CHINESE LATTICE DESIGNS, Daniel Sheets Dye. A collection of 1,239 beautiful geometric designs are shown, with titles, commentaries, and other information: 265 groups of designs based on parallelogram, octagon, hexagon, single-focus frames, wedge-lock, parallel waves, U-scroll, and more. 469pp. 6 1/8 x 9 1/4.   0-486-23096-1

DESIGNS FROM PRE-COLUMBIAN MEXICO, Jorge Enciso. 300 bold, rhythmic circle designs, originally incorporated on small clay spindle weights, depicting man-like deities, animals both real and fantastic, reptiles, birds, flowers, masks, geometrical figures, wheels, foliage, maze-like patterns, and frets. 105pp. 6 1/8 x 9 1/4.   0-486-22794-4

DESIGN MOTIFS OF ANCIENT MEXICO, Jorge Enciso. This catalog of ancient motifs contains over 760 vigorous, powerful, stark designs from pre-Columbian clay stamps made by Aztecs, Maya, Zapotecs, Toltec, Olmec, Mixtec. Depictions of serpents, gods, priests, dancers, florals, geometrics, more. 192pp. 6 1/8 x 9 1/4.   0-486-20084-1

ARGENTINE INDIAN ART, Alejandro Eduardo Fiadone. 284 rare designs include animal and totemic designs, geometric and rectilinear figures, abstracts, grids, and many other distinctive styles. Carefully adapted, authentic motifs; perfect for textile and print design. 96pp. 8 3/8 x 11.
0-486-29896-5

EGYPTIAN DESIGNS, Edited by Carol Belanger Grafton. 371 illustrations adapted from Egyptian sources, depicting gods and pharaohs, priests and priestesses, ordinary people, plants and animals, scenes of state occasion, battle, funerary custom, domestic life, and more. 48pp. 8 1/4 x 11.
0-486-27720-8

TREASURY OF JAPANESE DESIGNS AND MOTIFS FOR ARTISTS AND CRAFTSMEN, Edited by Carol Belanger Grafton. 360 traditional Japanese designs and motifs redrawn in clean, crisp black-and-white, royalty-free illustrations. 96pp. 8 1/4 x 11.   0-486-24435-0

AUTHENTIC CHINESE CUT-PAPER DESIGNS, Edited by Carol Belanger Grafton. Rich anthology of nearly 200 black-and-white motifs includes pandas, bamboo, cranes, dragons, peacocks, florals, landscapes, and many other traditional images in stylized, whimsical renderings. Royalty-free. 48pp. 8 1/4 x 11.   0-486-25775-4

MEXICAN PAINTERS: Rivera, Orozco, Siqueiros, and Other Artists of the Social Realist School, MacKinley Helm. Definitive introduction to art and artists of Mexico during great artistic movements of the '20s and '30s. Discussion of Rivera, Orozco, Siqueiros, Galvan, Cantú, Meza, many others. History, tradition, social movements, etc. 95 illustrations. 228pp. 6 1/2 x 9 1/4.   0-486-26028-3

TRADITIONAL JAPANESE FAMILY CRESTS FOR ARTISTS AND CRAFTSPEOPLE, Isao Honda. Over 1,700 compact, graceful, royalty-free designs depicting plant, leaf, animal, and fan designs in circular motifs; astronomical images, and more — for use by artists, designers, and craftworkers. 96pp. 8 3/8 x 11.   0-486-42273-9

TRADITIONAL JAPANESE CREST DESIGNS, Edited by Clarence Hornung. Over 500 royalty-free stylized motifs. Nature, abstracts, geometrics, more. Striking designs for logos, spots, other graphics. 48pp. 8 1/4 x 11.   0-486-25243-4

Art and Design from Many Cultures

TRADITIONAL JAPANESE STENCIL DESIGNS, Clarence Hornung. Versatile collection of 276 exquisite Japanese stencil designs — clouds, birds, butterflies, bamboo, plum and cherry blossoms, geometrics, more. Royalty-free illustrations are ideal for modern decorative and graphic needs. 128pp. 9 x 12. 0-486-24791-0

THE COMPLETE "CHINESE ORNAMENT": All 100 Color Plates, Owen Jones. From one of the most beautiful books on the decorative arts ever published: reproductions of classic full-color renderings by the great Victorian designer of design elements in Chinese porcelain and cloisonné antiquities. 112pp. 9 1/4 x 12 1/4. 0-486-26259-6

JAPANESE WOODBLOCK BIRD PRINTS, Numata Kashū. These lifelike images of birds and flowers first appeared in a now-rare 1883 portfolio. A magnificent reproduction of a 1938 facsimile of the original publication, this exquisite edition features 150 color illustrations. 160pp. 8 x 10. 0-486-47050-4

JAPANESE WOODBLOCK FLOWER PRINTS, Tanigami Kônan. Extraordinary collection of Japanese woodblock prints by a well-known artist features 120 plates in brilliant color. Realistic images from a rare edition include daffodils, tulips, and other familiar and unusual flowers. 128pp. 11 x 8 1/4. 0-486-46442-3

JAPANESE DESIGN MOTIFS, Matsuya Company. Definitive catalogue of Japanese heraldic crests featuring almost unlimited variety of plant, animal, bird, and geometric forms, from "wild goose" to "folding fan" to "mountain and mist," each with dozens of variations. 4,260 illustrations. 213pp. 11 3/8 x 8 1/4. 0-486-22874-6

CHINESE CUT-PAPER DESIGNS, Edited by Theodore Menten. 269 modern paper-cuttings from Mainland China: horses, pandas, butterflies, flowers, fish, peacocks, monkeys, phoenixes, lanterns, vases, landscapes, other traditional and modern motifs — printed solid red, black, blue, or green. 97pp. 8 3/8 x 11 1/4. 0-486-23198-4

TRADITIONAL AFRICAN DESIGNS, Gregory Mirow. Over 200 authentic designs from Dahomey, Sierra Leone, Burkina Faso, Mali, Kenya, Ghana, other African nations depict such unusual configurations as stylized lions, birds, fish, alligators, totemic figures, abstracts, geometrics, and zigzags. 48pp. 8 1/4 x 11. 0-486-29622-9

ANCIENT MEXICAN DESIGNS, Gregory Mirow. 240 meticulously reproduced motifs from the pre-Columbian world include Aztec calendars, animals, mythological characters, scores of other striking images — from codices, Maya hieroglyphs, mask panels, Olmec pottery figures, more. Royalty free. 48pp. 8 1/4 x 11. 0-486-40468-4

5000 DESIGNS AND MOTIFS FROM INDIA, Edited by Ajit Mookerjee. Incredibly rich treasury of authentic royalty-free designs from Harappa culture, Ajanta and Bagh murals, Muslim monuments, Buddhist temples, much more. Immediately usable or great for design inspiration. 208pp. 11 3/8 x 8 1/4. 0-486-29061-1

AUTHENTIC INDIAN DESIGNS, Edited by Maria Naylor. Largest collection anywhere: 2,500 authentic illustrations of bowls, bottles and pipes, geometric and floral patterns on beadwork, pictographs, symbolic tipi decorations, masks, basket weaves, Hopi katchina figures, much more. 219pp. 8 1/8 x 11. 0-486-23170-4

JAPANESE ANIMAL AND FLORAL CREST DESIGNS, Edited by Paul Negri. Drawn from traditional Japanese family crests, this collection presents 1,160 exotic black-and-white patterns, symbols, and decorative devices. They span a tremendous variety of styles, from utter simplicity to florid majesty. 64pp. 11 x 8 1/4. 0-486-45811-3

DESIGNS AND MOTIFS FROM INDIA, Marty Noble. Incredibly rich treasury of more than 200 traditional designs, developed by Indian artists over thousands of years. Exquisite adaptations from authentic embroideries and fabrics, pottery, mosaics, illuminated manuscripts, and other sources. 72pp. 8 1/4 x 11. 0-486-43403-6

Art and Design from Many Cultures

CHINESE DESIGNS AND MOTIFS, Marty Noble. With its dragons and fish, flowers and foo dogs, this magnificent compilation of 361 royalty-free designs offers an exotic archive of crisp black-and-white images in a variety of shapes and sizes. 84pp. 8 1/4 x 11. 0-486-42307-7

SOUTHEAST ASIAN DESIGNS, Marty Noble. Over 100 authentic motifs, among them serene Buddhas, sandstone sculptures, papier maché; masks, shadow puppets, tattoos, and details from temple ornaments. Approximately 125 black-and-white designs. 32pp. 8 1/4 x 11. 0-486-43106-1

TRADITIONAL CHINESE TEXTILE DESIGNS IN FULL COLOR, Northeast Drama Institute. Sixty authentic full-color motifs drawn from highly stylized opera traditions. Symbolic representations of dragons, lions, phoenixes, mandarin ducks, cranes, peonies, lotuses, much more. Vibrant color, subtle hues, beautiful renderings. 48pp. 9 3/8 x 12 1/4. 0-486-23979-9

THE CODEX NUTTALL, Edited by Zelia Nuttall. The only value-priced, full-color edition of the pre-Columbian Mexican (Mixtec) book. Features 88 color plates of kings, gods, heroes, temples, sacrifices, and more. New introduction. 96pp. 11 3/8 x 8 1/2. 0-486-23168-2

SOUTHWESTERN INDIAN DESIGNS, Madeleine Orban-Szontagh. Treasury of 250 royalty-free images, drawn from authentic motifs on Hopi ceremonial dress, Zuni shields, Anasazi pottery, Navajo jewelry, rugs and sand paintings, Pueblo pottery, and many more. 48pp. 8 1/4 x 11. 0-486-26985-X

JAPANESE FLORAL PATTERNS AND MOTIFS, Madeleine Orban-Szontagh. Archive of 45 designs adapted from kimonos, Noh costumes and screens: stripes, allover patterns, nature scenes, sprays of flowers and branches, much more, convey subtle elegance. Captions. 48pp. 8 1/4 x 11.

0-486-26330-4

NORTHWEST COAST INDIAN DESIGNS, Madeleine Orban-Szontagh. Over 270 designs from art of Nootka, Kwakiutl, Tlingit, other groups. Stylized plants, abstracts, repeating patterns, totemic images, more. 48pp. 8 1/4 x 11. 0-486-28179-5

261 NORTH AMERICAN INDIAN DESIGNS, Madeleine Orban-Szontagh. Clearly drawn royalty-free illustrations based on authentic design motifs of Sioux, Blackfoot, Apache, Cheyenne, other tribes. Abstract and floral motifs, human, animal and mythical figures. Ideal for many art and craft purposes. 48pp. 8 1/4 x 11. 0-486-27718-6

JAPANESE OPTICAL AND GEOMETRICAL ART, Hajime Ouchi. Some of the most ingenious and attractive modern motifs. 746 designs. 170pp. 8 1/4 x 11. 0-486-23553-X

JAPANESE NO MASKS: With 300 Illustrations of Authentic Historical Examples, Friedrich Perzynski. Edited and Translated by Stanley Appelbaum. 120 full-page plates of magnificent, elaborately carved, museum-quality masks worn by actors playing gods, warriors, beautiful women, feudal lords, and supernatural beings. Captions. 176pp. 6 1/8 x 9 1/4. 0-486-44014-1

POSADA'S POPULAR MEXICAN PRINTS, José Posada. 273 great 19th-century woodcuts: crimes, miracles, skeletons, ads, portraits, news cuts. Table of contents includes Calaveras; Disasters; National Events; Religion and Miracles; Don Chepito Marihuano; Chapbook Covers; Chapbook Illustrations; and Everyday Life. 156pp. 8 3/8 x 11 1/4. 0-486-22854-1

250 STENCIL DESIGNS FROM INDIA, K. Prakash. Authentic royalty-free designs include animal and floral motifs, paisleys, geometrics, border elements, spot illustrations, more. Ideal for textile design, home and furniture decoration, many other projects. 48pp. 8 1/4 x 10 7/8. 0-486-29026-3

PAISLEYS AND OTHER TEXTILE DESIGNS FROM INDIA, K. Prakash. This superb, comprehensive sourcebook features over 500 splendid motifs adapted from elegant brocades. It includes colorful block prints and woven designs inspired by nature — trees, leaves, flowers, buds, animals and birds. 156pp. 8 3/8 x 11. 0-486-27959-6

DECORATIVE ART OF THE SOUTHWESTERN INDIANS, Dorothy S. Sides. Nearly 300 royalty-free examples, ranging from 13th-century geometric art of Pueblo to contemporary designs, include motifs from pottery, basketry, beadwork, masks, dolls, sand paintings, and blankets. 50 plates. 128pp. 5 5/8 x 8 1/4. 0-486-20139-2

Art and Design from Many Cultures

THE CHINESE ON THE ART OF PAINTING: Texts by the Painter-Critics, from the Han through the Ch'ing Dynasties, Osvald Sirén. Comments by noted landscapists, poet-painters, historians, and theoreticians; discussions of Ch'an Buddhism and its relation to painting; methods of study and aesthetic principles, more. 288pp. 5 3/8 x 8 1/2. 0-486-44428-7

1000 DECORATIVE DESIGNS FROM INDIA, Devi Thapa, Kiran Chaudhri and V. S. Navalkar. This sourcebook showcases 1,000 decorative black-and-white motifs plucked from India's many sumptuous handicrafts: stonework, batik, embroidered fabrics, pottery, jewelry, personal adornments, carpets, more. 128pp. 8 3/8 x 11. 0-486-46040-1

AFRICAN DESIGN: An Illustrated Survey of Traditional Craftwork, Margaret Trowell. Nearly 200 handsome illustrations — from repetitive motifs in fabrics to carvings on bowls, drinking vessels, and door panels. Each object is identified and tribal source cited. 197 black-and-white illustrations. 160pp. 8 3/8 x 11. 0-486-42714-5

JAPANESE SILK DESIGNS IN FULL COLOR, Edited by M. P. Verneuil. Reproductions from rare portfolio portray intricate, subtly shaded images of florals, animal life, and geometrics in the manner of stylized Japanese art. 108 full-color designs. 64pp. 8 3/8 x 11. 0-486-43717-5

MEXICAN INDIAN FOLK DESIGNS: 252 Motifs from Textiles, Irmgard Weitlaner-Johnson. Incorporating abstract and geometric forms as well as highly stylized images of flowers, plants, animals, birds, and humans, these exacting illustrations represent more than 20 major Mexican Indian cultures. 96pp. 8 1/4 x 11. 0-486-27524-8

OUTLINES OF CHINESE SYMBOLISM AND ART MOTIVES, C. A. S. Williams. This standard reference, long familiar to students of Chinese culture, emphasizes the historical, legendary, or supernatural persons, animals, and objects as symbols in art and literature. 402 illustrations. 472pp. 5 3/8 x 8 1/2. 0-486-23372-3

AFRICAN DESIGNS FROM TRADITIONAL SOURCES, Geoffrey Williams. Linocut prints in crisp black-and-white designs reflect traditional work from Zulu, Masai, and dozens of other tribes. Masks, abstract motifs, and much more. 378 illustrations. 203pp. 6 1/2 x 9 1/4. 0-486-22752-9

ANCIENT EGYPTIAN DESIGNS FOR ARTISTS AND CRAFTSPEOPLE, Eva Wilson. Over 400 images of papyrus, sun god Re, lotus, scarabs, plant scrolls, many other authentic motifs. Notes. Captions. 128pp. 8 3/8 x 11 1/4. 0-486-25339-2

NORTH AMERICAN INDIAN DESIGNS FOR ARTISTS AND CRAFTSPEOPLE, Eva Wilson. Over 360 authentic royalty-free designs adapted from Navajo blankets, Hopi pottery, Sioux buffalo hides, more. Geometrics, symbolic figures, plant and animal motifs, much more. 128pp. 8 3/8 x 11. 0-486-25341-4

CHINESE ANIMAL DESIGNS, Edited by Chen Yan. Superb archive of more than 1,100 illustrations, grouped chronologically according to dynastic era, depicts dragons, tigers, fish, birds, horses, butterflies, waterfowl, and a host of other creatures — real and mythical. 144pp. 8 1/8 x 7 1/8. 0-486-44000-1